SGT FROG™
KERORO GUNSOU

VOL. #11 BY MINE YOSHIZAKI

TOKYOPOP®

HAMBURG // LONDON // LOS ANGELES // TOKYO

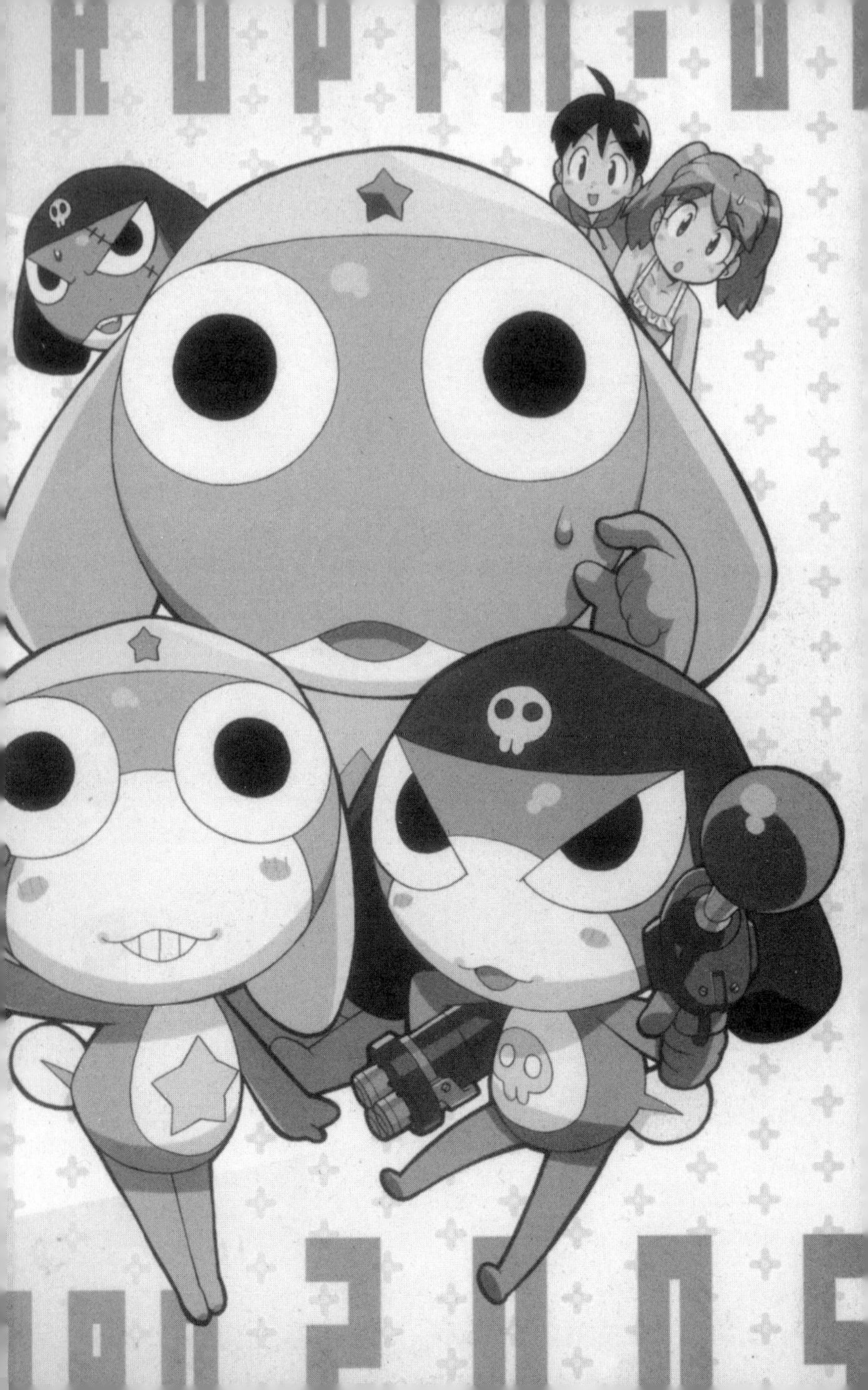

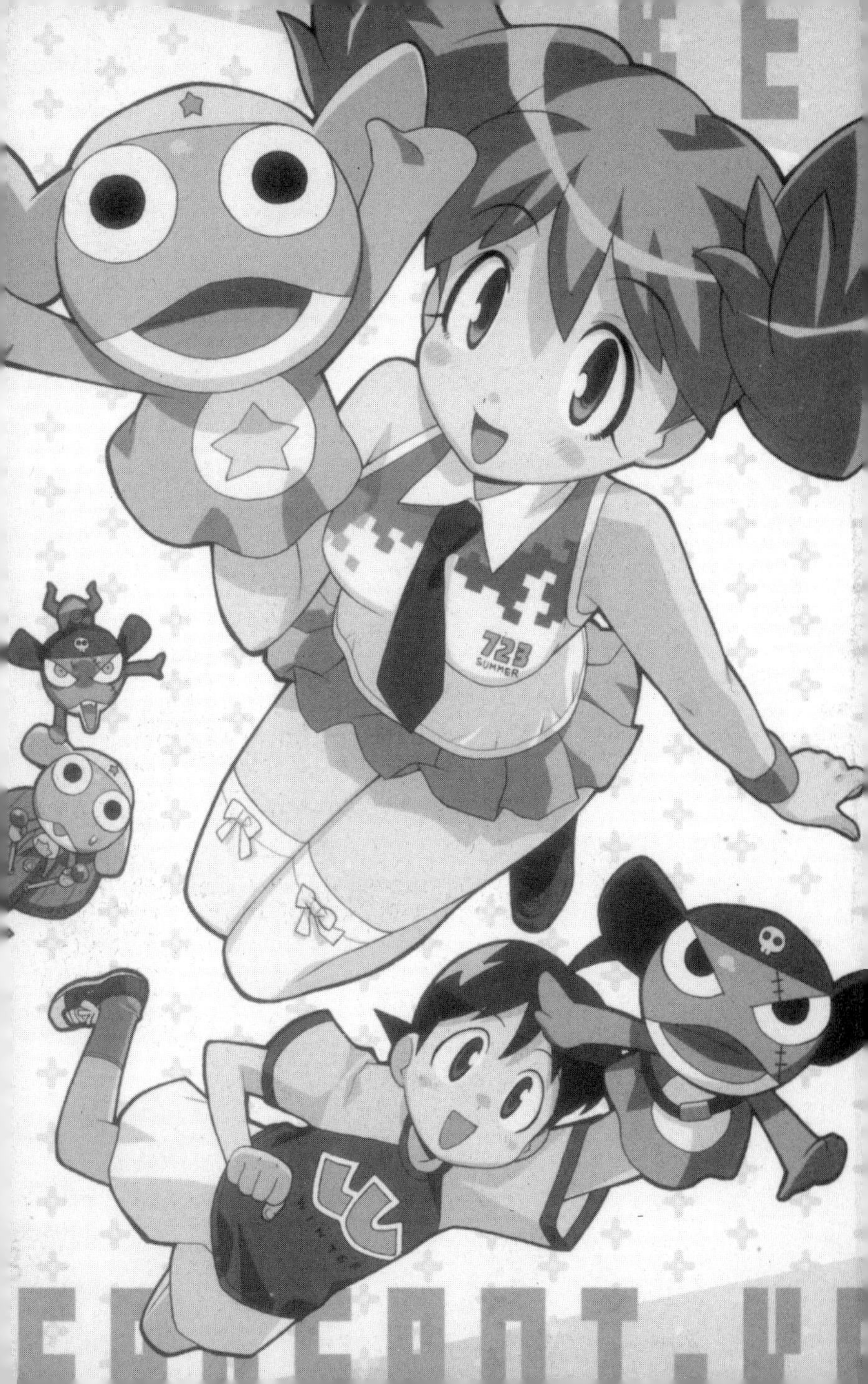
723
SUMMER

SGT. FROG 11 · TABLE OF CONTENTS

SGT FROG

KERORO GUNSOU

VOLUME #11

BY
MINE YOSHIZAKI

HAMBURG // LONDON // LOS ANGELES // TOKYO

SGT. Frog Vol. 11
Created by Mine Yoshizaki

Translation - Yuko Fukami
Associate Editor - Hope Donovan
Retouch and Lettering - Alyson Stetz and Jennifer Carbajal
Production Artist - Mike Estacio
Cover Design - James Lee

Editor - Paul Morrissey
Digital Imaging Manager - Chris Buford
Managing Editor - Lindsey Johnston
VP of Production - Ron Klamert
Publisher - Mike Kiley
Editor-in-Chief - Rob Tokar
President and C.O.O. - John Parker
C.E.O. and Chief Creative Officer - Stuart Levy

A  Manga

TOKYOPOP Inc.
5900 Wilshire Blvd. Suite 2000
Los Angeles, CA 90036

E-mail: info@TOKYOPOP.com
Come visit us online at www.TOKYOPOP.com

ISBN: 1-59816-596-8
First TOKYOPOP printing: July 2006
10 9 8 7 6 5 4 3 2 1
Printed in the USA

CHARACTER RELATIONSHIPS AND THE STORY SO FAR

(FACT-CHECKING PERFORMED BY SHONEN ACE MAGAZINE)

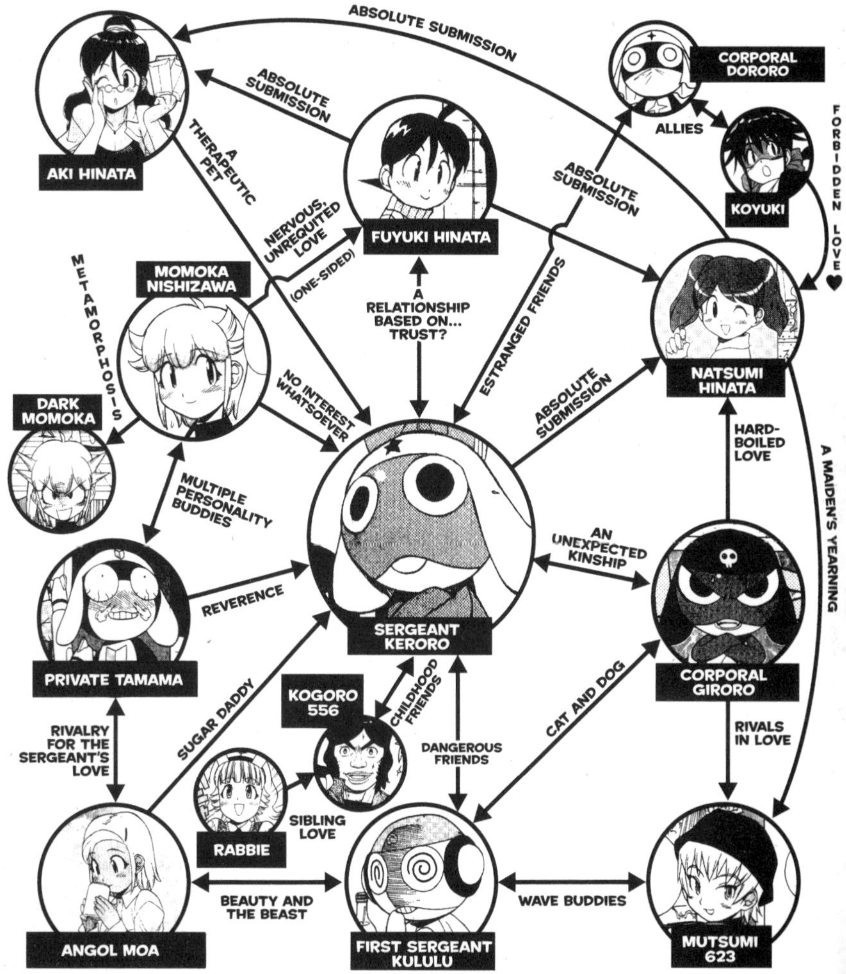

ABSOLUTE SUBMISSION
CORPORAL DORORO
AKI HINATA
ABSOLUTE SUBMISSION
A THERAPEUTIC PET
ALLIES
FORBIDDEN LOVE
KOYUKI
ABSOLUTE SUBMISSION
FUYUKI HINATA
NERVOUS, UNREQUITED LOVE
(ONE-SIDED)
METAMORPHOSIS
MOMOKA NISHIZAWA
A RELATIONSHIP BASED ON... TRUST?
ESTRANGED FRIENDS
NATSUMI HINATA
DARK MOMOKA
NO INTEREST WHATSOEVER
ABSOLUTE SUBMISSION
HARD-BOILED LOVE
A MAIDEN'S YEARNING
MULTIPLE PERSONALITY BUDDIES
AN UNEXPECTED KINSHIP
REVERENCE
SERGEANT KERORO
PRIVATE TAMAMA
CORPORAL GIRORO
KOGORO 556
CHILDHOOD FRIENDS
CAT AND DOG
RIVALRY FOR THE SERGEANT'S LOVE
SUGAR DADDY
DANGEROUS FRIENDS
RIVALS IN LOVE
SIBLING LOVE
RABBIE
BEAUTY AND THE BEAST
WAVE BUDDIES
ANGOL MOA
FIRST SERGEANT KULULU
MUTSUMI 623

AS CAPTAIN OF THE SPACE INVASION FORCE'S SPECIAL ADVANCE TEAM OF THE 58TH PLANET OF THE GAMMA STORM CLOUD SYSTEM, SGT. KERORO ENTERED THE HINATA FAMILY WHEN HIS PRE-ATTACK PREPARATION FOR THE INVASION OF EARTH RAN AFOUL VIA HIS EASY CAPTURE BY THE HINATA CHILDREN, FUYUKI AND NATSUMI. THANKS TO FUYUKI'S KINDNESS, OR AT LEAST HIS CURIOSITY, SGT. KERORO QUICKLY BECAME A BONA FIDE MEMBER OF THE HINATA FAMILY...IN OTHER WORDS, A TOTAL FREELOADER. THE SERGEANT'S SUBORDINATES--"DUAL PERSONALITY" PRIVATE TAMAMA; "BLAZING MILITARY MAN" CORPORATE GIRORO; THE "WAVISH" SERGEANT MAJOR KULULU; AND THE MUCH-HERALDED "LORD OF TERROR," ANGOL MOA--SOON JOINED HIM TO REFORM THE KERORO PLATOON, WHICH DOES AS IT PLEASES IN A TOP-SECRET BASE BENEATH THE HINATA HOME. AND WITH THE APPEARANCE OF ITS LONG-AWAITED FIFTH MEMBER, "ASSASSIN" CORPORAL DORORO, KERORO PLATOON IS COMPLETE, AND A FULL-SCALE INVASION OF POKOPEN IS ABOUT TO BEGIN...MAYBE? ONE THING'S FOR SURE--THEIR OPERATIONS WILL CONTINUE TO IRRITATE THE EARTH ON AN INTERGALACTIC SCALE!

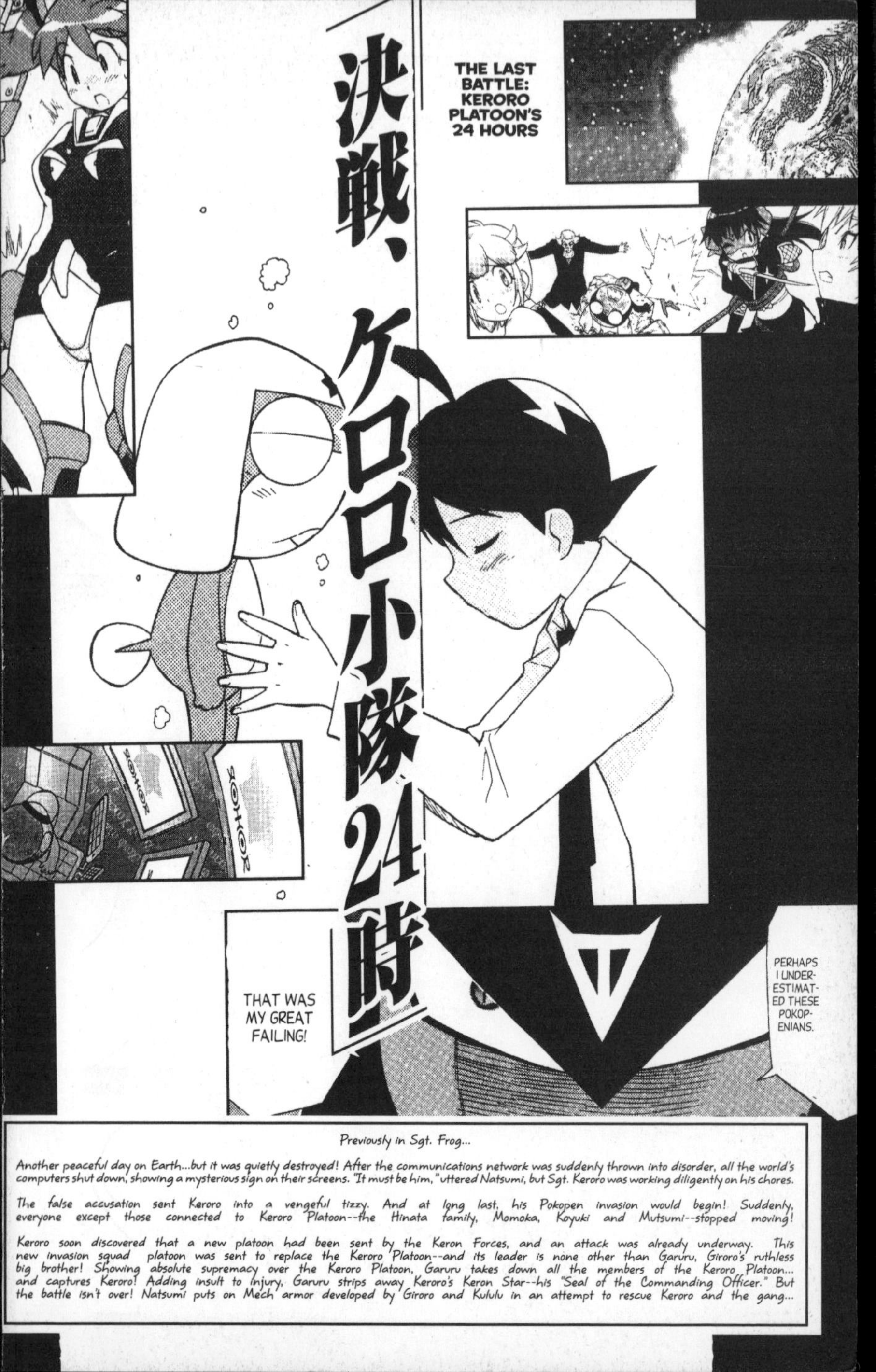
決戦、ケロロ小隊24時
THE LAST BATTLE: KERORO PLATOON'S 24 HOURS
PERHAPS I UNDER-ESTIMAT-ED THESE POKOP-ENIANS.
THAT WAS MY GREAT FAILING!

Previously in Sgt. Frog...

Another peaceful day on Earth...but it was quietly destroyed! After the communications network was suddenly thrown into disorder, all the world's computers shut down, showing a mysterious sign on their screens. "It must be him," uttered Natsumi, but Sgt. Keroro was working diligently on his chores.

The false accusation sent Keroro into a vengeful tizzy. And at long last, his Pokopen invasion would begin! Suddenly, everyone except those connected to Keroro Platoon--the Hinata family, Momoka, Koyuki and Mutsumi--stopped moving!

Keroro soon discovered that a new platoon had been sent by the Keron Forces, and an attack was already underway. This new invasion squad platoon was sent to replace the Keroro Platoon--and its leader is none other than Garuru, Giroro's ruthless big brother! Showing absolute supremacy over the Keroro Platoon, Garuru takes down all the members of the Keroro Platoon... and captures Keroro! Adding insult to injury, Garuru strips away Keroro's Keron Star--his "Seal of the Commanding Officer." But the battle isn't over! Natsumi puts on Mech armor developed by Giroro and Kululu in an attempt to rescue Keroro and the gang...

ENCOUNTER LXXXIV
THE LAST BATTLE: KERORO PLATOON'S 24 HOURS --PART FOUR

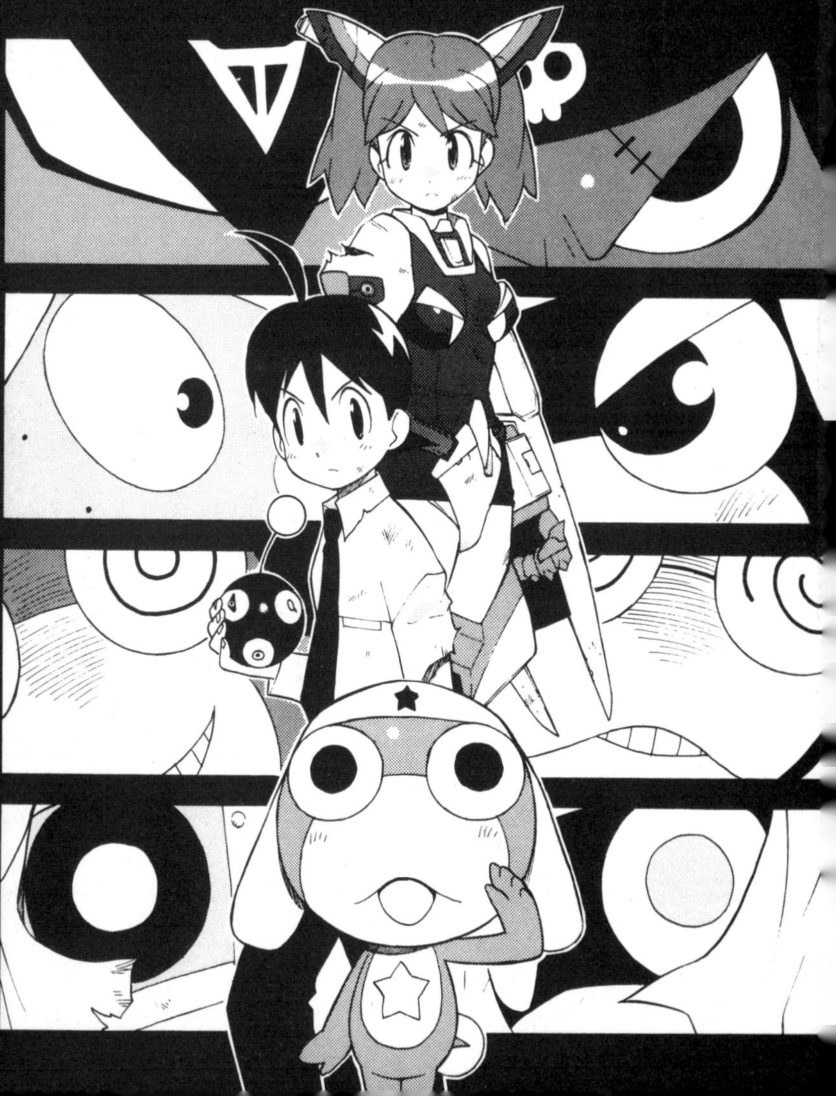

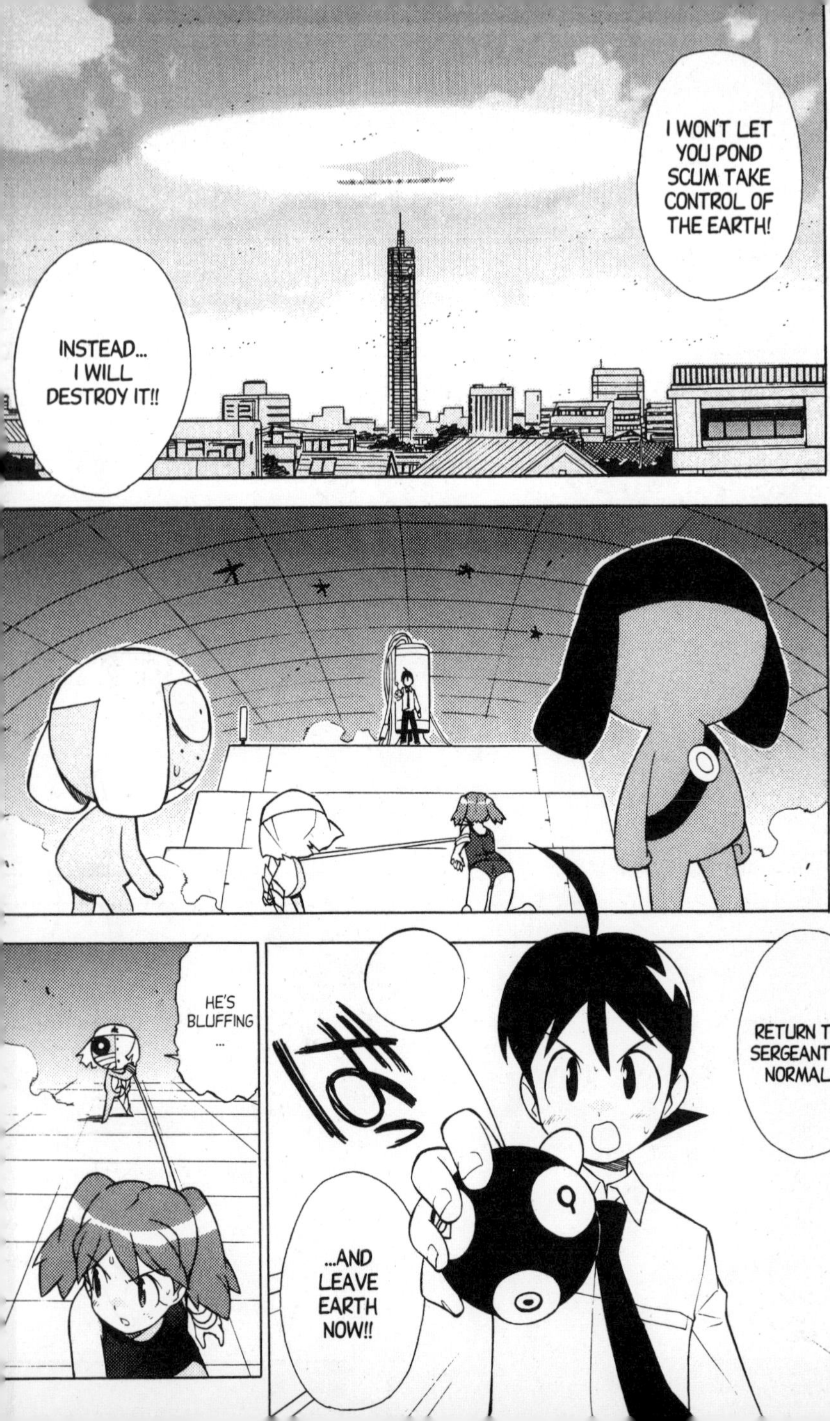
I WON'T LET YOU POND SCUM TAKE CONTROL OF THE EARTH!
INSTEAD... I WILL DESTROY IT!!
RETURN THE SERGEANT TO NORMAL...
...AND LEAVE EARTH NOW!!
HE'S BLUFFING ...

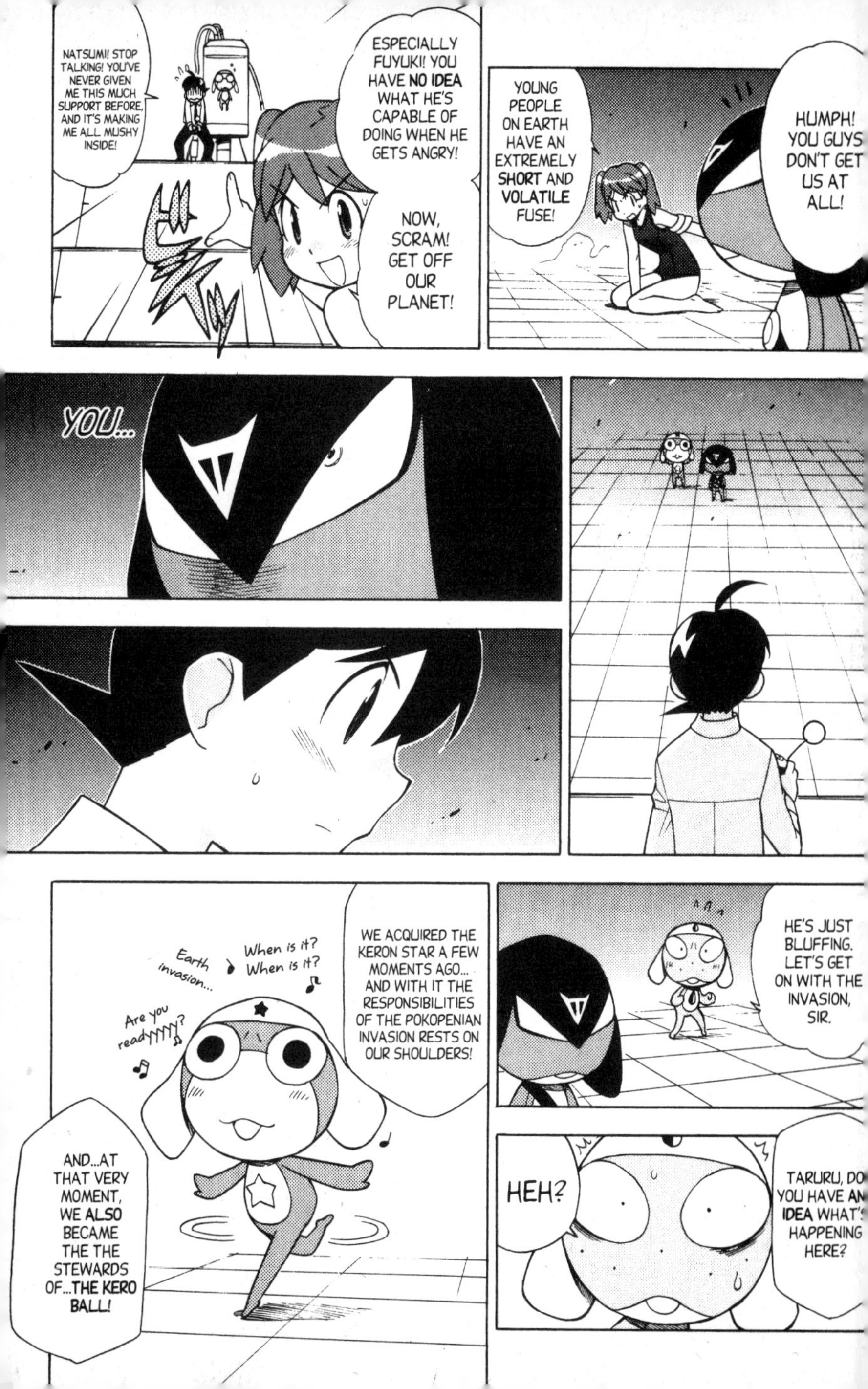
HUMPH! YOU GUYS DON'T GET US AT ALL!
YOUNG PEOPLE ON EARTH HAVE AN EXTREMELY SHORT AND VOLATILE FUSE!
ESPECIALLY FUYUKI! YOU HAVE NO IDEA WHAT HE'S CAPABLE OF DOING WHEN HE GETS ANGRY!
NOW, SCRAM! GET OFF OUR PLANET!
NATSUMI! STOP TALKING! YOU'VE NEVER GIVEN ME THIS MUCH SUPPORT BEFORE, AND IT'S MAKING ME ALL MUSHY INSIDE!
YOU...
HE'S JUST BLUFFING. LET'S GET ON WITH THE INVASION, SIR.
TARURU, DO YOU HAVE AN IDEA WHAT'S HAPPENING HERE?
HEH?
WE ACQUIRED THE KERON STAR A FEW MOMENTS AGO... AND WITH IT THE RESPONSIBILITIES OF THE POKOPENIAN INVASION RESTS ON OUR SHOULDERS!
Earth invasion...
When is it? When is it?
Are you readyyyyy?
AND...AT THAT VERY MOMENT, WE ALSO BECAME THE THE STEWARDS OF...THE KERO BALL!

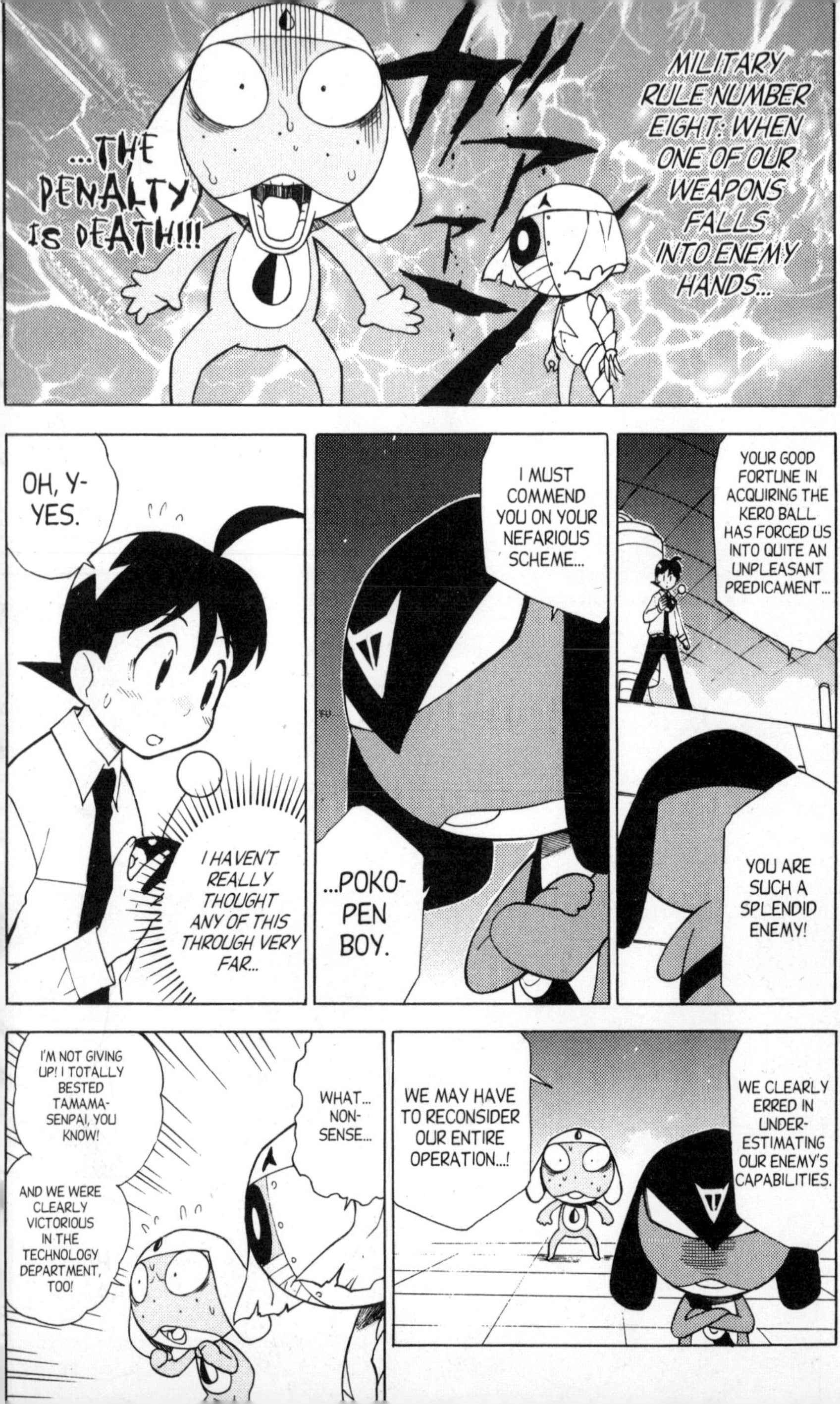
MILITARY RULE NUMBER EIGHT: WHEN ONE OF OUR WEAPONS FALLS INTO ENEMY HANDS...
...THE PENALTY IS DEATH!!!
YOUR GOOD FORTUNE IN ACQUIRING THE KERO BALL HAS FORCED US INTO QUITE AN UNPLEASANT PREDICAMENT...
YOU ARE SUCH A SPLENDID ENEMY!
I MUST COMMEND YOU ON YOUR NEFARIOUS SCHEME...
...POKO-PEN BOY.
OH, Y-YES.
I HAVEN'T REALLY THOUGHT ANY OF THIS THROUGH VERY FAR...
WE CLEARLY ERRED IN UNDER-ESTIMATING OUR ENEMY'S CAPABILITIES.
WE MAY HAVE TO RECONSIDER OUR ENTIRE OPERATION...!
WHAT... NON-SENSE...
I'M NOT GIVING UP! I TOTALLY BESTED TAMAMA-SENPAI, YOU KNOW!
AND WE WERE CLEARLY VICTORIOUS IN THE TECHNOLOGY DEPARTMENT, TOO!

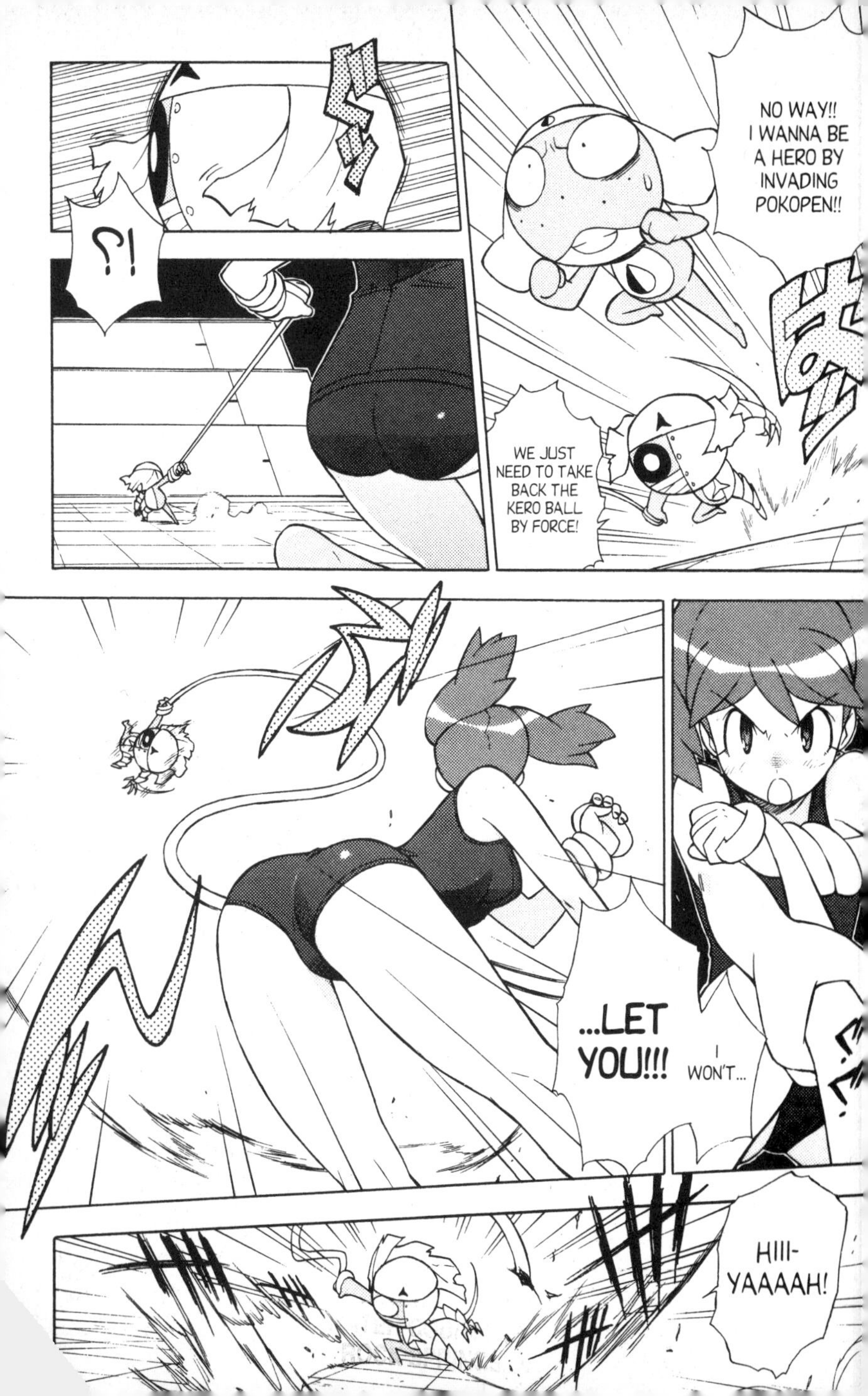
NO WAY!! I WANNA BE A HERO BY INVADING POKOPEN!!
WE JUST NEED TO TAKE BACK THE KERO BALL BY FORCE!
?!
I WON'T...
...LET YOU!!!
HIII-YAAAAH!

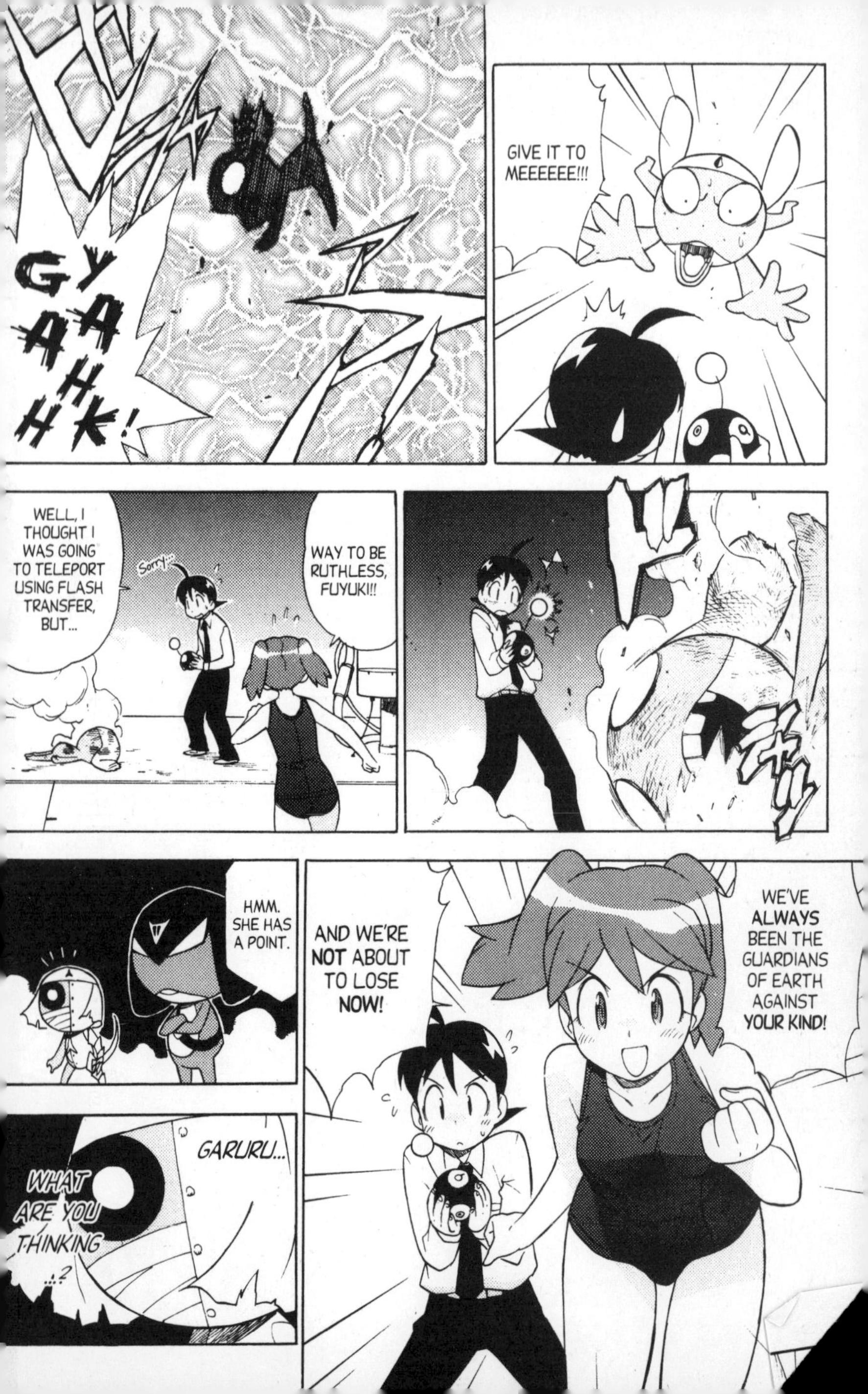
GIVE IT TO MEEEEEE!!!
GYAAHHHK!
WAY TO BE RUTHLESS, FUYUKI!!
Sorry...
WELL, I THOUGHT I WAS GOING TO TELEPORT USING FLASH TRANSFER, BUT...
WE'VE ALWAYS BEEN THE GUARDIANS OF EARTH AGAINST YOUR KIND!
AND WE'RE NOT ABOUT TO LOSE NOW!
HMM. SHE HAS A POINT.
GARURU...
WHAT ARE YOU THINKING ...?

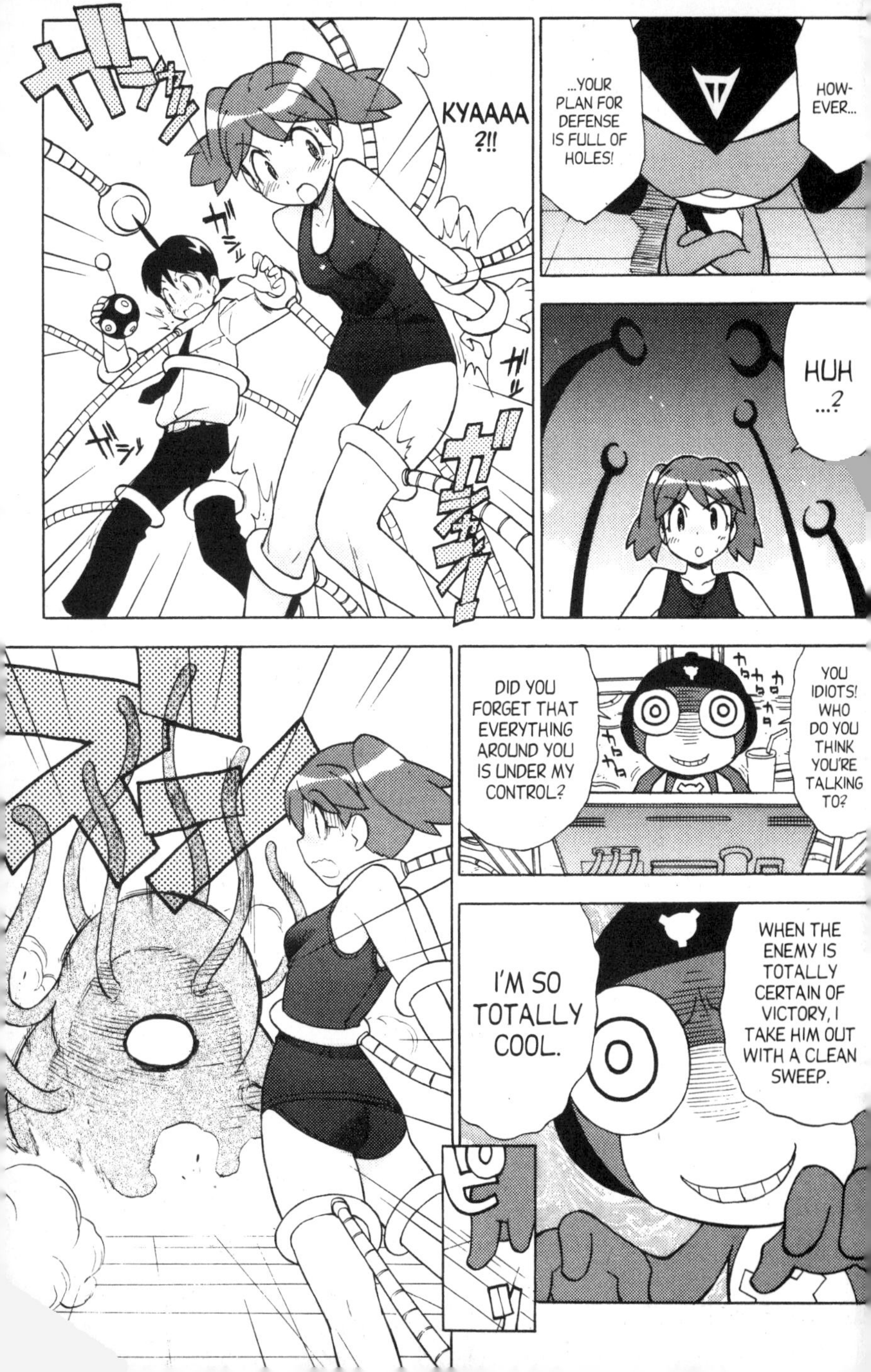
HOW-EVER...
...YOUR PLAN FOR DEFENSE IS FULL OF HOLES!
HUH ...?
KYAAAA ?!!
YOU IDIOTS! WHO DO YOU THINK YOU'RE TALKING TO?
DID YOU FORGET THAT EVERYTHING AROUND YOU IS UNDER MY CONTROL?
WHEN THE ENEMY IS TOTALLY CERTAIN OF VICTORY, I TAKE HIM OUT WITH A CLEAN SWEEP.
I'M SO TOTALLY COOL.

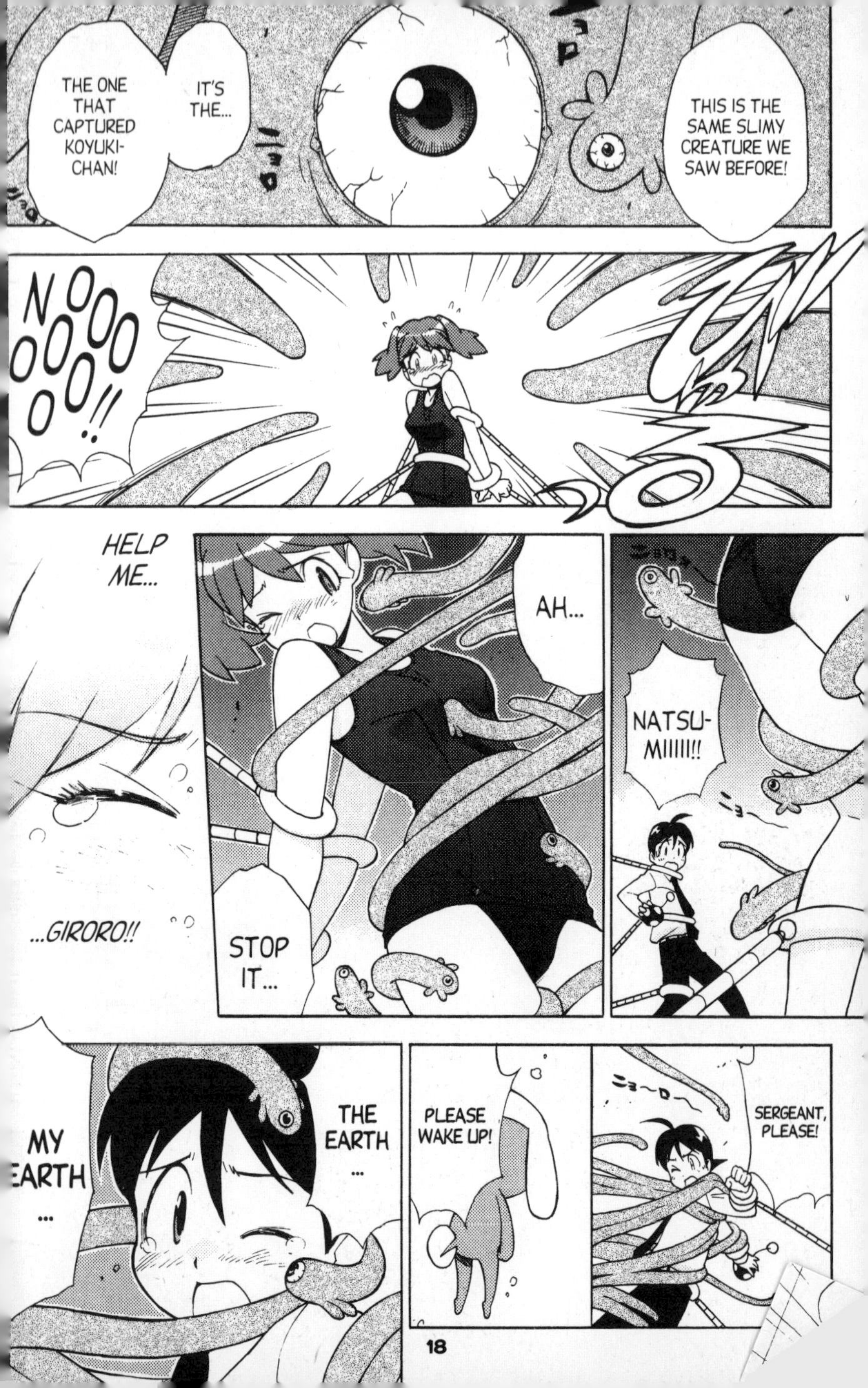

THIS IS THE SAME SLIMY CREATURE WE SAW BEFORE!
IT'S THE...
THE ONE THAT CAPTURED KOYUKI-CHAN!
NOOOOOOOOO!!
NATSU-MIIIII!!
AH...
STOP IT...
HELP ME...
...GIRORO!!
SERGEANT, PLEASE!
PLEASE WAKE UP!
THE EARTH ...
MY EARTH ...

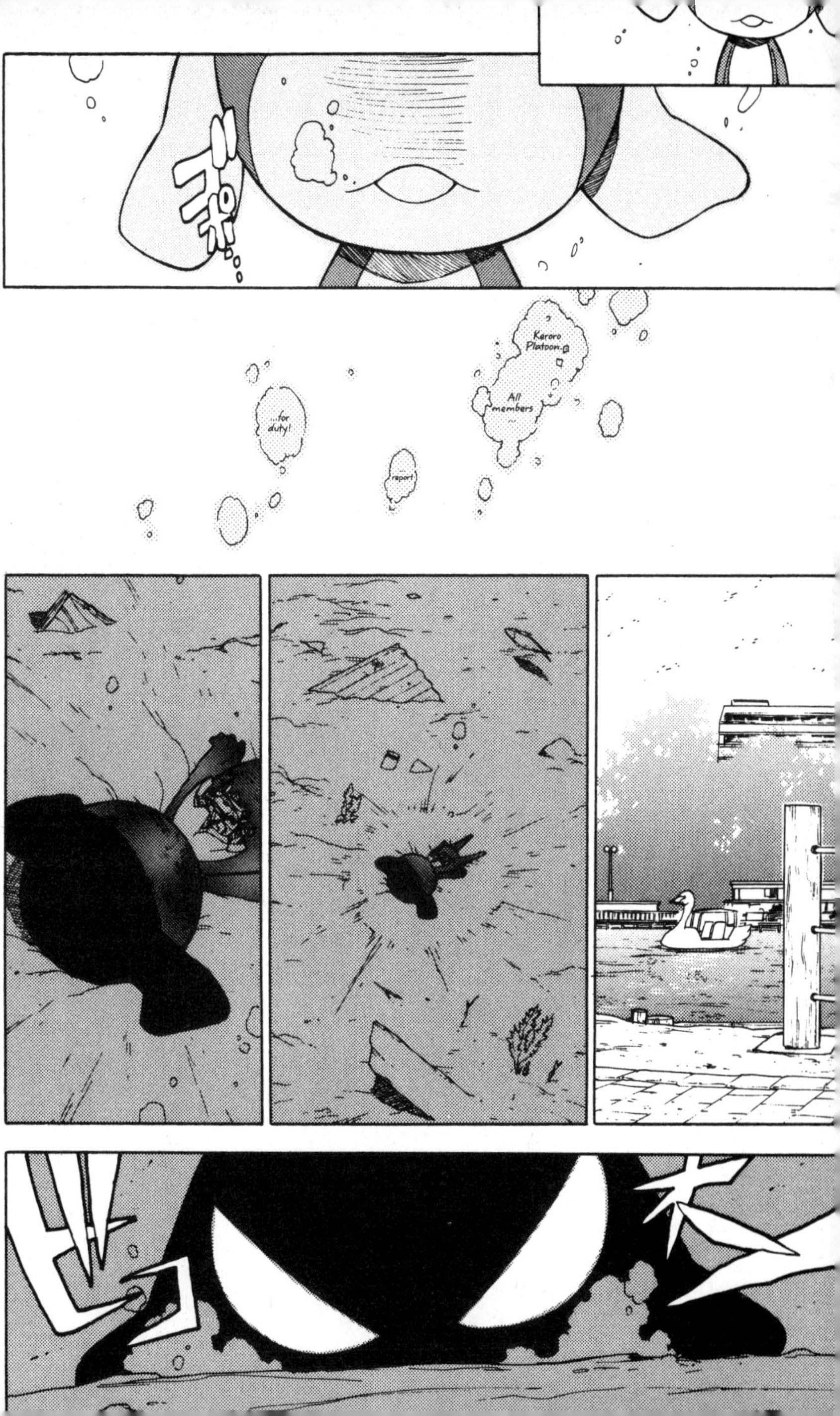
Keroro Platoon...
All members...
...report
...for duty!

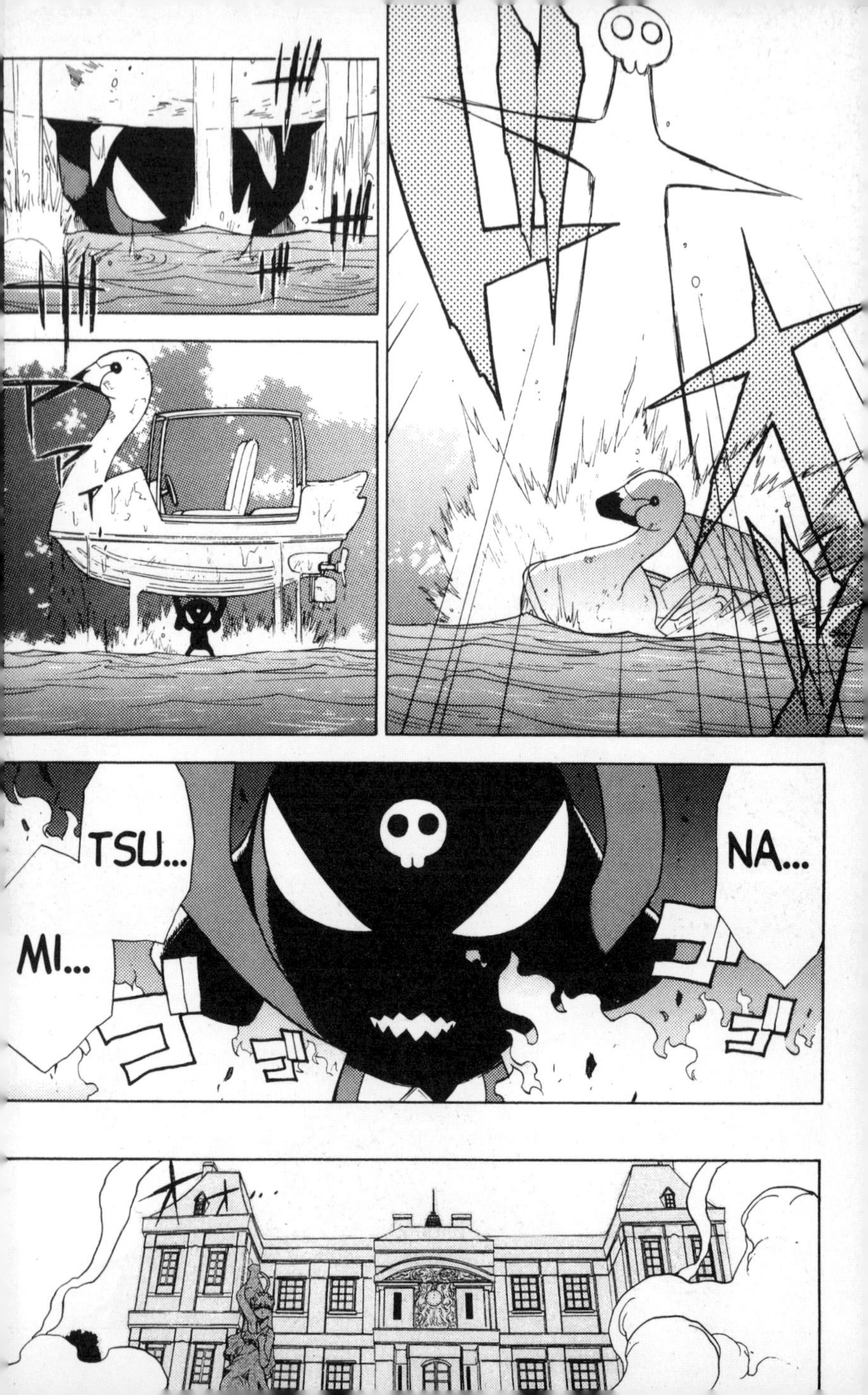
NA...
TSU...
MI...

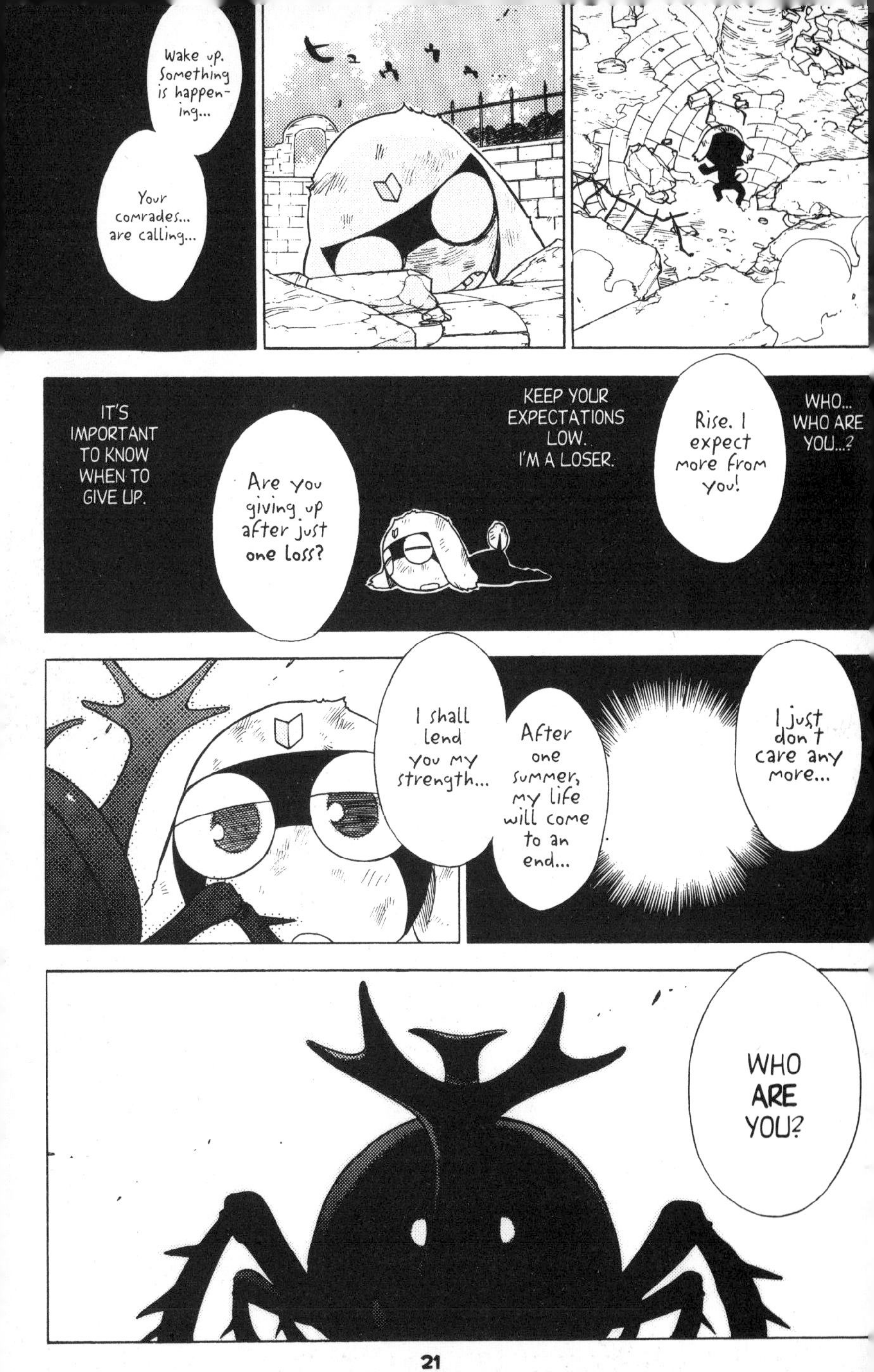
Wake up. Something is happening...
Your comrades... are calling...
WHO... WHO ARE YOU...?
Rise. I expect more from you!
KEEP YOUR EXPECTATIONS LOW. I'M A LOSER.
Are you giving up after just one loss?
IT'S IMPORTANT TO KNOW WHEN TO GIVE UP.
I just don't care any more...
After one summer, my life will come to an end...
I shall lend you my strength...
WHO ARE YOU?

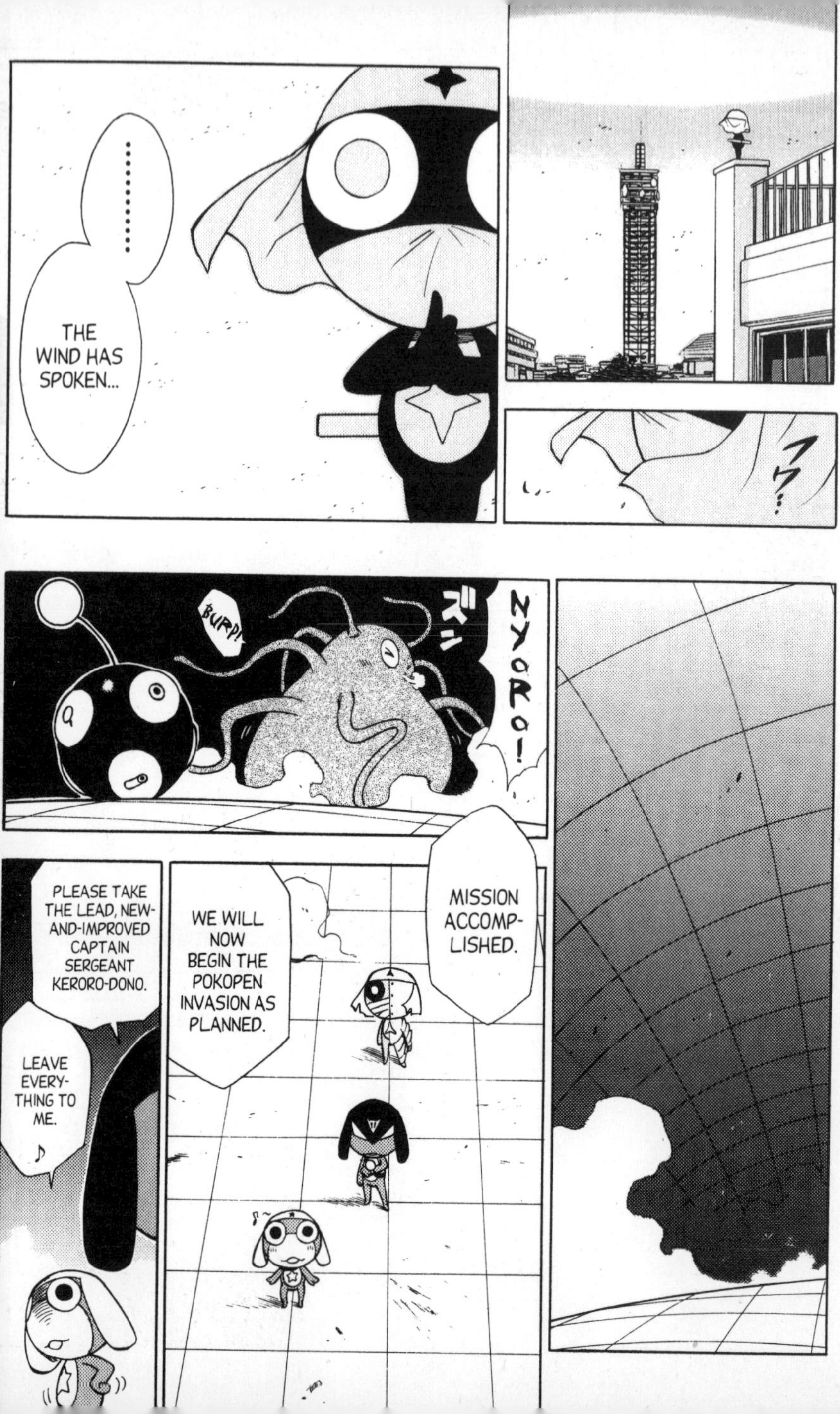

フワ…
......
THE WIND HAS SPOKEN...
NYORO!
ズッ
BURP!
MISSION ACCOMPLISHED.
WE WILL NOW BEGIN THE POKOPEN INVASION AS PLANNED.
PLEASE TAKE THE LEAD, NEW-AND-IMPROVED CAPTAIN SERGEANT KERORO-DONO.
LEAVE EVERYTHING TO ME. ♪

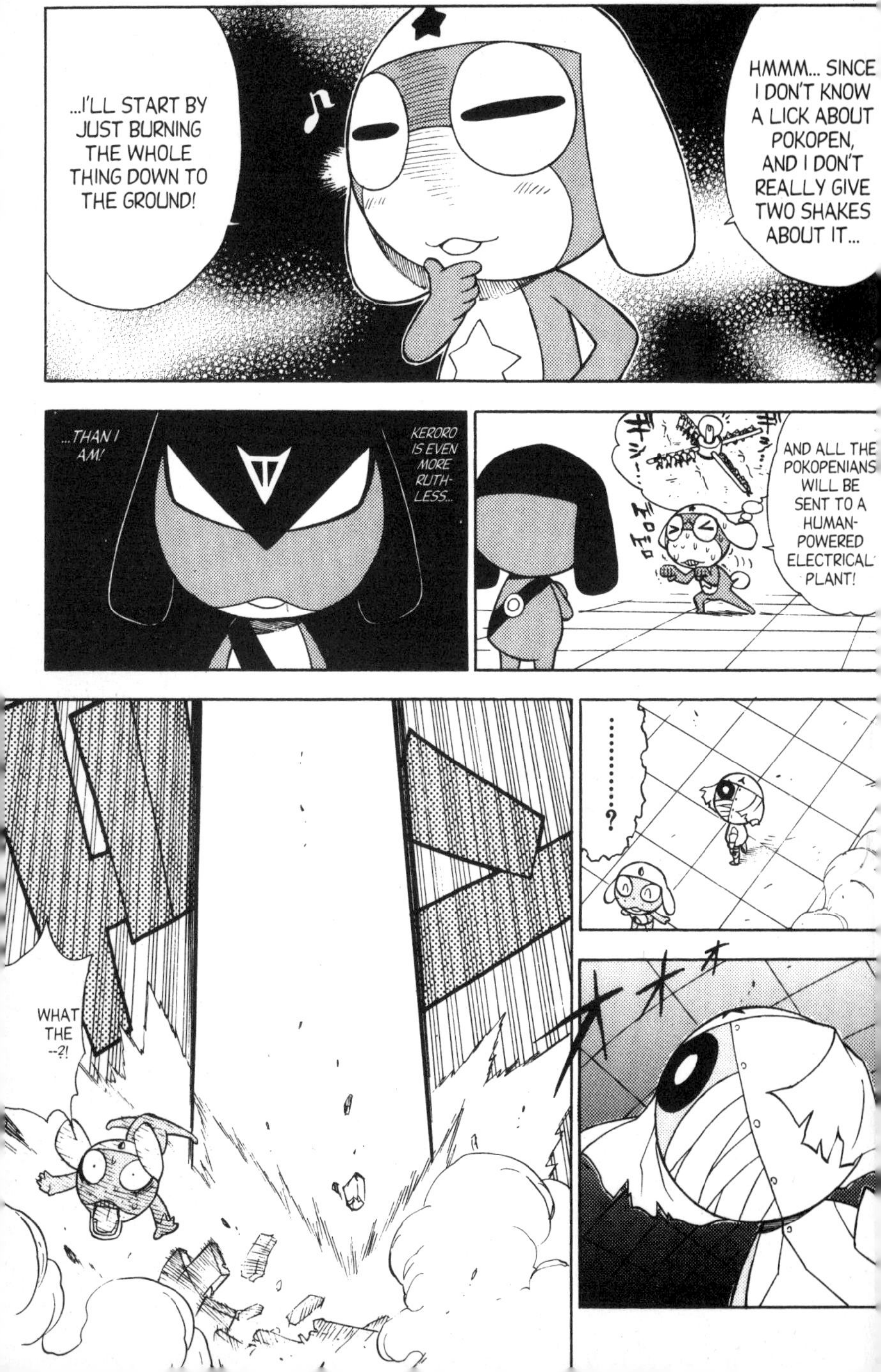
HMMM... SINCE I DON'T KNOW A LICK ABOUT POKOPEN, AND I DON'T REALLY GIVE TWO SHAKES ABOUT IT...
...I'LL START BY JUST BURNING THE WHOLE THING DOWN TO THE GROUND!
AND ALL THE POKOPENIANS WILL BE SENT TO A HUMAN-POWERED ELECTRICAL PLANT!
KERORO IS EVEN MORE RUTHLESS...
...THAN I AM!
......?
オオオ
WHAT THE --?!

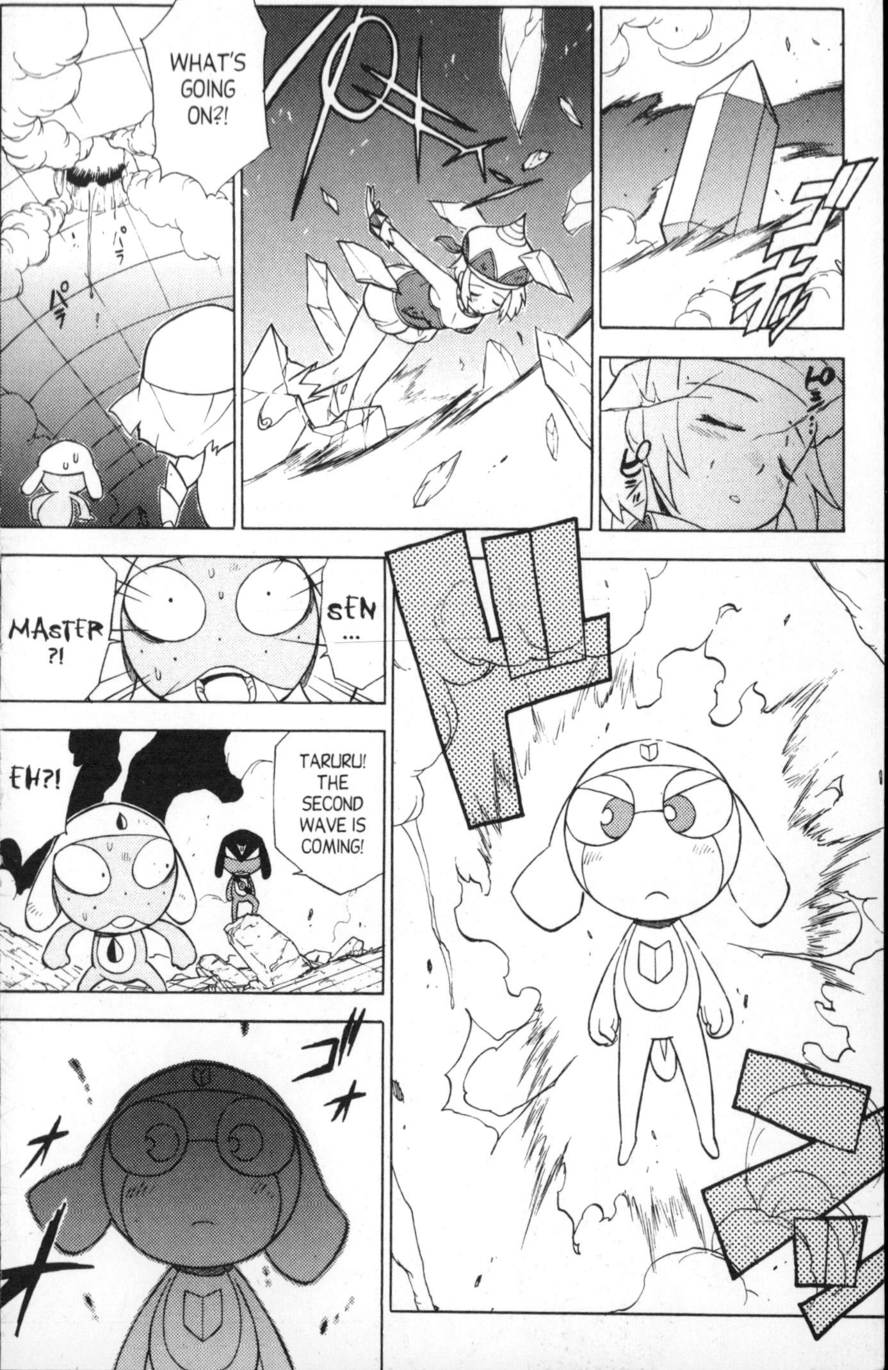
WHAT'S GOING ON?!
SEN...
MASTER?!
TARURU! THE SECOND WAVE IS COMING!
EH?!

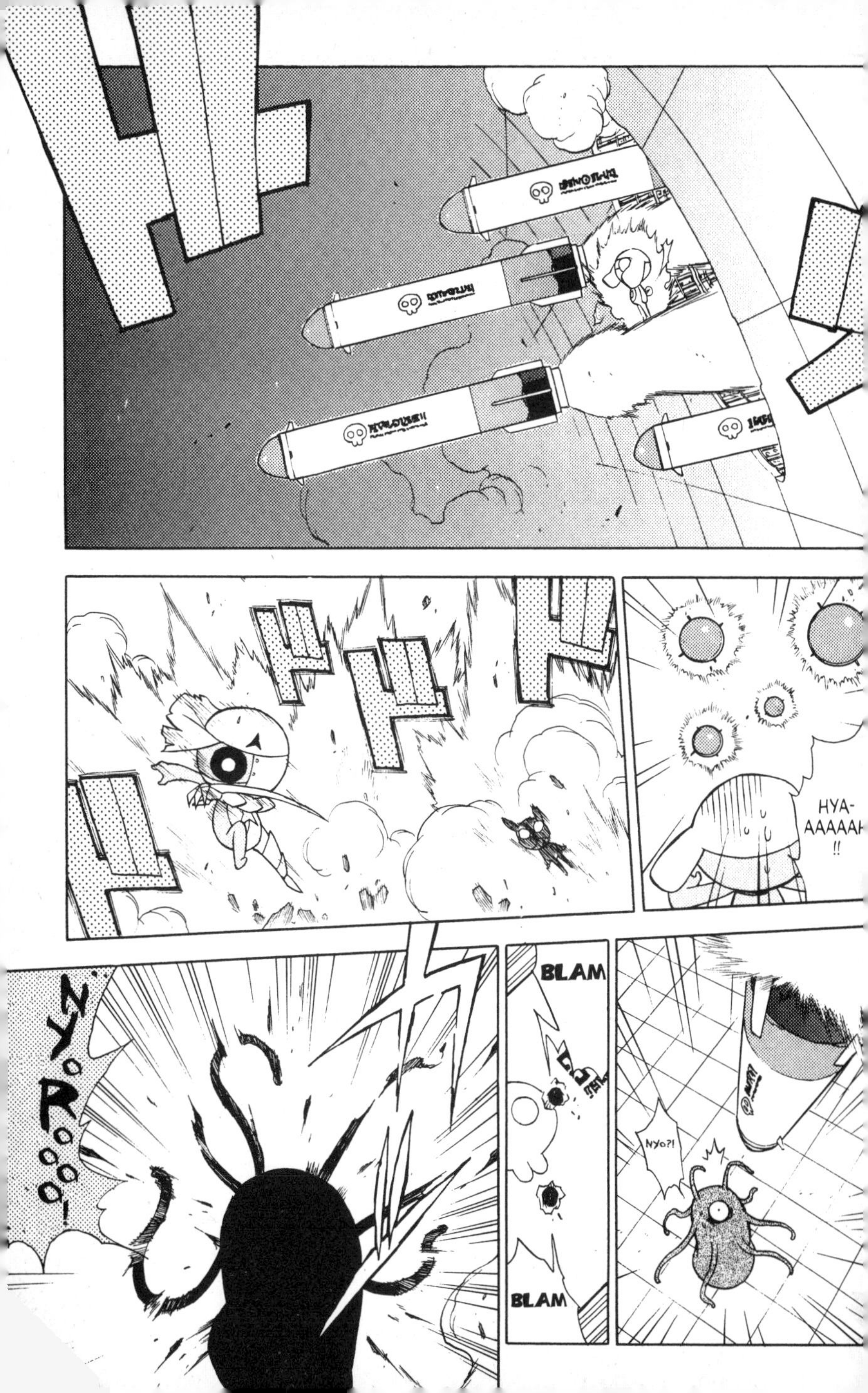
HYA-AAAAAH!!
NYO?!
BLAM
BLAM
NYOROOOO!

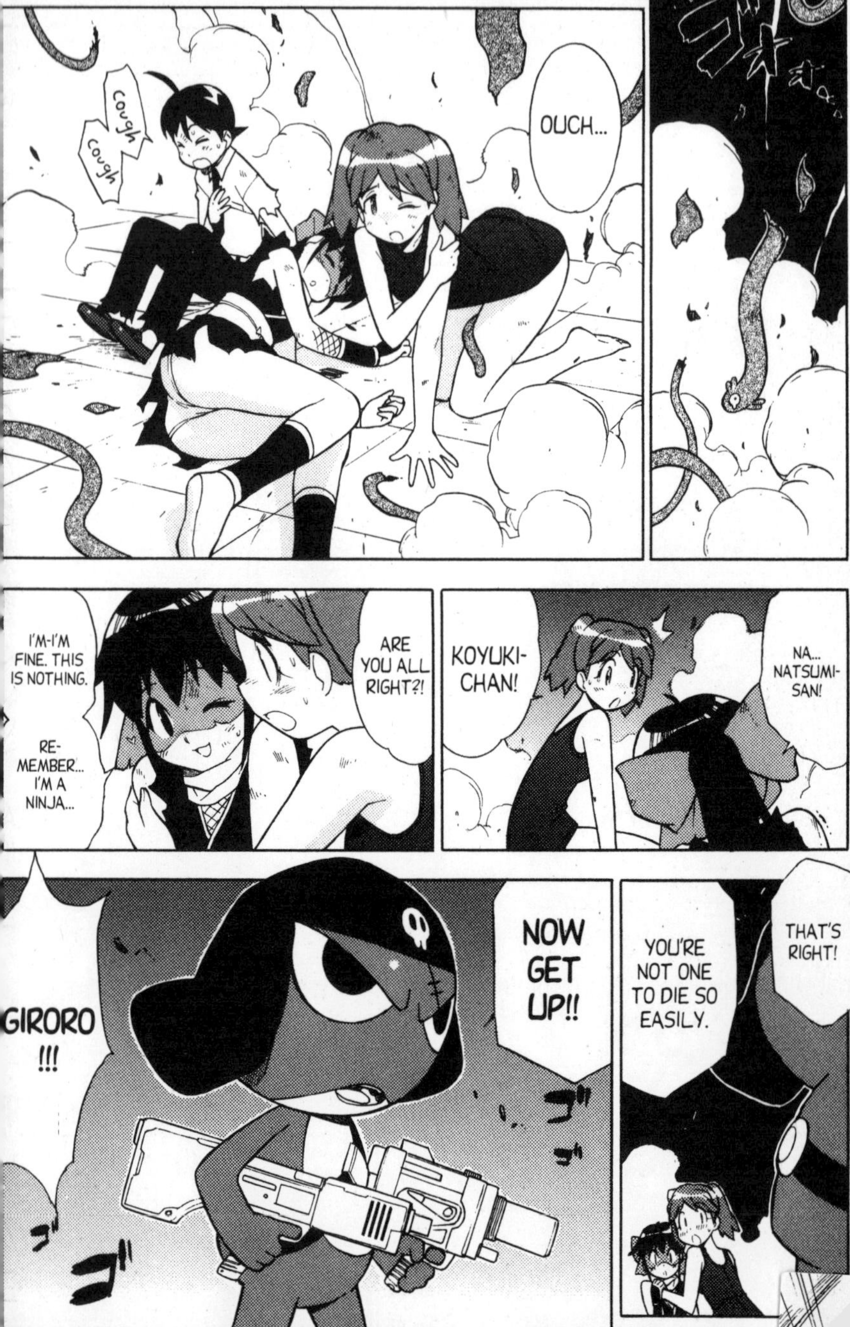
OUCH...
cough cough
NA... NATSUMI-SAN!
KOYUKI-CHAN!
ARE YOU ALL RIGHT?!
I'M-I'M FINE. THIS IS NOTHING.
RE-MEMBER... I'M A NINJA...
THAT'S RIGHT!
YOU'RE NOT ONE TO DIE SO EASILY.
NOW GET UP!!
GIRORO !!!

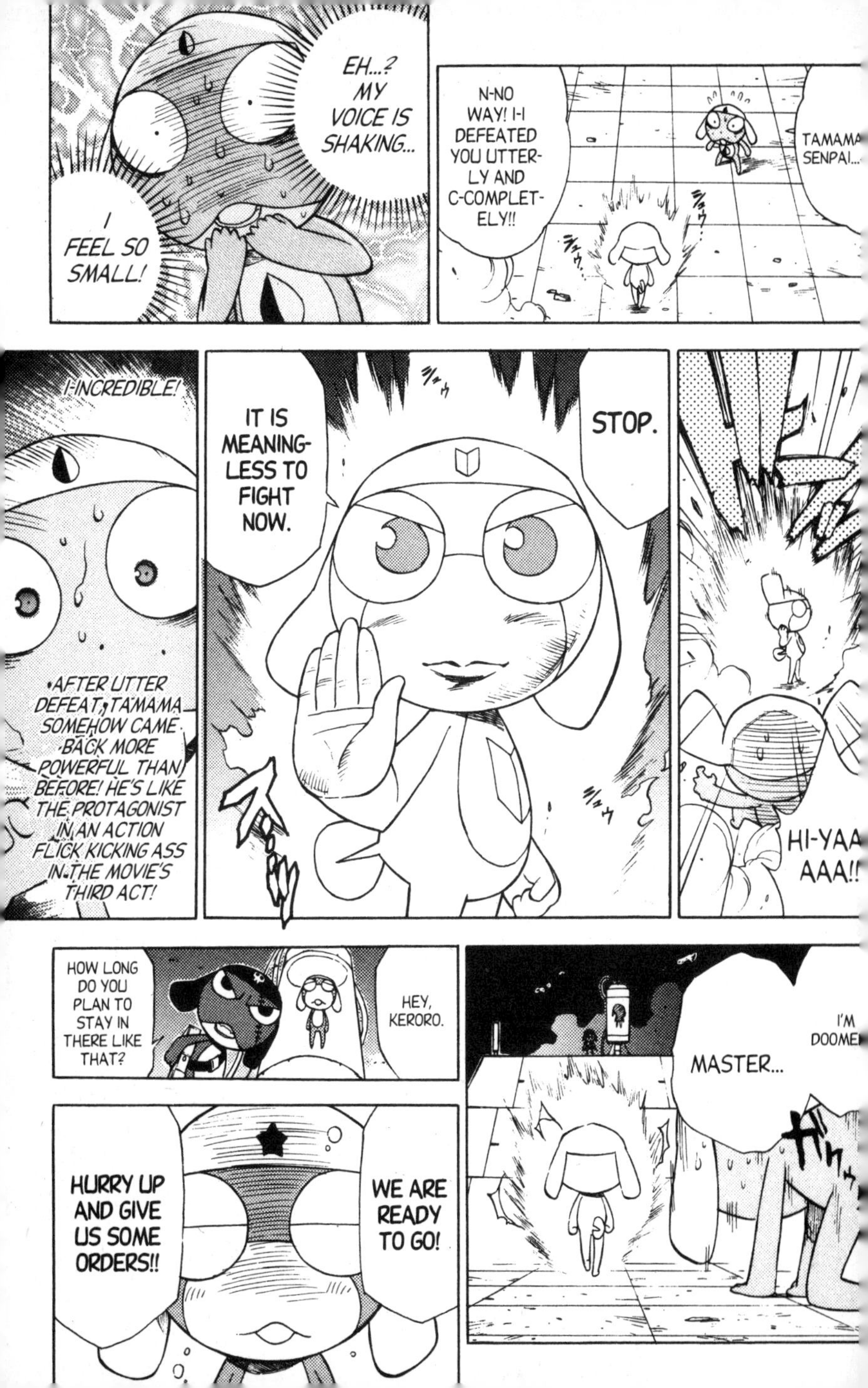
TAMAMA SENPAI...
N-NO WAY! I-I DEFEATED YOU UTTER-LY AND C-COMPLET-ELY!!
EH...? MY VOICE IS SHAKING...
I FEEL SO SMALL!
HI-YAA AAA!!
STOP.
IT IS MEANING-LESS TO FIGHT NOW.
I-INCREDIBLE!
•AFTER UTTER DEFEAT, TAMAMA SOMEHOW CAME BACK MORE POWERFUL THAN BEFORE! HE'S LIKE THE PROTAGONIST IN AN ACTION FLICK KICKING ASS IN THE MOVIE'S THIRD ACT!
I'M DOOME
MASTER...
HEY, KERORO.
HOW LONG DO YOU PLAN TO STAY IN THERE LIKE THAT?
WE ARE READY TO GO!
HURRY UP AND GIVE US SOME ORDERS!!

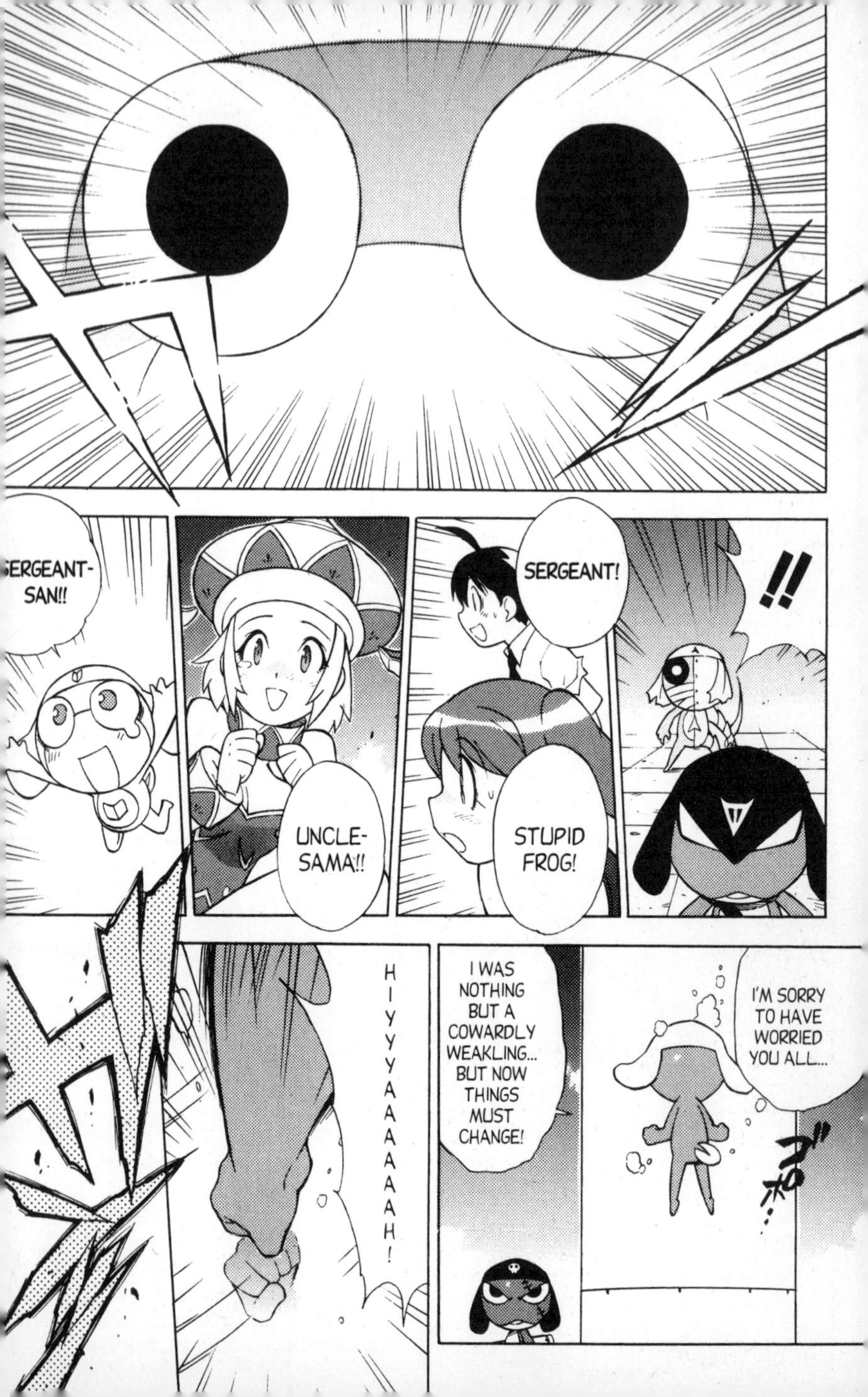
!!
SERGEANT!
STUPID FROG!
UNCLE-SAMA!!
SERGEANT-SAN!!
I'M SORRY TO HAVE WORRIED YOU ALL...
I WAS NOTHING BUT A COWARDLY WEAKLING... BUT NOW THINGS MUST CHANGE!
HIYYYAAAAAAH!

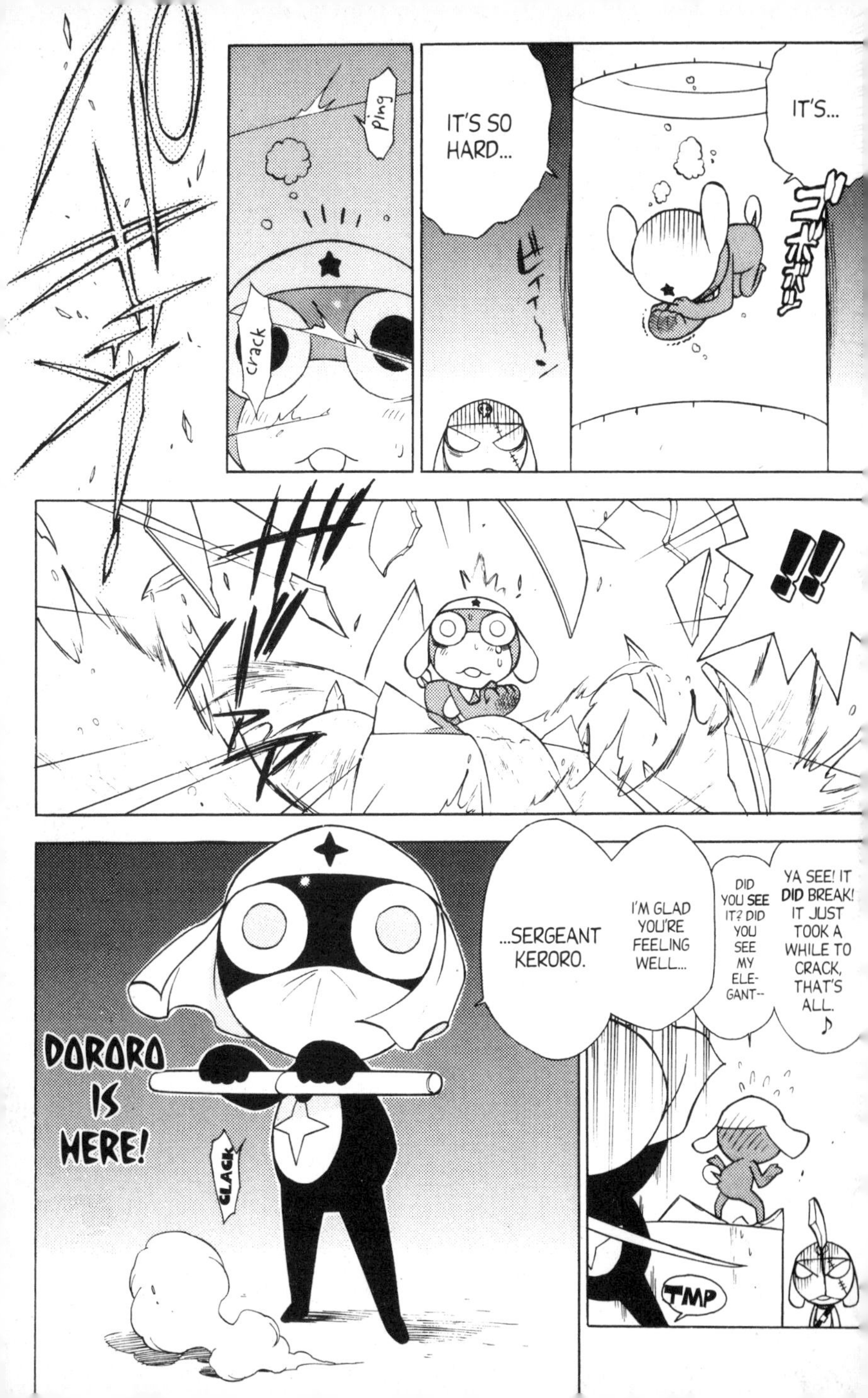
IT'S...
IT'S SO HARD...
ping
crack
!!
YA SEE! IT DID BREAK! IT JUST TOOK A WHILE TO CRACK, THAT'S ALL. ♪
DID YOU SEE IT? DID YOU SEE MY ELE-GANT--
I'M GLAD YOU'RE FEELING WELL...
...SERGEANT KERORO.
TMP
DORORO IS HERE!
CLACK

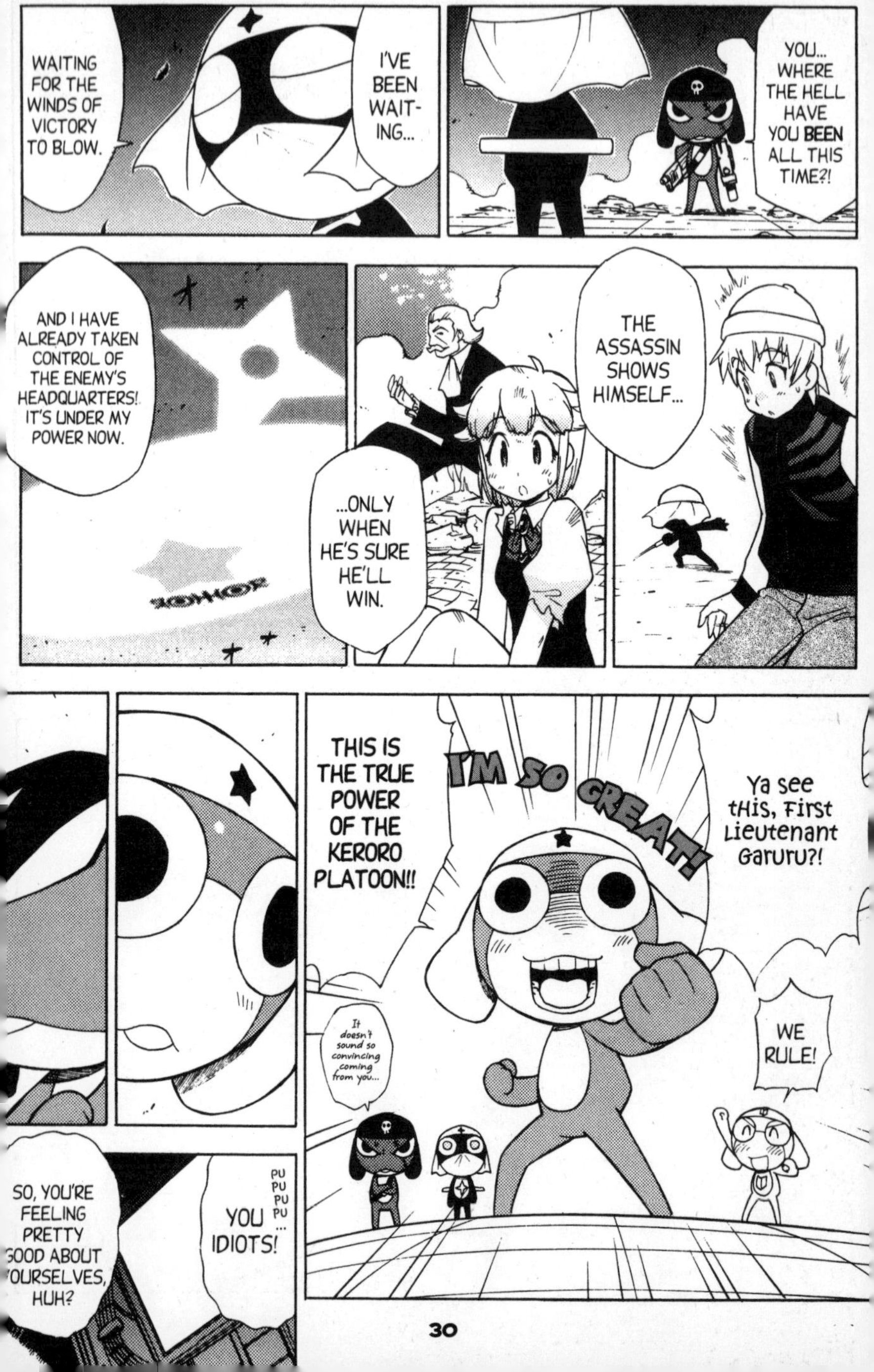
YOU... WHERE THE HELL HAVE YOU BEEN ALL THIS TIME?!
I'VE BEEN WAITING...
WAITING FOR THE WINDS OF VICTORY TO BLOW.
THE ASSASSIN SHOWS HIMSELF...
...ONLY WHEN HE'S SURE HE'LL WIN.
AND I HAVE ALREADY TAKEN CONTROL OF THE ENEMY'S HEADQUARTERS! IT'S UNDER MY POWER NOW.
Ya see tHIS, First Lieutenant Garuru?!
I'M SO GREAT!
THIS IS THE TRUE POWER OF THE KERORO PLATOON!!
WE RULE!
It doesn't sound so convincing coming from you...
PU PU PU PU...
YOU IDIOTS!
SO, YOU'RE FEELING PRETTY GOOD ABOUT YOURSELVES, HUH?

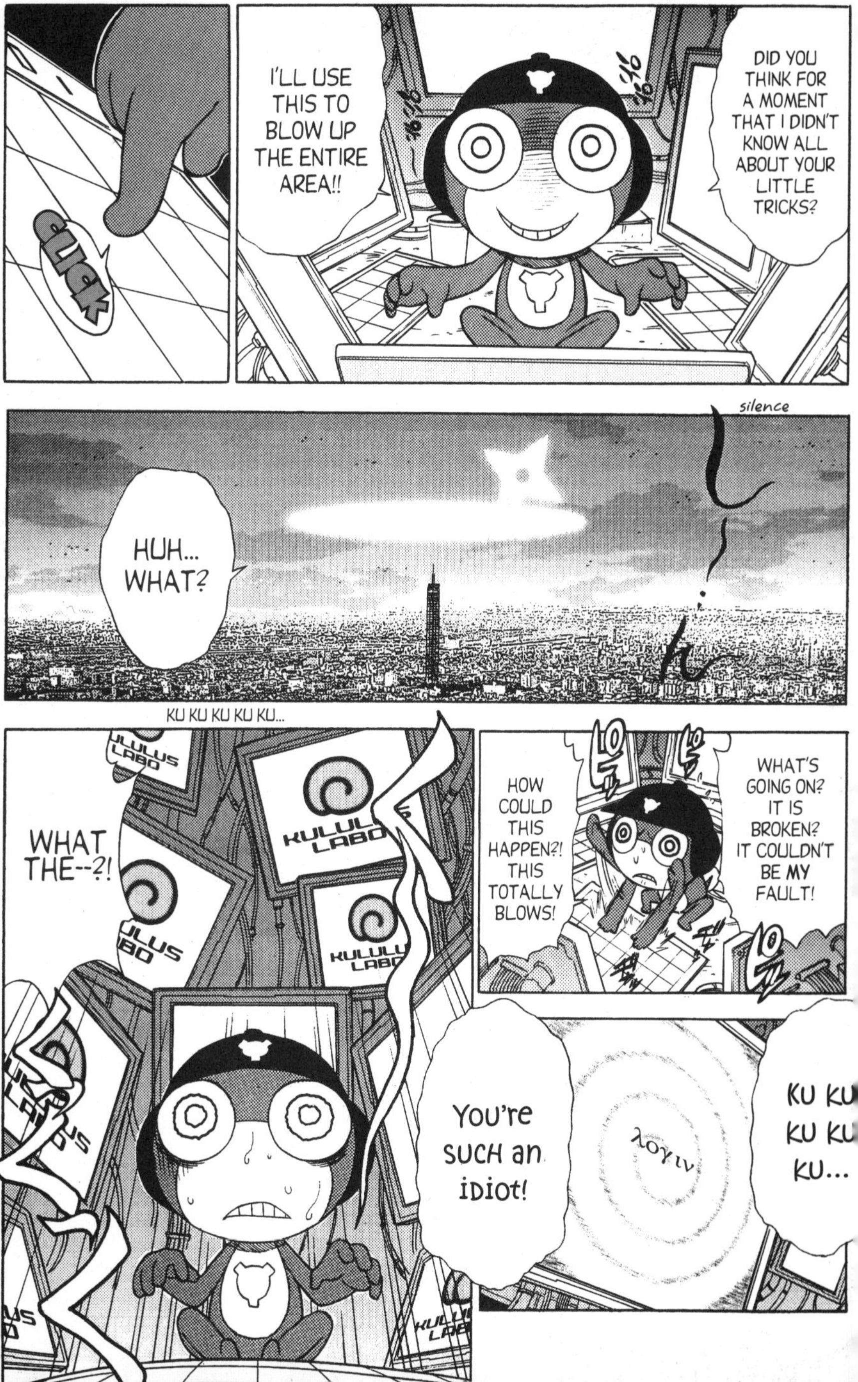
DID YOU THINK FOR A MOMENT THAT I DIDN'T KNOW ALL ABOUT YOUR LITTLE TRICKS?
I'LL USE THIS TO BLOW UP THE ENTIRE AREA!!
CLICK
silence
HUH... WHAT?
KU KU KU KU KU...
WHAT'S GOING ON? IT IS BROKEN? IT COULDN'T BE MY FAULT!
HOW COULD THIS HAPPEN?! THIS TOTALLY BLOWS!
KU KU KU KU KU...
λογιν
You're SUCH an idiot!
KULULUS LABO
WHAT THE--?!

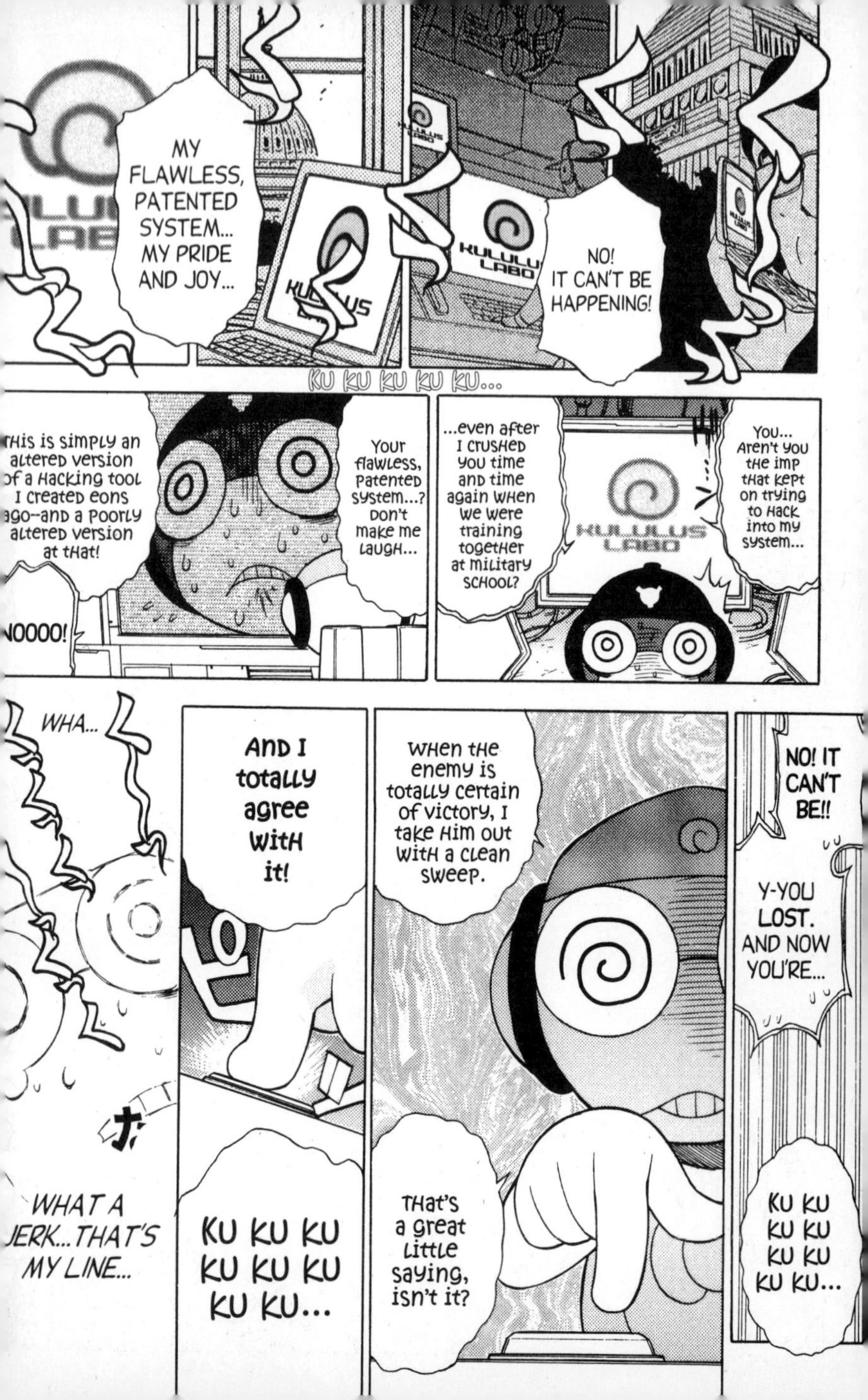
NO! IT CAN'T BE HAPPENING!
MY FLAWLESS, PATENTED SYSTEM... MY PRIDE AND JOY...
KU KU KU KU KU KU...
You... Aren't you the imp that kept on trying to hack into my system...
...even after I crushed you time and time again when we were training together at military school?
Your flawless, patented system...? Don't make me laugh...
This is simply an altered version of a hacking tool I created eons ago--and a poorly altered version at that!
NOOOO!
NO! IT CAN'T BE!!
Y-YOU LOST. AND NOW YOU'RE...
KU KU KU KU KU KU KU KU...
When the enemy is totally certain of victory, I take him out with a clean sweep.
That's a great little saying, isn't it?
And I totally agree with it!
KU KU KU KU KU KU KU KU...
WHA...
WHAT A JERK...THAT'S MY LINE...

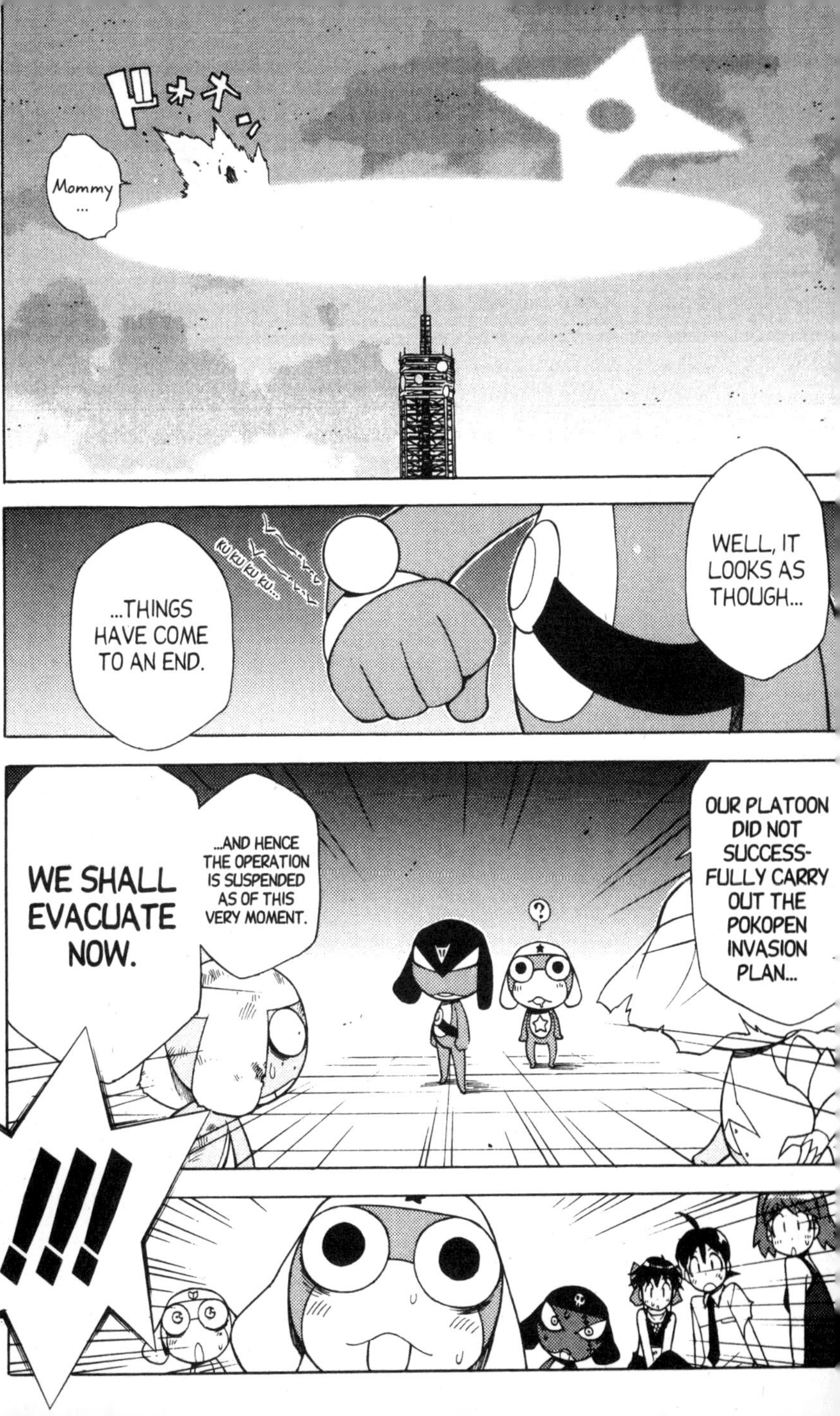
Mommy ...
WELL, IT LOOKS AS THOUGH...
KU KU KU KU...
...THINGS HAVE COME TO AN END.
OUR PLATOON DID NOT SUCCESS-FULLY CARRY OUT THE POKOPEN INVASION PLAN...
?
...AND HENCE THE OPERATION IS SUSPENDED AS OF THIS VERY MOMENT.
WE SHALL EVACUATE NOW.
!!!

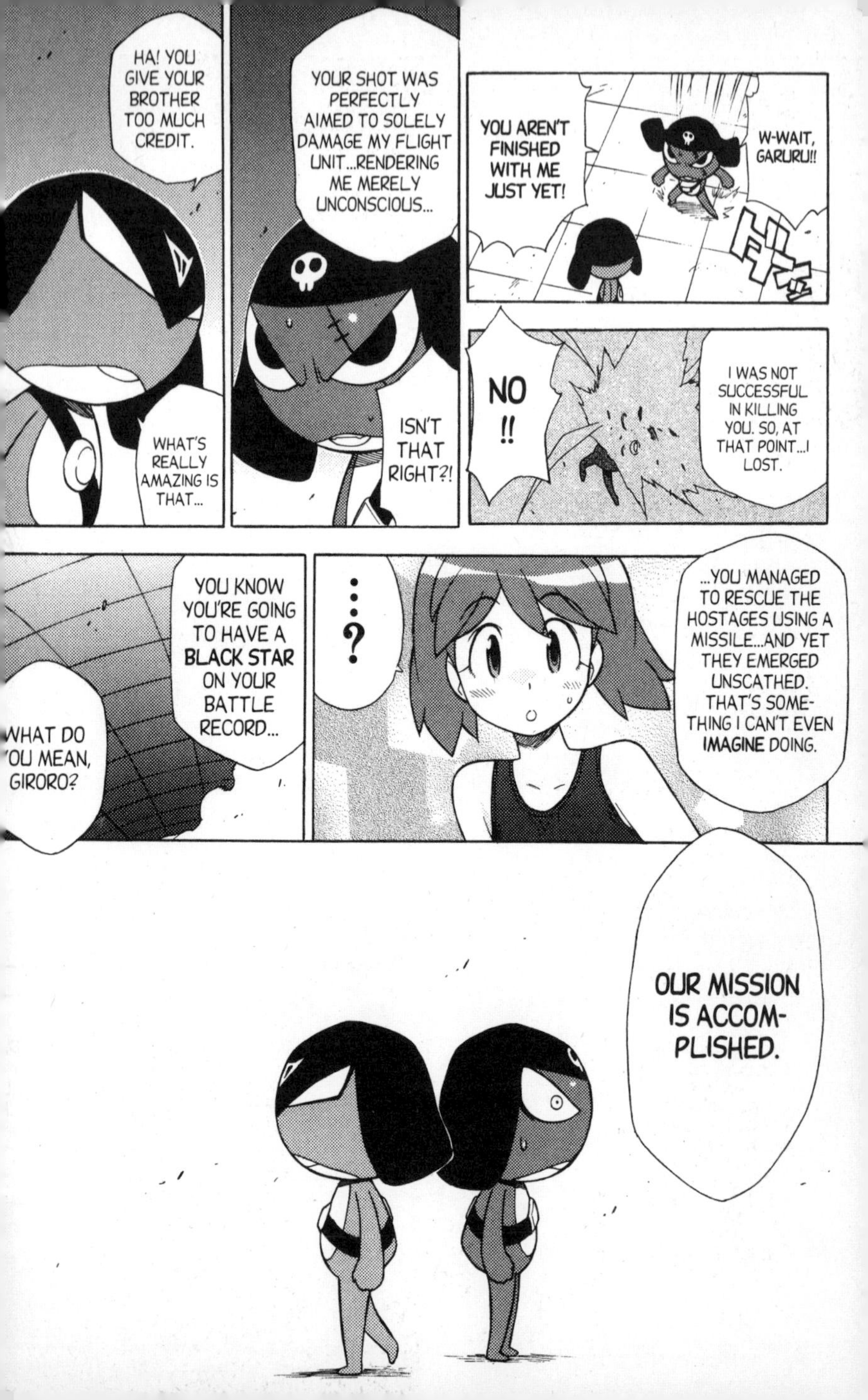

W-WAIT, GARURU!!
YOU AREN'T FINISHED WITH ME JUST YET!
I WAS NOT SUCCESSFUL IN KILLING YOU. SO, AT THAT POINT...I LOST.
NO !!
YOUR SHOT WAS PERFECTLY AIMED TO SOLELY DAMAGE MY FLIGHT UNIT...RENDERING ME MERELY UNCONSCIOUS...
ISN'T THAT RIGHT?!
HA! YOU GIVE YOUR BROTHER TOO MUCH CREDIT.
WHAT'S REALLY AMAZING IS THAT...
...YOU MANAGED TO RESCUE THE HOSTAGES USING A MISSILE...AND YET THEY EMERGED UNSCATHED. THAT'S SOME-THING I CAN'T EVEN IMAGINE DOING.
...?
YOU KNOW YOU'RE GOING TO HAVE A BLACK STAR ON YOUR BATTLE RECORD...
WHAT DO YOU MEAN, GIRORO?
OUR MISSION IS ACCOM-PLISHED.

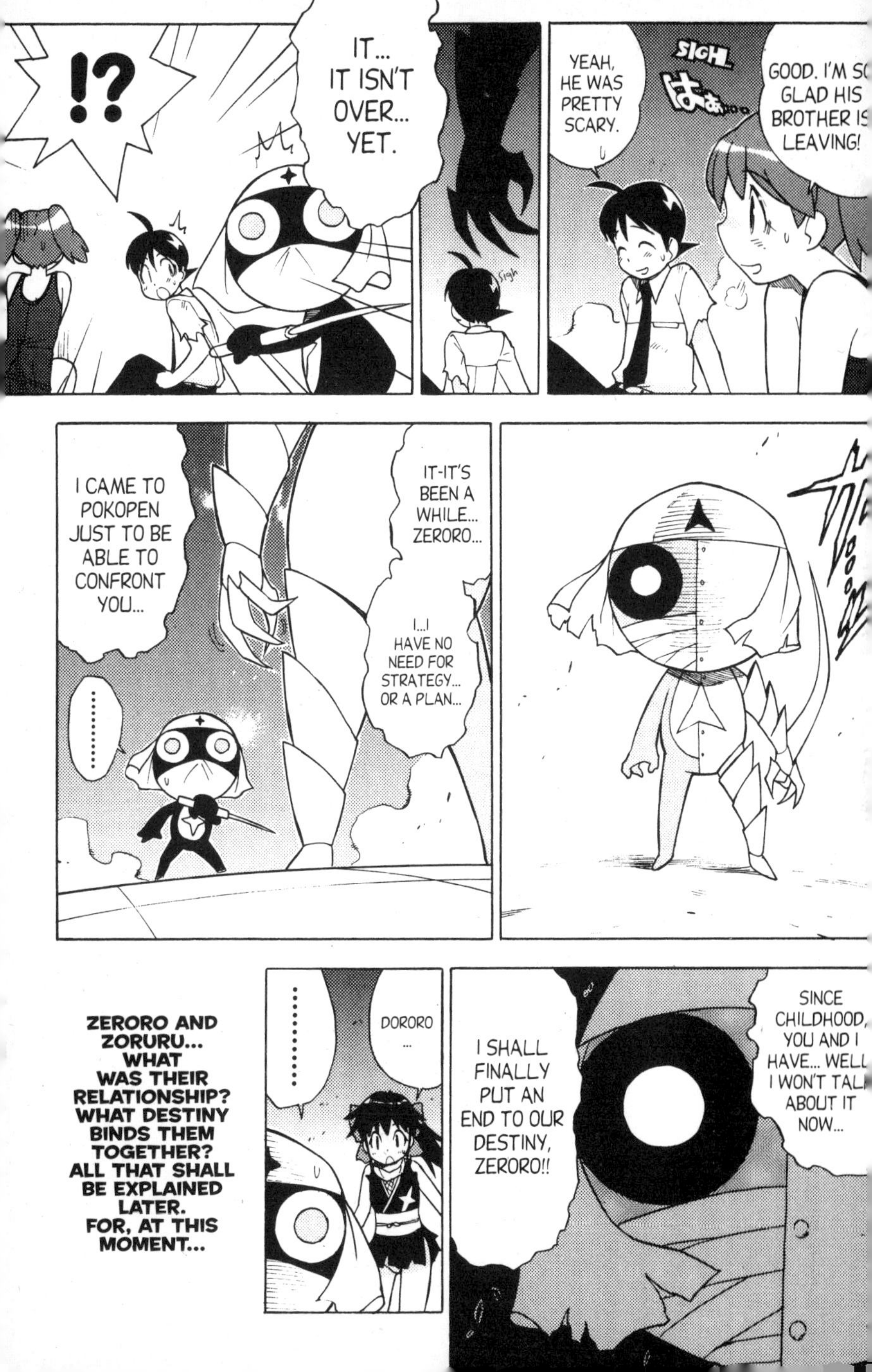
GOOD. I'M SO GLAD HIS BROTHER IS LEAVING!
SIGH
はぁ…
YEAH, HE WAS PRETTY SCARY.
Sigh
IT... IT ISN'T OVER... YET.
!?
IT-IT'S BEEN A WHILE... ZERORO...
I...I HAVE NO NEED FOR STRATEGY... OR A PLAN...
I CAME TO POKOPEN JUST TO BE ABLE TO CONFRONT YOU...
....
SINCE CHILDHOOD, YOU AND I HAVE... WELL I WON'T TALK ABOUT IT NOW...
I SHALL FINALLY PUT AN END TO OUR DESTINY, ZERORO!!
DORORO ...
....
ZERORO AND ZORURU... WHAT WAS THEIR RELATIONSHIP? WHAT DESTINY BINDS THEM TOGETHER? ALL THAT SHALL BE EXPLAINED LATER. FOR, AT THIS MOMENT...

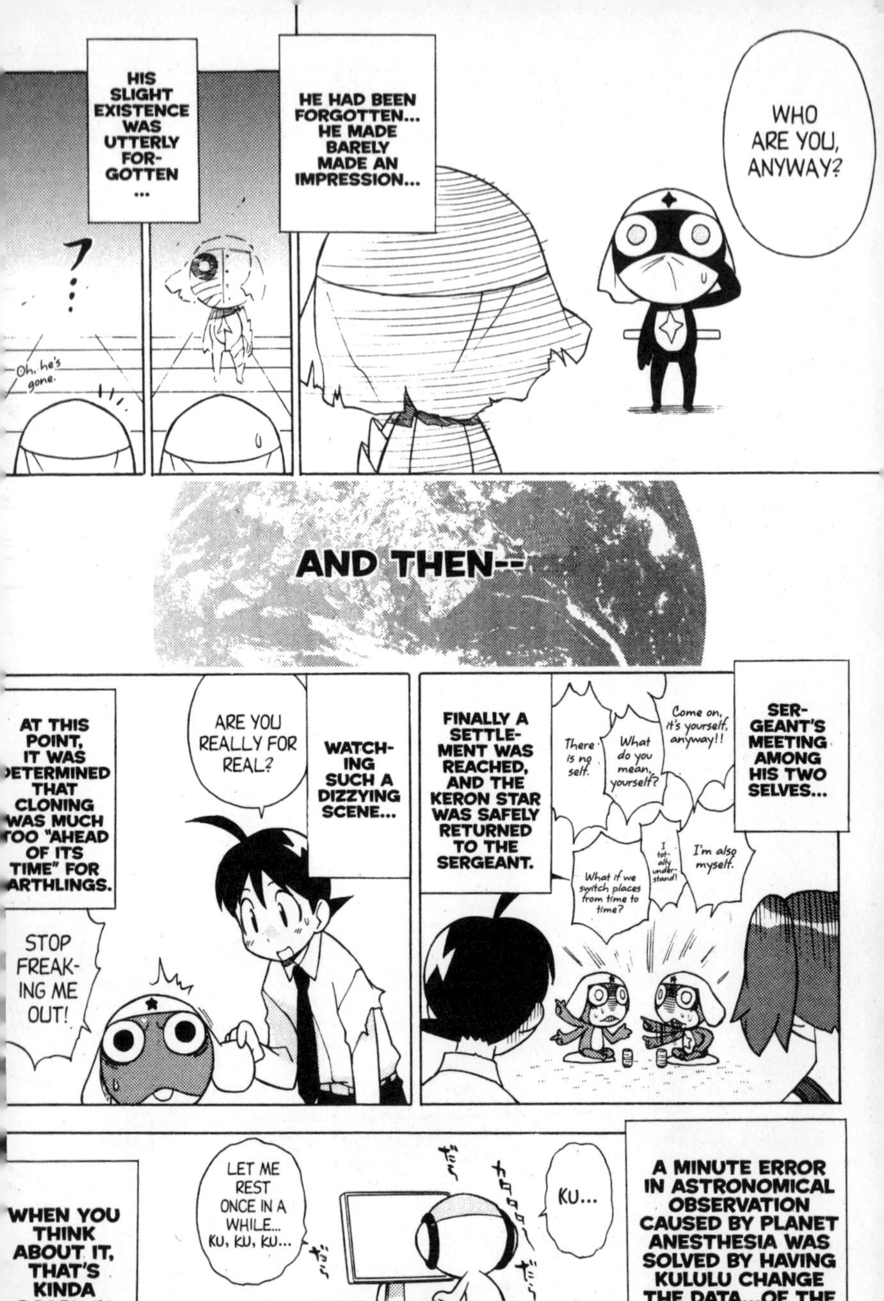
WHO ARE YOU, ANYWAY?
HE HAD BEEN FORGOTTEN... HE MADE BARELY MADE AN IMPRESSION...
HIS SLIGHT EXISTENCE WAS UTTERLY FORGOTTEN ...
?...
Oh, he's gone.
AND THEN--
SERGEANT'S MEETING AMONG HIS TWO SELVES...
Come on, it's yourself, anyway!!
What do you mean, yourself?
There is no self.
I'm also myself.
I totally understand!
What if we switch places from time to time?
FINALLY A SETTLEMENT WAS REACHED, AND THE KERON STAR WAS SAFELY RETURNED TO THE SERGEANT.
WATCHING SUCH A DIZZYING SCENE...
ARE YOU REALLY FOR REAL?
AT THIS POINT, IT WAS ETERMINED THAT CLONING WAS MUCH OO "AHEAD OF ITS TIME" FOR ARTHLINGS.
STOP FREAKING ME OUT!
A MINUTE ERROR IN ASTRONOMICAL OBSERVATION CAUSED BY PLANET ANESTHESIA WAS SOLVED BY HAVING KULULU CHANGE THE DATA...OF THE ENTIRE WORLD!
KU...
LET ME REST ONCE IN A WHILE... KU, KU, KU...
WHEN YOU THINK ABOUT IT, THAT'S KINDA SCARY IN ITSELF...

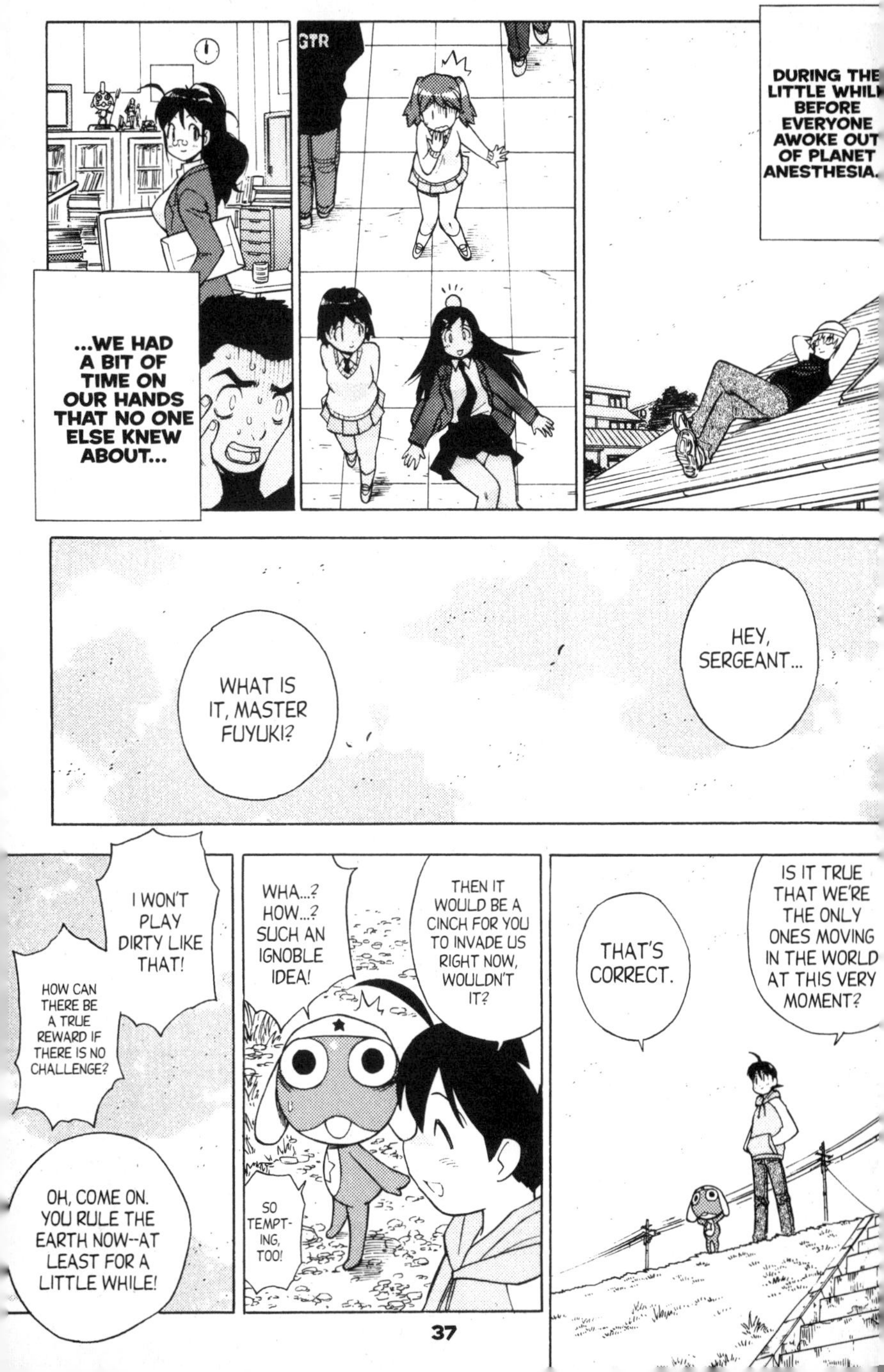
DURING THE LITTLE WHIL BEFORE EVERYONE AWOKE OUT OF PLANET ANESTHESIA.
...WE HAD A BIT OF TIME ON OUR HANDS THAT NO ONE ELSE KNEW ABOUT...
HEY, SERGEANT...
WHAT IS IT, MASTER FUYUKI?
IS IT TRUE THAT WE'RE THE ONLY ONES MOVING IN THE WORLD AT THIS VERY MOMENT?
THAT'S CORRECT.
THEN IT WOULD BE A CINCH FOR YOU TO INVADE US RIGHT NOW, WOULDN'T IT?
WHA...? HOW...? SUCH AN IGNOBLE IDEA!
SO TEMPT-ING, TOO!
I WON'T PLAY DIRTY LIKE THAT!
HOW CAN THERE BE A TRUE REWARD IF THERE IS NO CHALLENGE?
OH, COME ON. YOU RULE THE EARTH NOW--AT LEAST FOR A LITTLE WHILE!

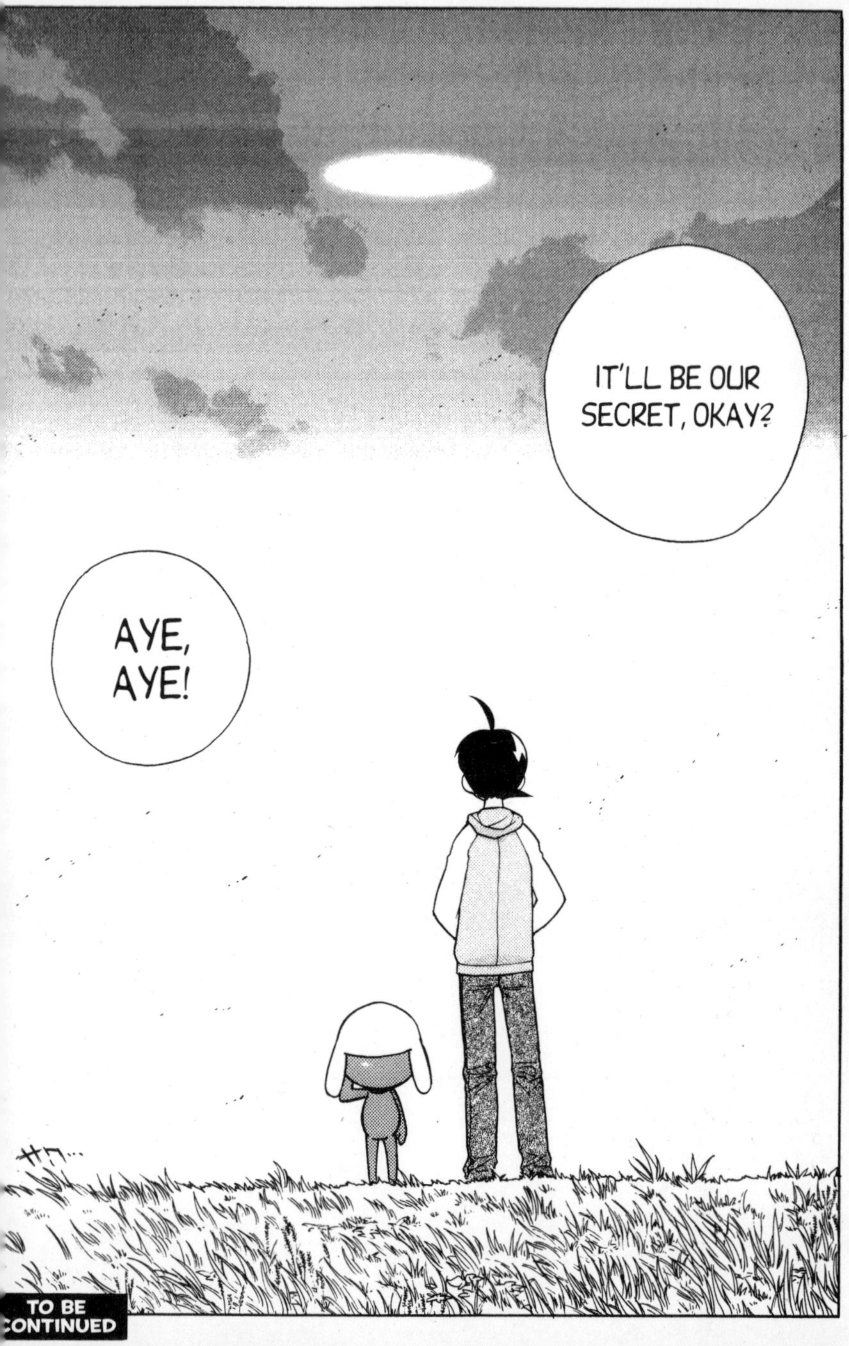
IT'LL BE OUR SECRET, OKAY?
AYE, AYE!
TO BE CONTINUED

ENCOUNTER LXXXV
THE TALE OF KOYUKI AZUMAYA & DORORO

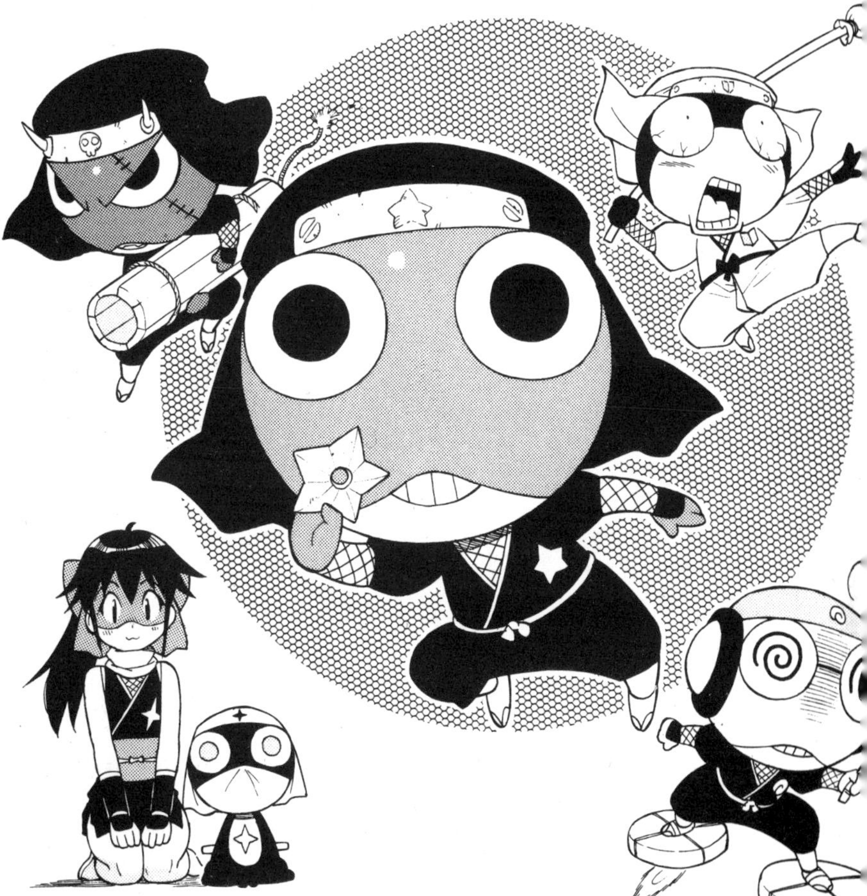

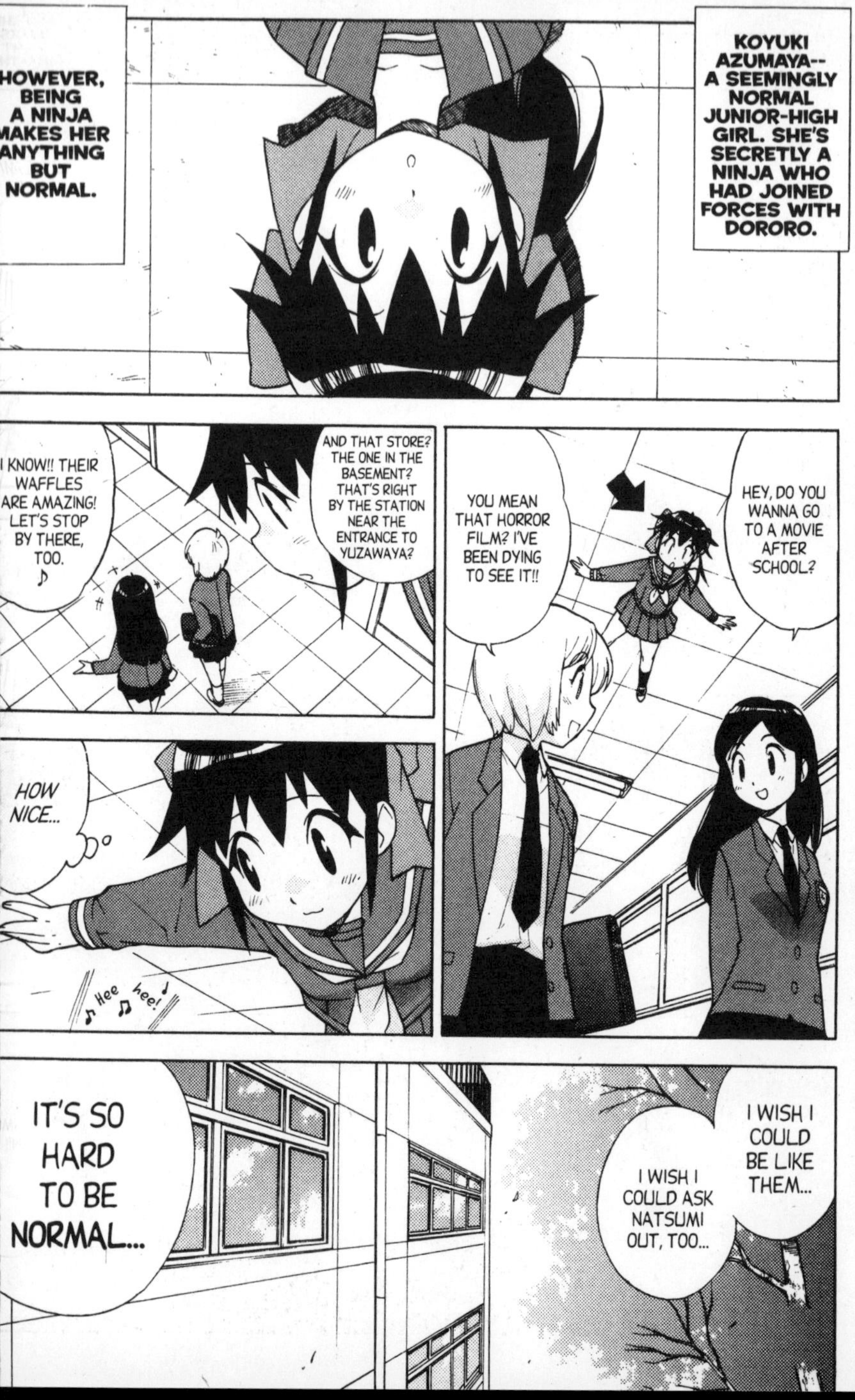
KOYUKI AZUMAYA-- A SEEMINGLY NORMAL JUNIOR-HIGH GIRL. SHE'S SECRETLY A NINJA WHO HAD JOINED FORCES WITH DORORO.
HOWEVER, BEING A NINJA MAKES HER ANYTHING BUT NORMAL.
HEY, DO YOU WANNA GO TO A MOVIE AFTER SCHOOL?
YOU MEAN THAT HORROR FILM? I'VE BEEN DYING TO SEE IT!!
AND THAT STORE? THE ONE IN THE BASEMENT? THAT'S RIGHT BY THE STATION NEAR THE ENTRANCE TO YUZAWAYA?
I KNOW!! THEIR WAFFLES ARE AMAZING! LET'S STOP BY THERE, TOO. ♪
HOW NICE...
♪ Hee ♫ hee! ♩
I WISH I COULD BE LIKE THEM...
I WISH I COULD ASK NATSUMI OUT, TOO...
IT'S SO HARD TO BE NORMAL...

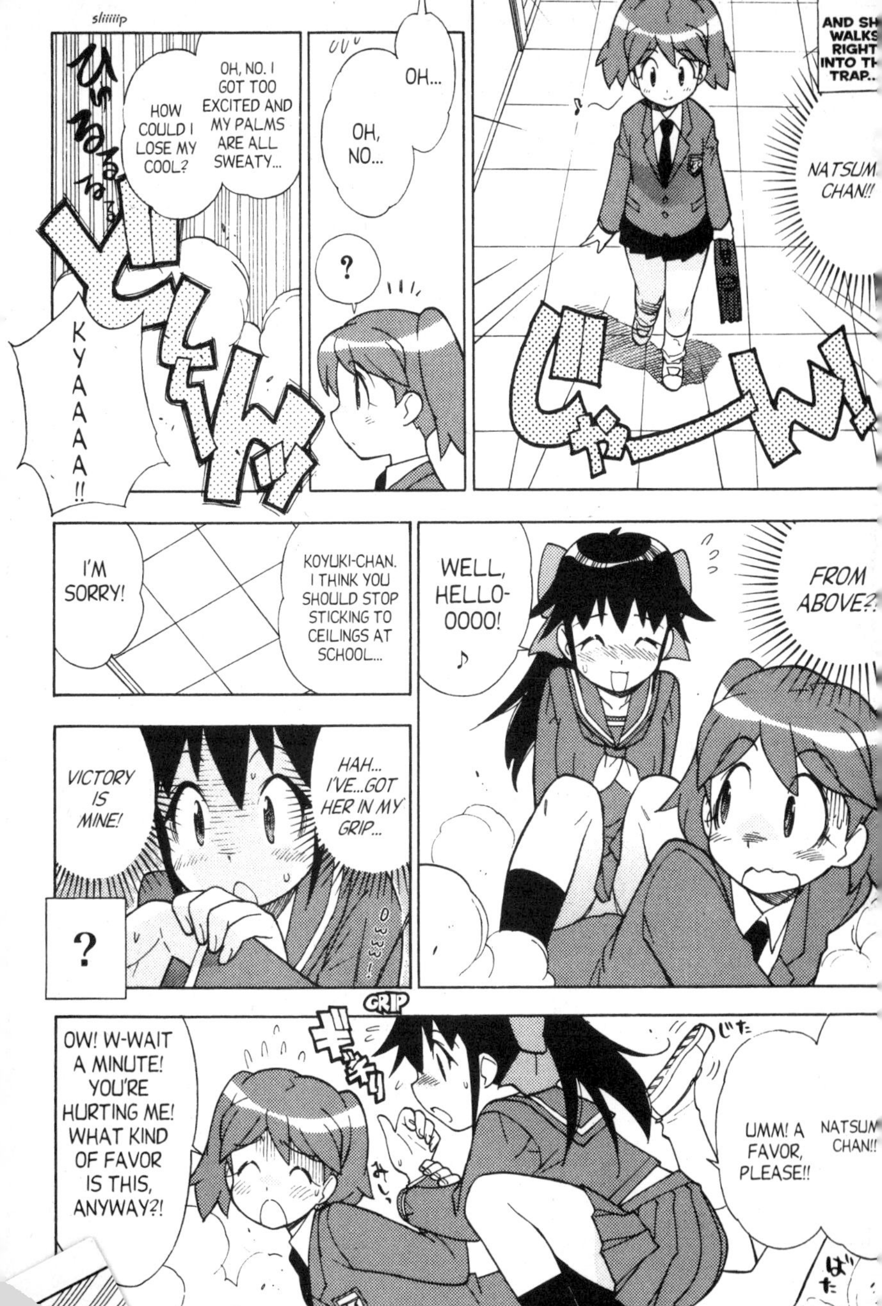
AND SH WALKS RIGHT INTO TH TRAP..
NATSUM CHAN!!
OH...
OH, NO...
?
OH, NO. I GOT TOO EXCITED AND MY PALMS ARE ALL SWEATY...
HOW COULD I LOSE MY COOL?
sliiiip
KYAAAAA!!
FROM ABOVE?!
WELL, HELLO-OOOO! ♪
KOYUKI-CHAN. I THINK YOU SHOULD STOP STICKING TO CEILINGS AT SCHOOL...
I'M SORRY!
HAH... I'VE...GOT HER IN MY GRIP...
VICTORY IS MINE!
?
NATSUM CHAN!!
UMM! A FAVOR, PLEASE!!
GRIP
OW! W-WAIT A MINUTE! YOU'RE HURTING ME! WHAT KIND OF FAVOR IS THIS, ANYWAY?!

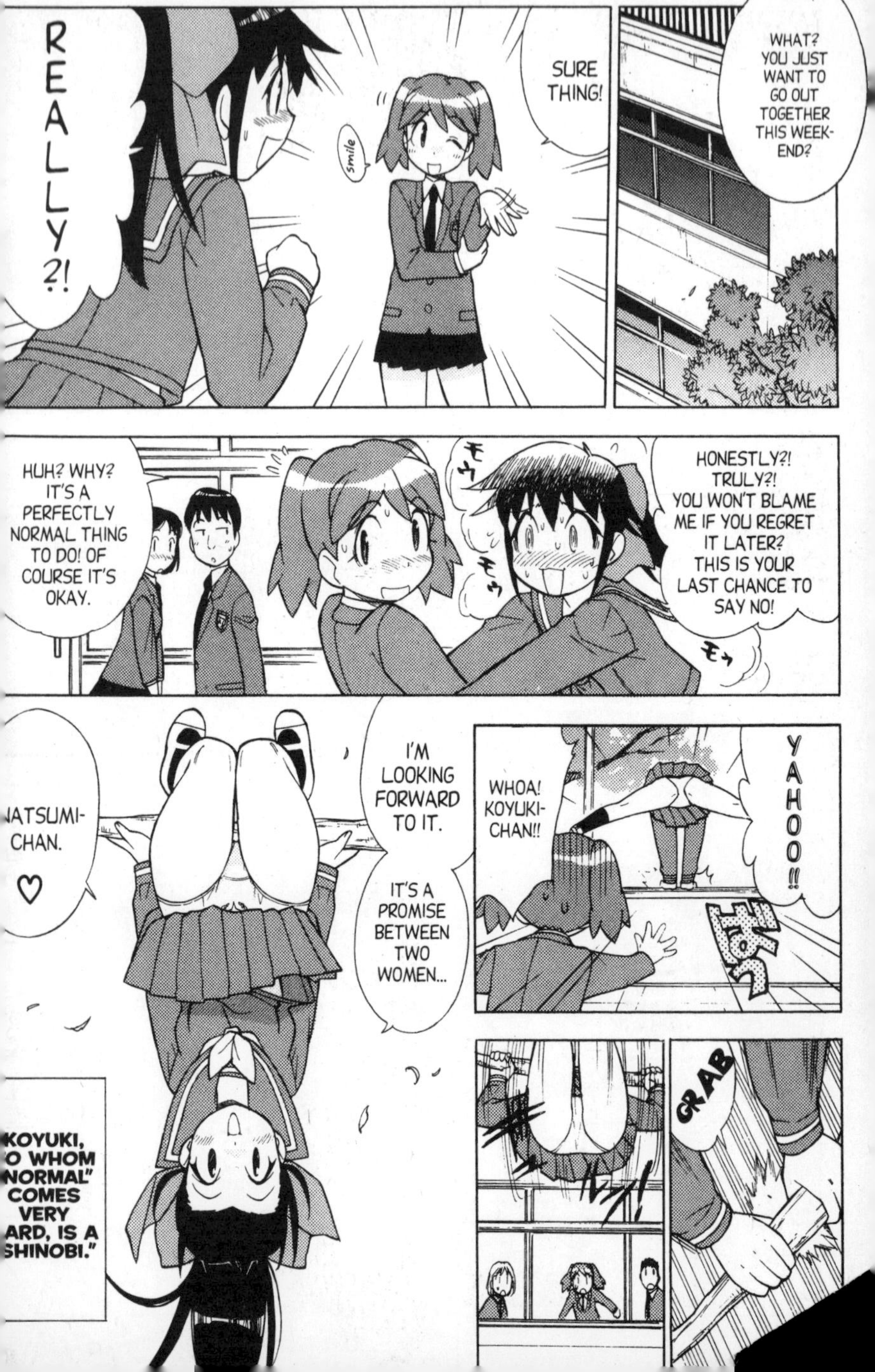
WHAT? YOU JUST WANT TO GO OUT TOGETHER THIS WEEK-END?
SURE THING!
smile
REALLY?!
HONESTLY?! TRULY?! YOU WON'T BLAME ME IF YOU REGRET IT LATER? THIS IS YOUR LAST CHANCE TO SAY NO!
HUH? WHY? IT'S A PERFECTLY NORMAL THING TO DO! OF COURSE IT'S OKAY.
YAHOO!!
WHOA! KOYUKI-CHAN!!
GRAB
I'M LOOKING FORWARD TO IT.
IT'S A PROMISE BETWEEN TWO WOMEN...
ATSUMI-CHAN. ♡
KOYUKI, O WHOM NORMAL" COMES VERY ARD, IS A SHINOBI."

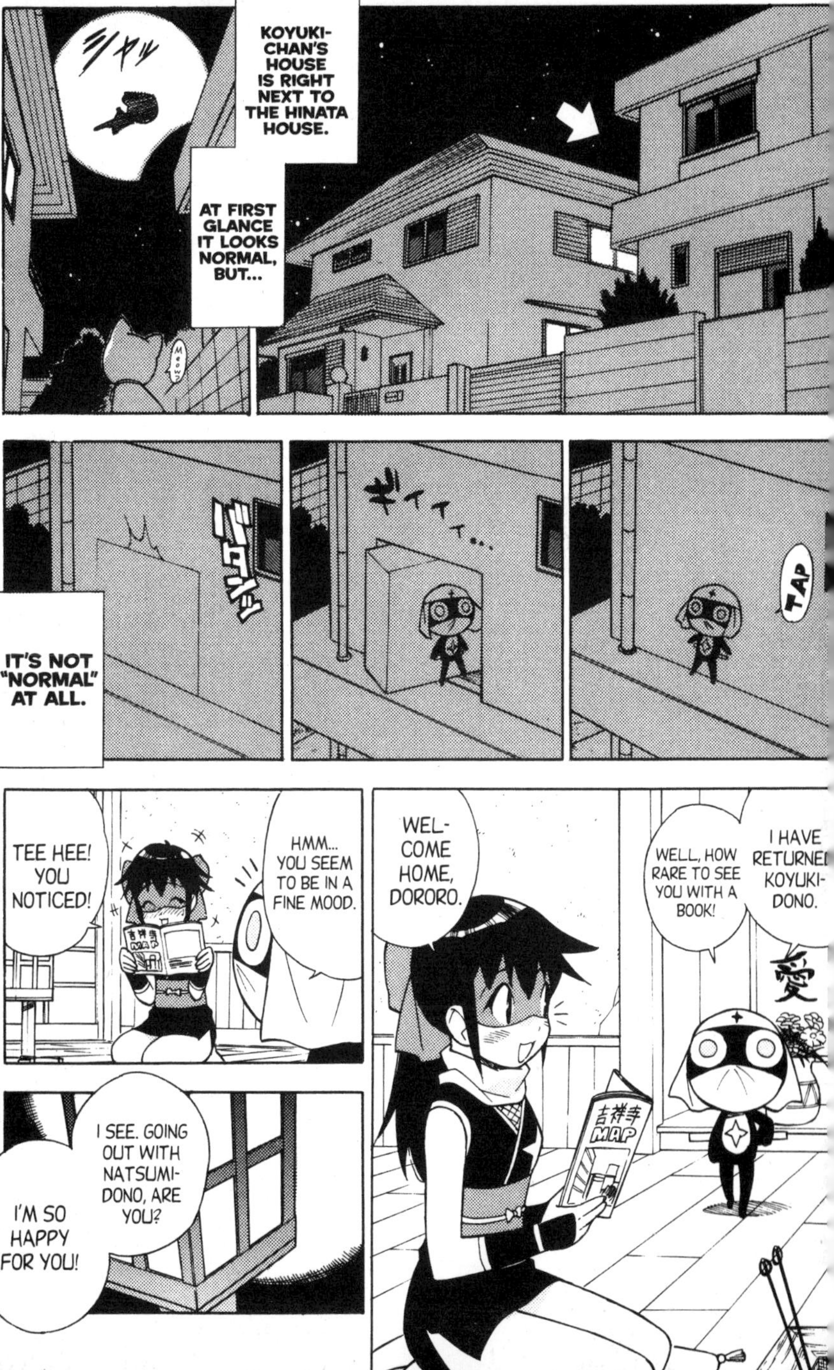
KOYUKI-CHAN'S HOUSE IS RIGHT NEXT TO THE HINATA HOUSE.
シャッ
AT FIRST GLANCE IT LOOKS NORMAL, BUT...
Meow?
TAP
ギィィィ...
バタンッ
IT'S NOT "NORMAL" AT ALL.
I HAVE RETURNED KOYUKI-DONO.
WELL, HOW RARE TO SEE YOU WITH A BOOK!
WEL-COME HOME, DORORO.
愛
吉祥寺 MAP
HMM... YOU SEEM TO BE IN A FINE MOOD.
TEE HEE! YOU NOTICED!
吉祥寺 MAP
I SEE. GOING OUT WITH NATSUMI-DONO, ARE YOU?
I'M SO HAPPY FOR YOU!

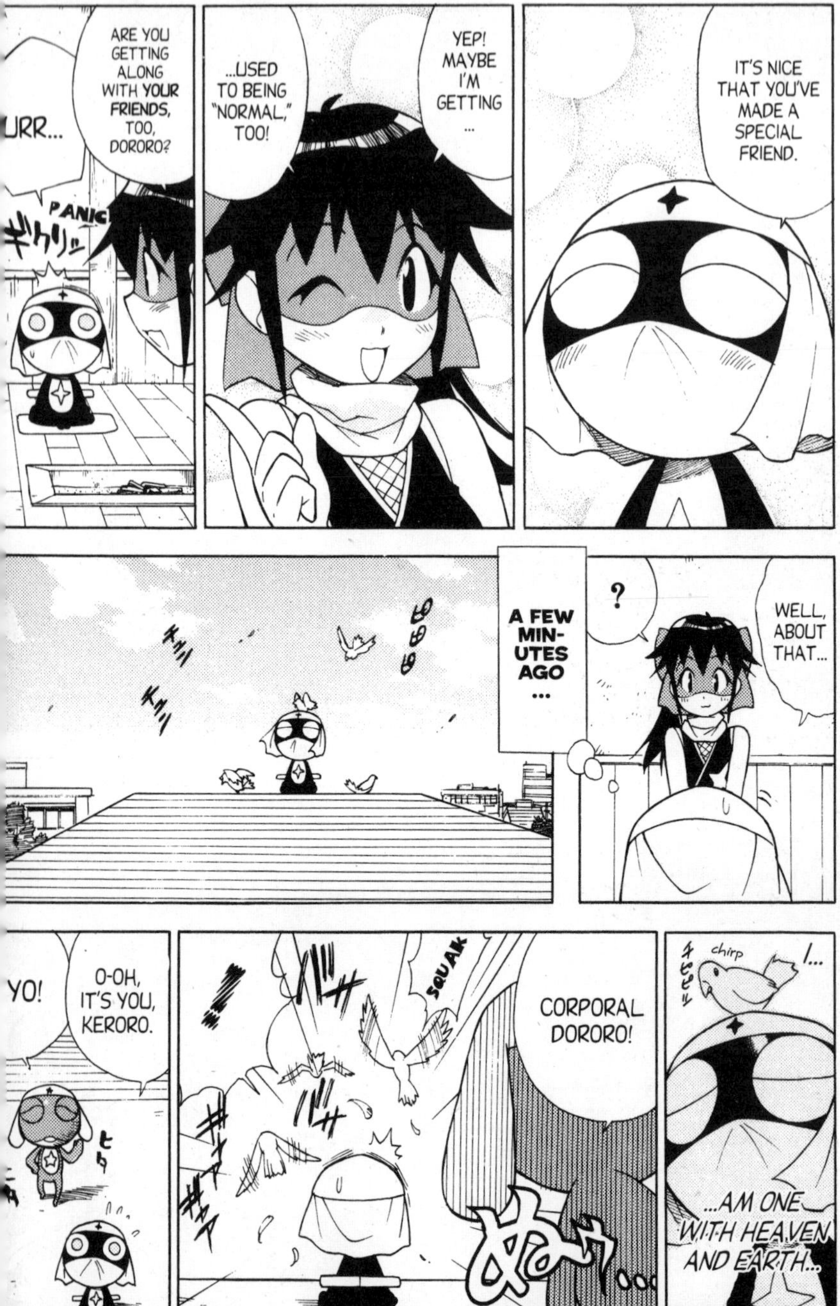
IT'S NICE THAT YOU'VE MADE A SPECIAL FRIEND.
YEP! MAYBE I'M GETTING ...
...USED TO BEING "NORMAL," TOO!
ARE YOU GETTING ALONG WITH YOUR FRIENDS, TOO, DORORO?
URR...
PANIC
WELL, ABOUT THAT...
?
A FEW MIN-UTES AGO ...
chirp
I...
...AM ONE WITH HEAVEN AND EARTH...
SQUAWK
CORPORAL DORORO!
O-OH, IT'S YOU, KERORO.
YO!

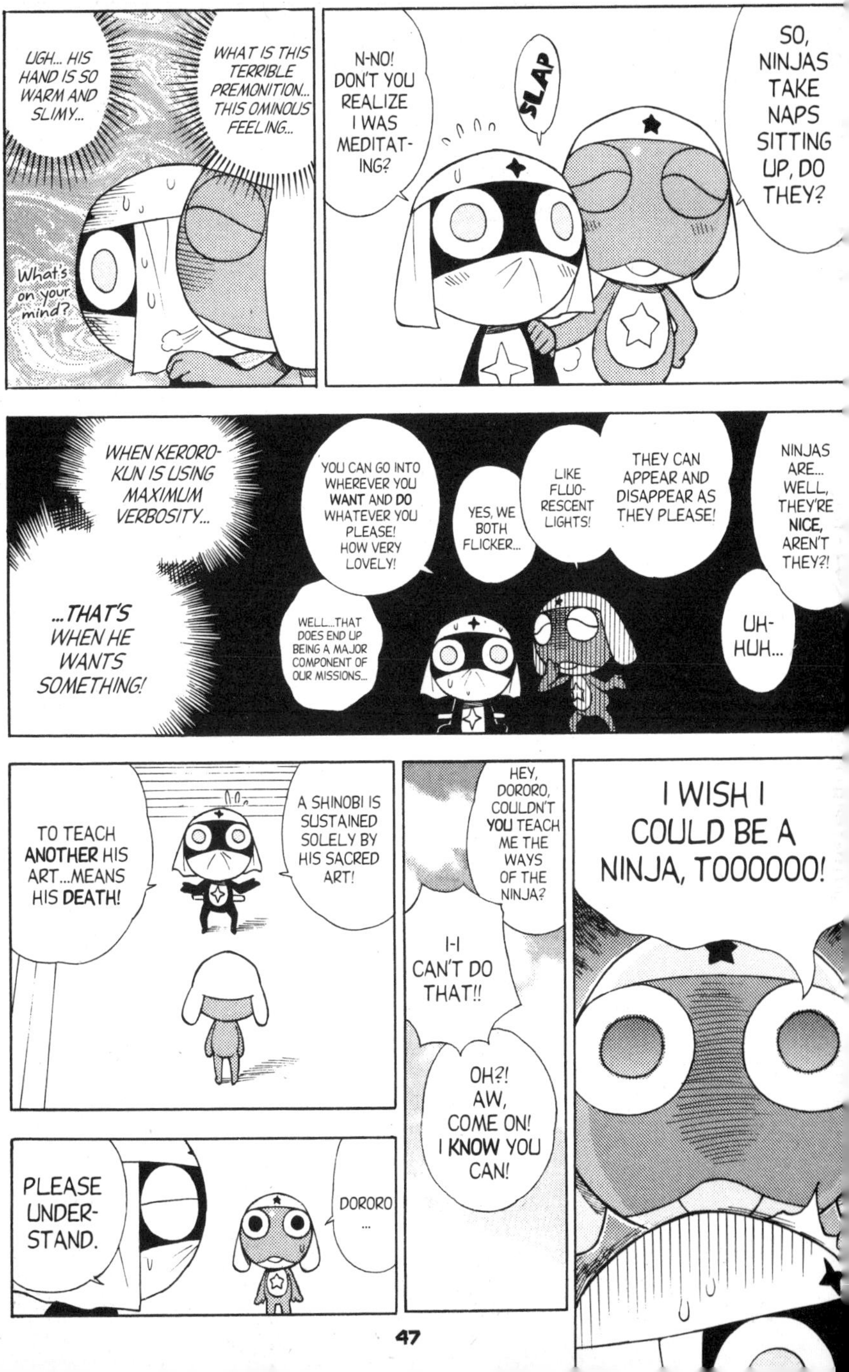
SO, NINJAS TAKE NAPS SITTING UP, DO THEY?
SLAP
N-NO! DON'T YOU REALIZE I WAS MEDITAT-ING?
WHAT IS THIS TERRIBLE PREMONITION... THIS OMINOUS FEELING...
UGH... HIS HAND IS SO WARM AND SLIMY...
What's on your mind?
NINJAS ARE... WELL, THEY'RE **NICE,** AREN'T THEY?!
THEY CAN APPEAR AND DISAPPEAR AS THEY PLEASE!
LIKE FLUO-RESCENT LIGHTS!
YES, WE BOTH FLICKER...
YOU CAN GO INTO WHEREVER YOU **WANT** AND **DO** WHATEVER YOU PLEASE! HOW VERY LOVELY!
UH-HUH...
WELL...THAT DOES END UP BEING A MAJOR COMPONENT OF OUR MISSIONS...
WHEN KERORO-KUN IS USING MAXIMUM VERBOSITY...
...THAT'S WHEN HE WANTS SOMETHING!
I WISH I COULD BE A NINJA, TOOOOOO!
HEY, DORORO, COULDN'T **YOU** TEACH ME THE WAYS OF THE NINJA?
I-I CAN'T DO THAT!!
OH?! AW, COME ON! I **KNOW** YOU CAN!
A SHINOBI IS SUSTAINED SOLELY BY HIS SACRED ART!
TO TEACH **ANOTHER** HIS ART...MEANS HIS **DEATH!**
DORORO ...
PLEASE UNDER-STAND.

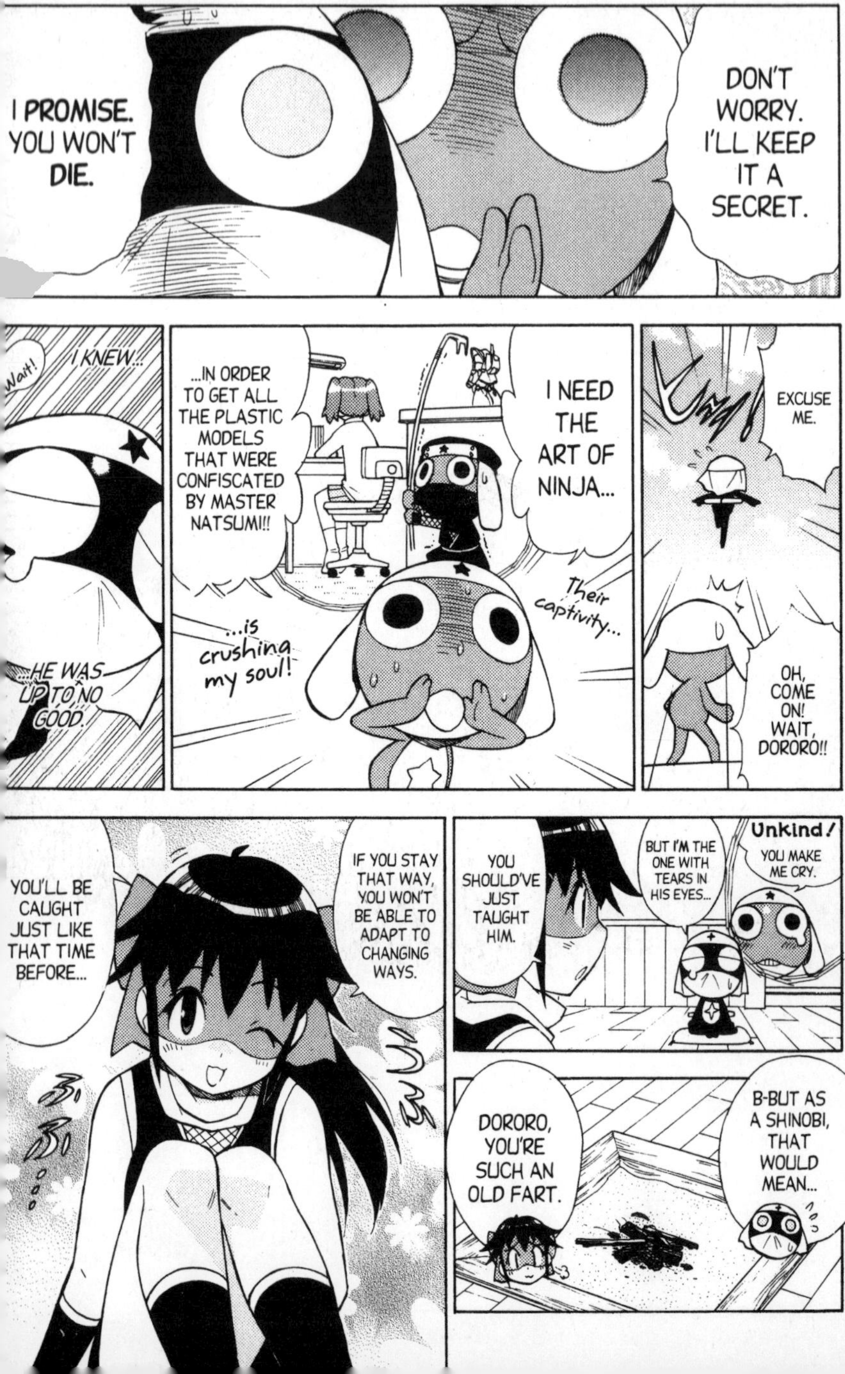
DON'T WORRY. I'LL KEEP IT A SECRET.
I PROMISE. YOU WON'T DIE.
EXCUSE ME.
OH, COME ON! WAIT, DORORO!!
I NEED THE ART OF NINJA...
...IN ORDER TO GET ALL THE PLASTIC MODELS THAT WERE CONFISCATED BY MASTER NATSUMI!!
Their captivity...
...is crushing my soul!
I KNEW...
Wait!
...HE WAS UP TO NO GOOD.
Unkind!
YOU MAKE ME CRY.
BUT I'M THE ONE WITH TEARS IN HIS EYES...
YOU SHOULD'VE JUST TAUGHT HIM.
B-BUT AS A SHINOBI, THAT WOULD MEAN...
DORORO, YOU'RE SUCH AN OLD FART.
IF YOU STAY THAT WAY, YOU WON'T BE ABLE TO ADAPT TO CHANGING WAYS.
YOU'LL BE CAUGHT JUST LIKE THAT TIME BEFORE...

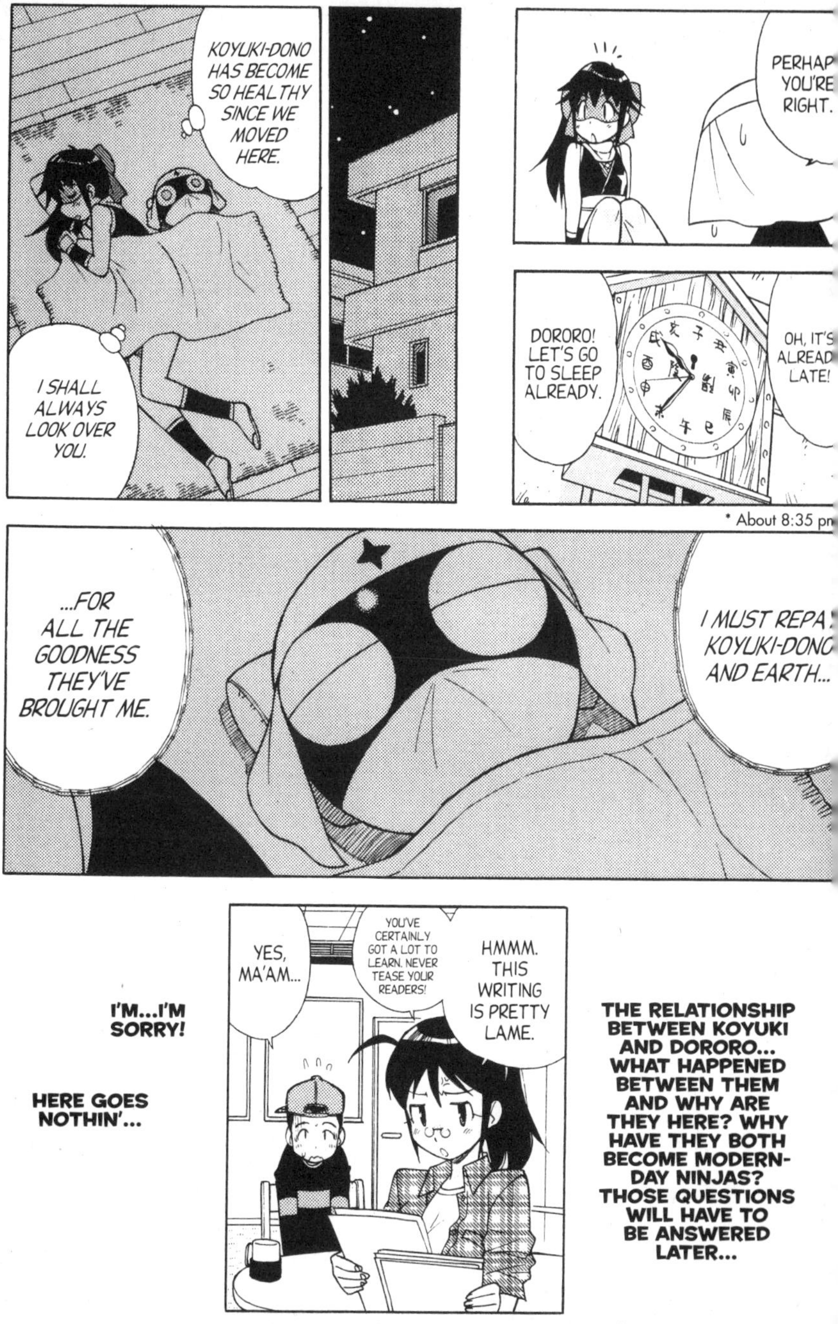
PERHAP YOU'RE RIGHT.
OH, IT'S ALREAD LATE!
DORORO! LET'S GO TO SLEEP ALREADY.
* About 8:35 p
KOYUKI-DONO HAS BECOME SO HEALTHY SINCE WE MOVED HERE.
I SHALL ALWAYS LOOK OVER YOU.
I MUST REPA KOYUKI-DONO AND EARTH...
...FOR ALL THE GOODNESS THEY'VE BROUGHT ME.
THE RELATIONSHIP BETWEEN KOYUKI AND DORORO... WHAT HAPPENED BETWEEN THEM AND WHY ARE THEY HERE? WHY HAVE THEY BOTH BECOME MODERN-DAY NINJAS? THOSE QUESTIONS WILL HAVE TO BE ANSWERED LATER...
HMMM. THIS WRITING IS PRETTY LAME.
YOU'VE CERTAINLY GOT A LOT TO LEARN. NEVER TEASE YOUR READERS!
YES, MA'AM...
I'M...I'M SORRY!
HERE GOES NOTHIN'...

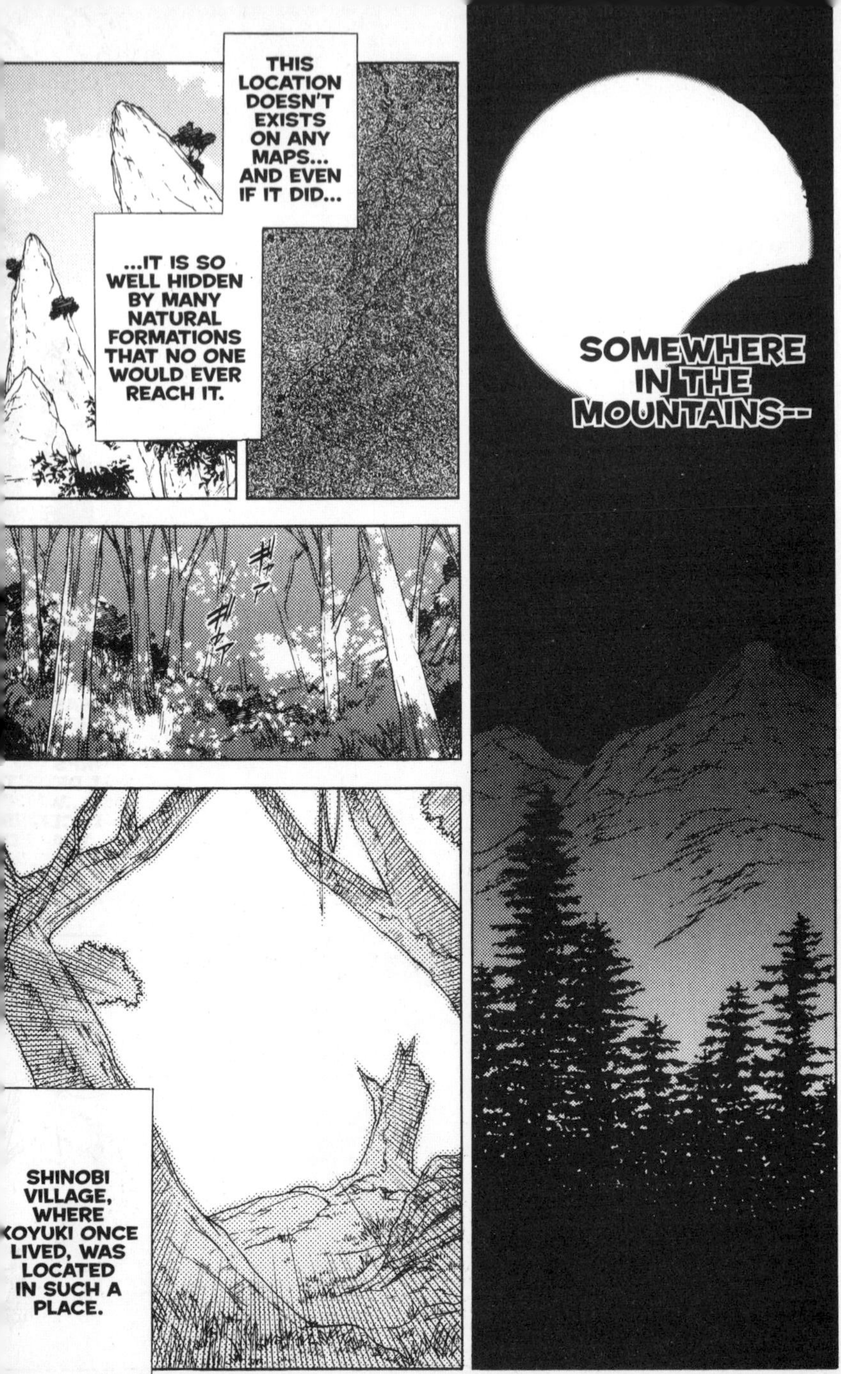
SOMEWHERE IN THE MOUNTAINS--
THIS LOCATION DOESN'T EXISTS ON ANY MAPS... AND EVEN IF IT DID...
...IT IS SO WELL HIDDEN BY MANY NATURAL FORMATIONS THAT NO ONE WOULD EVER REACH IT.
SHINOBI VILLAGE, WHERE KOYUKI ONCE LIVED, WAS LOCATED IN SUCH A PLACE.

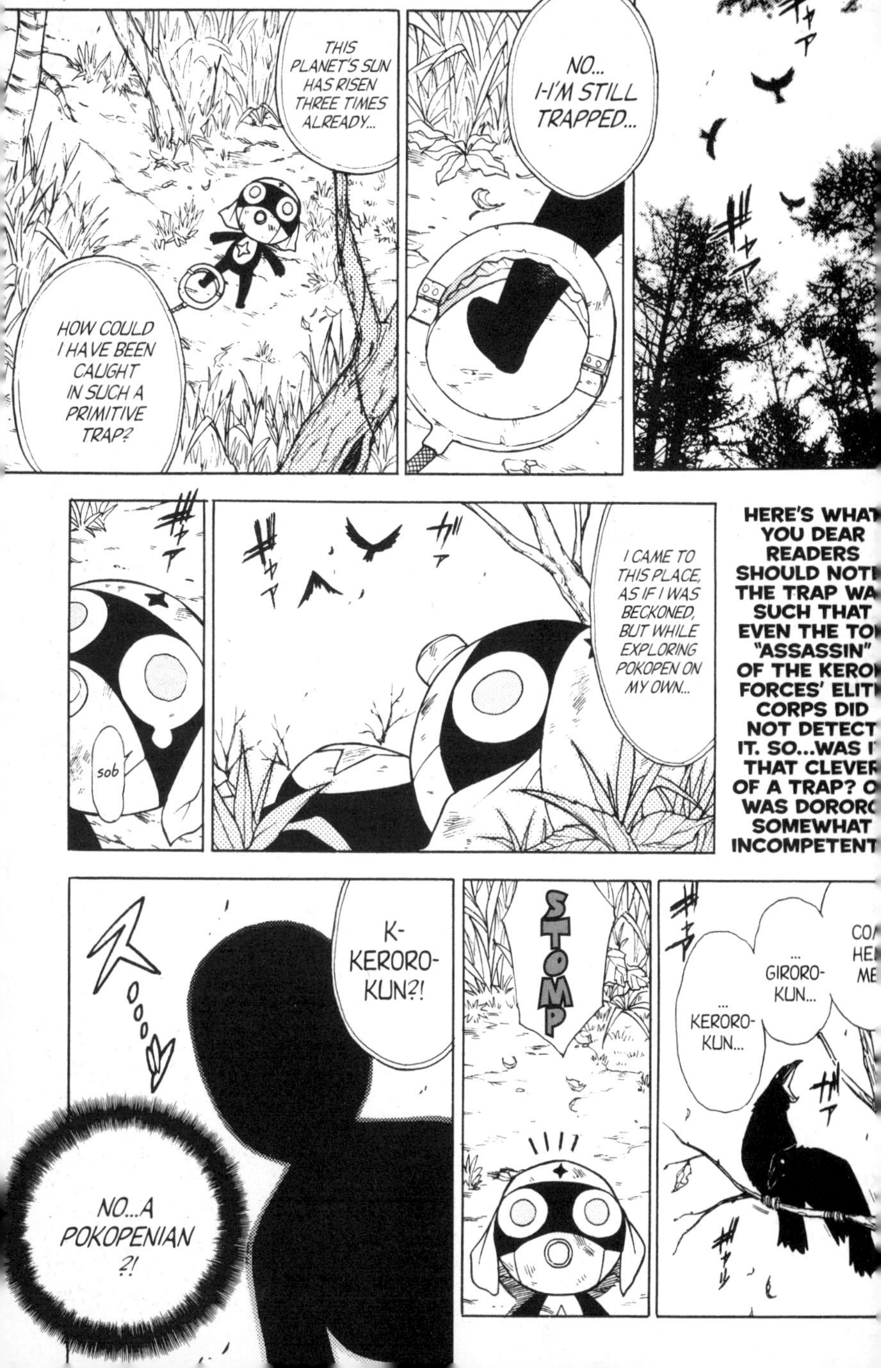
NO... I-I'M STILL TRAPPED...
THIS PLANET'S SUN HAS RISEN THREE TIMES ALREADY...
HOW COULD I HAVE BEEN CAUGHT IN SUCH A PRIMITIVE TRAP?
HERE'S WHAT YOU DEAR READERS SHOULD NOTE THE TRAP WA SUCH THAT EVEN THE TO "ASSASSIN" OF THE KERO FORCES' ELIT CORPS DID NOT DETECT IT. SO...WAS I THAT CLEVER OF A TRAP? O WAS DORORO SOMEWHAT INCOMPETENT
I CAME TO THIS PLACE, AS IF I WAS BECKONED, BUT WHILE EXPLORING POKOPEN ON MY OWN...
sob
... GIRORO-KUN...
... KERORO-KUN...
STOMP
K-KERORO-KUN?!
NO...A POKOPENIAN ?!

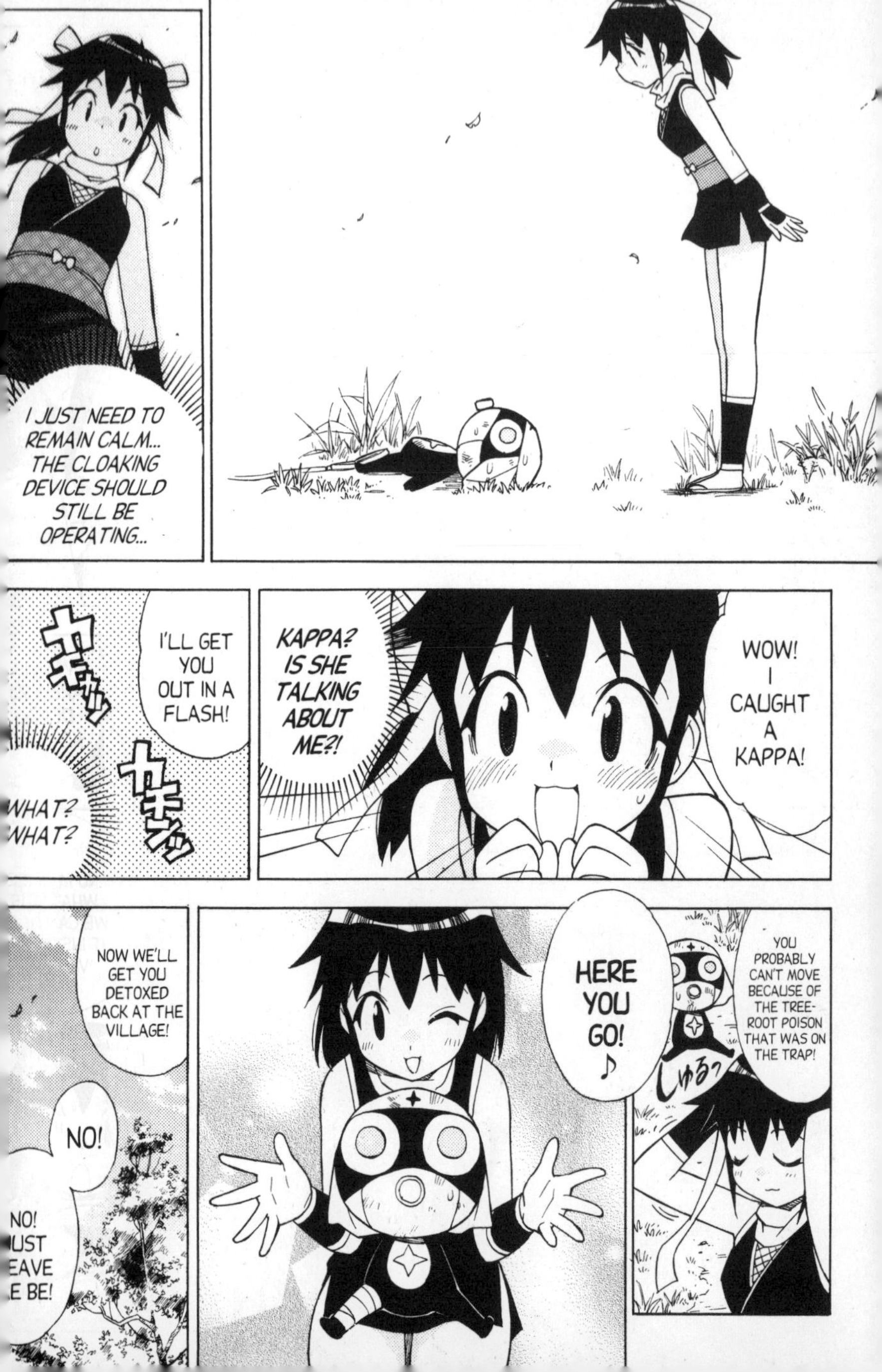
I JUST NEED TO REMAIN CALM... THE CLOAKING DEVICE SHOULD STILL BE OPERATING...
WOW! I CAUGHT A KAPPA!
KAPPA? IS SHE TALKING ABOUT ME?!
I'LL GET YOU OUT IN A FLASH!
WHAT? WHAT?
YOU PROBABLY CAN'T MOVE BECAUSE OF THE TREE-ROOT POISON THAT WAS ON THE TRAP!
しゅるっ
HERE YOU GO! ♪
NOW WE'LL GET YOU DETOXED BACK AT THE VILLAGE!
NO!
NO! UST EAVE E BE!

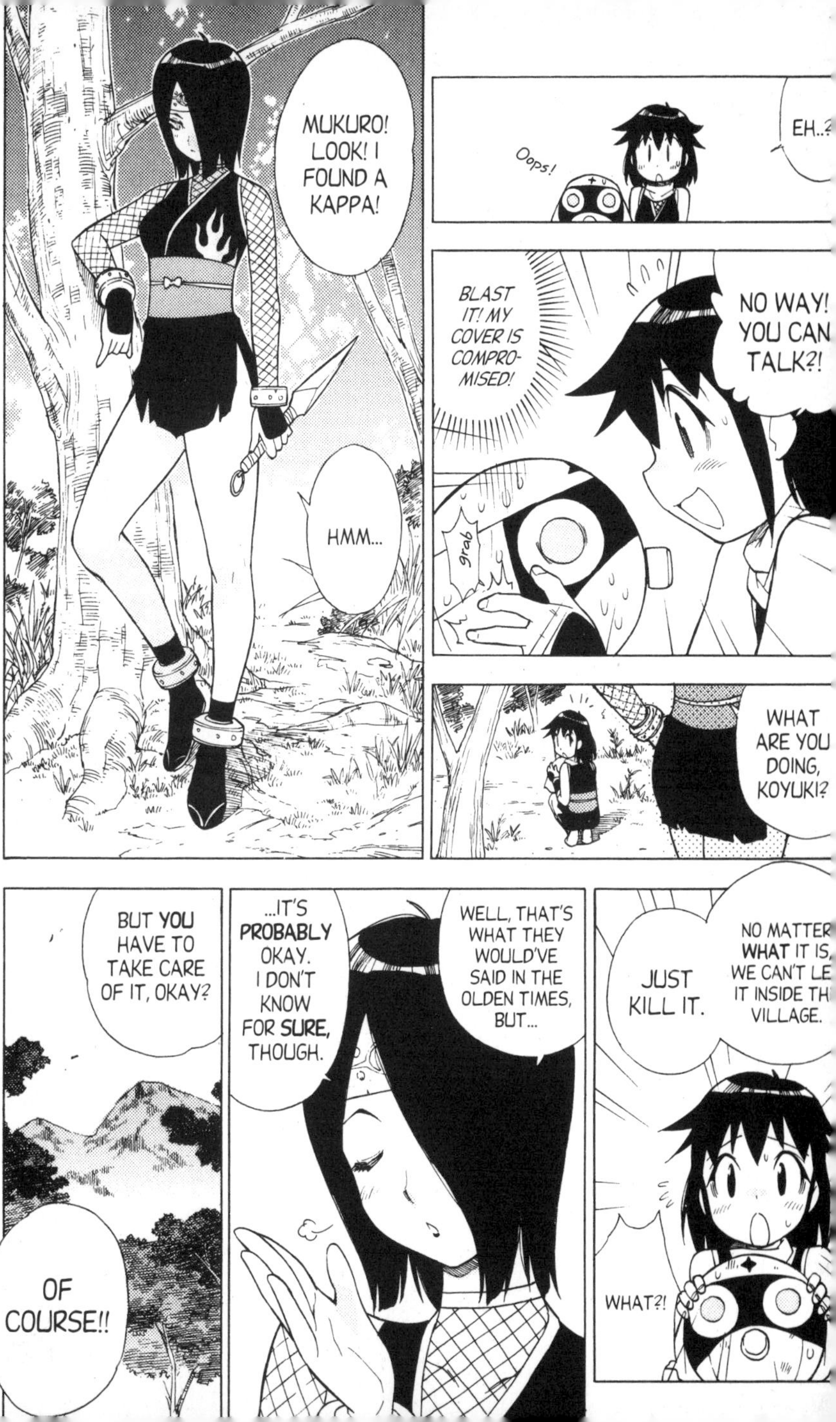
EH..?
Oops!
NO WAY! YOU CAN TALK?!
BLAST IT! MY COVER IS COMPRO-MISED!
grab
WHAT ARE YOU DOING, KOYUKI?
MUKURO! LOOK! I FOUND A KAPPA!
HMM...
NO MATTER WHAT IT IS, WE CAN'T LE IT INSIDE TH VILLAGE.
JUST KILL IT.
WHAT?!
WELL, THAT'S WHAT THEY WOULD'VE SAID IN THE OLDEN TIMES, BUT...
...IT'S PROBABLY OKAY. I DON'T KNOW FOR SURE, THOUGH.
BUT YOU HAVE TO TAKE CARE OF IT, OKAY?
OF COURSE!!

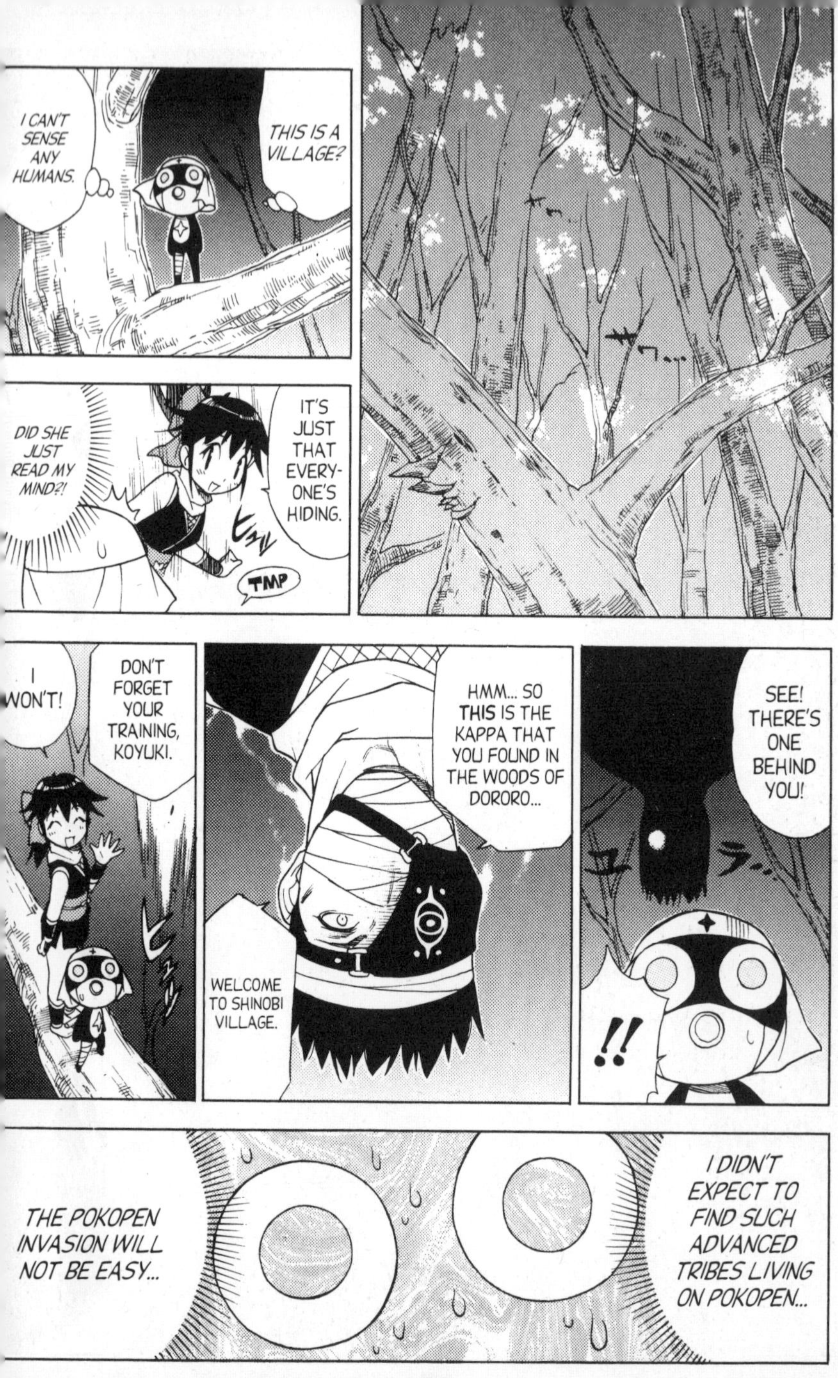
THIS IS A VILLAGE?
I CAN'T SENSE ANY HUMANS.
IT'S JUST THAT EVERYONE'S HIDING.
TMP
DID SHE JUST READ MY MIND?!
SEE! THERE'S ONE BEHIND YOU!
!!
HMM... SO THIS IS THE KAPPA THAT YOU FOUND IN THE WOODS OF DORORO...
WELCOME TO SHINOBI VILLAGE.
DON'T FORGET YOUR TRAINING, KOYUKI.
I WON'T!
I DIDN'T EXPECT TO FIND SUCH ADVANCED TRIBES LIVING ON POKOPEN...
THE POKOPEN INVASION WILL NOT BE EASY...

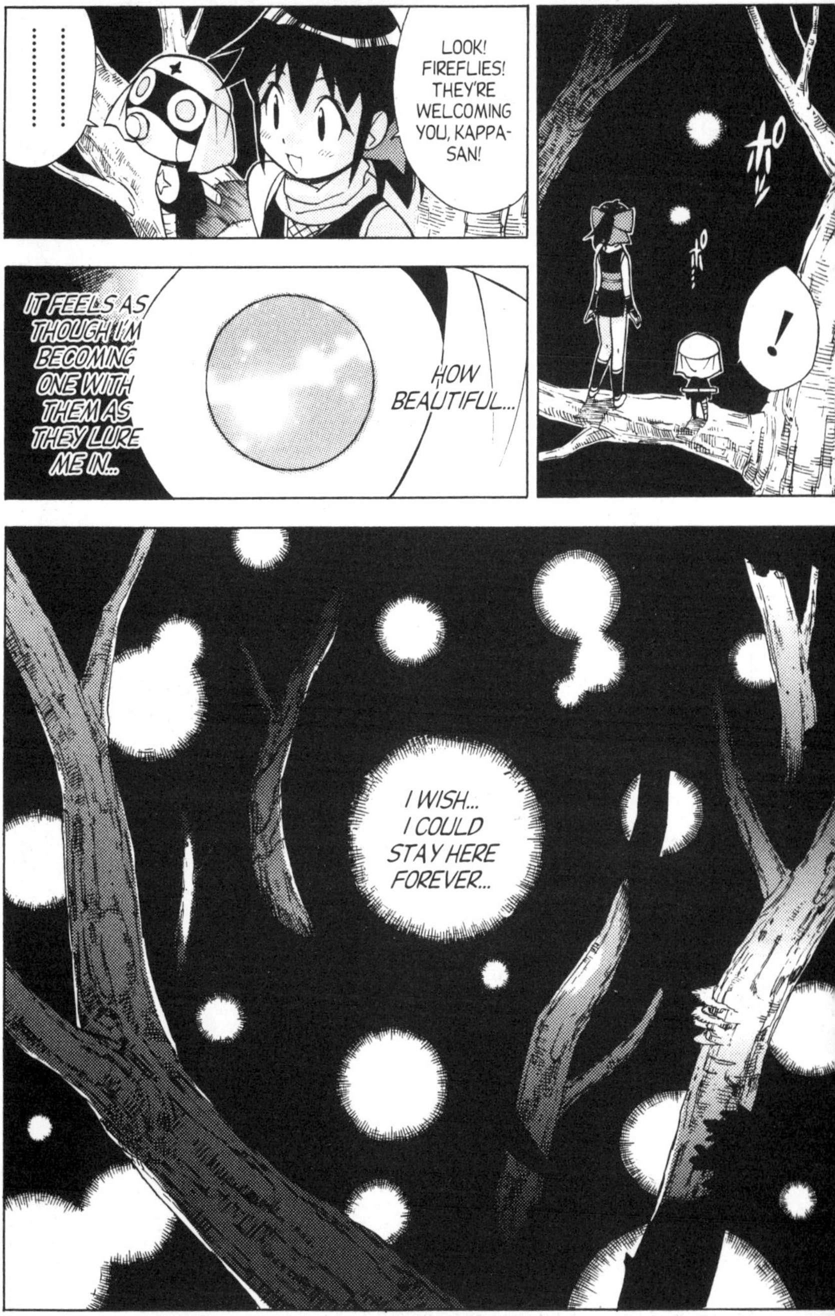
!
LOOK! FIREFLIES! THEY'RE WELCOMING YOU, KAPPA-SAN!
......
HOW BEAUTIFUL...
IT FEELS AS THOUGH I'M BECOMING ONE WITH THEM AS THEY LURE ME IN...
I WISH... I COULD STAY HERE FOREVER...

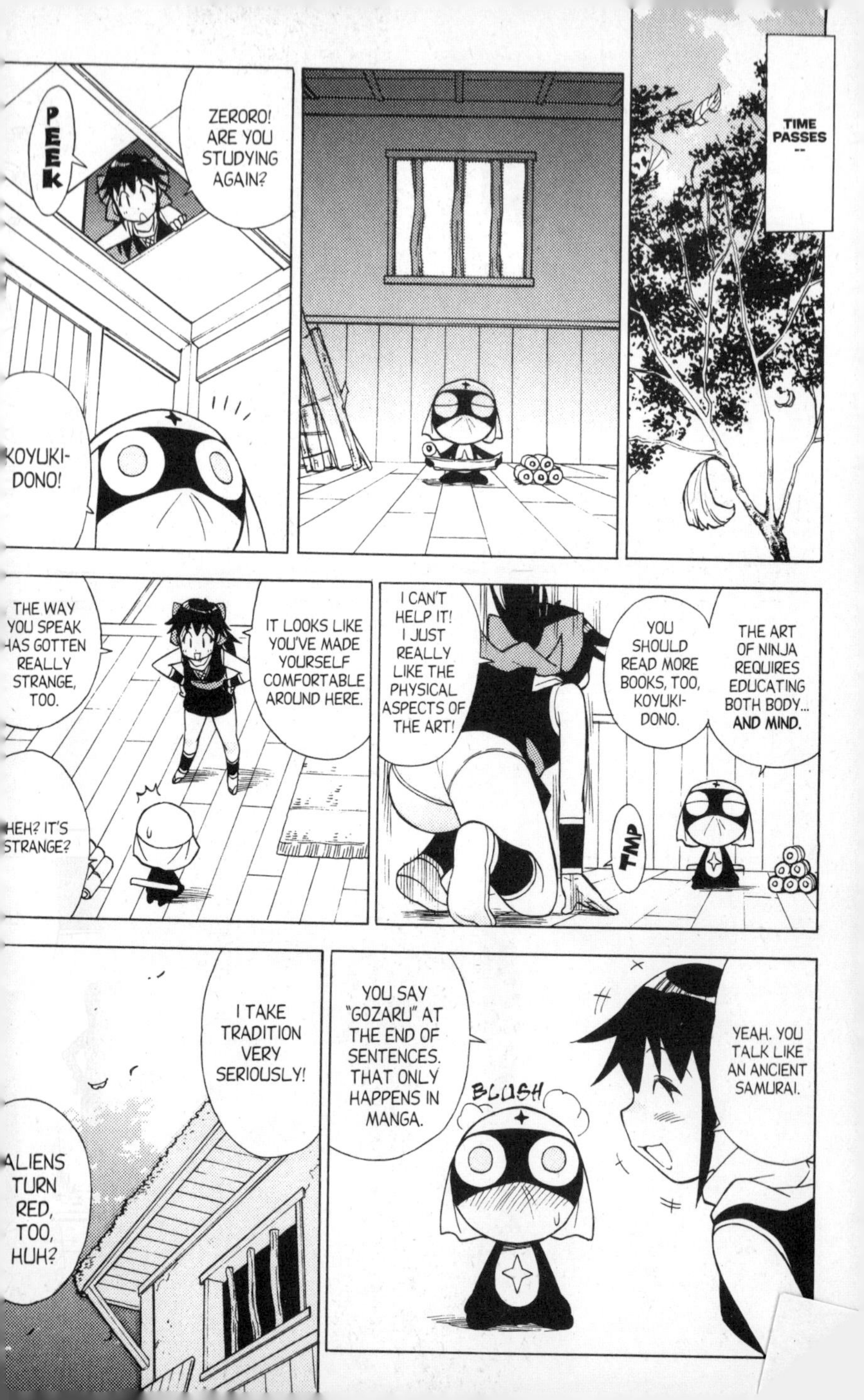
TIME PASSES --
ZERORO! ARE YOU STUDYING AGAIN?
PEEK
KOYUKI-DONO!
THE ART OF NINJA REQUIRES EDUCATING BOTH BODY... AND MIND.
YOU SHOULD READ MORE BOOKS, TOO, KOYUKI-DONO.
I CAN'T HELP IT! I JUST REALLY LIKE THE PHYSICAL ASPECTS OF THE ART!
TMP
IT LOOKS LIKE YOU'VE MADE YOURSELF COMFORTABLE AROUND HERE.
THE WAY YOU SPEAK HAS GOTTEN REALLY STRANGE, TOO.
HEH? IT'S STRANGE?
YEAH. YOU TALK LIKE AN ANCIENT SAMURAI.
YOU SAY "GOZARU" AT THE END OF SENTENCES. THAT ONLY HAPPENS IN MANGA.
BLUSH
I TAKE TRADITION VERY SERIOUSLY!
ALIENS TURN RED, TOO, HUH?

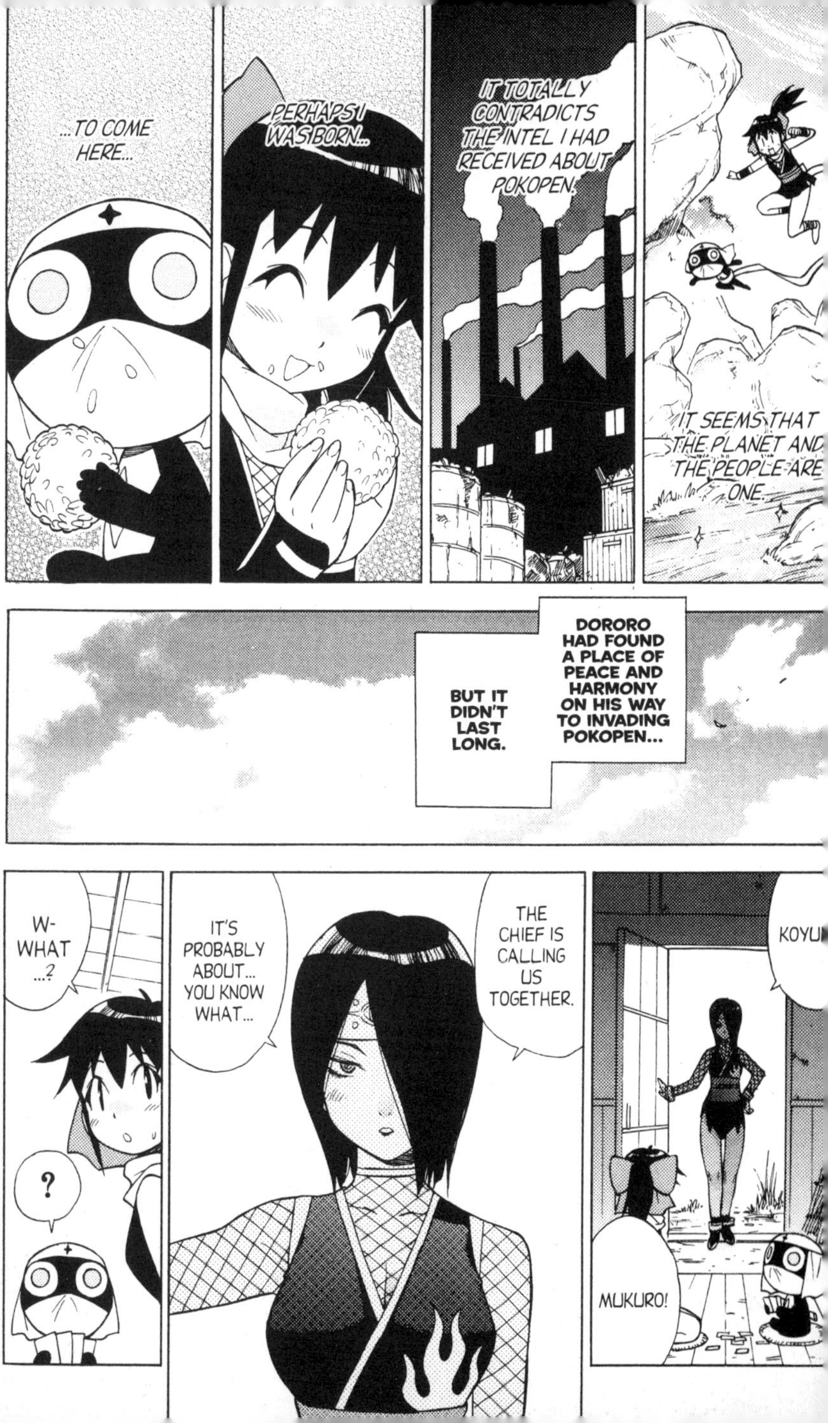
IT SEEMS THAT THE PLANET AND THE PEOPLE ARE ONE.
IT TOTALLY CONTRADICTS THE INTEL I HAD RECEIVED ABOUT POKOPEN.
PERHAPS I WAS BORN...
...TO COME HERE...
DORORO HAD FOUND A PLACE OF PEACE AND HARMONY ON HIS WAY TO INVADING POKOPEN...
BUT IT DIDN'T LAST LONG.
KOYU
MUKURO!
THE CHIEF IS CALLING US TOGETHER.
IT'S PROBABLY ABOUT... YOU KNOW WHAT...
W-WHAT...?
?

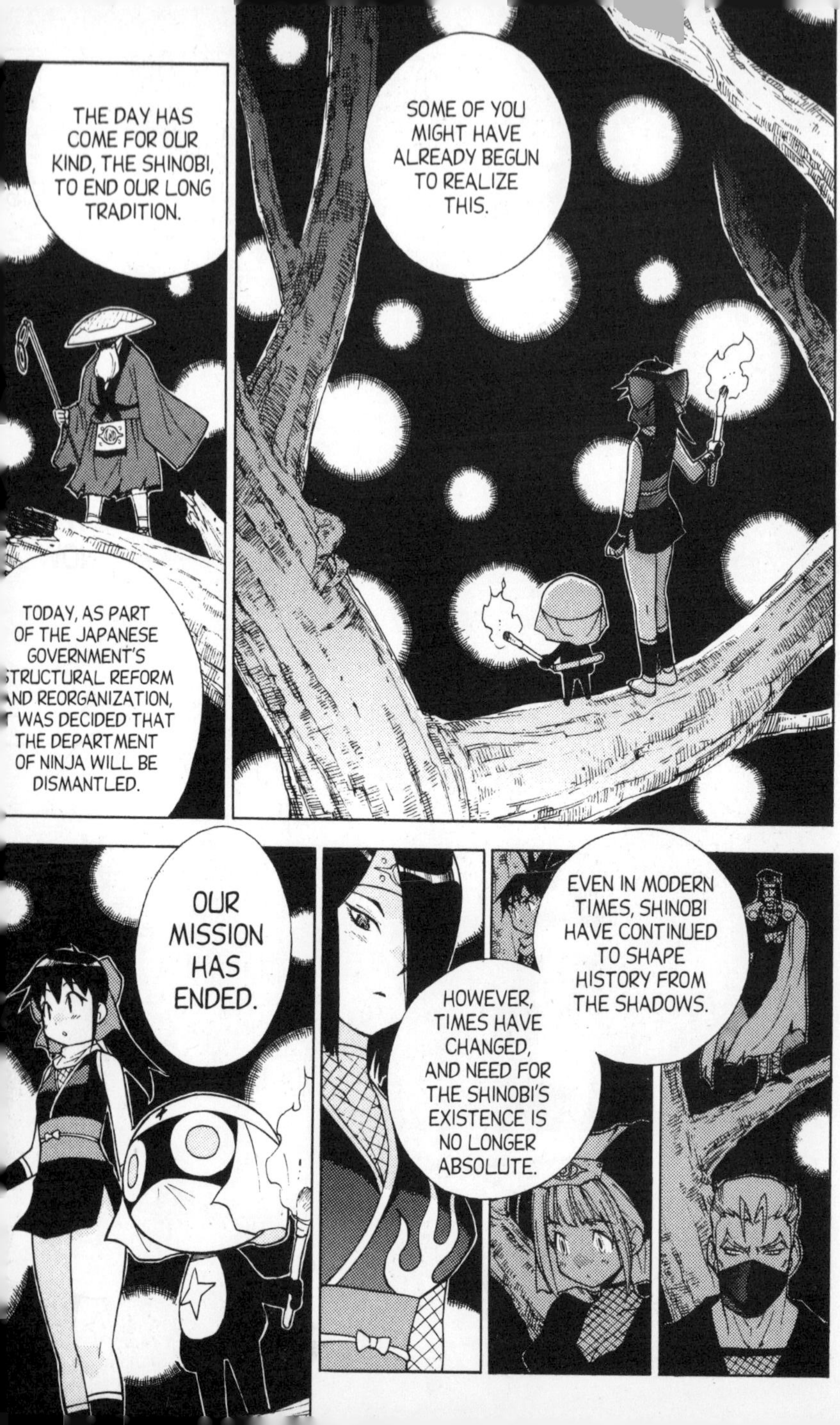
SOME OF YOU MIGHT HAVE ALREADY BEGUN TO REALIZE THIS.
THE DAY HAS COME FOR OUR KIND, THE SHINOBI, TO END OUR LONG TRADITION.
TODAY, AS PART OF THE JAPANESE GOVERNMENT'S STRUCTURAL REFORM AND REORGANIZATION, IT WAS DECIDED THAT THE DEPARTMENT OF NINJA WILL BE DISMANTLED.
EVEN IN MODERN TIMES, SHINOBI HAVE CONTINUED TO SHAPE HISTORY FROM THE SHADOWS.
HOWEVER, TIMES HAVE CHANGED, AND NEED FOR THE SHINOBI'S EXISTENCE IS NO LONGER ABSOLUTE.
OUR MISSION HAS ENDED.

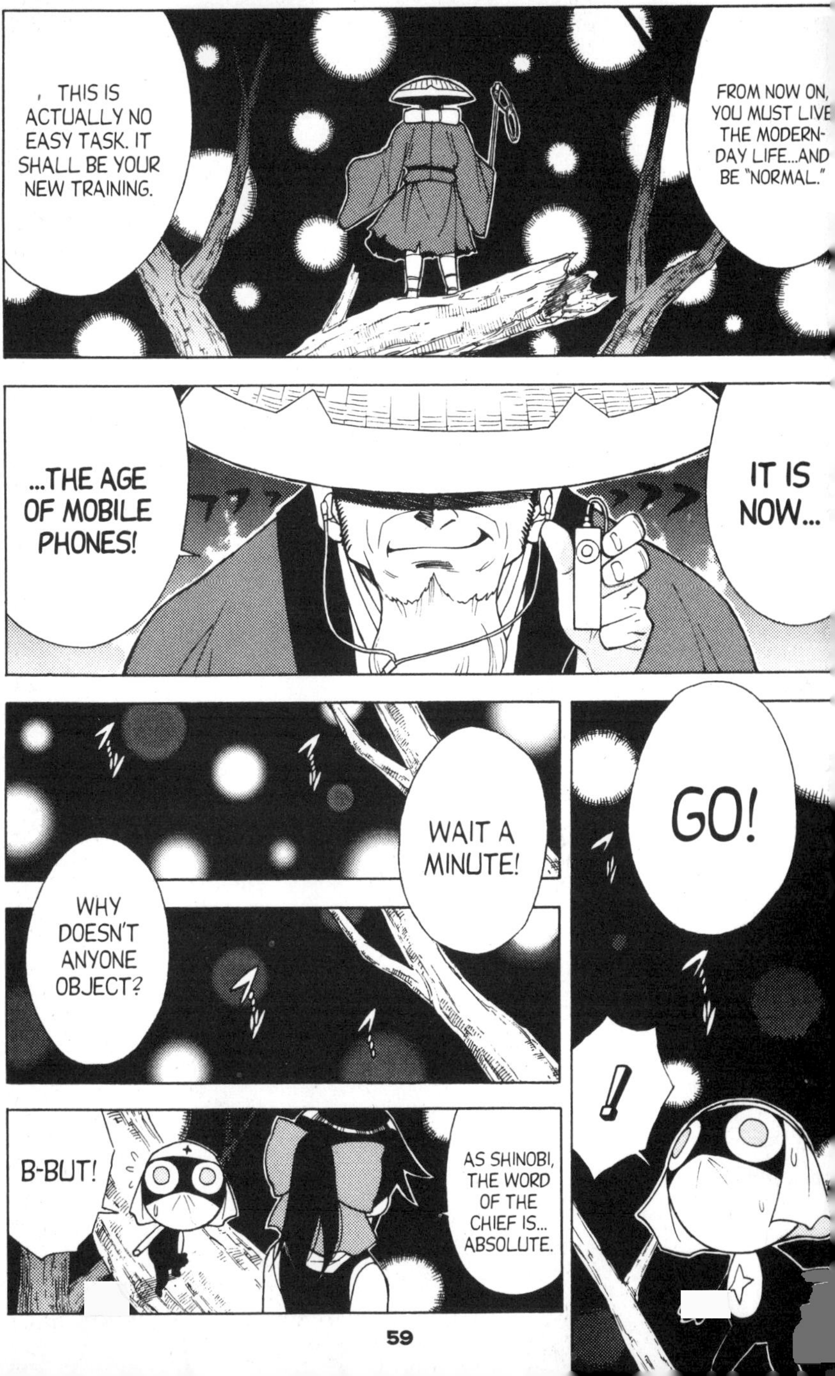
FROM NOW ON, YOU MUST LIVE THE MODERN-DAY LIFE...AND BE "NORMAL."
THIS IS ACTUALLY NO EASY TASK. IT SHALL BE YOUR NEW TRAINING.
IT IS NOW...
...THE AGE OF MOBILE PHONES!
GO!
!
WAIT A MINUTE!
WHY DOESN'T ANYONE OBJECT?
AS SHINOBI, THE WORD OF THE CHIEF IS... ABSOLUTE.
B-BUT!

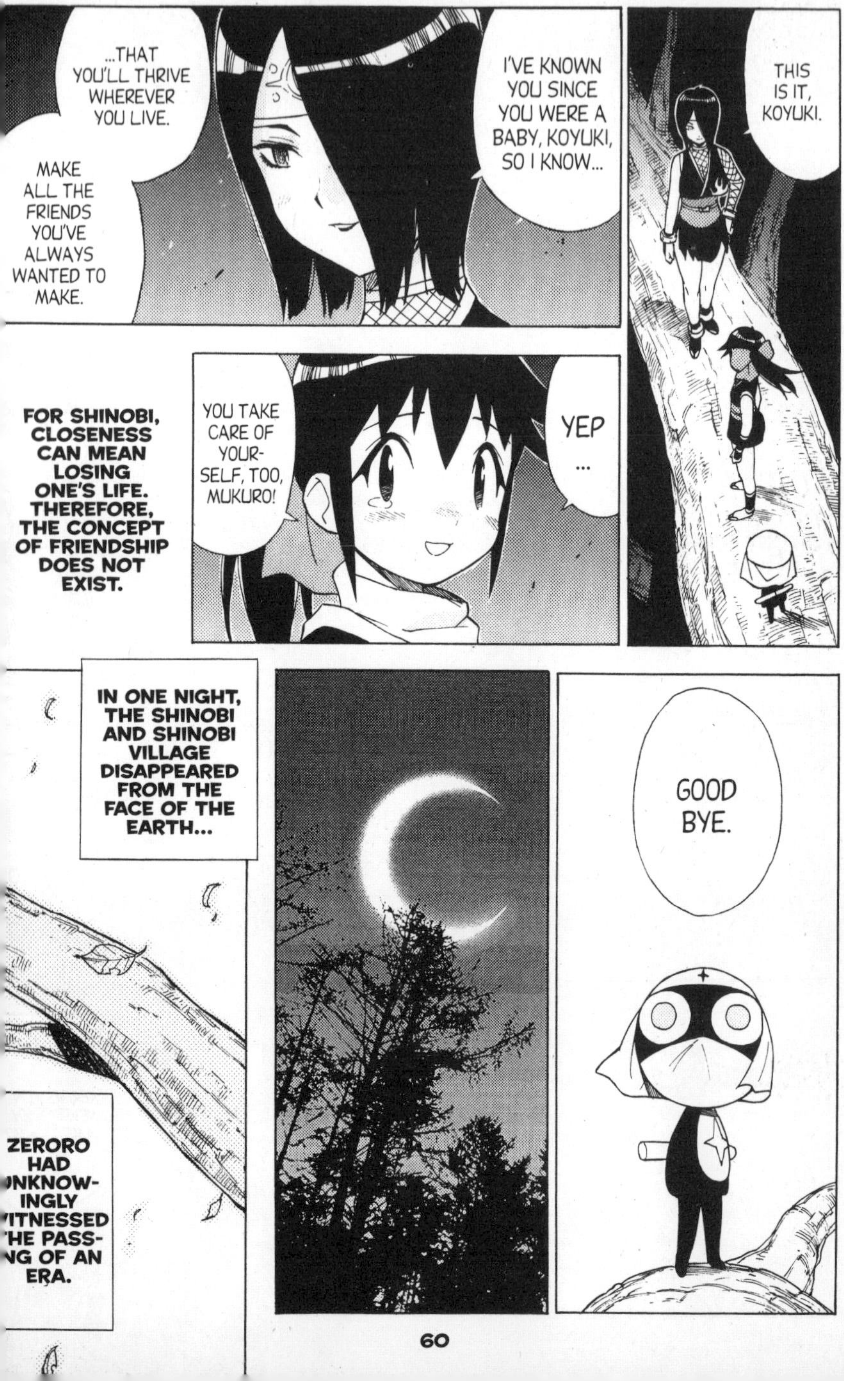
THIS IS IT, KOYUKI.
I'VE KNOWN YOU SINCE YOU WERE A BABY, KOYUKI, SO I KNOW...
...THAT YOU'LL THRIVE WHEREVER YOU LIVE.
MAKE ALL THE FRIENDS YOU'VE ALWAYS WANTED TO MAKE.
YEP ...
YOU TAKE CARE OF YOUR-SELF, TOO, MUKURO!
FOR SHINOBI, CLOSENESS CAN MEAN LOSING ONE'S LIFE. THEREFORE, THE CONCEPT OF FRIENDSHIP DOES NOT EXIST.
GOOD BYE.
IN ONE NIGHT, THE SHINOBI AND SHINOBI VILLAGE DISAPPEARED FROM THE FACE OF THE EARTH...
ZERORO HAD NKNOW-INGLY ITNESSED HE PASS-NG OF AN ERA.

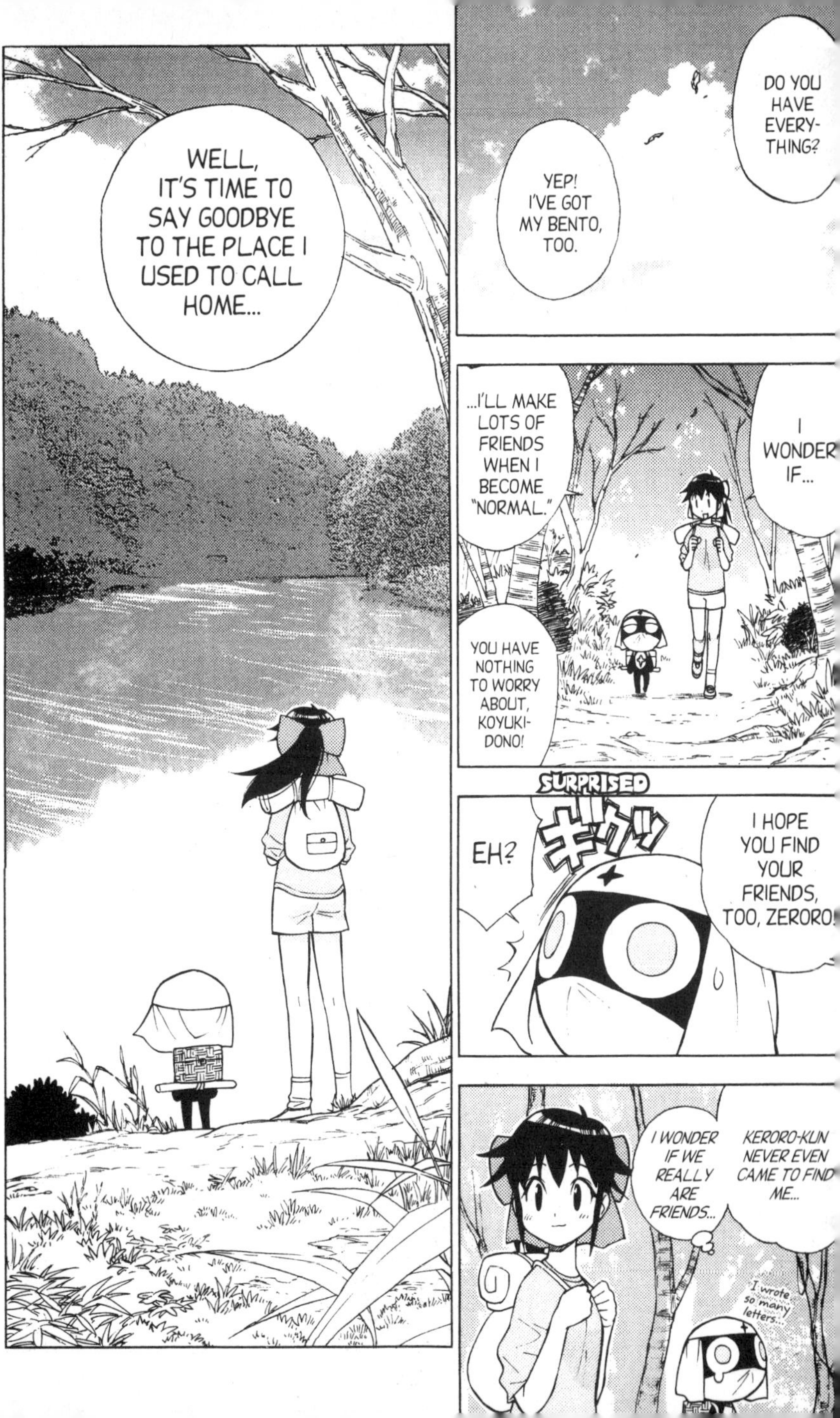
DO YOU HAVE EVERYTHING?
YEP! I'VE GOT MY BENTO, TOO.
I WONDER IF...
...I'LL MAKE LOTS OF FRIENDS WHEN I BECOME "NORMAL."
YOU HAVE NOTHING TO WORRY ABOUT, KOYUKI-DONO!
I HOPE YOU FIND YOUR FRIENDS, TOO, ZERORO!
SURPRISED
ギクッ
EH?
KERORO-KUN NEVER EVEN CAME TO FIND ME...
I WONDER IF WE REALLY ARE FRIENDS...
I wrote so many letters...
WELL, IT'S TIME TO SAY GOODBYE TO THE PLACE I USED TO CALL HOME...

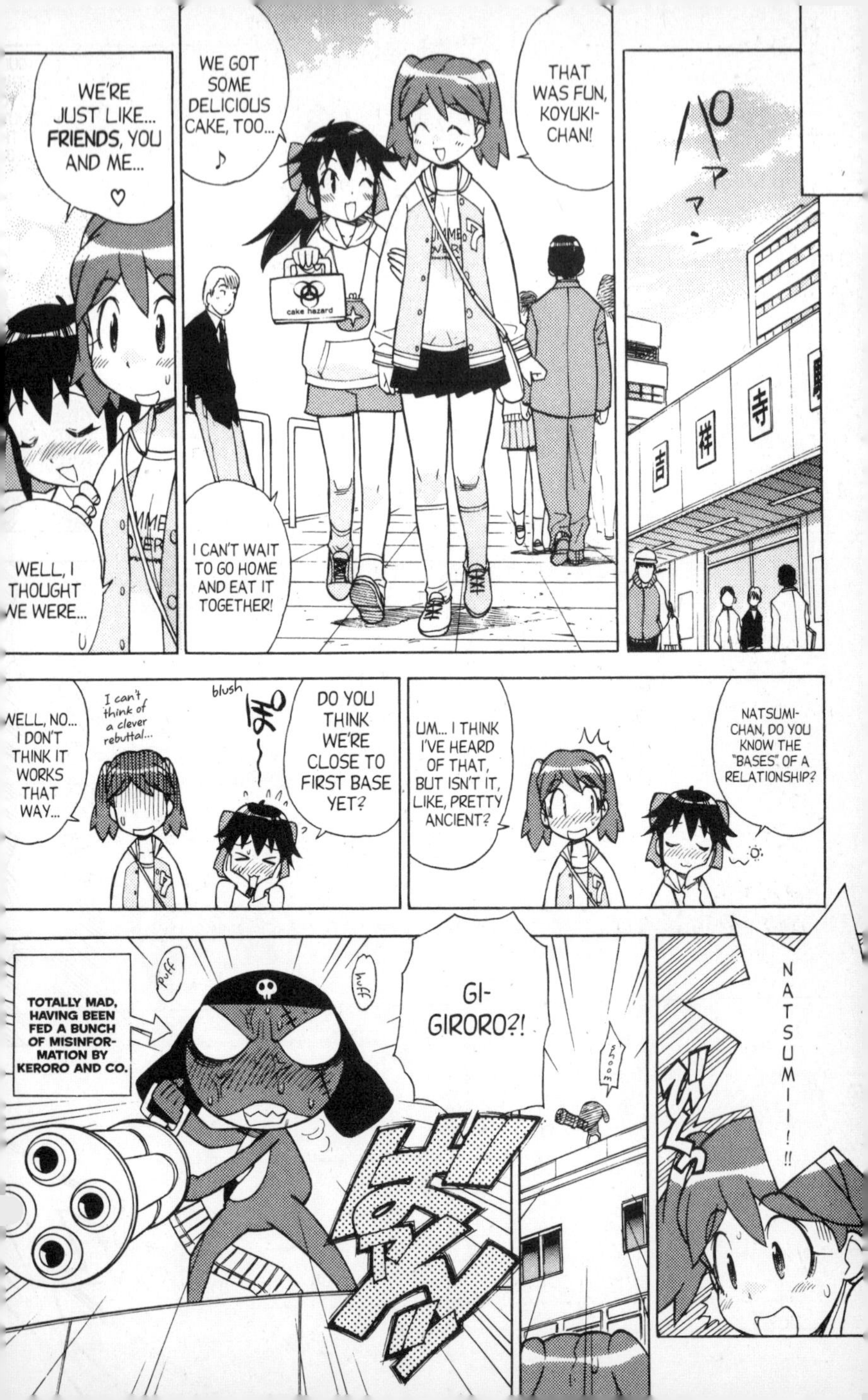
パァァン
吉祥寺
THAT WAS FUN, KOYUKI-CHAN!
WE GOT SOME DELICIOUS CAKE, TOO... ♪
cake hazard
I CAN'T WAIT TO GO HOME AND EAT IT TOGETHER!
WE'RE JUST LIKE... **FRIENDS**, YOU AND ME... ♡
WELL, I THOUGHT WE WERE...
NATSUMI-CHAN, DO YOU KNOW THE "BASES" OF A RELATIONSHIP?
UM... I THINK I'VE HEARD OF THAT, BUT ISN'T IT, LIKE, PRETTY ANCIENT?
DO YOU THINK WE'RE CLOSE TO FIRST BASE YET?
blush
ぽ~~
I can't think of a clever rebuttal...
WELL, NO... I DON'T THINK IT WORKS THAT WAY...
NATSUMI!!!
GI-GIRORO?!
shoom
huff
puff
TOTALLY MAD, HAVING BEEN FED A BUNCH OF MISINFORMATION BY KERORO AND CO.

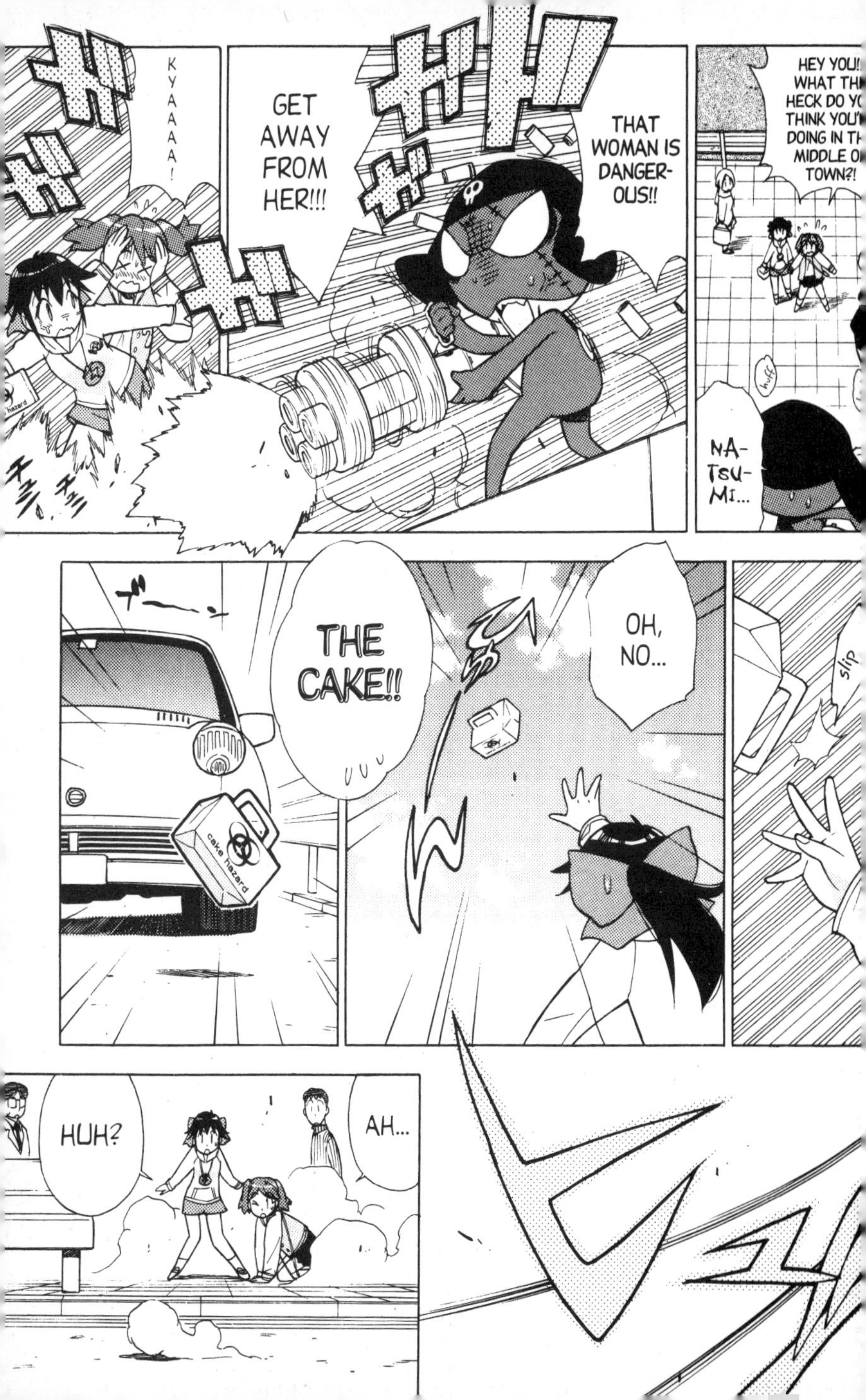
HEY YOU!! WHAT THE HECK DO YOU THINK YOU'RE DOING IN THE MIDDLE OF TOWN?!
huff
NA- TSU- MI...
THAT WOMAN IS DANGER- OUS!!
GET AWAY FROM HER!!!
KYAAAAA!
hazard
slip
OH, NO...
THE CAKE!!
cake hazard
AH...
HUH?

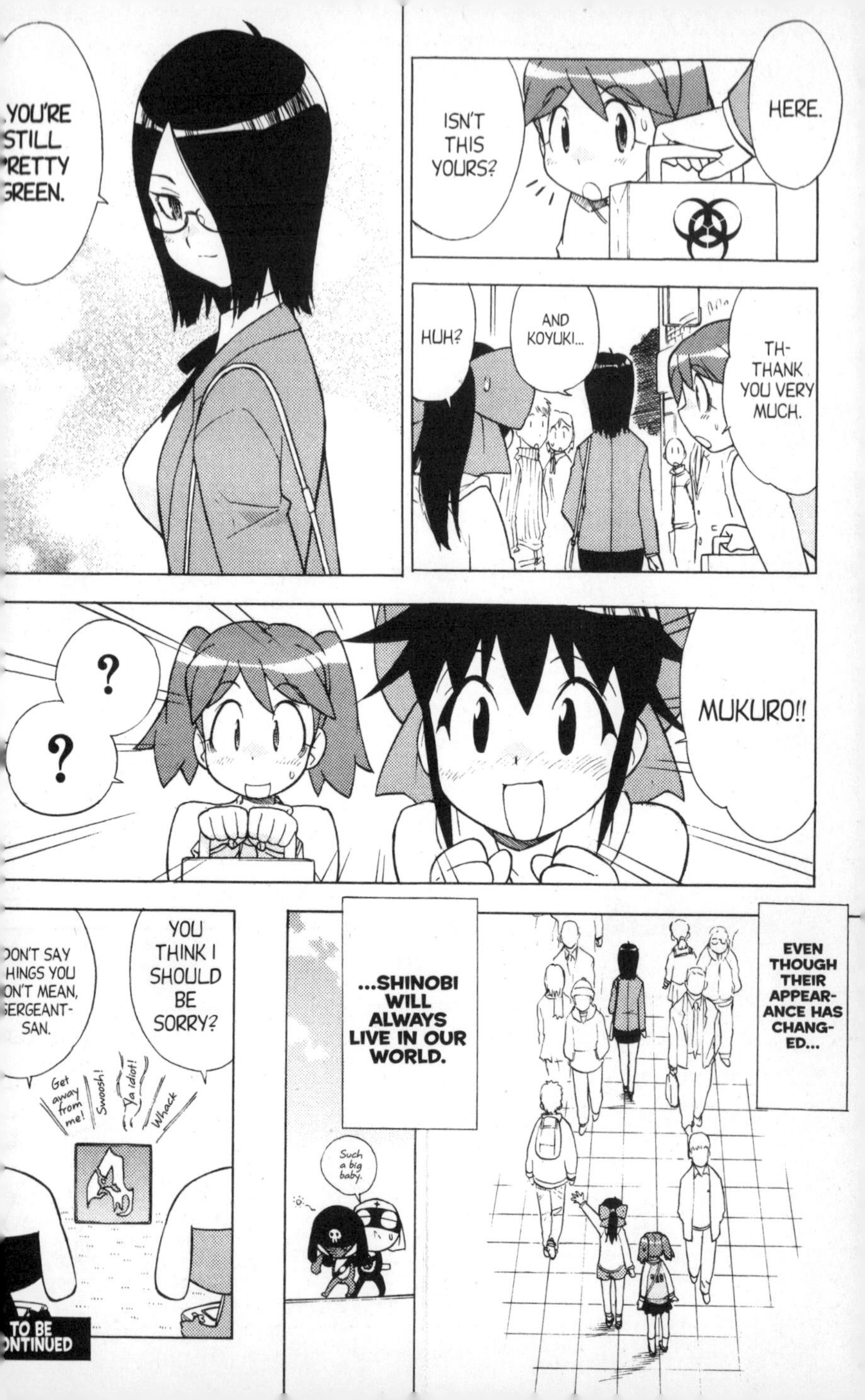
HERE.
ISN'T THIS YOURS?
TH-THANK YOU VERY MUCH.
AND KOYUKI...
HUH?
YOU'RE STILL RETTY REEN.
MUKURO!!
?
?
EVEN THOUGH THEIR APPEAR-ANCE HAS CHANG-ED...
...SHINOBI WILL ALWAYS LIVE IN OUR WORLD.
Such a big baby.
YOU THINK I SHOULD BE SORRY?
ON'T SAY HINGS YOU ON'T MEAN, ERGEANT-SAN.
Whack
Ya idiot!
Swoosh!
Get away from me!
TO BE ONTINUED

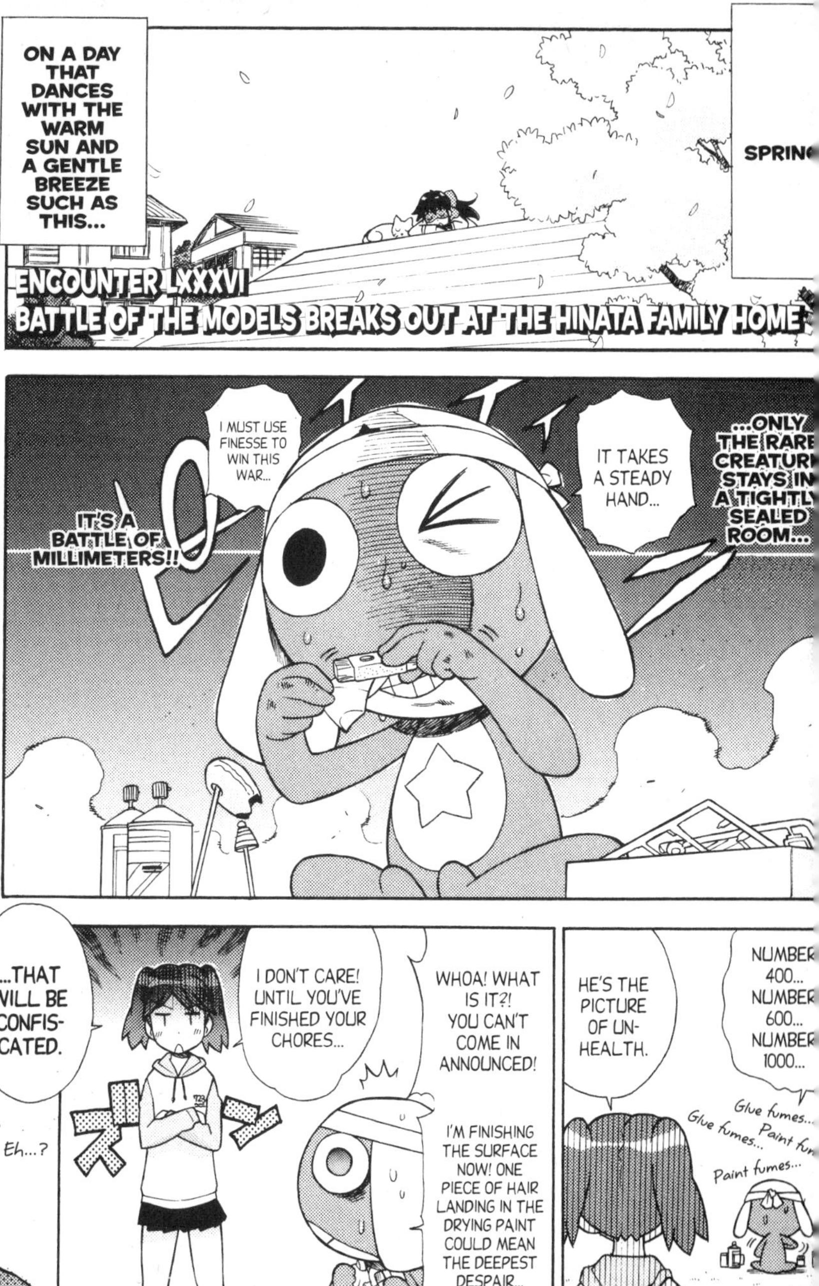
SPRIN
ON A DAY THAT DANCES WITH THE WARM SUN AND A GENTLE BREEZE SUCH AS THIS...
ENCOUNTER LXXXVI
BATTLE OF THE MODELS BREAKS OUT AT THE HINATA FAMILY HOME
...ONLY THE RARE CREATUR STAYS IN A TIGHTL SEALED ROOM...
IT TAKES A STEADY HAND...
I MUST USE FINESSE TO WIN THIS WAR...
IT'S A BATTLE OF MILLIMETERS!!
NUMBER 400... NUMBER 600... NUMBER 1000...
HE'S THE PICTURE OF UN-HEALTH.
Glue fumes...
Glue fumes...
Paint fu
Paint fumes...
WHOA! WHAT IS IT?! YOU CAN'T COME IN ANNOUNCED!
I'M FINISHING THE SURFACE NOW! ONE PIECE OF HAIR LANDING IN THE DRYING PAINT COULD MEAN THE DEEPEST DESPAIR...
I DON'T CARE! UNTIL YOU'VE FINISHED YOUR CHORES...
...THAT WILL BE CONFIS-CATED.
Eh...?

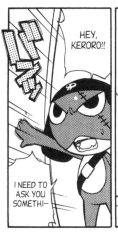

IT'S NOT RIGHT!!
THIS MONTH'S PAY HAS NOT BEEN DEPOSITED IN MY ACCOUNT...
HOW AM I SUPPOSED TO SEND MONEY TO MY FOLKS LIKE THIS ...?!
HEY, KERORO!!
I NEED TO ASK YOU SOMETHI--
GENTLE ...
GENTLE ...
TAKES A STEADY HAND...
WHAT'S WRONG, KERORO?!
STOP THAT! THERE ARE NO GUNDAM MODELS HERE!!
CAREFUL! YOU'LL MAKE THE GLUE SQUEEZE OUT...
WHAT? NATSUMI CONFISCATED YOUR GUNDAM MODEL?
NOT JUST ANY MODEL. IT'S THE GREATEST ONE IN MY COLLECTION. I WAS SAVING IT FOR THE PERFECT DAY...
I ALREADY PUT ALL OF THIS MONTH'S PAY INTO THE OPERATION BUDGET, AND...
COMING FROM YOU, THAT'S A SURPRISINGLY NOBLE WAY TO SPEND YOUR MONEY...
AND WHAT IS THE OPERATION YOU SPEAK OF?

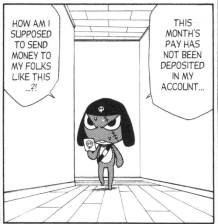

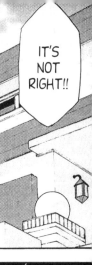

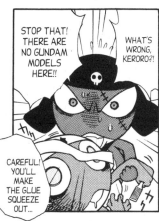

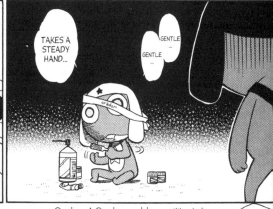

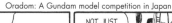

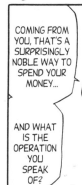

Oradom: A Gundam model competition in Japan

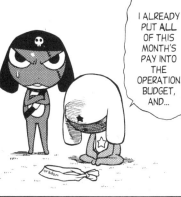

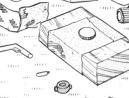

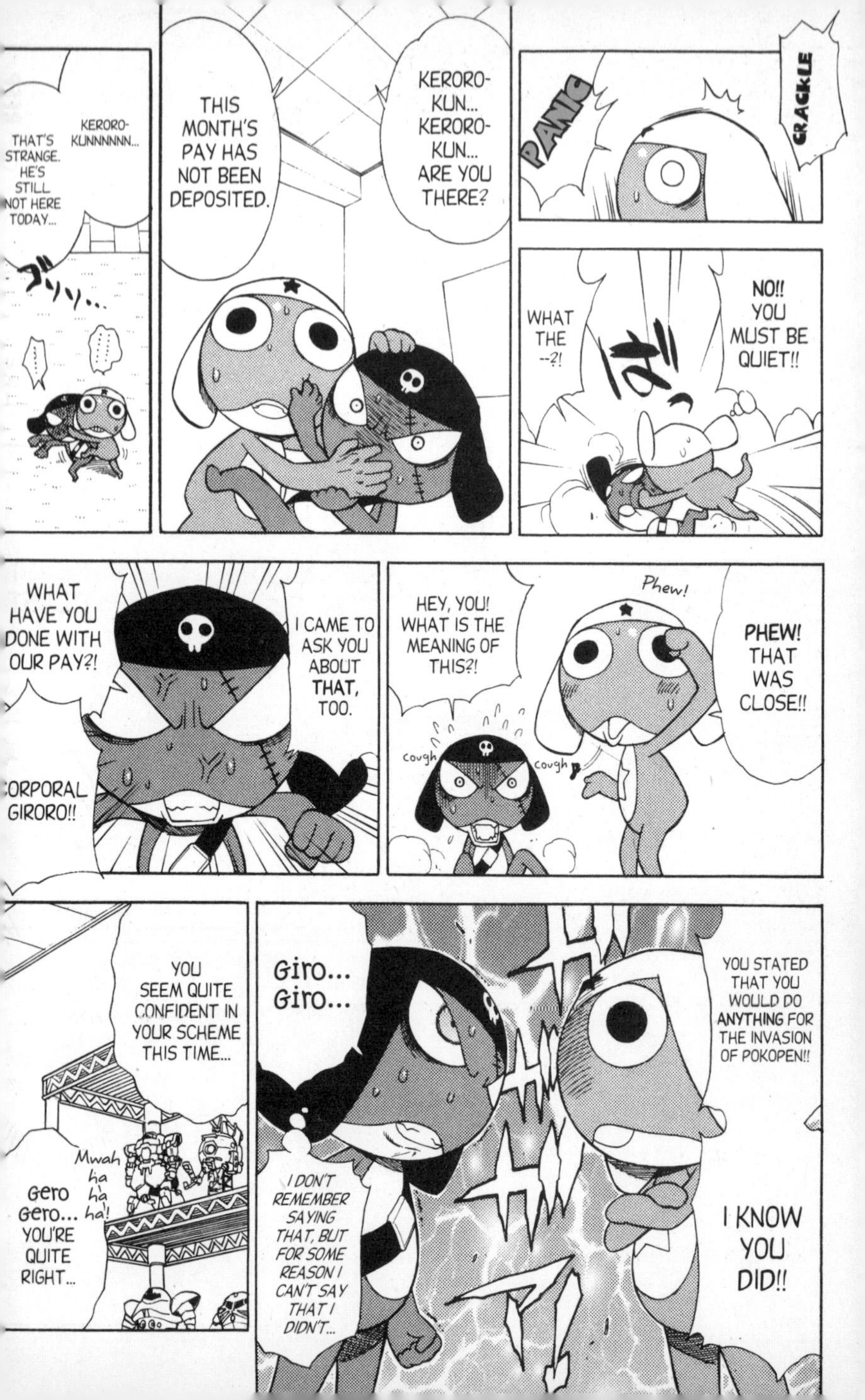

PANIC
CRACKLE
NO!! YOU MUST BE QUIET!!
WHAT THE --?!
KERORO-KUN... KERORO-KUN... ARE YOU THERE?
THIS MONTH'S PAY HAS NOT BEEN DEPOSITED.
KERORO-KUNNNNNNN...
THAT'S STRANGE. HE'S STILL NOT HERE TODAY...
Phew!
PHEW! THAT WAS CLOSE!!
HEY, YOU! WHAT IS THE MEANING OF THIS?!
cough
cough
I CAME TO ASK YOU ABOUT THAT, TOO.
WHAT HAVE YOU DONE WITH OUR PAY?!
ORPORAL GIRORO!!
YOU STATED THAT YOU WOULD DO ANYTHING FOR THE INVASION OF POKOPEN!!
Giro... Giro...
I DON'T REMEMBER SAYING THAT, BUT FOR SOME REASON I CAN'T SAY THAT I DIDN'T...
I KNOW YOU DID!!
YOU SEEM QUITE CONFIDENT IN YOUR SCHEME THIS TIME...
Mwah ha ha ha!
Gero Gero... YOU'RE QUITE RIGHT...

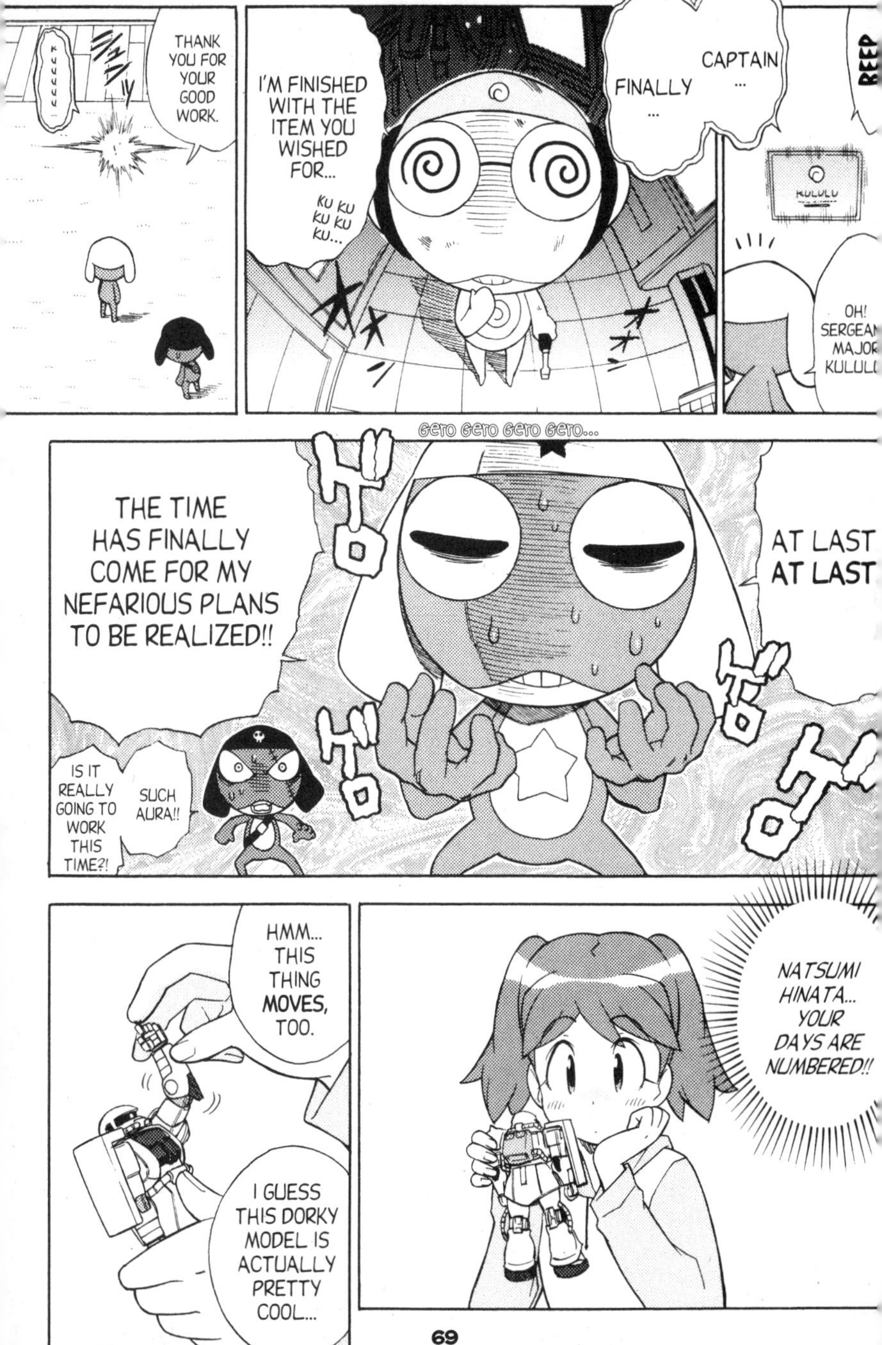
BEEP
KULULU
OH! SERGEAN MAJOR KULUL
CAPTAIN ... FINALLY ...
I'M FINISHED WITH THE ITEM YOU WISHED FOR...
KU KU KU KU KU...
THANK YOU FOR YOUR GOOD WORK.
Gero Gero Gero Gero...
AT LAST AT LAST
THE TIME HAS FINALLY COME FOR MY NEFARIOUS PLANS TO BE REALIZED!!
SUCH AURA!!
IS IT REALLY GOING TO WORK THIS TIME?!
NATSUMI HINATA... YOUR DAYS ARE NUMBERED!!
HMM... THIS THING MOVES, TOO.
I GUESS THIS DORKY MODEL IS ACTUALLY PRETTY COOL...

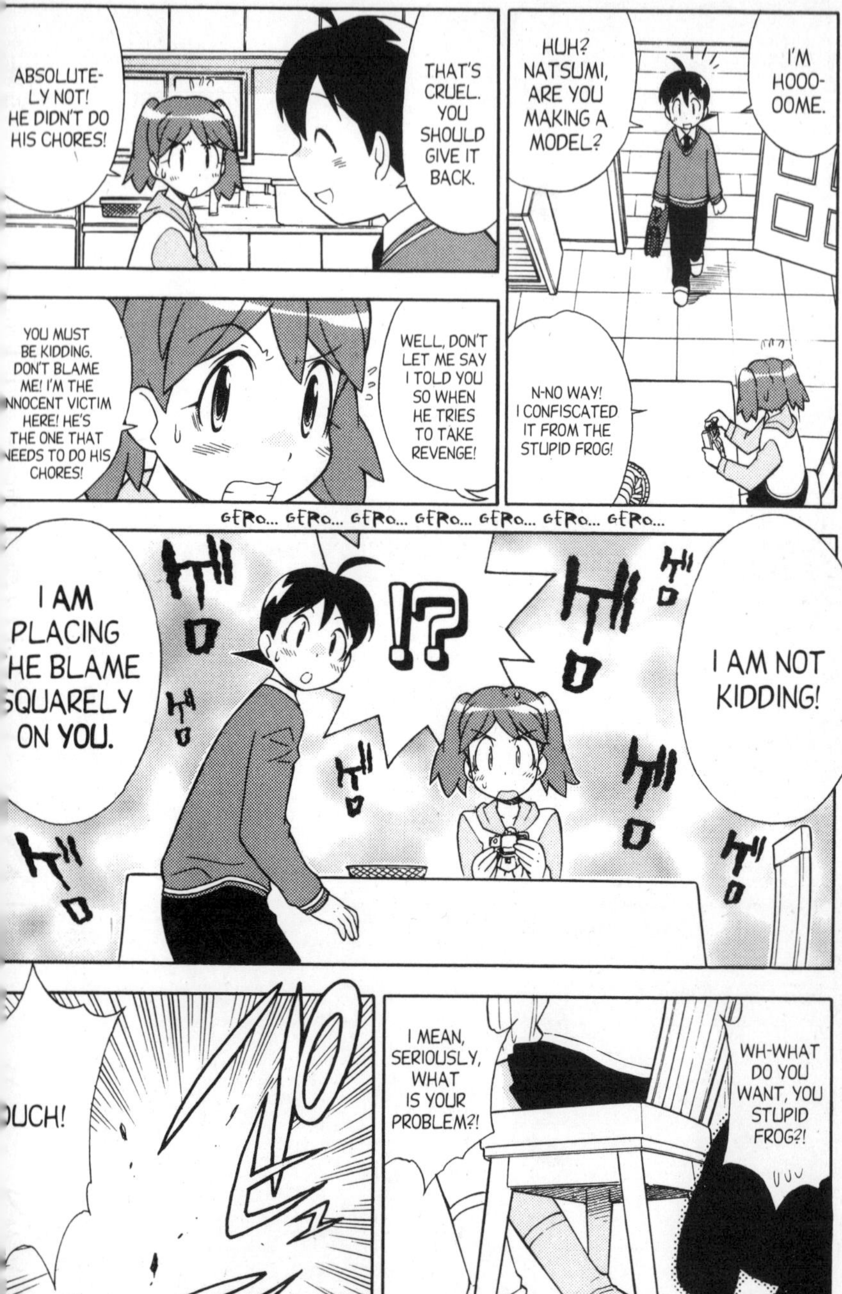
I'M HOOOOOME.
HUH? NATSUMI, ARE YOU MAKING A MODEL?
N-NO WAY! I CONFISCATED IT FROM THE STUPID FROG!
THAT'S CRUEL. YOU SHOULD GIVE IT BACK.
ABSOLUTE-LY NOT! HE DIDN'T DO HIS CHORES!
WELL, DON'T LET ME SAY I TOLD YOU SO WHEN HE TRIES TO TAKE REVENGE!
YOU MUST BE KIDDING. DON'T BLAME ME! I'M THE NNOCENT VICTIM HERE! HE'S THE ONE THAT EEDS TO DO HIS CHORES!
GERO... GERO... GERO... GERO... GERO... GERO... GERO...
I AM NOT KIDDING!
!?
I AM PLACING HE BLAME QUARELY ON YOU.
WH-WHAT DO YOU WANT, YOU STUPID FROG?!
I MEAN, SERIOUSLY, WHAT IS YOUR PROBLEM?!
UCH!

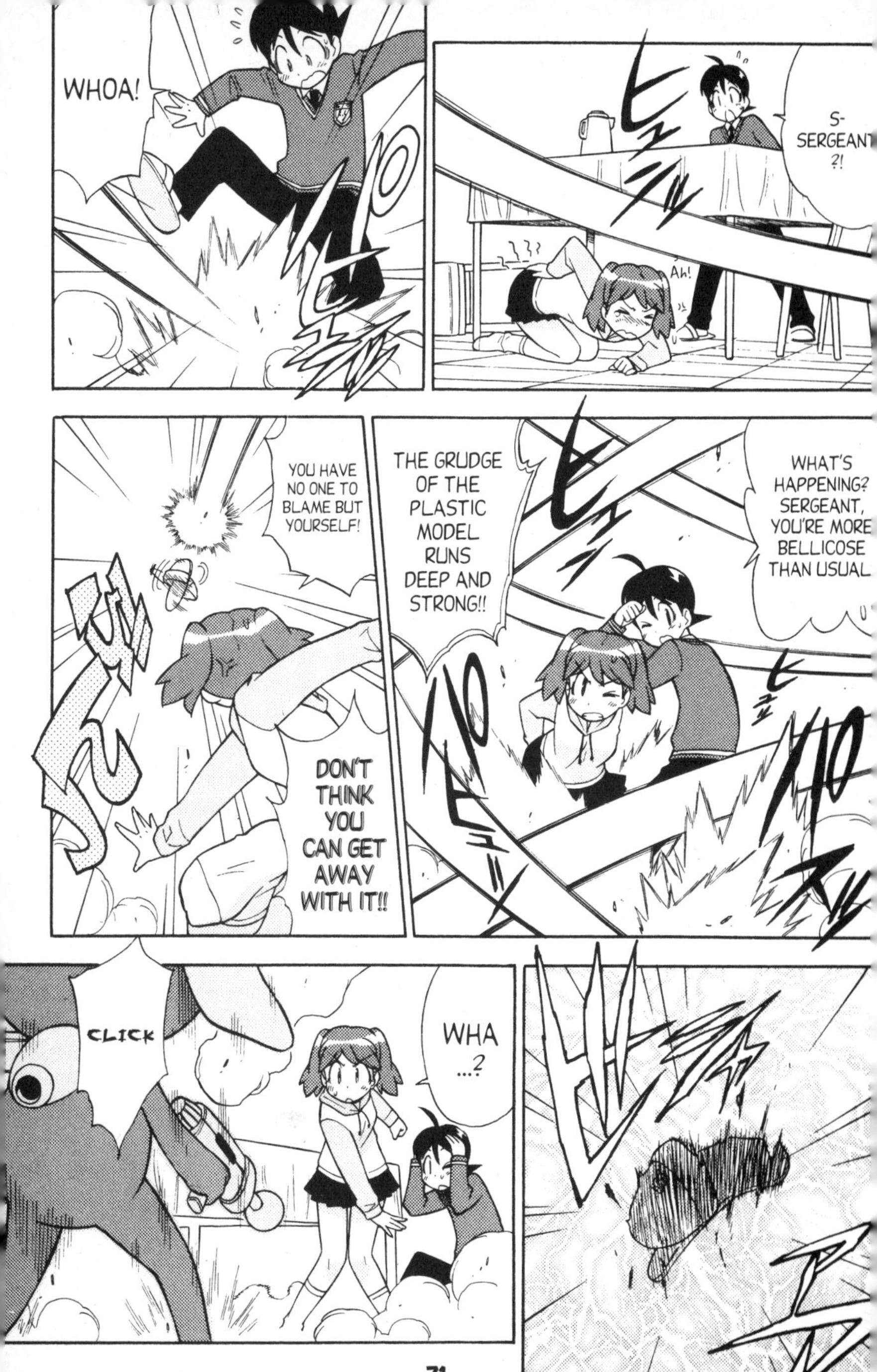
S-SERGEANT?!
Ah!
WHOA!
WHAT'S HAPPENING? SERGEANT, YOU'RE MORE BELLICOSE THAN USUAL.
THE GRUDGE OF THE PLASTIC MODEL RUNS DEEP AND STRONG!!
YOU HAVE NO ONE TO BLAME BUT YOURSELF!
DON'T THINK YOU CAN GET AWAY WITH IT!!
WHA ...?
CLICK

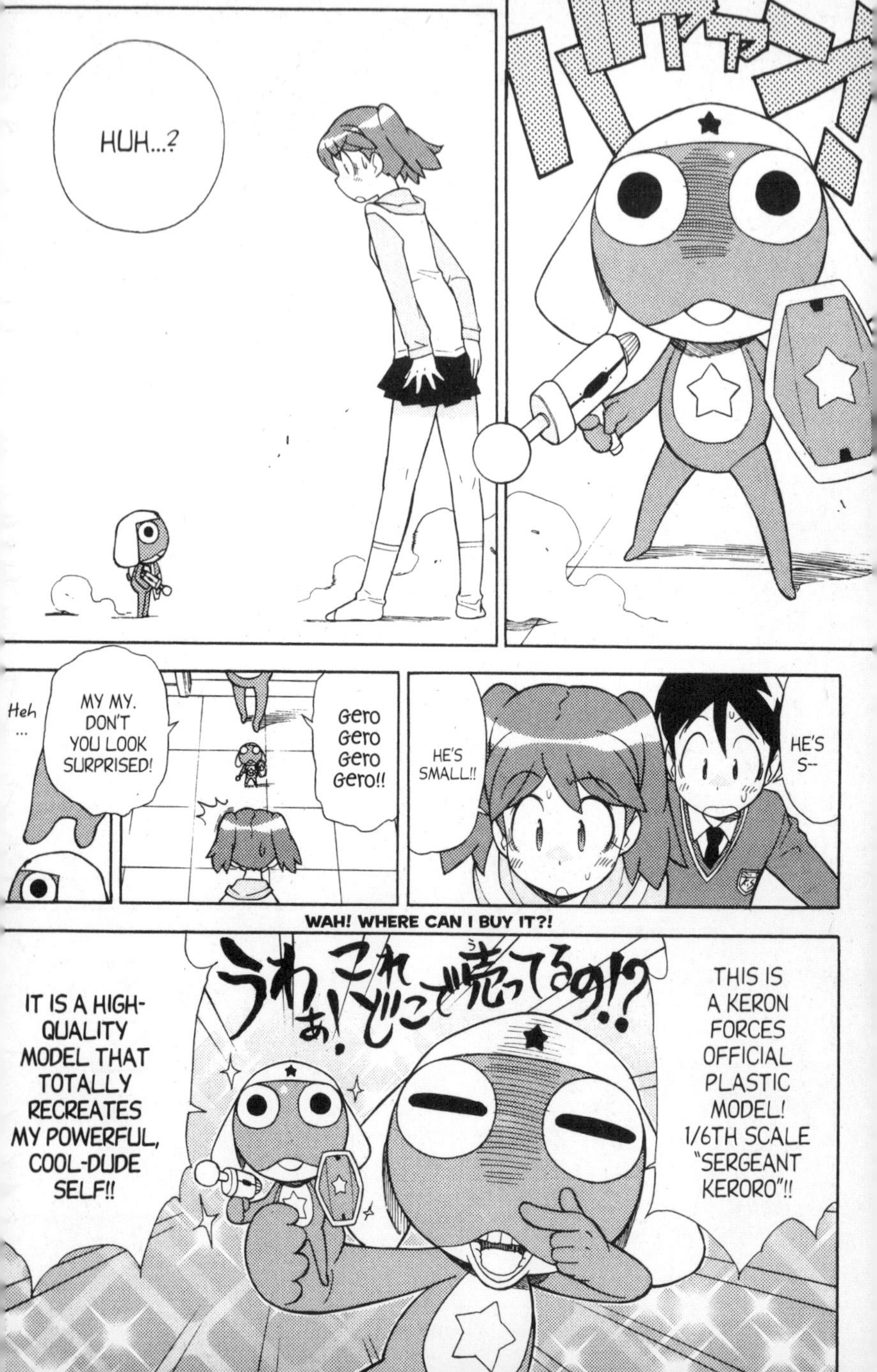
HUH...?
HE'S S--
HE'S SMALL!!
Gero Gero Gero Gero!!
MY MY. DON'T YOU LOOK SURPRISED!
Heh ...
WAH! WHERE CAN I BUY IT?!
うわあ！これどこで売ってるの!?
THIS IS A KERON FORCES OFFICIAL PLASTIC MODEL! 1/6TH SCALE "SERGEANT KERORO"!!
IT IS A HIGH-QUALITY MODEL THAT TOTALLY RECREATES MY POWERFUL, COOL-DUDE SELF!!

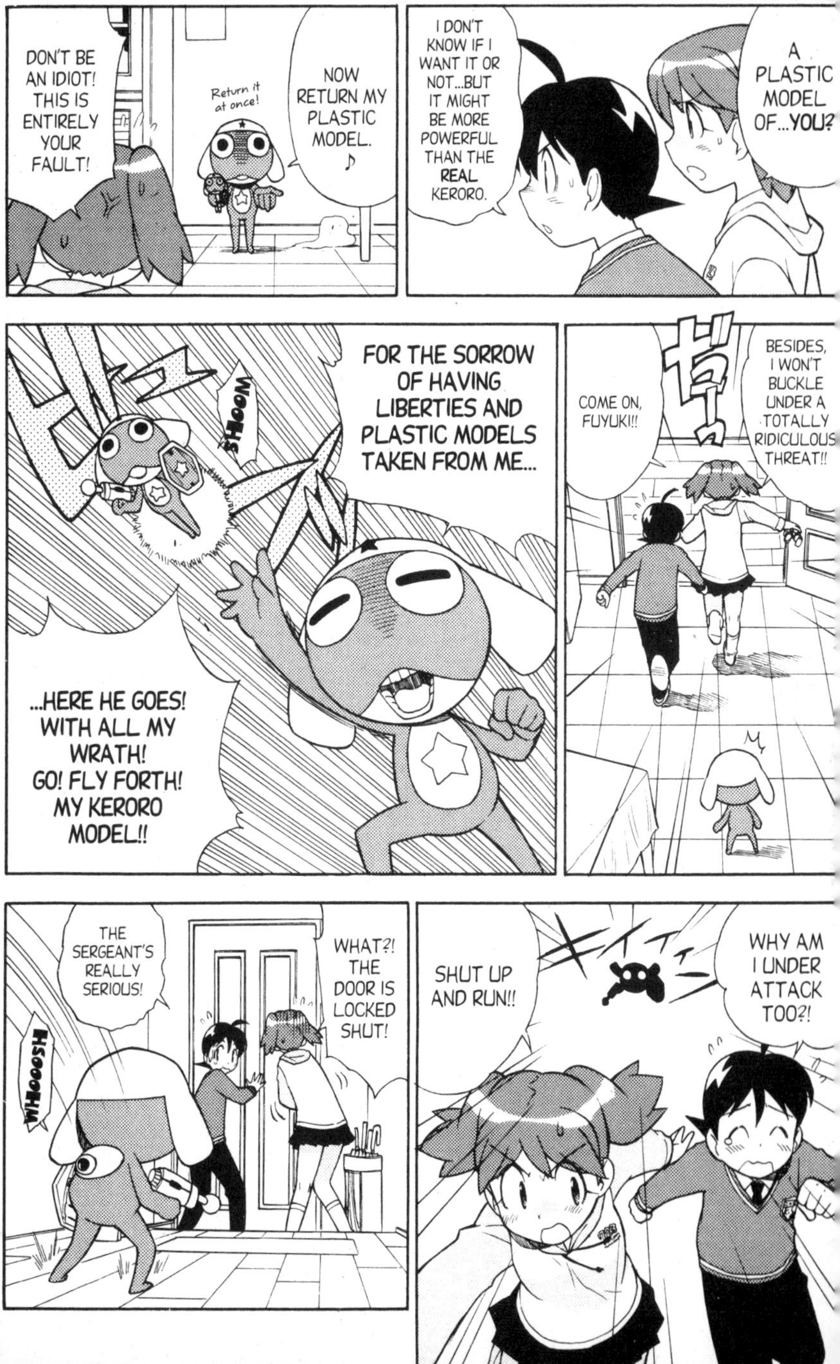
A PLASTIC MODEL OF...YOU?
I DON'T KNOW IF I WANT IT OR NOT...BUT IT MIGHT BE MORE POWERFUL THAN THE REAL KERORO.
NOW RETURN MY PLASTIC MODEL. ♪
Return it at once!
DON'T BE AN IDIOT! THIS IS ENTIRELY YOUR FAULT!
BESIDES, I WON'T BUCKLE UNDER A TOTALLY RIDICULOUS THREAT!!
COME ON, FUYUKI!!
FOR THE SORROW OF HAVING LIBERTIES AND PLASTIC MODELS TAKEN FROM ME...
WHOOSH
...HERE HE GOES! WITH ALL MY WRATH! GO! FLY FORTH! MY KERORO MODEL!!
WHY AM I UNDER ATTACK TOO?!
SHUT UP AND RUN!!
WHAT?! THE DOOR IS LOCKED SHUT!
THE SERGEANT'S REALLY SERIOUS!
WHOOOOSH

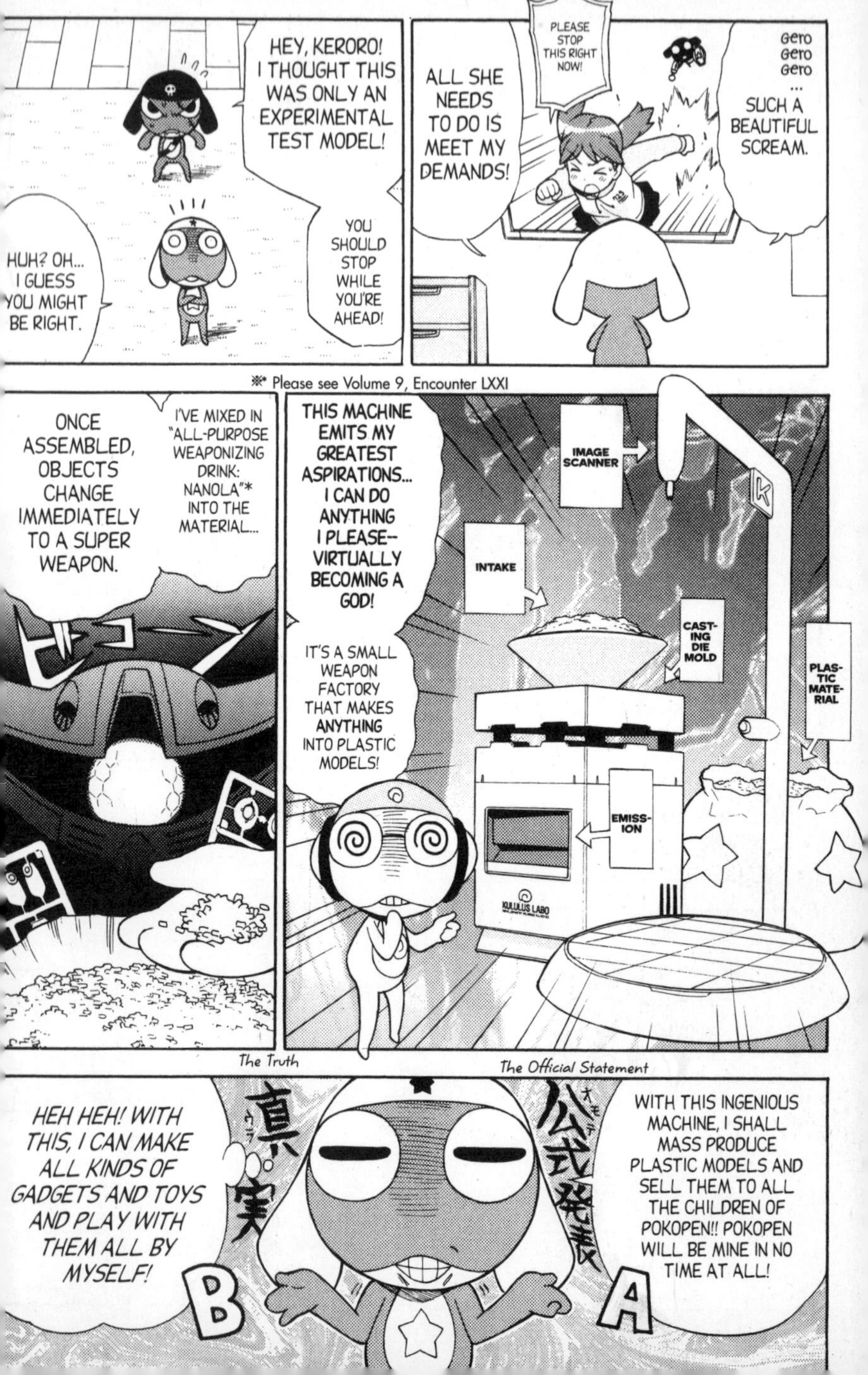
PLEASE STOP THIS RIGHT NOW!
Gero Gero Gero ... SUCH A BEAUTIFUL SCREAM.
ALL SHE NEEDS TO DO IS MEET MY DEMANDS!
HEY, KERORO! I THOUGHT THIS WAS ONLY AN EXPERIMENTAL TEST MODEL!
YOU SHOULD STOP WHILE YOU'RE AHEAD!
HUH? OH... I GUESS YOU MIGHT BE RIGHT.
※* Please see Volume 9, Encounter LXXI
THIS MACHINE EMITS MY GREATEST ASPIRATIONS... I CAN DO ANYTHING I PLEASE-- VIRTUALLY BECOMING A GOD!
IMAGE SCANNER
INTAKE
CASTING DIE MOLD
PLASTIC MATERIAL
EMISSION
KULULUS LABO
IT'S A SMALL WEAPON FACTORY THAT MAKES ANYTHING INTO PLASTIC MODELS!
I'VE MIXED IN "ALL-PURPOSE WEAPONIZING DRINK: NANOLA"* INTO THE MATERIAL...
ONCE ASSEMBLED, OBJECTS CHANGE IMMEDIATELY TO A SUPER WEAPON.
The Official Statement
公式発表
A
WITH THIS INGENIOUS MACHINE, I SHALL MASS PRODUCE PLASTIC MODELS AND SELL THEM TO ALL THE CHILDREN OF POKOPEN!! POKOPEN WILL BE MINE IN NO TIME AT ALL!
The Truth
真実
B
HEH HEH! WITH THIS, I CAN MAKE ALL KINDS OF GADGETS AND TOYS AND PLAY WITH THEM ALL BY MYSELF!

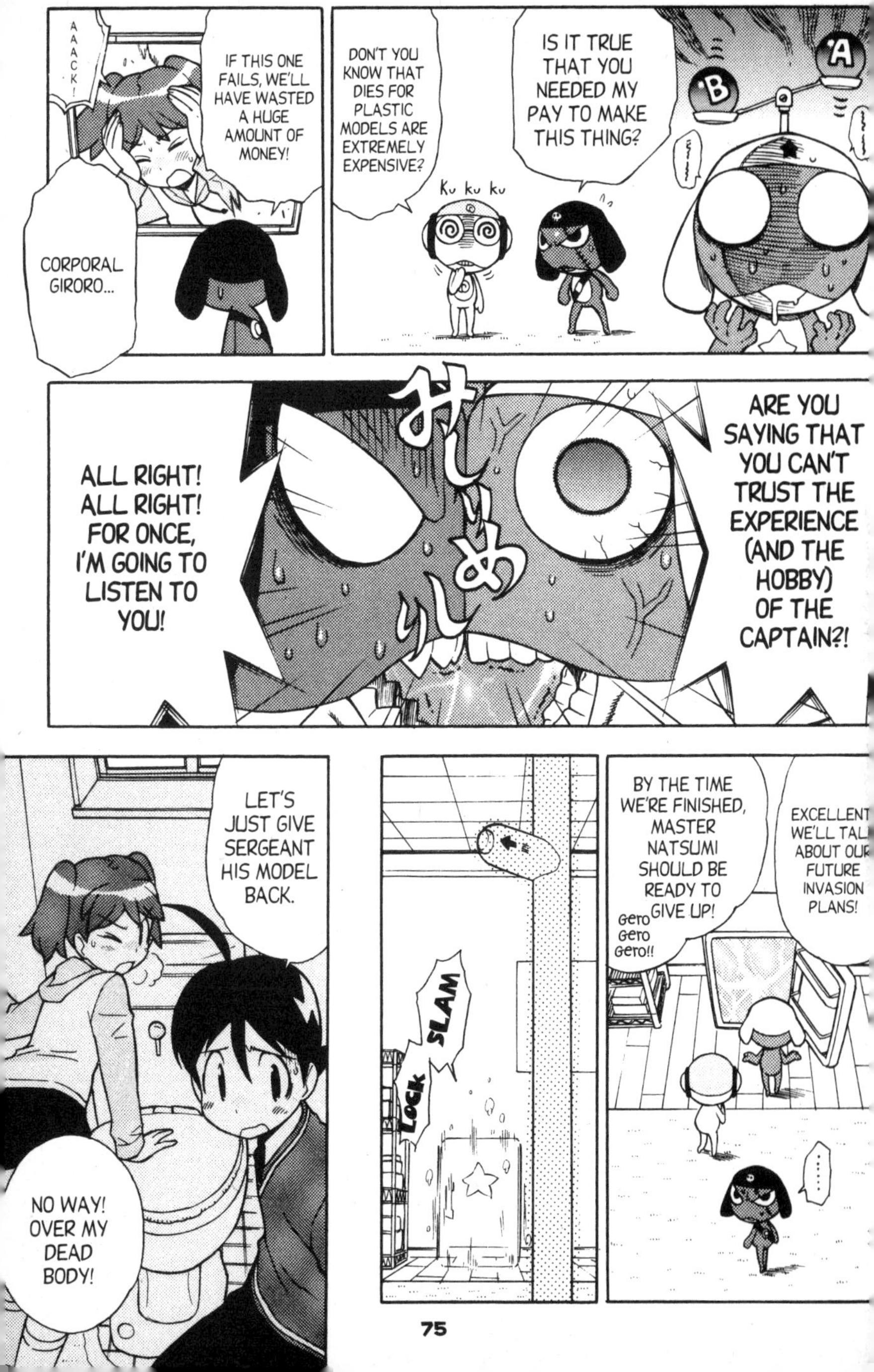
IS IT TRUE THAT YOU NEEDED MY PAY TO MAKE THIS THING?
DON'T YOU KNOW THAT DIES FOR PLASTIC MODELS ARE EXTREMELY EXPENSIVE?
Ku ku ku
IF THIS ONE FAILS, WE'LL HAVE WASTED A HUGE AMOUNT OF MONEY!
AAACK!
CORPORAL GIRORO...
ARE YOU SAYING THAT YOU CAN'T TRUST THE EXPERIENCE (AND THE HOBBY) OF THE CAPTAIN?!
みしめりし
ALL RIGHT! ALL RIGHT! FOR ONCE, I'M GOING TO LISTEN TO YOU!
EXCELLENT WE'LL TAL ABOUT OUR FUTURE INVASION PLANS!
BY THE TIME WE'RE FINISHED, MASTER NATSUMI SHOULD BE READY TO GIVE UP!
Gero Gero Gero!!
......
SLAM
LOCK
LET'S JUST GIVE SERGEANT HIS MODEL BACK.
NO WAY! OVER MY DEAD BODY!

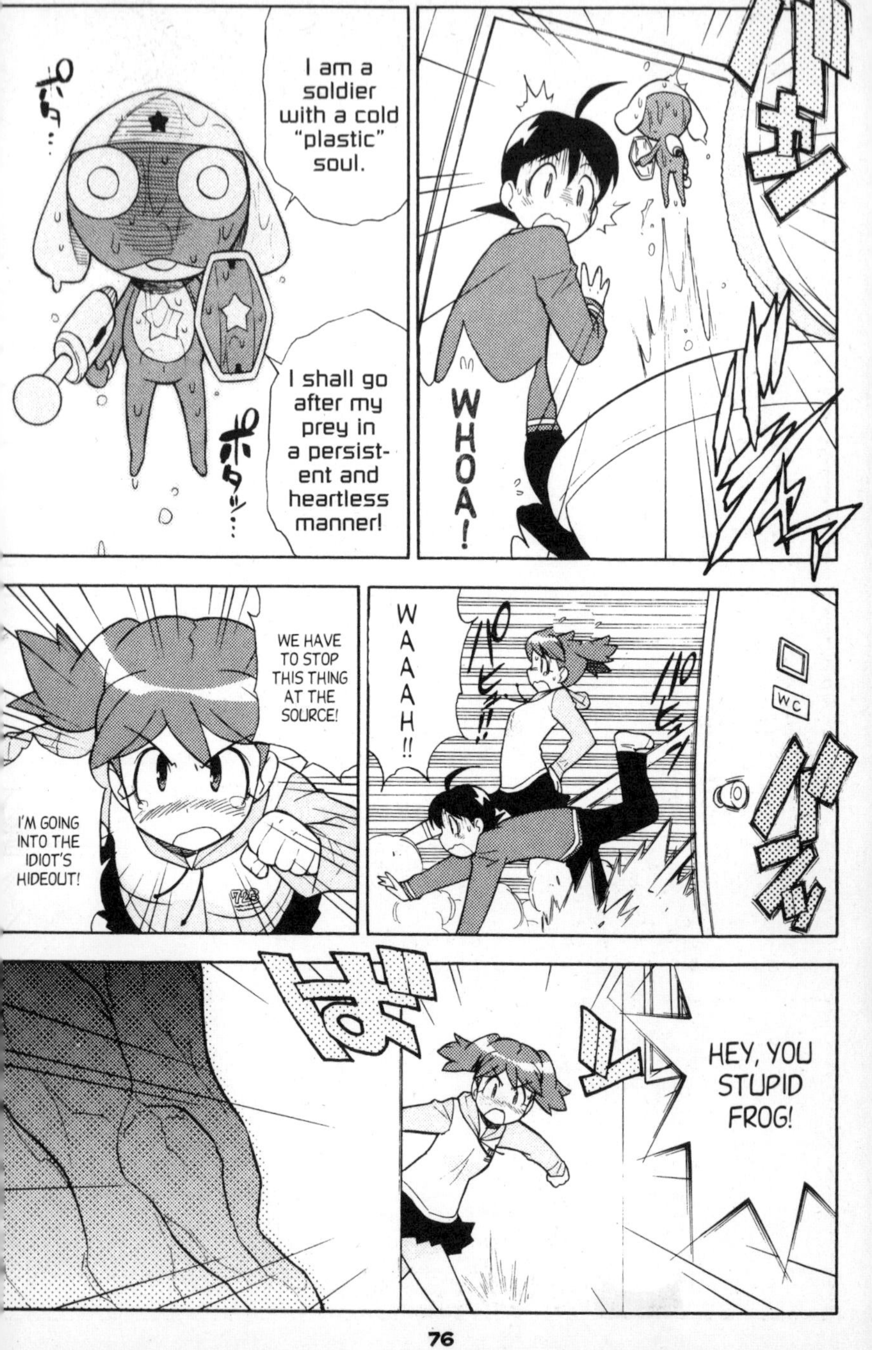
WHOA!
I am a soldier with a cold "plastic" soul.
I shall go after my prey in a persistent and heartless manner!
WAAAAH!!
WE HAVE TO STOP THIS THING AT THE SOURCE!
I'M GOING INTO THE IDIOT'S HIDEOUT!
WC
HEY, YOU STUPID FROG!

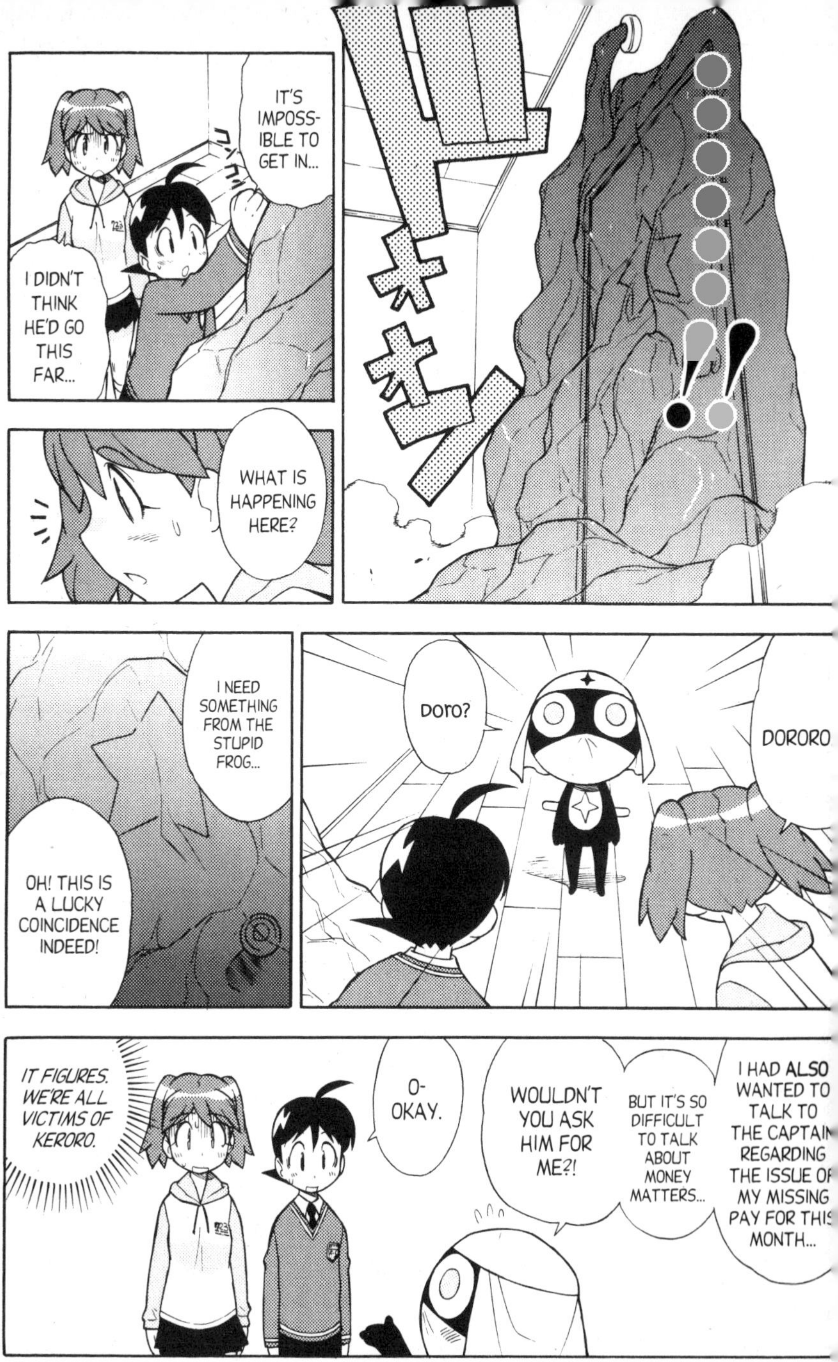
IT'S IMPOSS-IBLE TO GET IN...
I DIDN'T THINK HE'D GO THIS FAR...
WHAT IS HAPPENING HERE?
DORORO.
Doro?
I NEED SOMETHING FROM THE STUPID FROG...
OH! THIS IS A LUCKY COINCIDENCE INDEED!
I HAD **ALSO** WANTED TO TALK TO THE CAPTAIN REGARDING THE ISSUE OF MY MISSING PAY FOR THIS MONTH...
BUT IT'S SO DIFFICULT TO TALK ABOUT MONEY MATTERS...
WOULDN'T YOU ASK HIM FOR ME?!
O-OKAY.
IT FIGURES. WE'RE ALL VICTIMS OF KERORO.

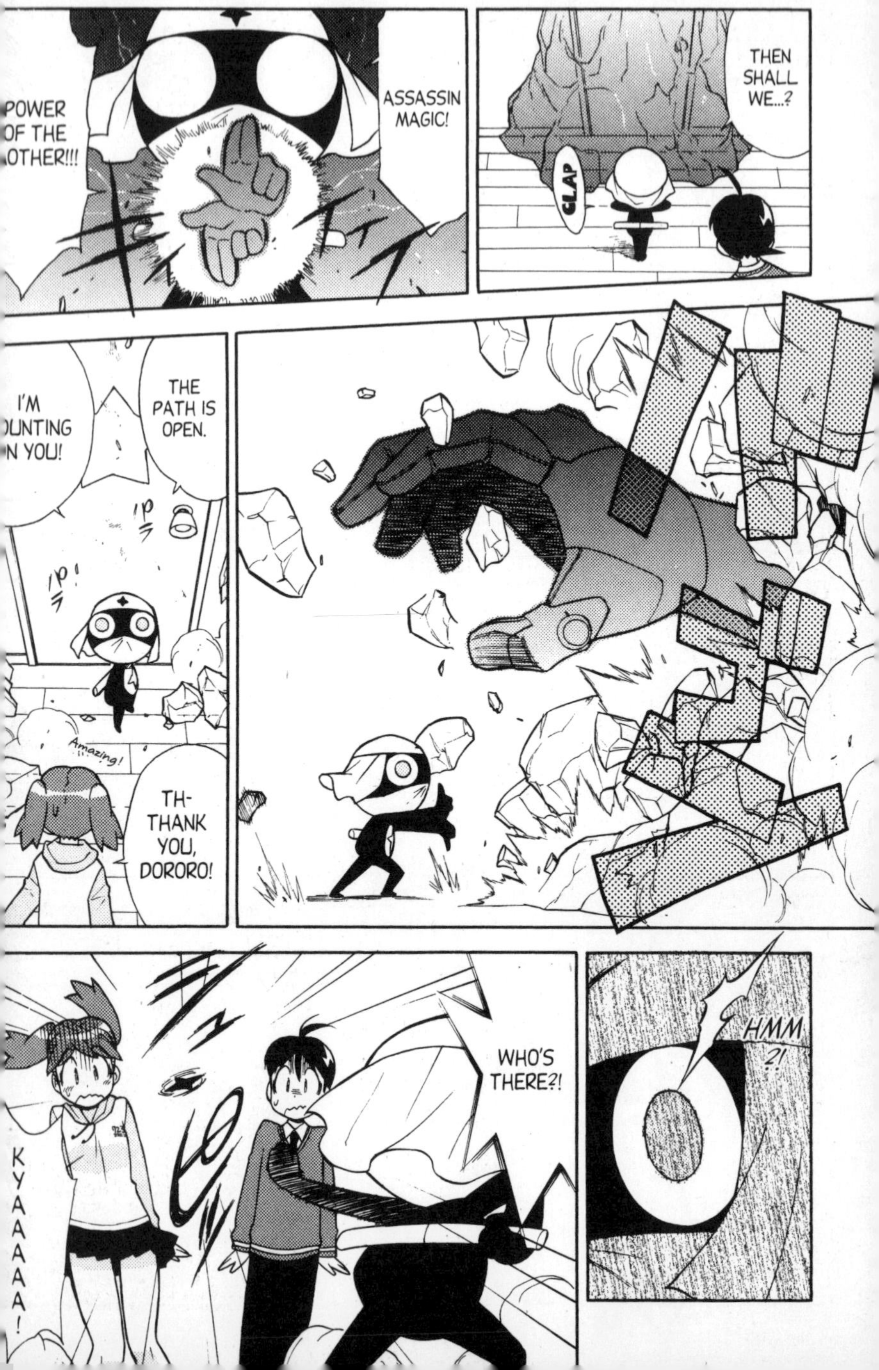
THEN SHALL WE...?
CLAP
ASSASSIN MAGIC!
POWER OF THE OTHER!!!
THE PATH IS OPEN.
I'M UNTING N YOU!
Amazing!
TH-THANK YOU, DORORO!
HMM?!
WHO'S THERE?!
KYAAAAAA!

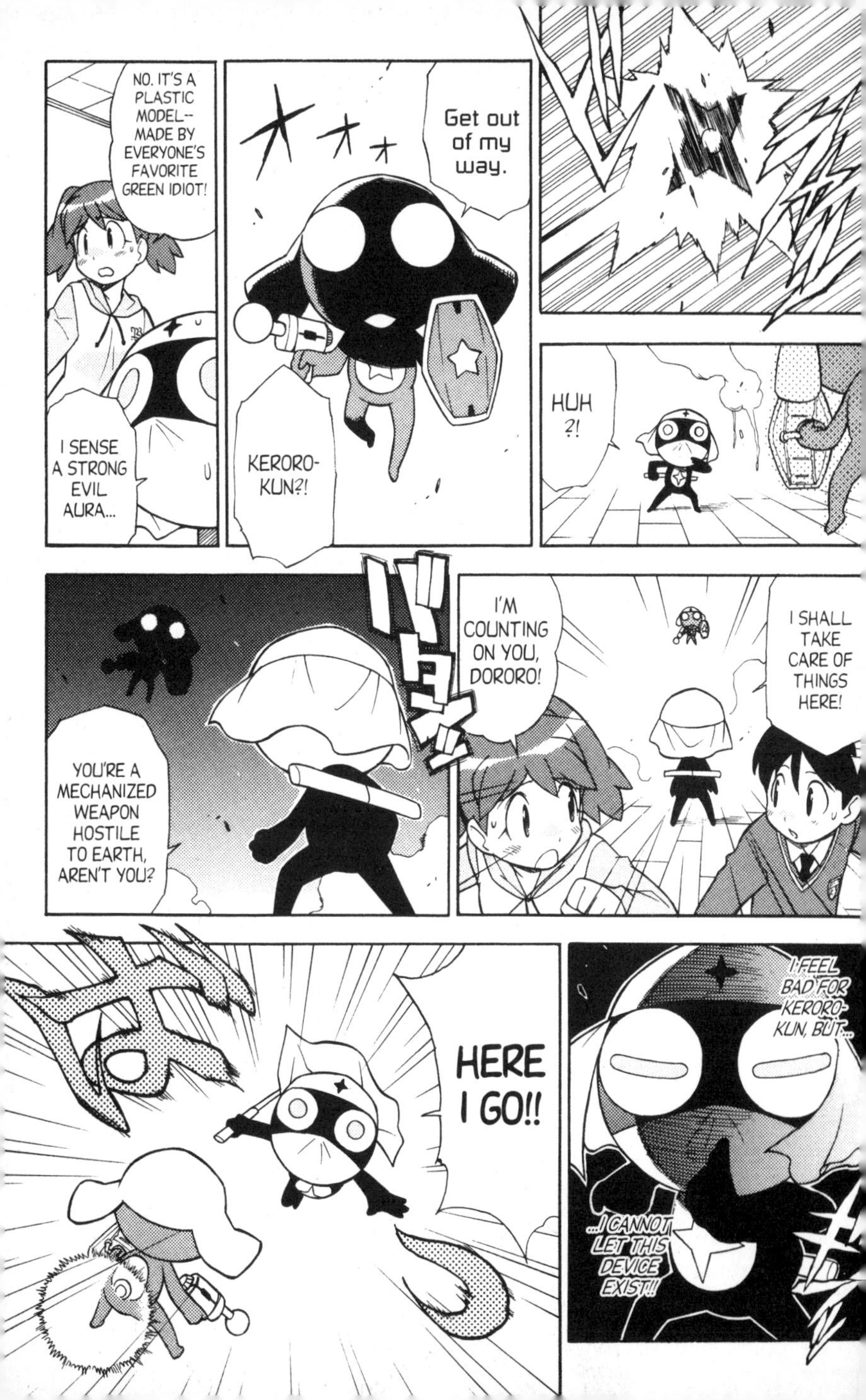
HUH ?!
Get out of my way.
KERORO-KUN?!
NO. IT'S A PLASTIC MODEL-- MADE BY EVERYONE'S FAVORITE GREEN IDIOT!
I SENSE A STRONG EVIL AURA...
I SHALL TAKE CARE OF THINGS HERE!
I'M COUNTING ON YOU, DORORO!
YOU'RE A MECHANIZED WEAPON HOSTILE TO EARTH, AREN'T YOU?
I FEEL BAD FOR KERORO-KUN, BUT...
...I CANNOT LET THIS DEVICE EXIST!!
HERE I GO!!

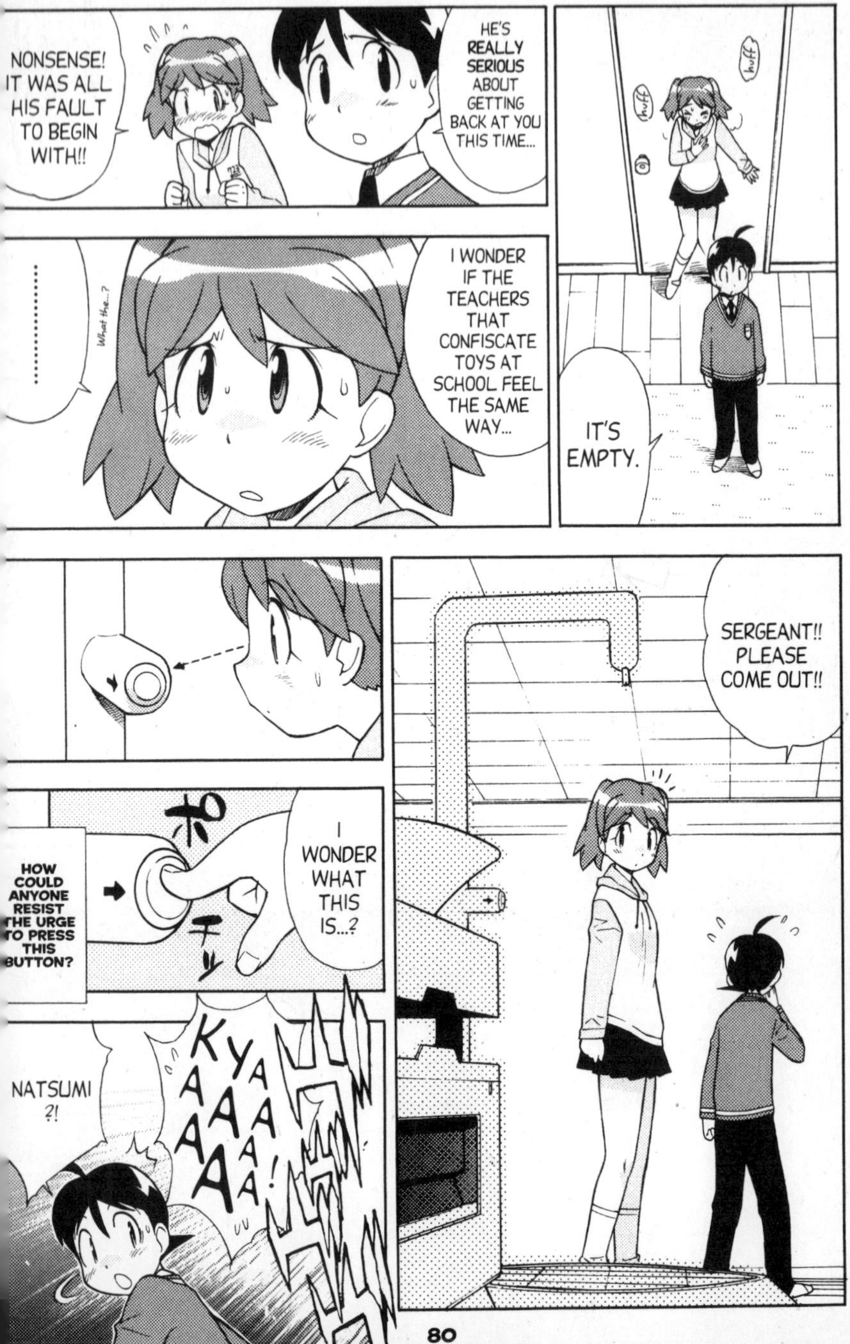

huff
huff
IT'S EMPTY.
HE'S REALLY SERIOUS ABOUT GETTING BACK AT YOU THIS TIME...
NONSENSE! IT WAS ALL HIS FAULT TO BEGIN WITH!!
I WONDER IF THE TEACHERS THAT CONFISCATE TOYS AT SCHOOL FEEL THE SAME WAY...
....
What the...?
SERGEANT!! PLEASE COME OUT!!
I WONDER WHAT THIS IS...?
ポ
チッ
HOW COULD ANYONE RESIST THE URGE TO PRESS THIS BUTTON?
KYAAAAAAAAAA!
NATSUMI ?!

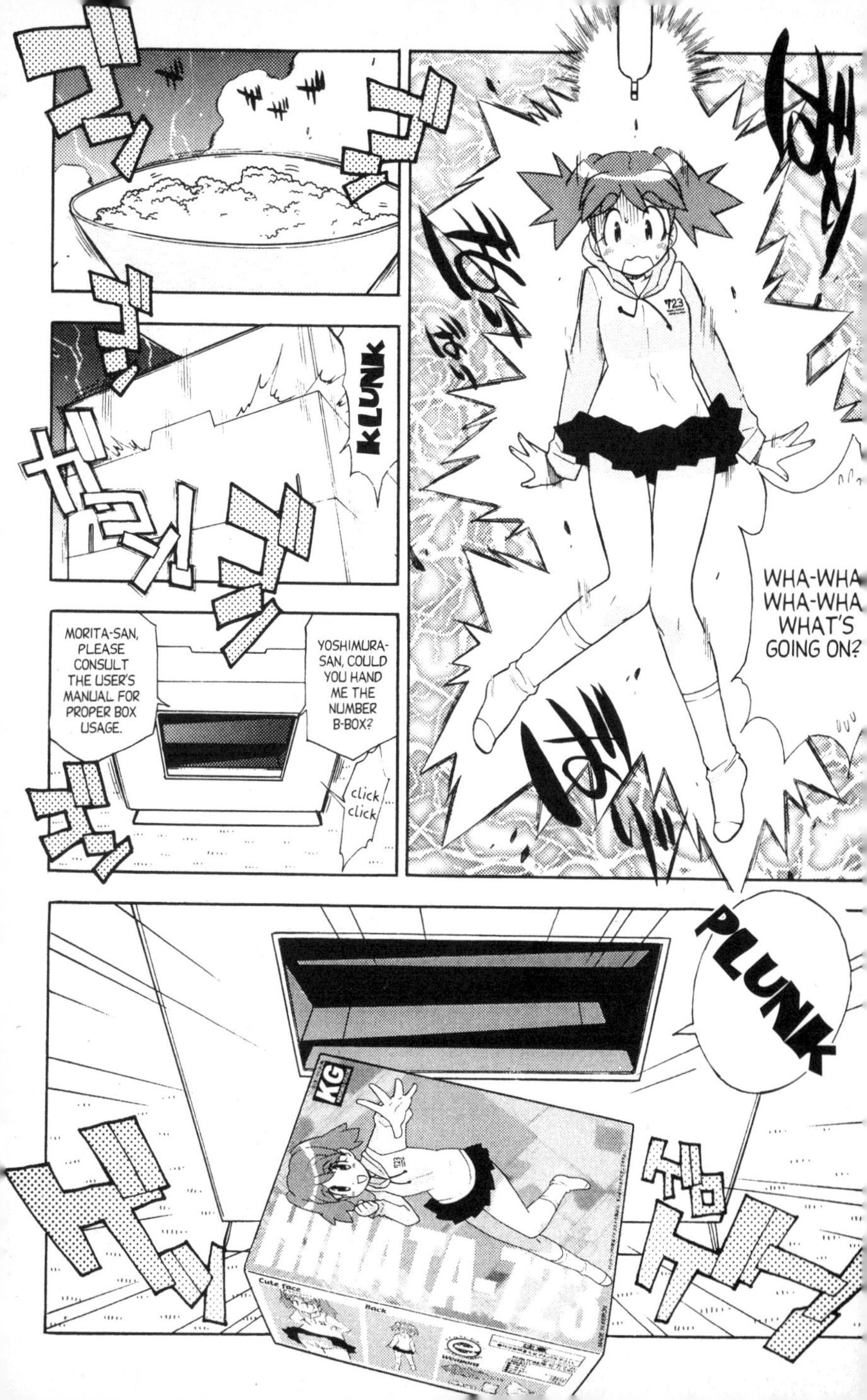
WHA-WHA
WHA-WHA
WHAT'S
GOING ON?
KLUNK
YOSHIMURA-SAN, COULD YOU HAND ME THE NUMBER B-BOX?
MORITA-SAN, PLEASE CONSULT THE USER'S MANUAL FOR PROPER BOX USAGE.
click
click
PLUNK
KG
Cute face
Back

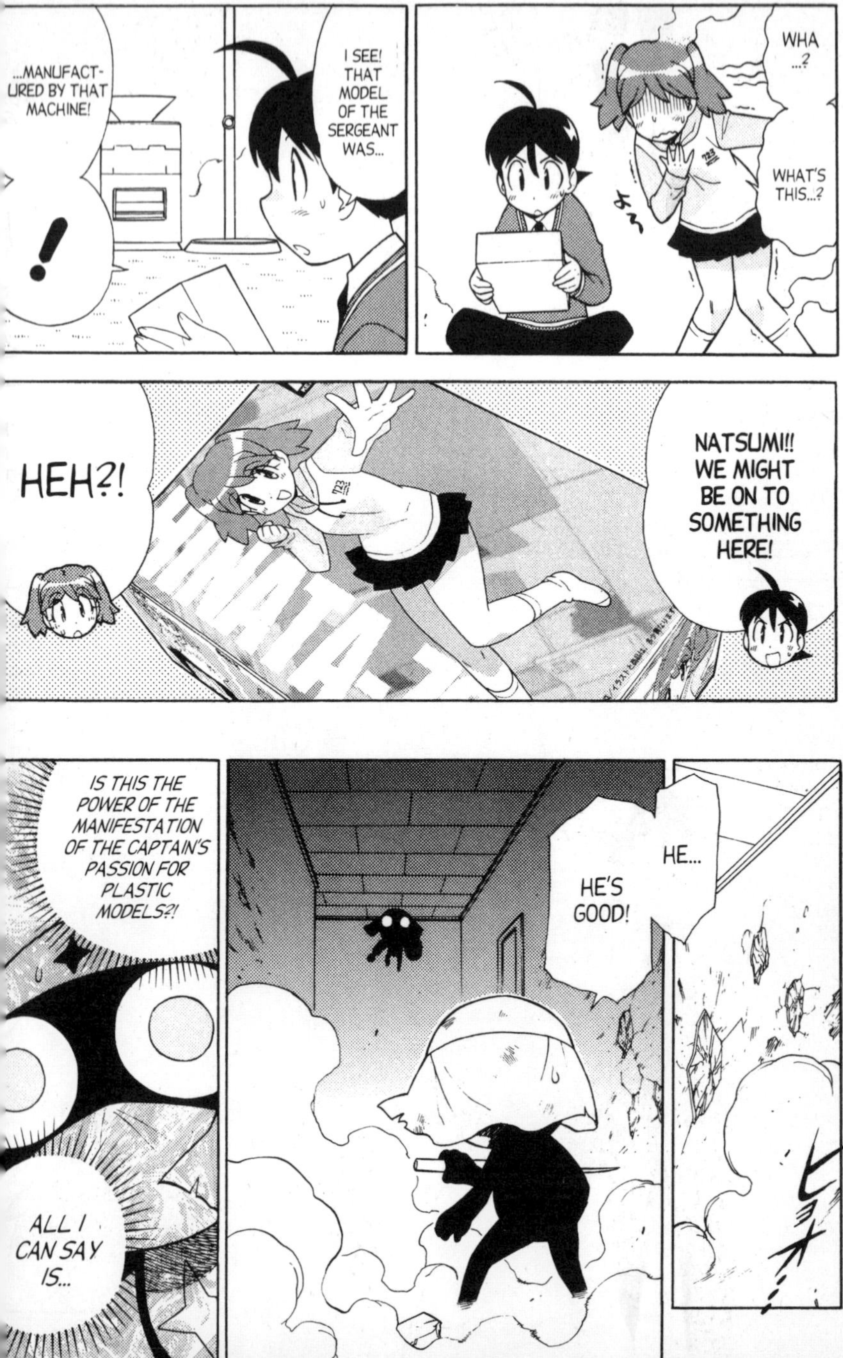
WHA ...?
WHAT'S THIS...?
I SEE! THAT MODEL OF THE SERGEANT WAS...
...MANUFACT-URED BY THAT MACHINE!
!
NATSUMI!! WE MIGHT BE ON TO SOMETHING HERE!
HEH?!
HE...
HE'S GOOD!
IS THIS THE POWER OF THE MANIFESTATION OF THE CAPTAIN'S PASSION FOR PLASTIC MODELS?!
ALL I CAN SAY IS...

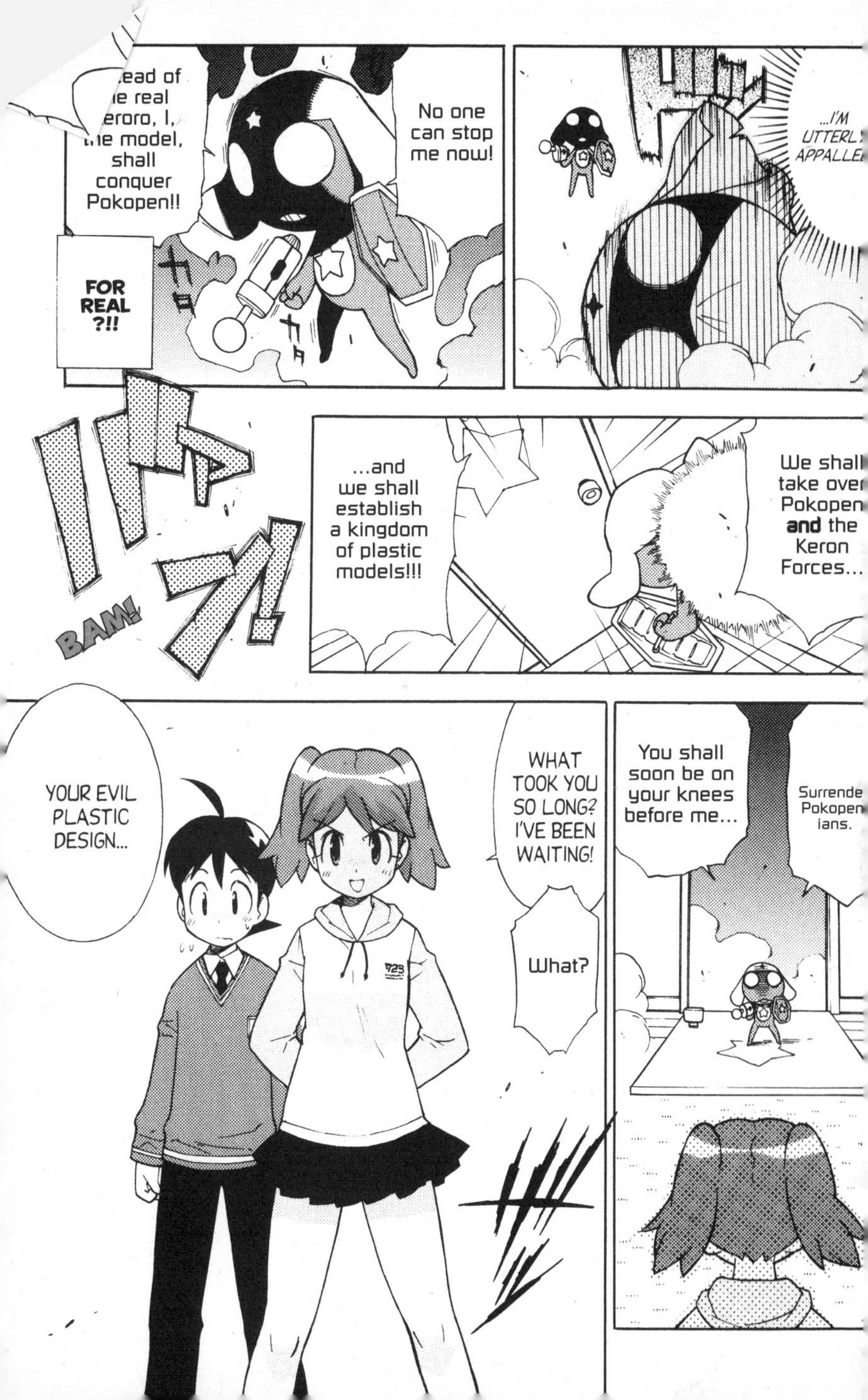
...I'M UTTERL APPALLE
ead of e real eroro, I, the model, shall conquer Pokopen!!
No one can stop me now!
FOR REAL ?!!
We shall take ove Pokopen and the Keron Forces...
...and we shall establish a kingdom of plastic models!!!
BAM!
Surrende Pokopen ians.
You shall soon be on your knees before me...
WHAT TOOK YOU SO LONG? I'VE BEEN WAITING!
What?
YOUR EVIL PLASTIC DESIGN...

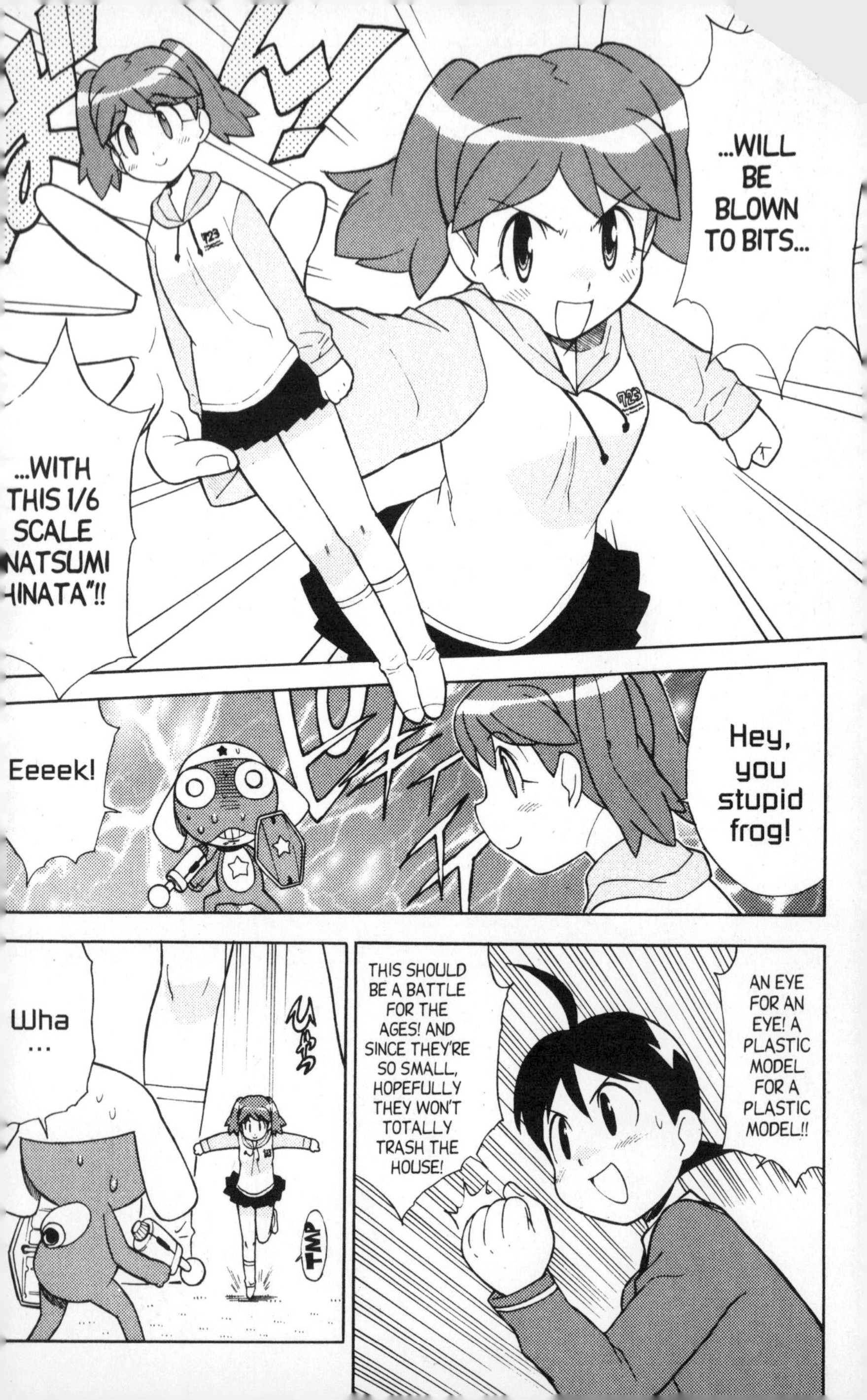
...WILL BE BLOWN TO BITS...
...WITH THIS 1/6 SCALE NATSUMI HINATA"!!
Hey, you stupid frog!
Eeeek!
AN EYE FOR AN EYE! A PLASTIC MODEL FOR A PLASTIC MODEL!!
THIS SHOULD BE A BATTLE FOR THE AGES! AND SINCE THEY'RE SO SMALL, HOPEFULLY THEY WON'T TOTALLY TRASH THE HOUSE!
Wha ...
TMP

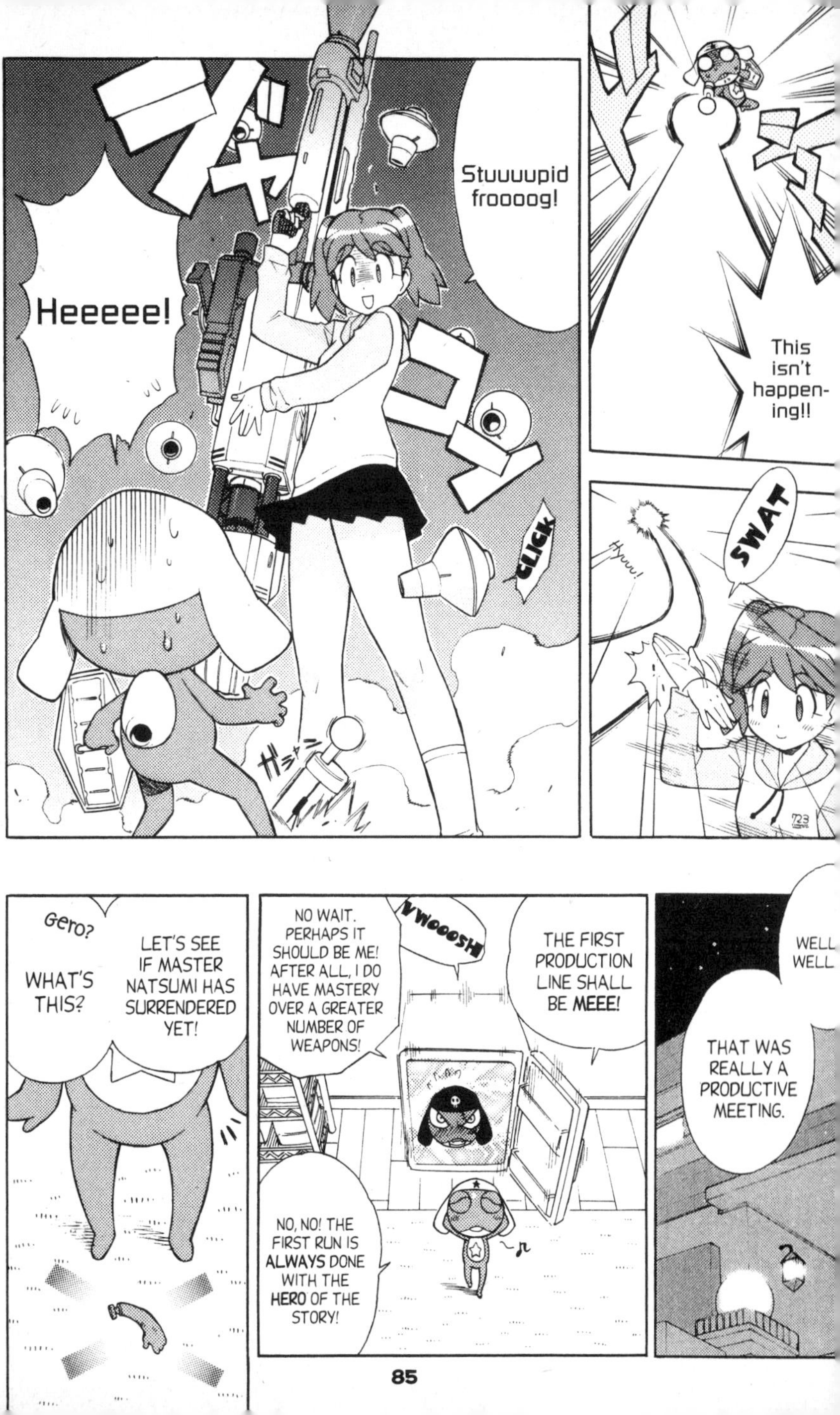
This isn't happen-ing!!
SWAT
Hyuuu!
Stuuuupid froooog!
Heeeee!
CLICK
WELL WELL
THAT WAS REALLY A PRODUCTIVE MEETING.
THE FIRST PRODUCTION LINE SHALL BE MEEE!
VWOOOSH
NO WAIT. PERHAPS IT SHOULD BE ME! AFTER ALL, I DO HAVE MASTERY OVER A GREATER NUMBER OF WEAPONS!
NO, NO! THE FIRST RUN IS ALWAYS DONE WITH THE HERO OF THE STORY!
LET'S SEE IF MASTER NATSUMI HAS SURRENDERED YET!
Gero?
WHAT'S THIS?

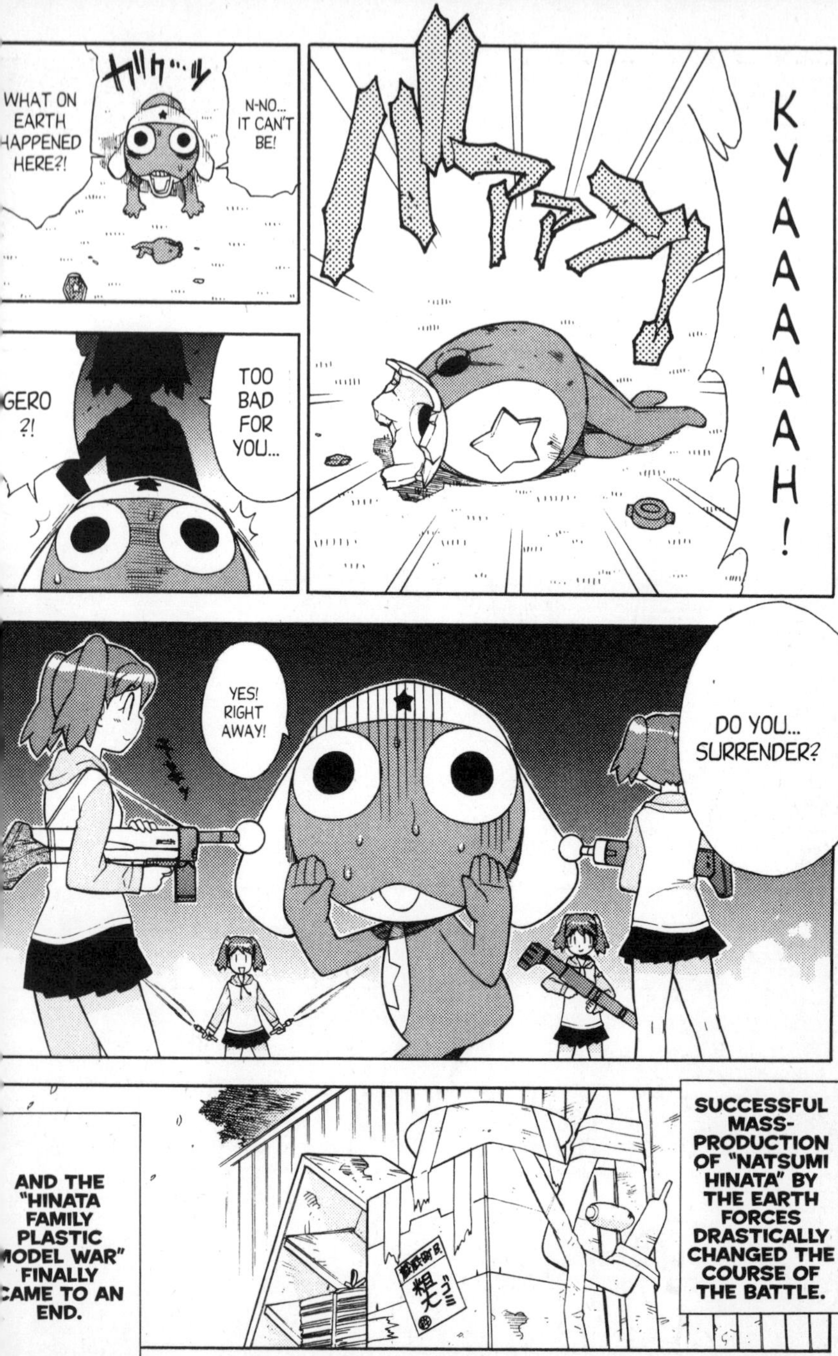
KYAAAAAH!
N-NO... IT CAN'T BE!
WHAT ON EARTH HAPPENED HERE?!
TOO BAD FOR YOU...
GERO?!
DO YOU... SURRENDER?
YES! RIGHT AWAY!
SUCCESSFUL MASS-PRODUCTION OF "NATSUMI HINATA" BY THE EARTH FORCES DRASTICALLY CHANGED THE COURSE OF THE BATTLE.
AND THE "HINATA FAMILY PLASTIC MODEL WAR" FINALLY CAME TO AN END.

Over-Sized Refuse

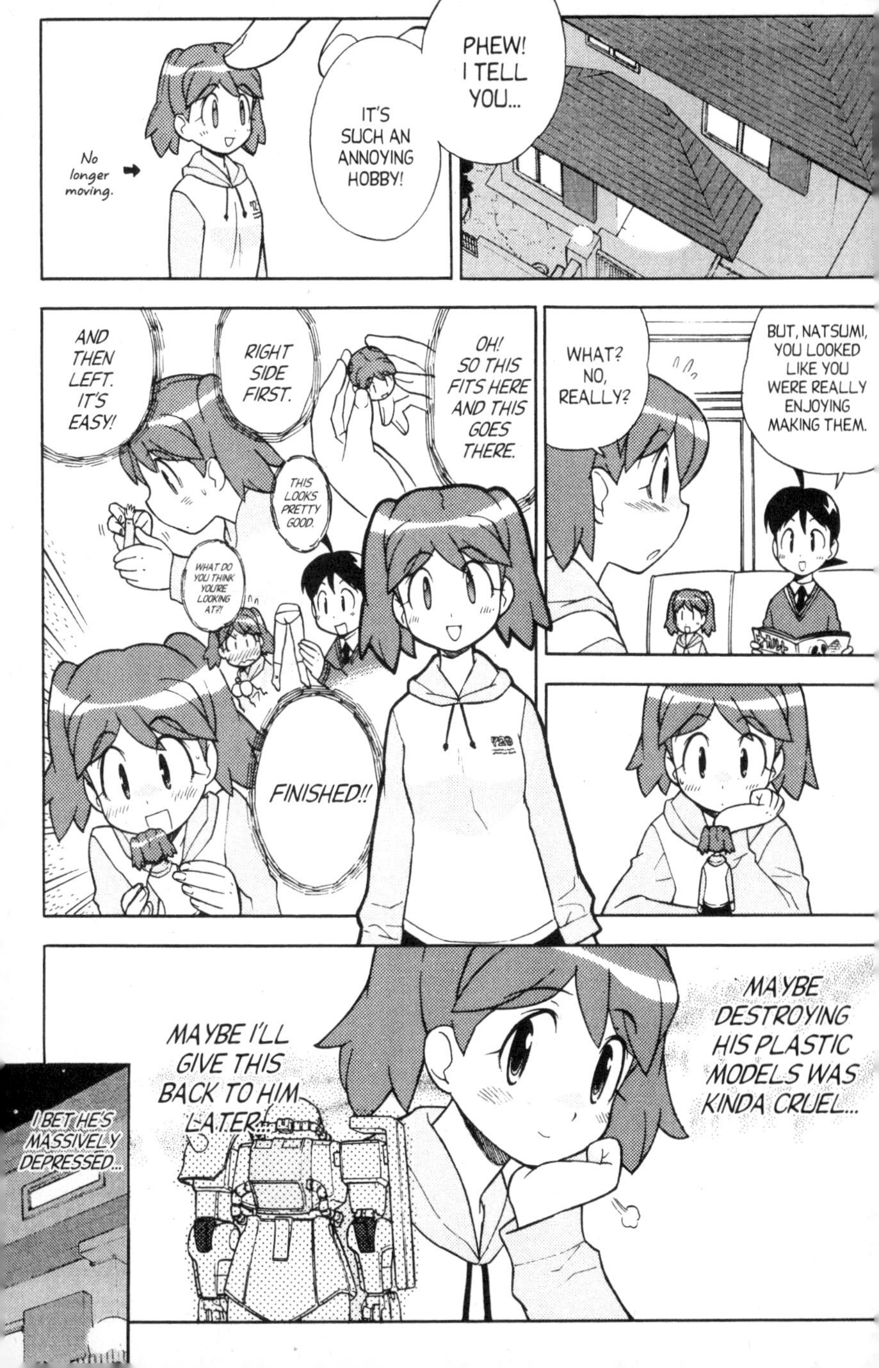
PHEW! I TELL YOU...
IT'S SUCH AN ANNOYING HOBBY!
No longer moving.
BUT, NATSUMI, YOU LOOKED LIKE YOU WERE REALLY ENJOYING MAKING THEM.
WHAT? NO, REALLY?
OH! SO THIS FITS HERE AND THIS GOES THERE.
RIGHT SIDE FIRST.
AND THEN LEFT. IT'S EASY!
THIS LOOKS PRETTY GOOD.
WHAT DO YOU THINK YOU'RE LOOKING AT?!
FINISHED!!
MAYBE DESTROYING HIS PLASTIC MODELS WAS KINDA CRUEL...
MAYBE I'LL GIVE THIS BACK TO HIM LATER...
I BET HE'S MASSIVELY DEPRESSED...

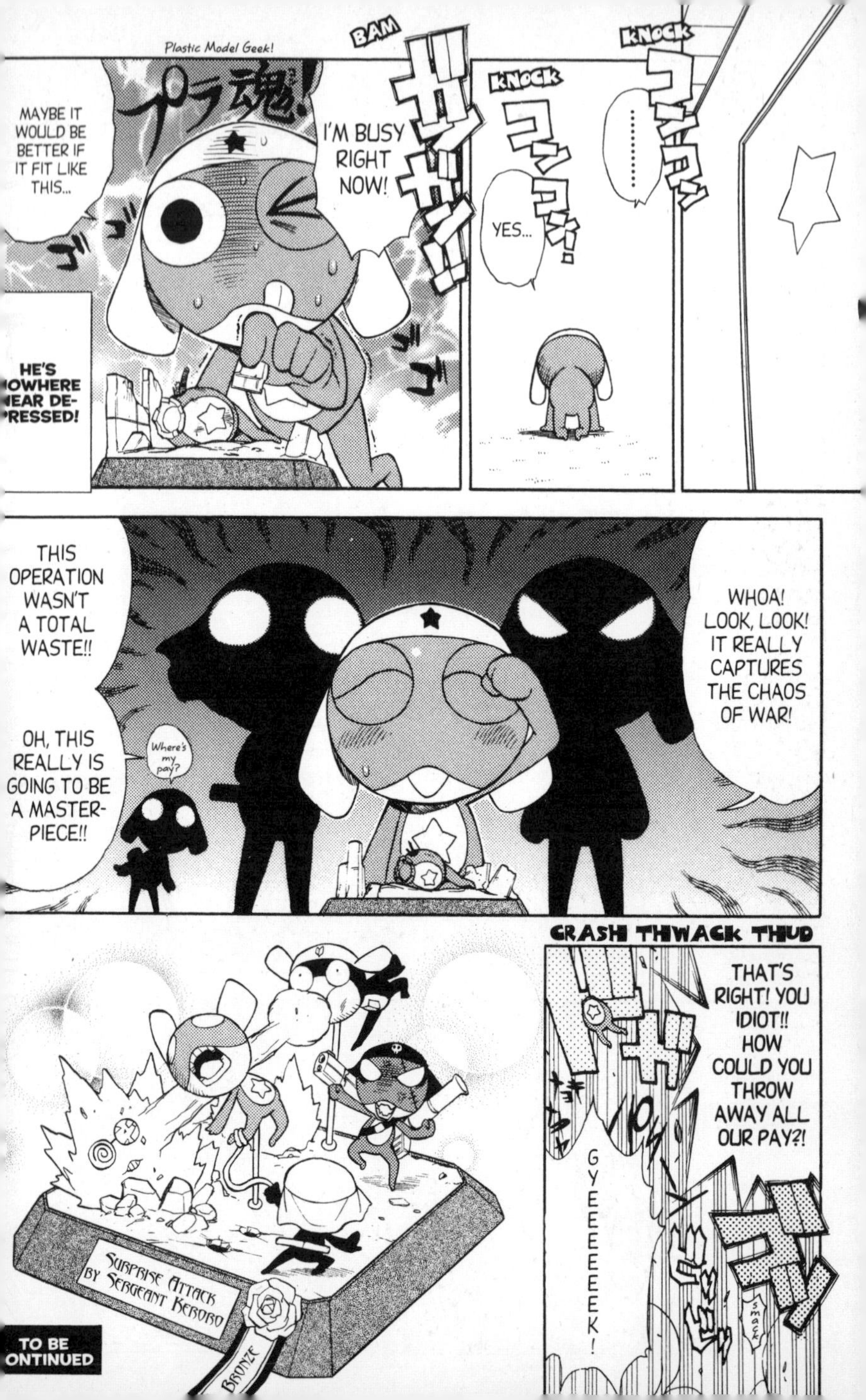
KNOCK
......
KNOCK
YES...
BAM
Plastic Model Geek!
プラ魂!
I'M BUSY RIGHT NOW!
MAYBE IT WOULD BE BETTER IF IT FIT LIKE THIS...
HE'S OWHERE EAR DE-RESSED!
WHOA! LOOK, LOOK! IT REALLY CAPTURES THE CHAOS OF WAR!
THIS OPERATION WASN'T A TOTAL WASTE!!
OH, THIS REALLY IS GOING TO BE A MASTER-PIECE!!
Where's my pay?
CRASH THWACK THUD
THAT'S RIGHT! YOU IDIOT!! HOW COULD YOU THROW AWAY ALL OUR PAY?!
GYEEEEEEEK!
smack
SURPRISE ATTACK BY SERGEANT KERORO
BRONZE
TO BE ONTINUED

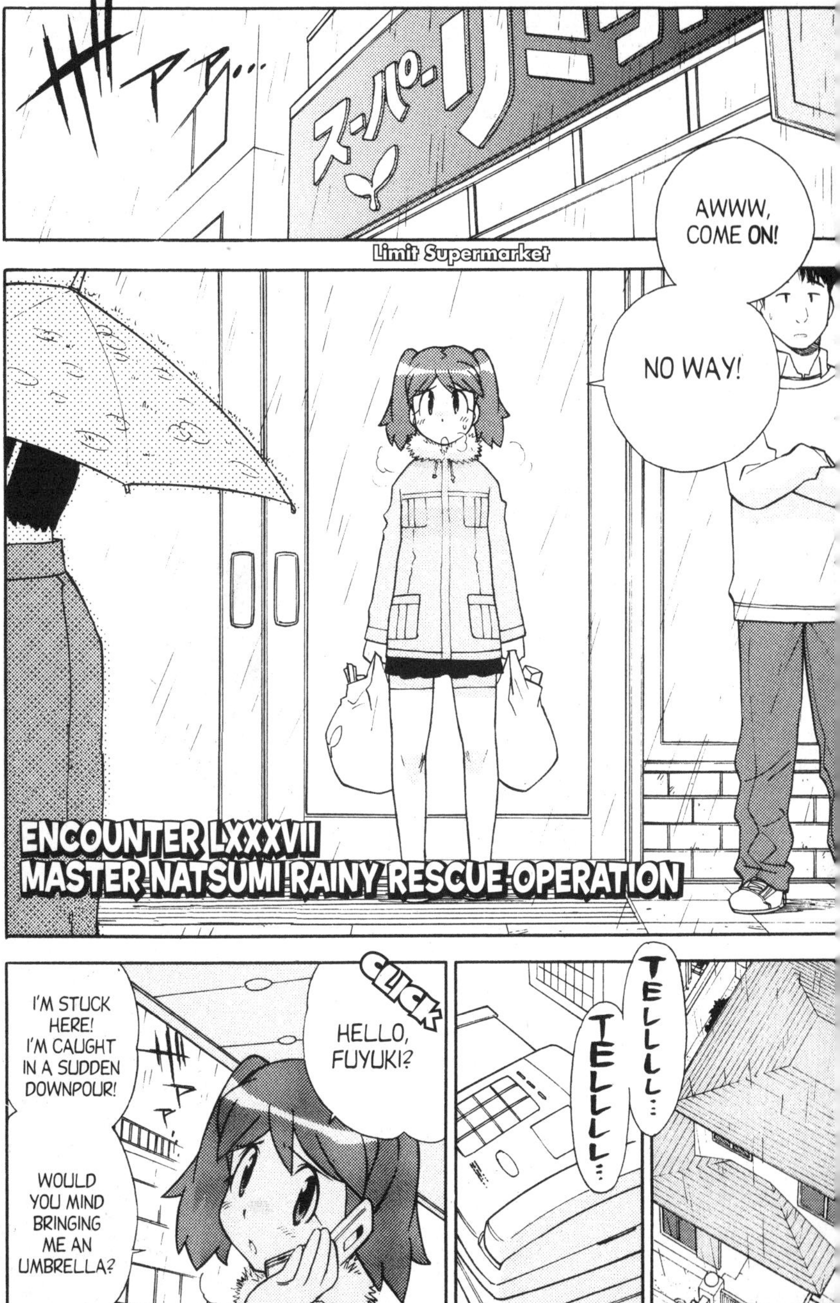
Limit Supermarket
AWWW, COME ON!
NO WAY!
ENCOUNTER LXXXVII
MASTER NATSUMI RAINY RESCUE OPERATION
TELLLL...
TELLLLL...
CLICK
HELLO, FUYUKI?
I'M STUCK HERE! I'M CAUGHT IN A SUDDEN DOWNPOUR!
WOULD YOU MIND BRINGING ME AN UMBRELLA?

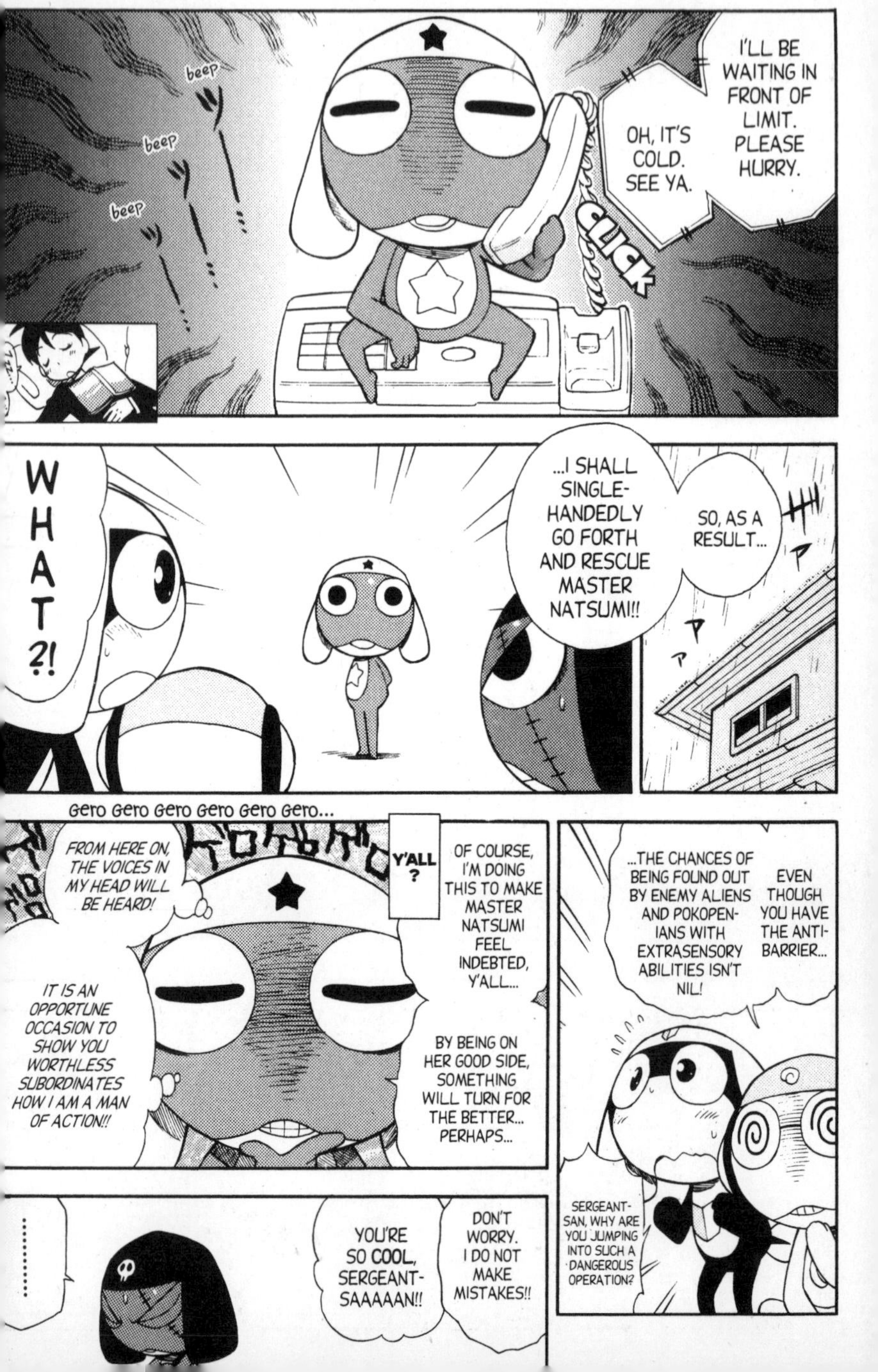
I'LL BE WAITING IN FRONT OF LIMIT. PLEASE HURRY.
OH, IT'S COLD. SEE YA.
CLICK
beep
beep
beep
SO, AS A RESULT...
...I SHALL SINGLE-HANDEDLY GO FORTH AND RESCUE MASTER NATSUMI!!
WHAT?!
Gero Gero Gero Gero Gero Gero...
EVEN THOUGH YOU HAVE THE ANTI-BARRIER...
...THE CHANCES OF BEING FOUND OUT BY ENEMY ALIENS AND POKOPEN-IANS WITH EXTRASENSORY ABILITIES ISN'T NIL!
SERGEANT-SAN, WHY ARE YOU JUMPING INTO SUCH A DANGEROUS OPERATION?
OF COURSE, I'M DOING THIS TO MAKE MASTER NATSUMI FEEL INDEBTED, Y'ALL...
Y'ALL ?
BY BEING ON HER GOOD SIDE, SOMETHING WILL TURN FOR THE BETTER... PERHAPS...
FROM HERE ON, THE VOICES IN MY HEAD WILL BE HEARD!
IT IS AN OPPORTUNE OCCASION TO SHOW YOU WORTHLESS SUBORDINATES HOW I AM A MAN OF ACTION!!
DON'T WORRY. I DO NOT MAKE MISTAKES!!
YOU'RE SO COOL, SERGEANT-SAAAAAN!!
....

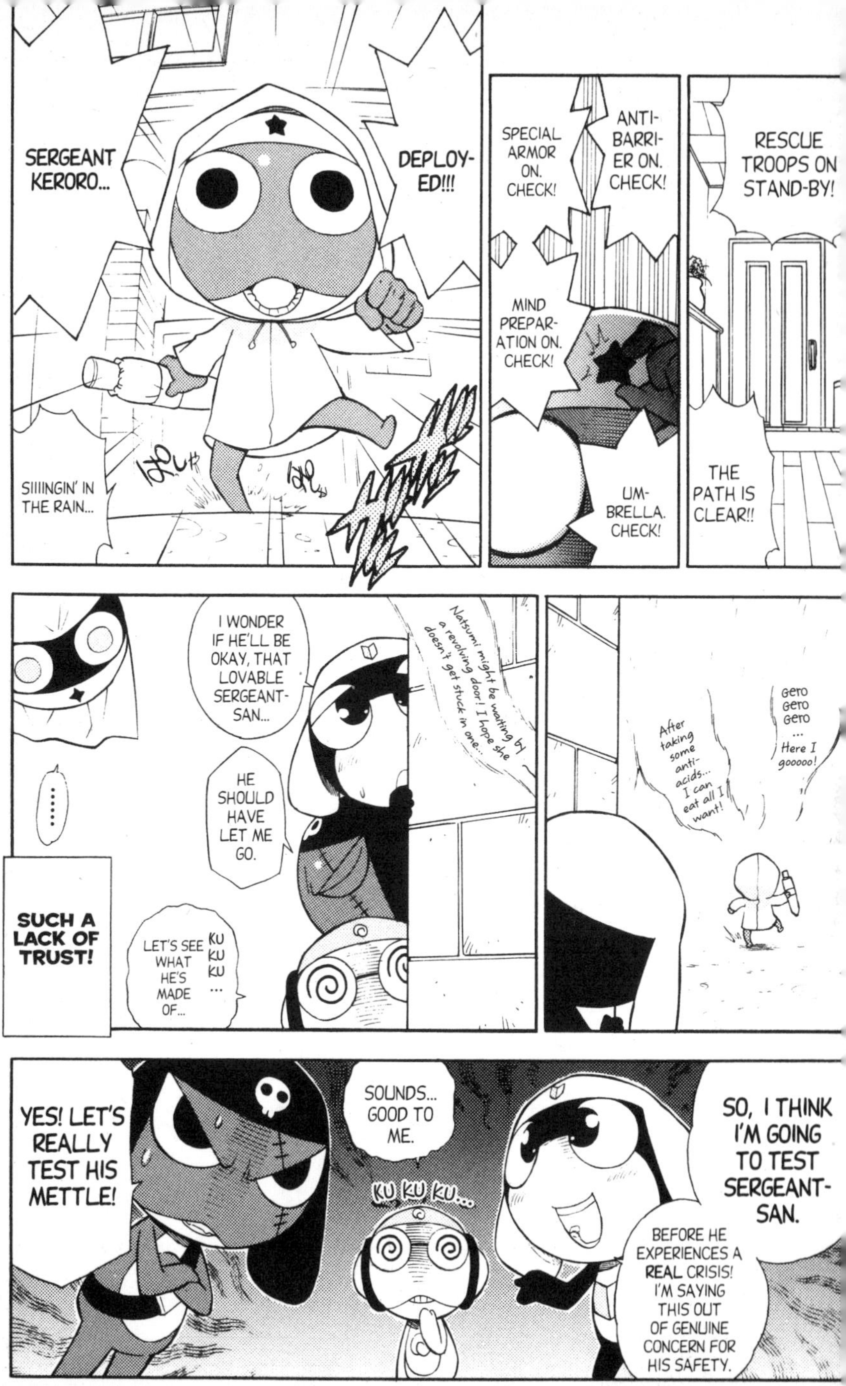

RESCUE TROOPS ON STAND-BY!
THE PATH IS CLEAR!!
ANTI-BARRIER ON. CHECK!
SPECIAL ARMOR ON. CHECK!
MIND PREPARATION ON. CHECK!
UMBRELLA. CHECK!
DEPLOYED!!!
SERGEANT KERORO...
SIIIINGIN' IN THE RAIN...
Gero Gero Gero ... Here I gooooo!
After taking some anti-acids... I can eat all I want!
Natsumi might be waiting by a revolving door! I hope she doesn't get stuck in one...
I WONDER IF HE'LL BE OKAY, THAT LOVABLE SERGEANT-SAN...
HE SHOULD HAVE LET ME GO.
KU KU KU ...
LET'S SEE WHAT HE'S MADE OF...
......
SUCH A LACK OF TRUST!
SO, I THINK I'M GOING TO TEST SERGEANT-SAN.
BEFORE HE EXPERIENCES A REAL CRISIS! I'M SAYING THIS OUT OF GENUINE CONCERN FOR HIS SAFETY.
SOUNDS... GOOD TO ME.
KU KU KU...
YES! LET'S REALLY TEST HIS METTLE!

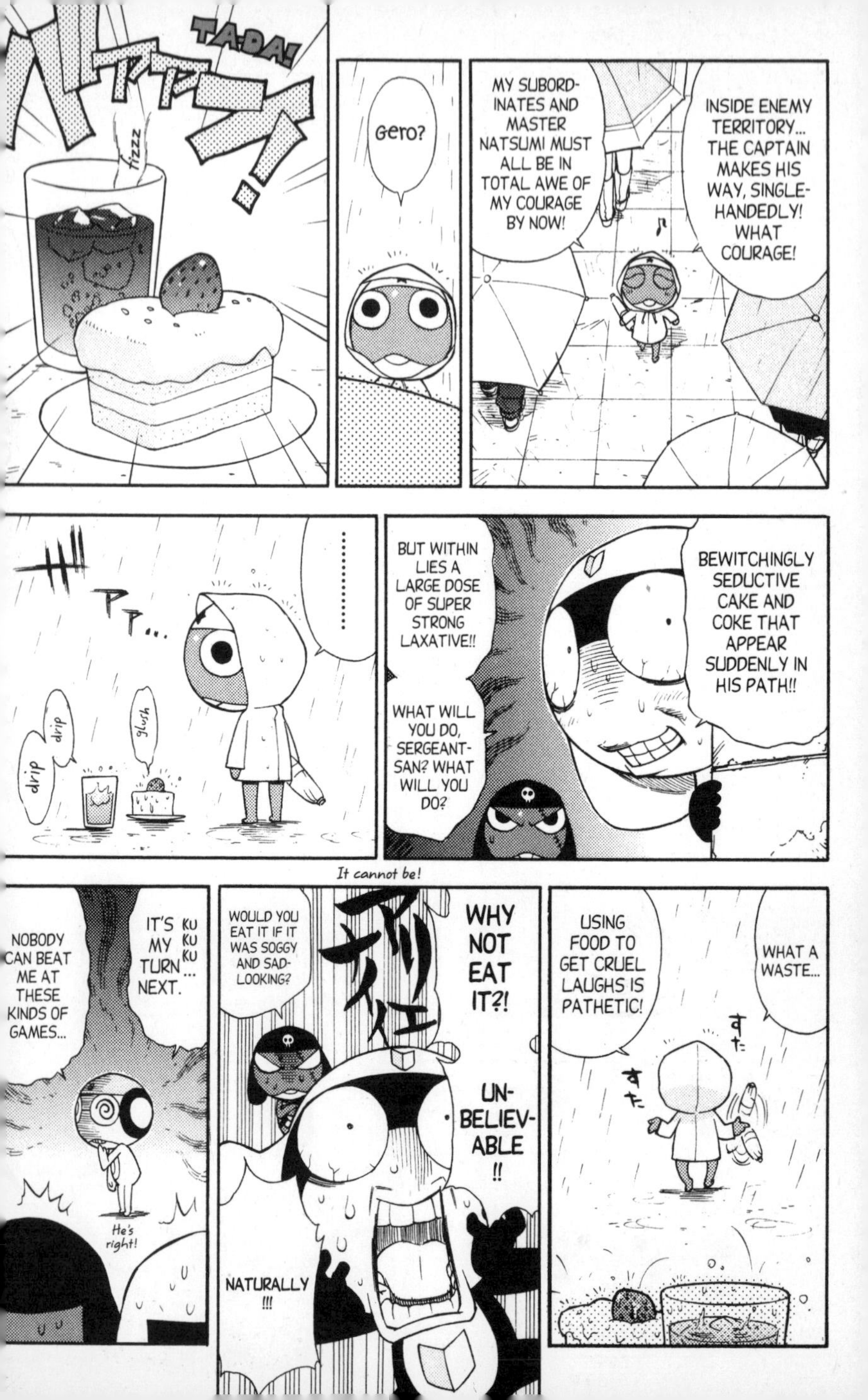
INSIDE ENEMY TERRITORY... THE CAPTAIN MAKES HIS WAY, SINGLE-HANDEDLY! WHAT COURAGE!
MY SUBORDINATES AND MASTER NATSUMI MUST ALL BE IN TOTAL AWE OF MY COURAGE BY NOW!
Gero?
TA-DA!
fizzz
BEWITCHINGLY SEDUCTIVE CAKE AND COKE THAT APPEAR SUDDENLY IN HIS PATH!!
BUT WITHIN LIES A LARGE DOSE OF SUPER STRONG LAXATIVE!!
WHAT WILL YOU DO, SERGEANT-SAN? WHAT WILL YOU DO?
....
drip
drip
glush
It cannot be!
WHAT A WASTE...
USING FOOD TO GET CRUEL LAUGHS IS PATHETIC!
WHY NOT EAT IT?!
WOULD YOU EAT IT IF IT WAS SOGGY AND SAD-LOOKING?
UN-BELIEV-ABLE !!
NATURALLY !!!
KU KU KU...
IT'S MY TURN NEXT.
NOBODY CAN BEAT ME AT THESE KINDS OF GAMES...
He's right!

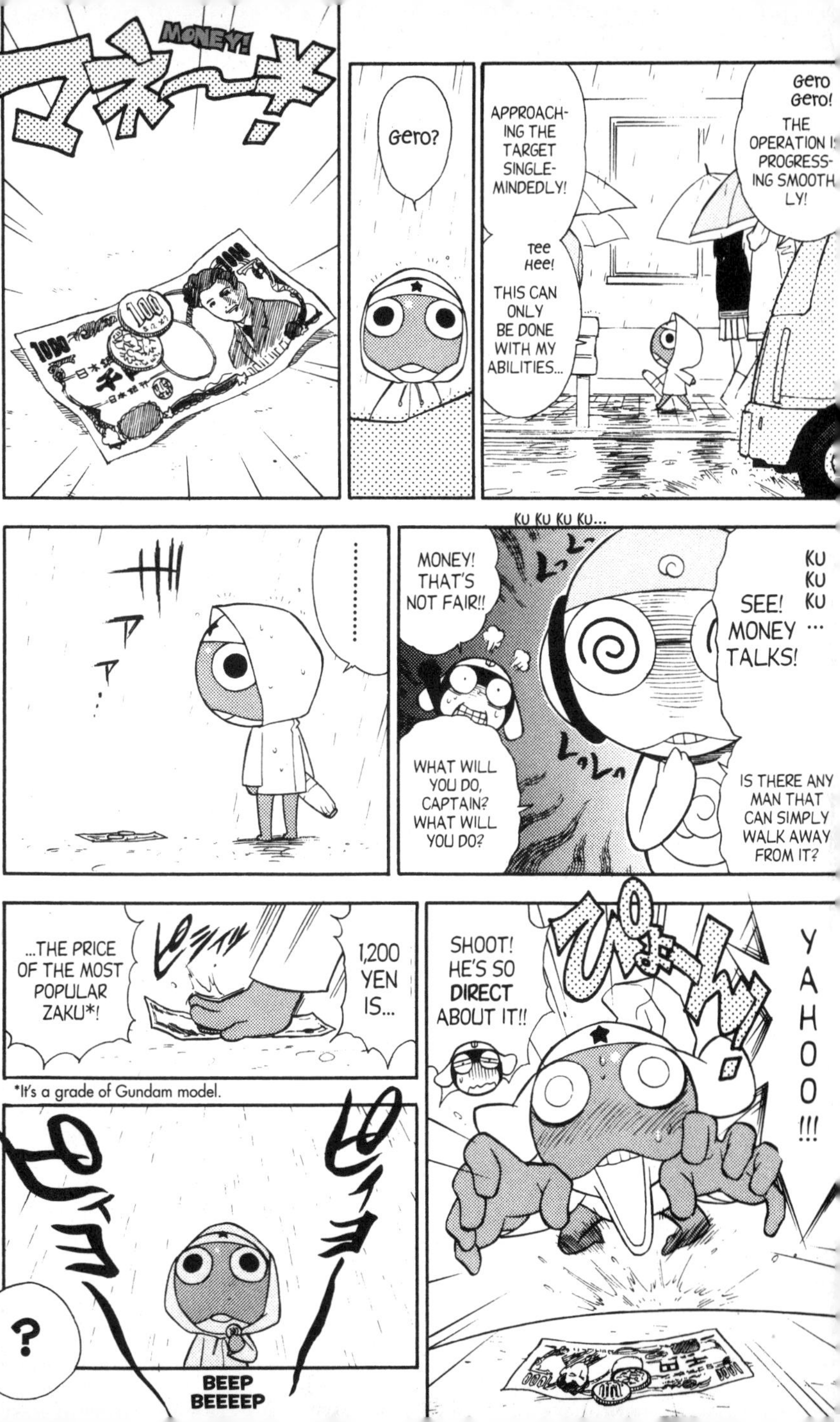
Gero Gero! THE OPERATION IS PROGRESSING SMOOTHLY!
APPROACHING THE TARGET SINGLE-MINDEDLY!
TEE HEE!
THIS CAN ONLY BE DONE WITH MY ABILITIES...
Gero?
MONEY!
KU KU KU KU...
SEE! MONEY TALKS!
KU KU KU ...
MONEY! THAT'S NOT FAIR!!
IS THERE ANY MAN THAT CAN SIMPLY WALK AWAY FROM IT?
WHAT WILL YOU DO, CAPTAIN? WHAT WILL YOU DO?
....
YAHOO!!!
SHOOT! HE'S SO DIRECT ABOUT IT!!
1,200 YEN IS...
...THE PRICE OF THE MOST POPULAR ZAKU*!
?
BEEP BEEEEP

*It's a grade of Gundam model.

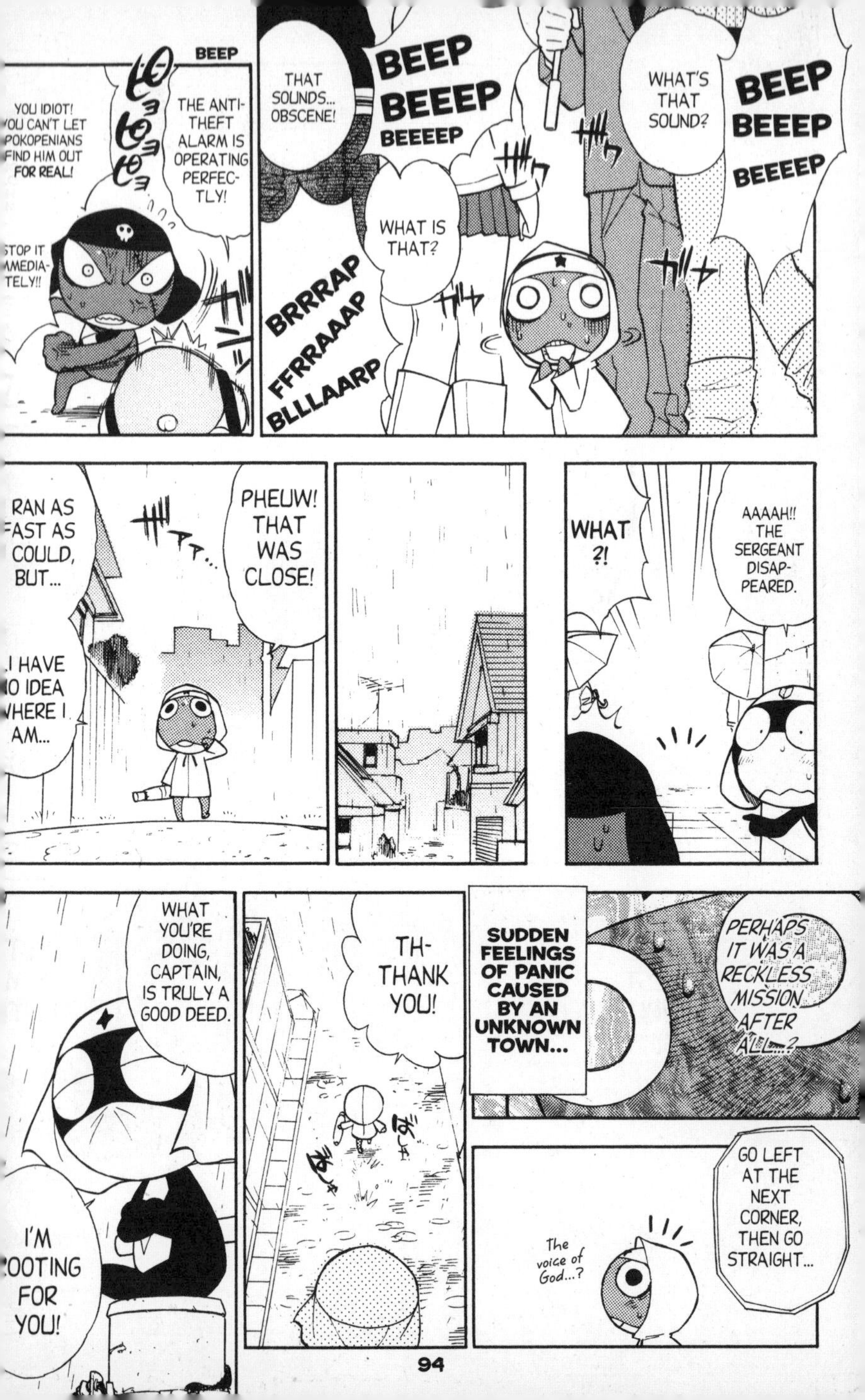
WHAT'S THAT SOUND?
BEEP BEEEP BEEEEP
THAT SOUNDS... OBSCENE!
BEEP BEEEP BEEEEP
WHAT IS THAT?
BRRRAP FFRRAAAP BLLLAARP
BEEP
THE ANTI-THEFT ALARM IS OPERATING PERFECTLY!
YOU IDIOT! OU CAN'T LET POKOPENIANS FIND HIM OUT FOR REAL!
TOP IT MEDIA-TELY!!
AAAAH!! THE SERGEANT DISAP-PEARED.
WHAT?!
PHEUW! THAT WAS CLOSE!
RAN AS FAST AS COULD, BUT...
.I HAVE O IDEA HERE I AM...
PERHAPS IT WAS A RECKLESS MISSION AFTER ALL...?
SUDDEN FEELINGS OF PANIC CAUSED BY AN UNKNOWN TOWN...
GO LEFT AT THE NEXT CORNER, THEN GO STRAIGHT...
The voice of God...?
TH-THANK YOU!
WHAT YOU'RE DOING, CAPTAIN, IS TRULY A GOOD DEED.
I'M OOTING FOR YOU!

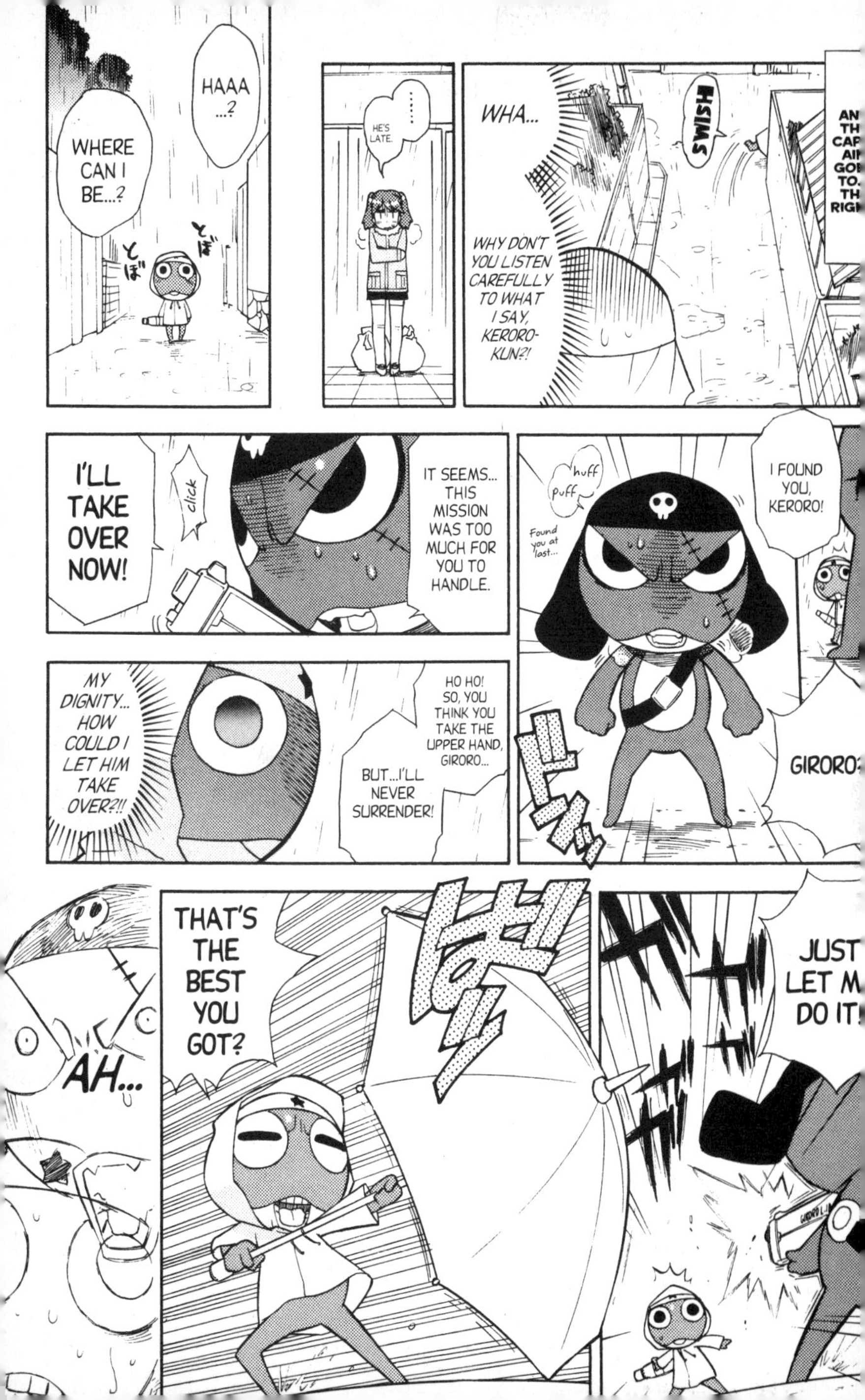
SWISH
WHA...
WHY DON'T YOU LISTEN CAREFULLY TO WHAT I SAY, KERORO-KUN?!
......
HE'S LATE.
HAAA ...?
WHERE CAN I BE...?
とぼ
とぼ
I FOUND YOU, KERORO!
huff
puff
Found you at last...
GIRORO?
IT SEEMS... THIS MISSION WAS TOO MUCH FOR YOU TO HANDLE.
click
I'LL TAKE OVER NOW!
HO HO! SO, YOU THINK YOU TAKE THE UPPER HAND, GIRORO...
BUT...I'LL NEVER SURRENDER!
MY DIGNITY... HOW COULD I LET HIM TAKE OVER?!!
THAT'S THE BEST YOU GOT?
AH...

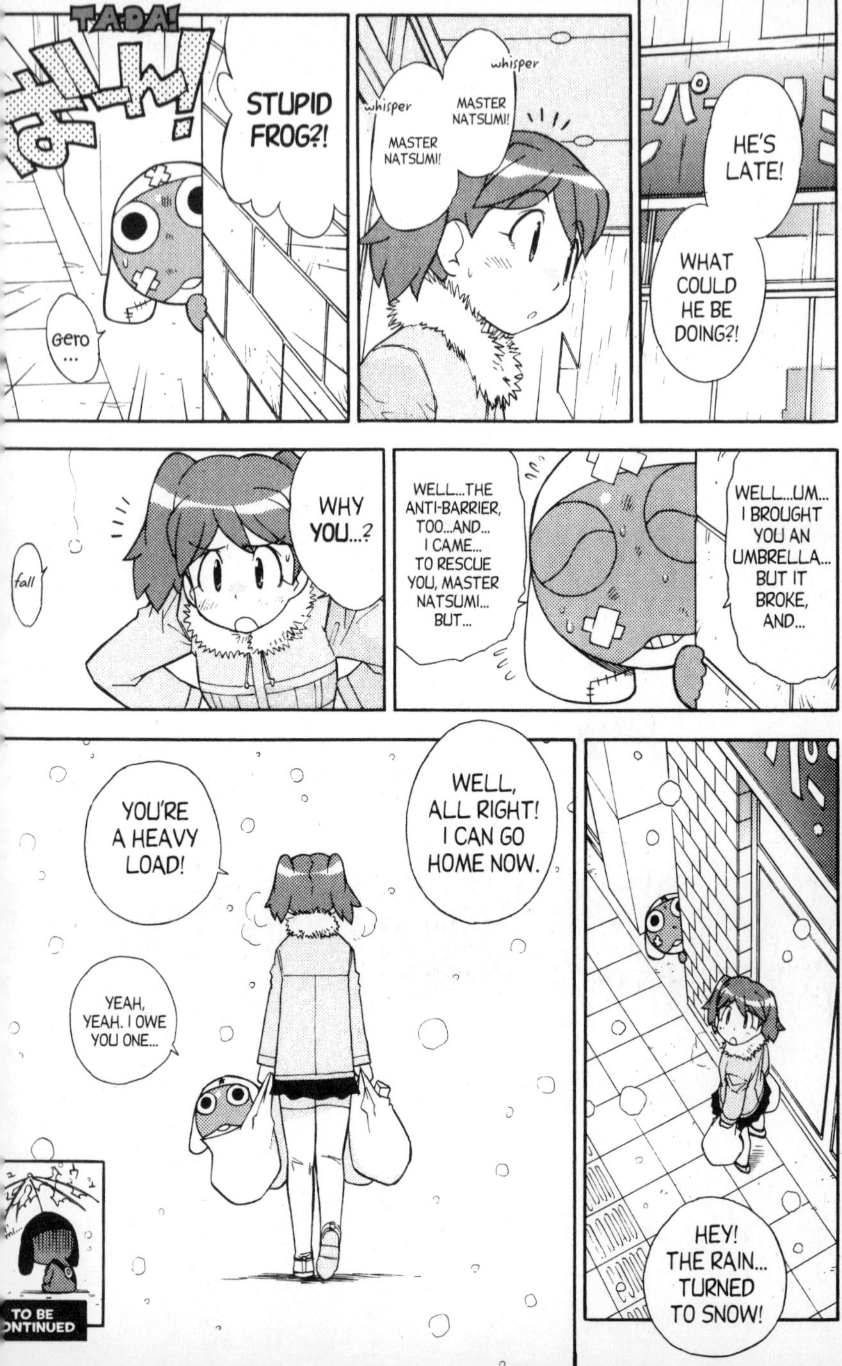
HE'S LATE!
WHAT COULD HE BE DOING?!
whisper
MASTER NATSUMI!
whisper
MASTER NATSUMI!
STUPID FROG?!
TADA!
Gero...
WELL...UM... I BROUGHT YOU AN UMBRELLA... BUT IT BROKE, AND...
WELL...THE ANTI-BARRIER, TOO...AND... I CAME... TO RESCUE YOU, MASTER NATSUMI... BUT...
WHY YOU...?
fall
HEY! THE RAIN... TURNED TO SNOW!
WELL, ALL RIGHT! I CAN GO HOME NOW.
YOU'RE A HEAVY LOAD!
YEAH, YEAH. I OWE YOU ONE...
TO BE ONTINUED

ENCOUNTER LXXXVIII
A NEW BEGINNING? A DETERMINED SERGEANT LEAVES HOME

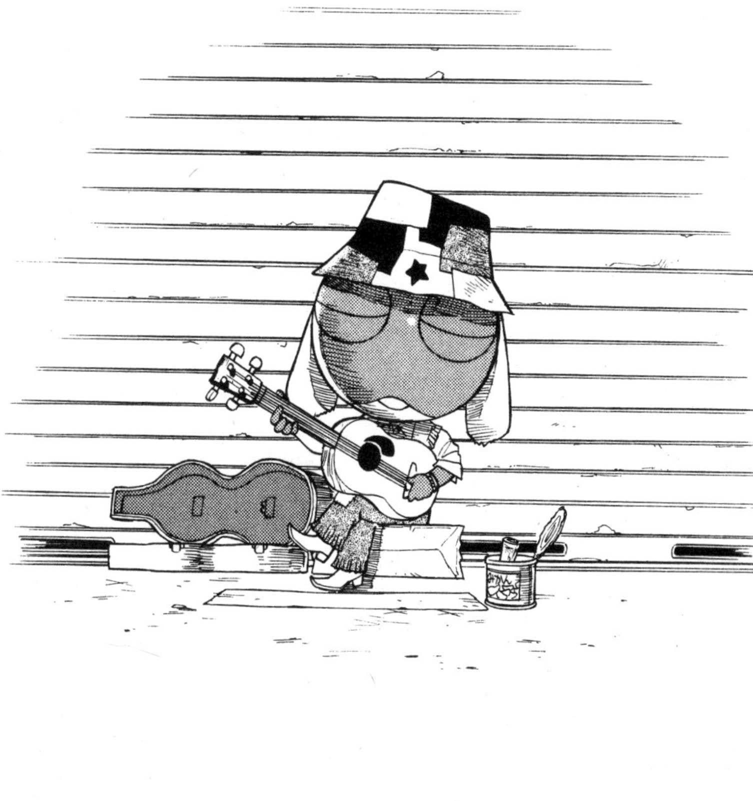

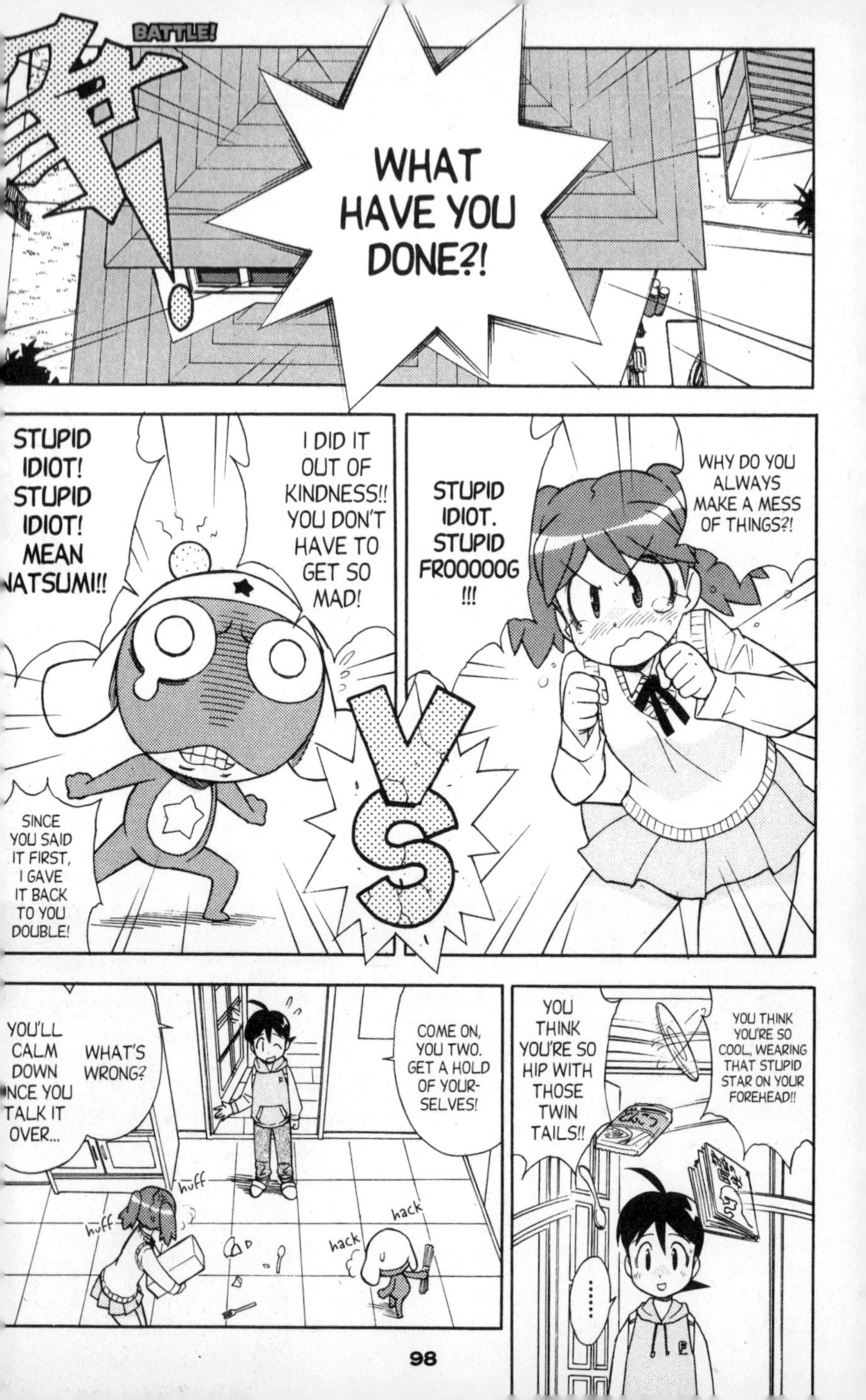
BATTLE!
WHAT HAVE YOU DONE?!
WHY DO YOU ALWAYS MAKE A MESS OF THINGS?!
STUPID IDIOT. STUPID FROOOOOG !!!
I DID IT OUT OF KINDNESS!! YOU DON'T HAVE TO GET SO MAD!
STUPID IDIOT! STUPID IDIOT! MEAN NATSUMI!!
VS
SINCE YOU SAID IT FIRST, I GAVE IT BACK TO YOU DOUBLE!
YOU THINK YOU'RE SO COOL, WEARING THAT STUPID STAR ON YOUR FOREHEAD!!
YOU THINK YOU'RE SO HIP WITH THOSE TWIN TAILS!!
......
COME ON, YOU TWO. GET A HOLD OF YOUR-SELVES!
WHAT'S WRONG?
YOU'LL CALM DOWN ONCE YOU TALK IT OVER...
huff
huff
hack
hack

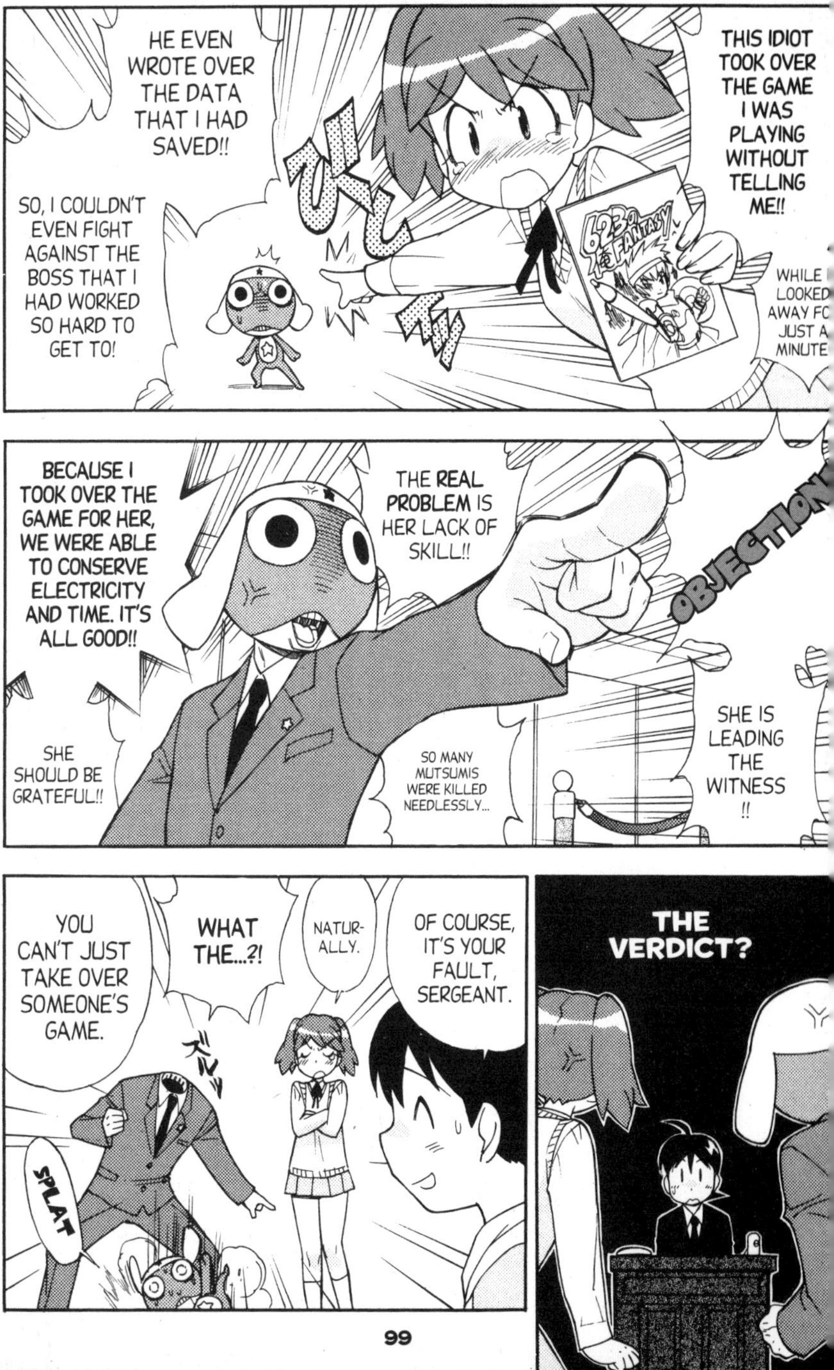
THIS IDIOT TOOK OVER THE GAME I WAS PLAYING WITHOUT TELLING ME!!
WHILE I LOOKED AWAY FO JUST A MINUTE
623の俺FANTASY
HE EVEN WROTE OVER THE DATA THAT I HAD SAVED!!
SO, I COULDN'T EVEN FIGHT AGAINST THE BOSS THAT I HAD WORKED SO HARD TO GET TO!
OBJECTION
SHE IS LEADING THE WITNESS !!
THE REAL PROBLEM IS HER LACK OF SKILL!!
BECAUSE I TOOK OVER THE GAME FOR HER, WE WERE ABLE TO CONSERVE ELECTRICITY AND TIME. IT'S ALL GOOD!!
SO MANY MUTSUMIS WERE KILLED NEEDLESSLY...
SHE SHOULD BE GRATEFUL!!
THE VERDICT?
OF COURSE, IT'S YOUR FAULT, SERGEANT.
NATUR-ALLY.
WHAT THE...?!
YOU CAN'T JUST TAKE OVER SOMEONE'S GAME.
ズルッ
SPLAT

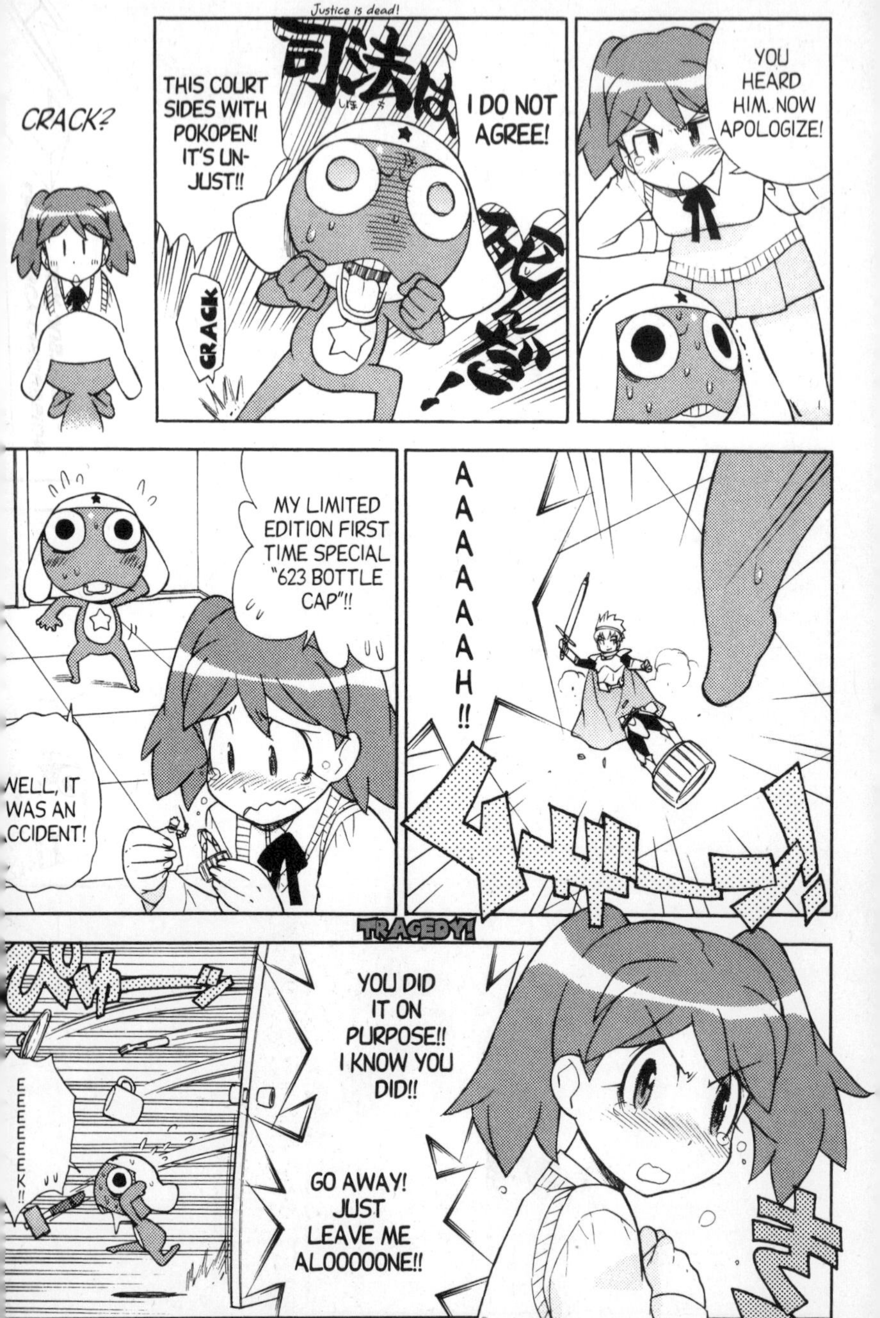
YOU HEARD HIM. NOW APOLOGIZE!
Justice is dead!
I DO NOT AGREE!
THIS COURT SIDES WITH POKOPEN! IT'S UN-JUST!!
CRACK
CRACK?
AAAAAAAAH!!
MY LIMITED EDITION FIRST TIME SPECIAL "623 BOTTLE CAP"!!
WELL, IT WAS AN CCIDENT!
TRAGEDY!
YOU DID IT ON PURPOSE!! I KNOW YOU DID!!
GO AWAY! JUST LEAVE ME ALOOOOONE!!
EEEEEEEK!!

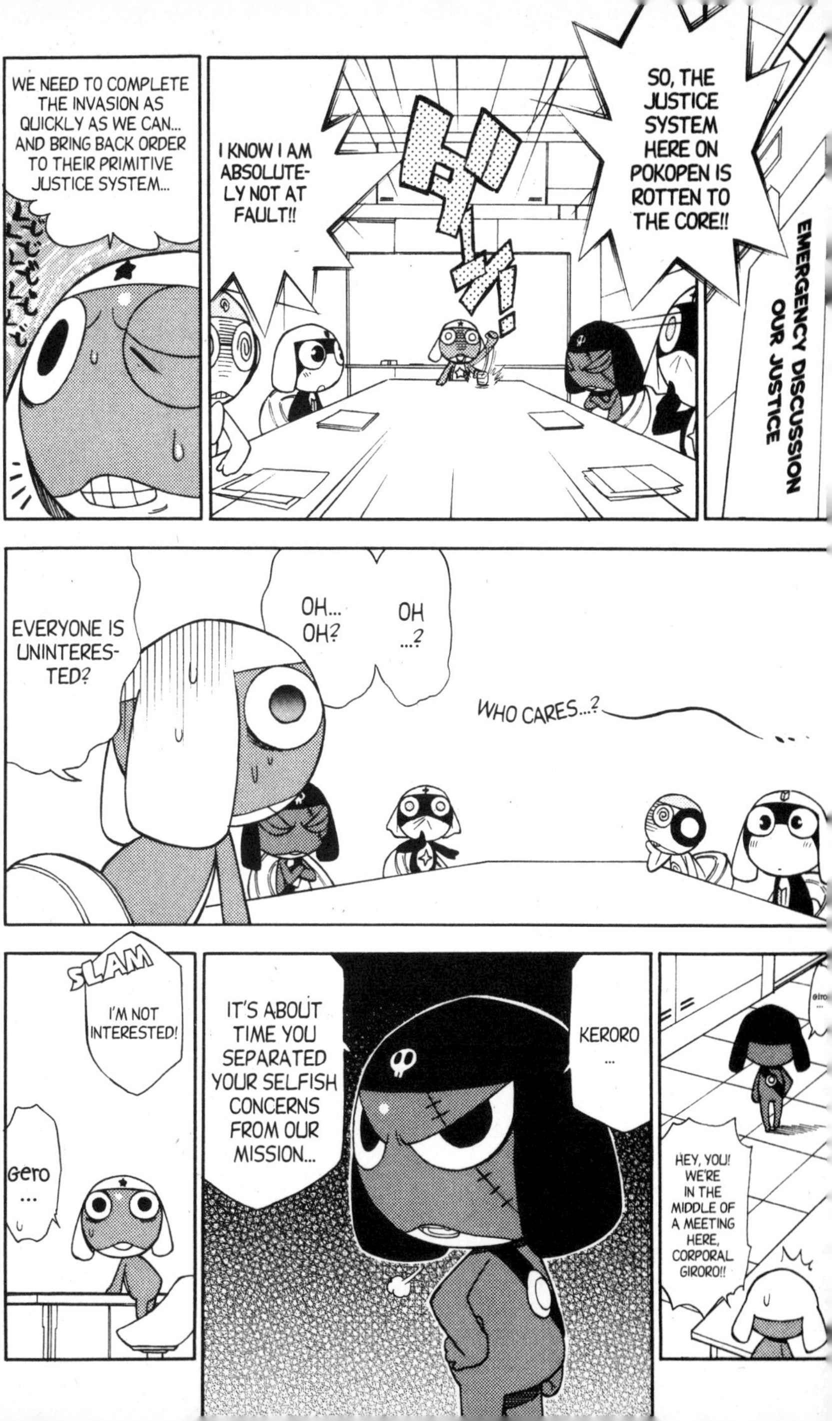

EMERGENCY DISCUSSION OUR JUSTICE
SO, THE JUSTICE SYSTEM HERE ON POKOPEN IS ROTTEN TO THE CORE!!
I KNOW I AM ABSOLUTE-LY NOT AT FAULT!!
WE NEED TO COMPLETE THE INVASION AS QUICKLY AS WE CAN... AND BRING BACK ORDER TO THEIR PRIMITIVE JUSTICE SYSTEM...
WHO CARES...?
OH ...?
OH... OH?
EVERYONE IS UNINTERES-TED?
Giro ...
HEY, YOU! WE'RE IN THE MIDDLE OF A MEETING HERE, CORPORAL GIRORO!!
KERORO ...
IT'S ABOUT TIME YOU SEPARATED YOUR SELFISH CONCERNS FROM OUR MISSION...
SLAM
I'M NOT INTERESTED!
Gero ...

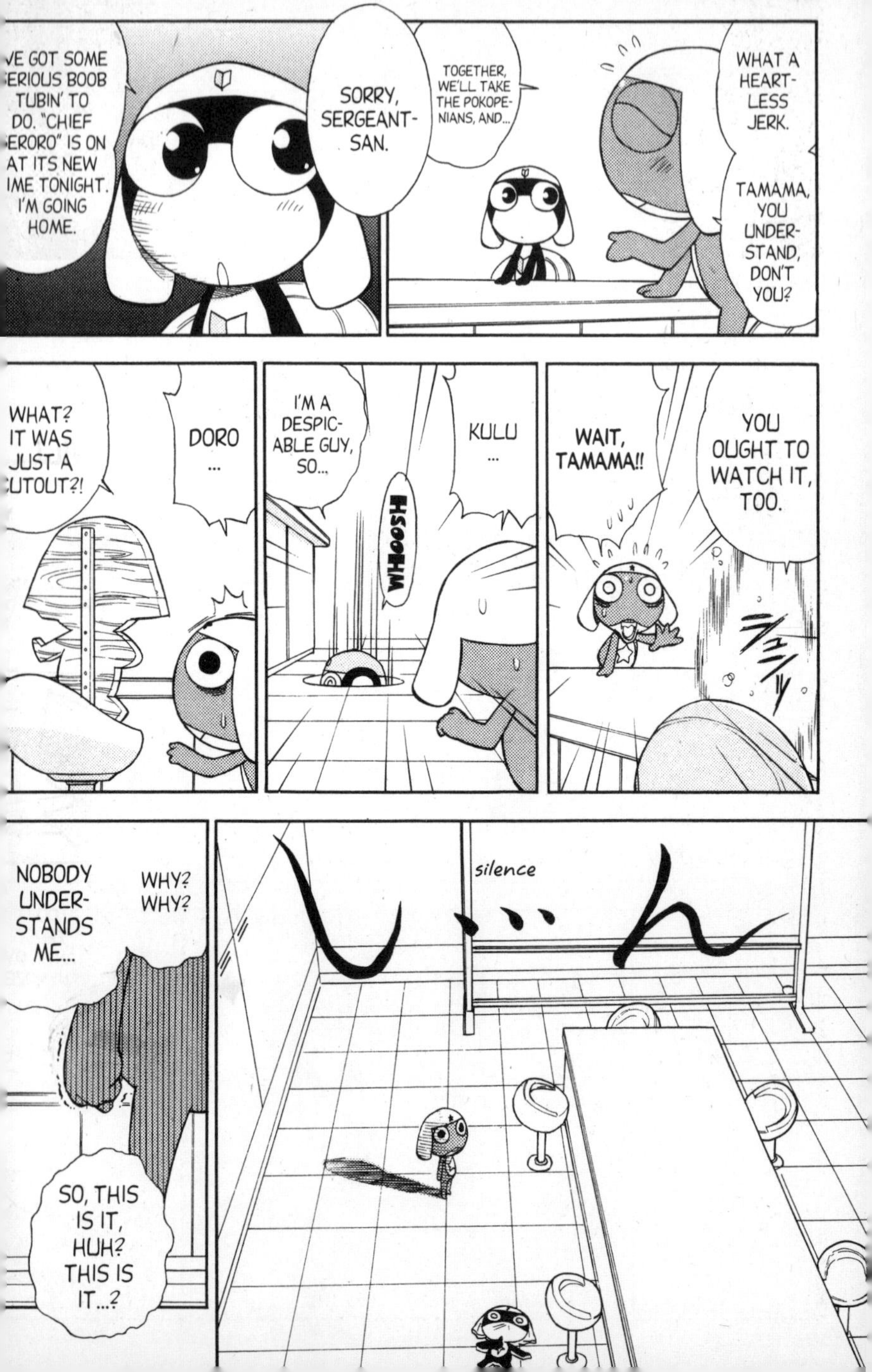
WHAT A HEART-LESS JERK.
TAMAMA, YOU UNDER-STAND, DON'T YOU?
TOGETHER, WE'LL TAKE THE POKOPE-NIANS, AND...
SORRY, SERGEANT-SAN.
VE GOT SOME ERIOUS BOOB TUBIN' TO DO. "CHIEF ERORO" IS ON AT ITS NEW IME TONIGHT. I'M GOING HOME.
YOU OUGHT TO WATCH IT, TOO.
WAIT, TAMAMA!!
KULU ...
I'M A DESPIC-ABLE GUY, SO...
WHOOSH
DORO ...
WHAT? IT WAS JUST A UTOUT?!
silence
しいん
WHY? WHY?
NOBODY UNDER-STANDS ME...
SO, THIS IS IT, HUH? THIS IS IT...?

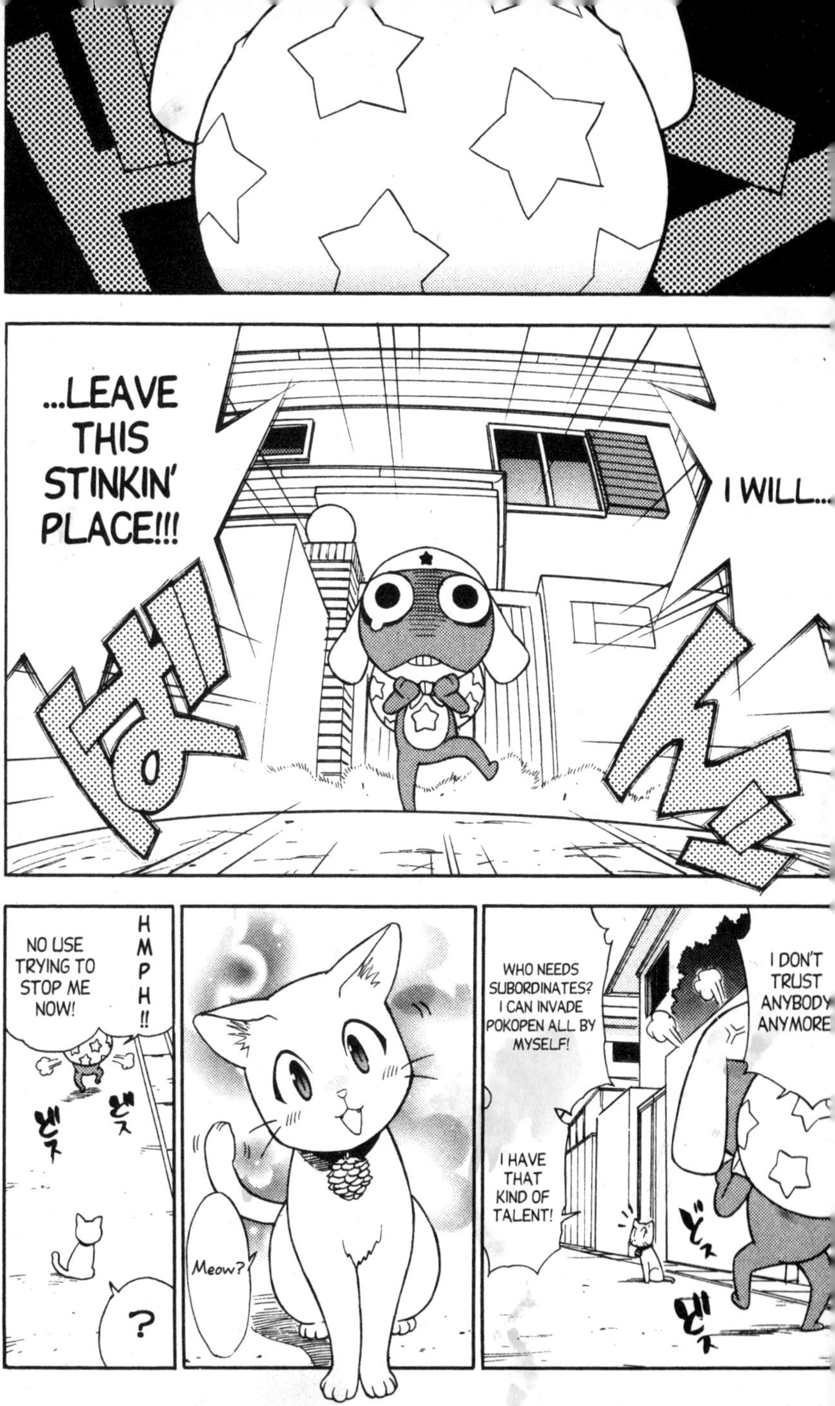
I WILL...
...LEAVE THIS STINKIN' PLACE!!!
I DON'T TRUST ANYBODY ANYMORE
WHO NEEDS SUBORDINATES? I CAN INVADE POKOPEN ALL BY MYSELF!
I HAVE THAT KIND OF TALENT!
どス
どス
Meow?
HMPH!!
NO USE TRYING TO STOP ME NOW!
どス
どス
?

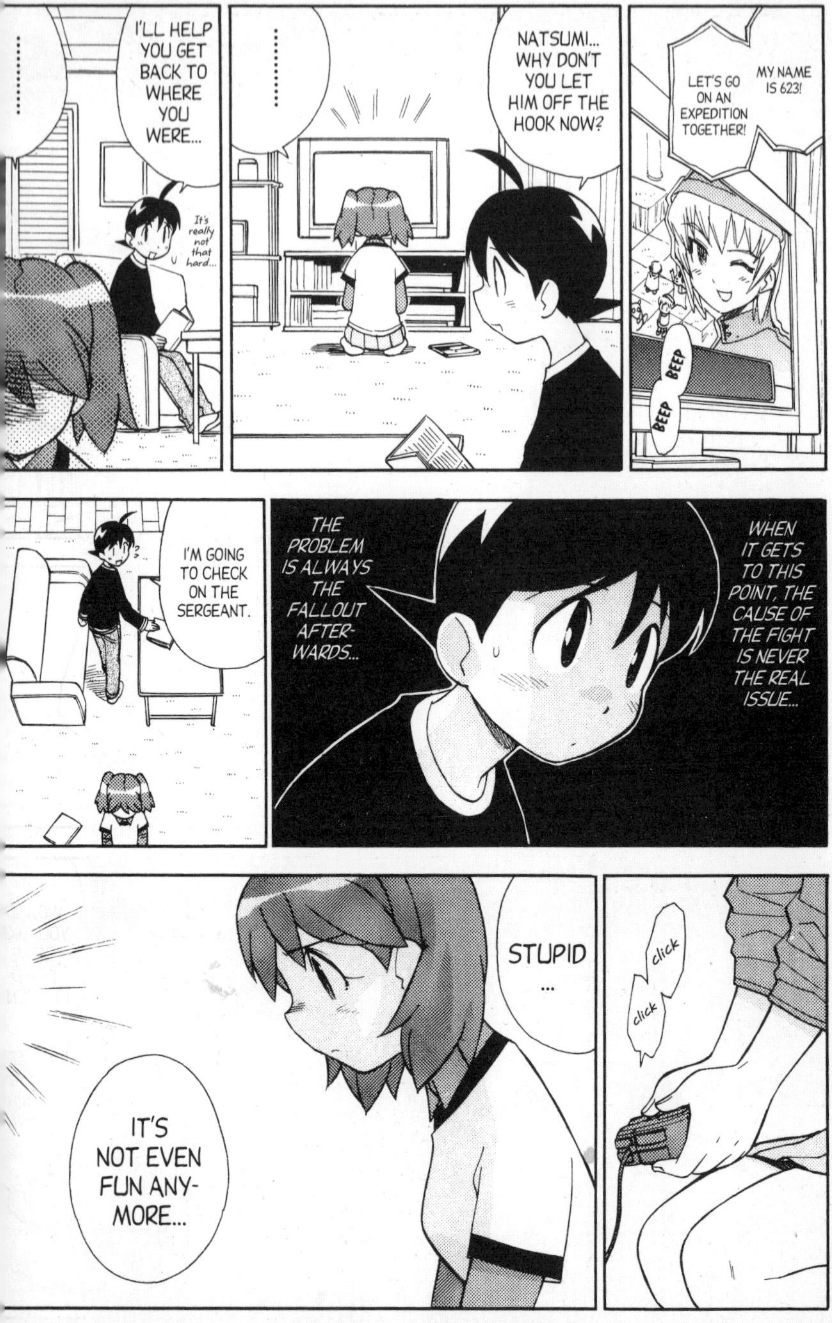
MY NAME IS 623!
LET'S GO ON AN EXPEDITION TOGETHER!
BEEP
BEEP
NATSUMI... WHY DON'T YOU LET HIM OFF THE HOOK NOW?
....
I'LL HELP YOU GET BACK TO WHERE YOU WERE...
It's really not that hard...
....
WHEN IT GETS TO THIS POINT, THE CAUSE OF THE FIGHT IS NEVER THE REAL ISSUE...
THE PROBLEM IS ALWAYS THE FALLOUT AFTER-WARDS...
I'M GOING TO CHECK ON THE SERGEANT.
click
click
STUPID ...
IT'S NOT EVEN FUN ANY-MORE...

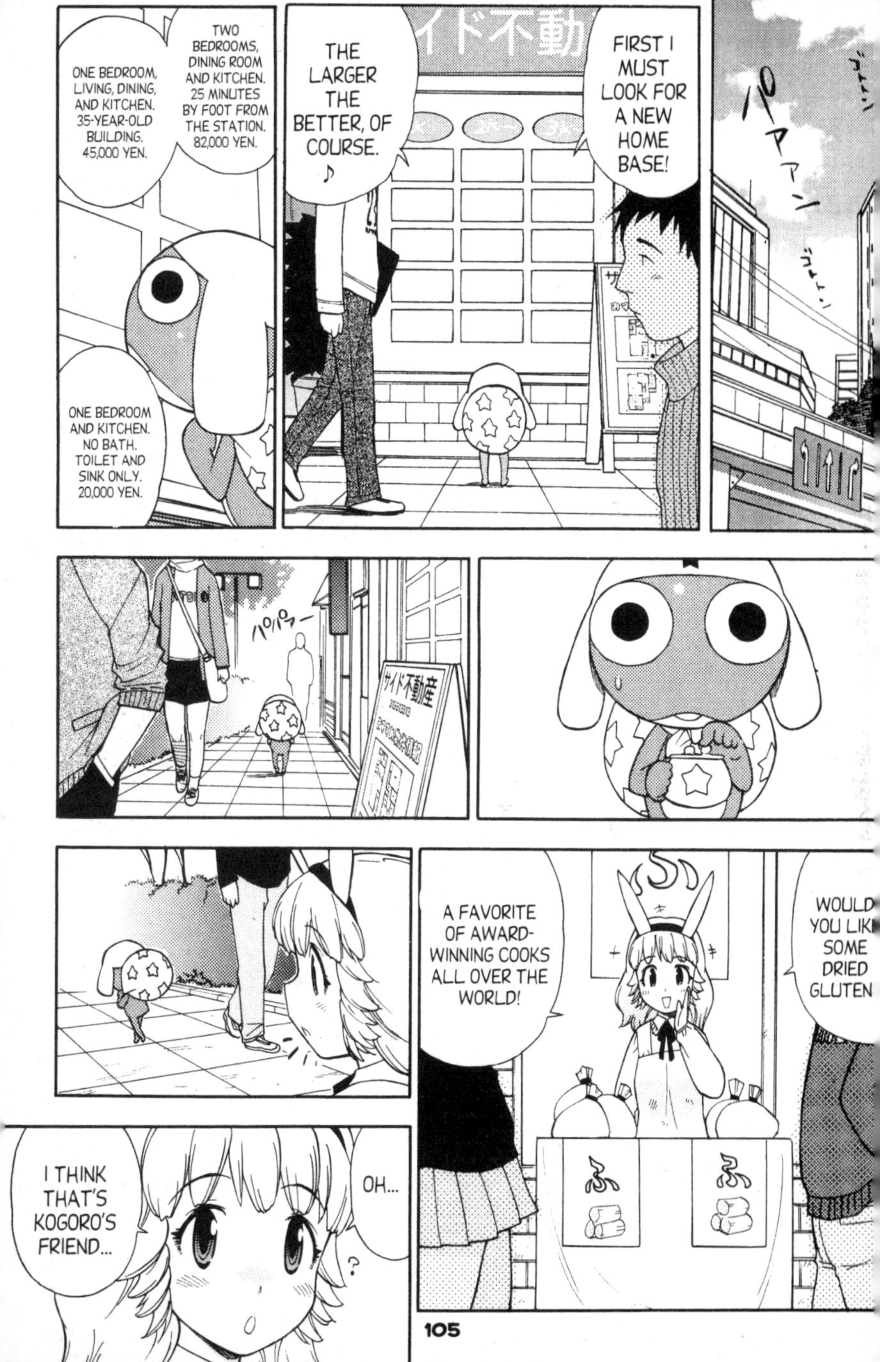
パアァーン
FIRST I MUST LOOK FOR A NEW HOME BASE!
THE LARGER THE BETTER, OF COURSE. ♪
TWO BEDROOMS, DINING ROOM AND KITCHEN. 25 MINUTES BY FOOT FROM THE STATION. 82,000 YEN.
ONE BEDROOM, LIVING, DINING, AND KITCHEN. 35-YEAR-OLD BUILDING. 45,000 YEN.
ONE BEDROOM AND KITCHEN. NO BATH. TOILET AND SINK ONLY. 20,000 YEN.
サイド不動産
パパァー
WOULD YOU LIK SOME DRIED GLUTEN
A FAVORITE OF AWARD-WINNING COOKS ALL OVER THE WORLD!
ふ
ふ
OH...
I THINK THAT'S KOGORO'S FRIEND...
?

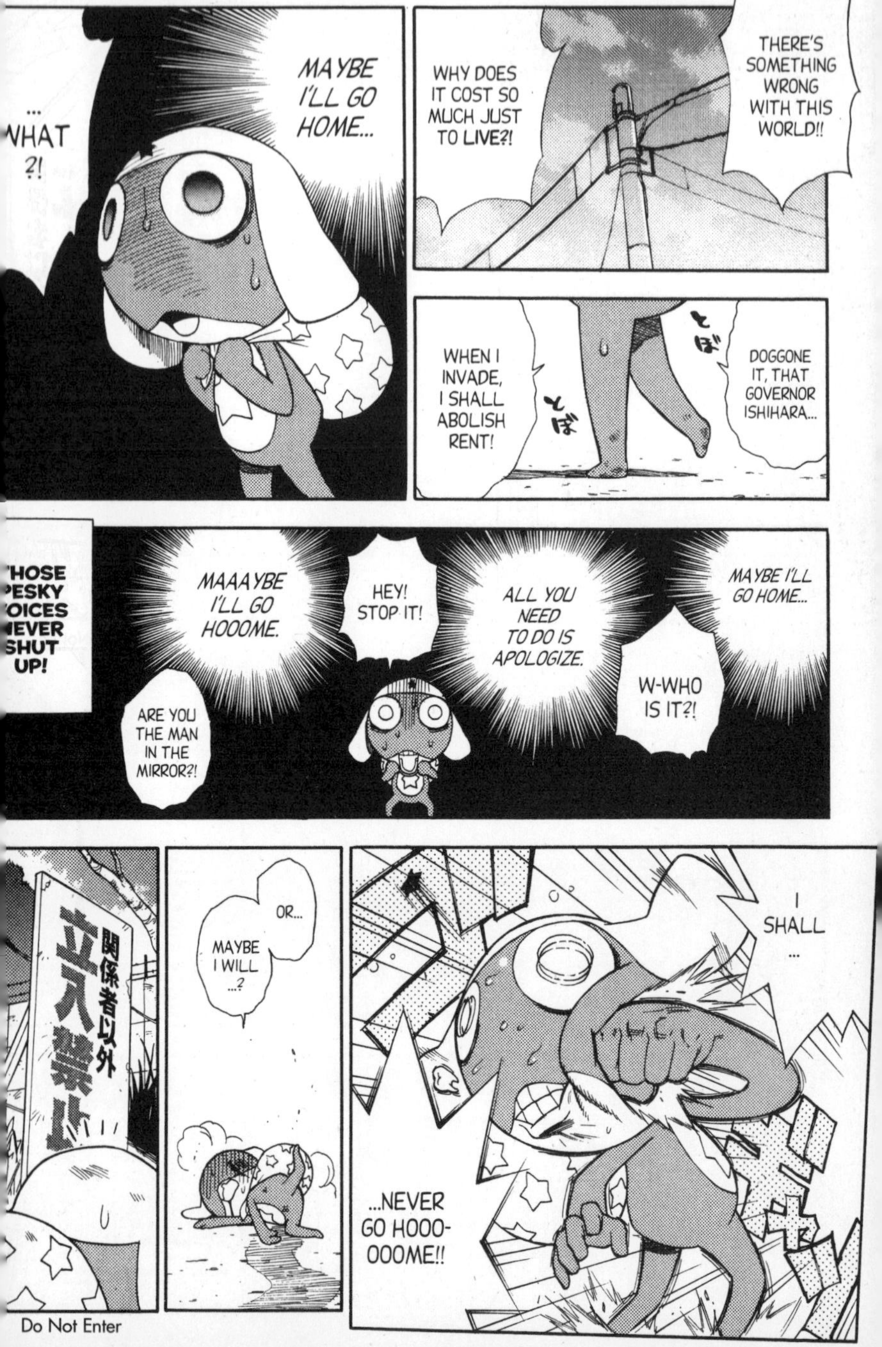
THERE'S SOMETHING WRONG WITH THIS WORLD!!
WHY DOES IT COST SO MUCH JUST TO LIVE?!
DOGGONE IT, THAT GOVERNOR ISHIHARA...
とぼ
WHEN I INVADE, I SHALL ABOLISH RENT!
とぼ
MAYBE I'LL GO HOME...
...WHAT?!
MAYBE I'LL GO HOME...
W-WHO IS IT?!
ALL YOU NEED TO DO IS APOLOGIZE.
HEY! STOP IT!
MAAAYBE I'LL GO HOOOME.
ARE YOU THE MAN IN THE MIRROR?!
THOSE PESKY VOICES NEVER SHUT UP!
I SHALL ...
...NEVER GO HOOO-OOOME!!
OR...
MAYBE I WILL ...?
関係者以外
立入禁止
Do Not Enter

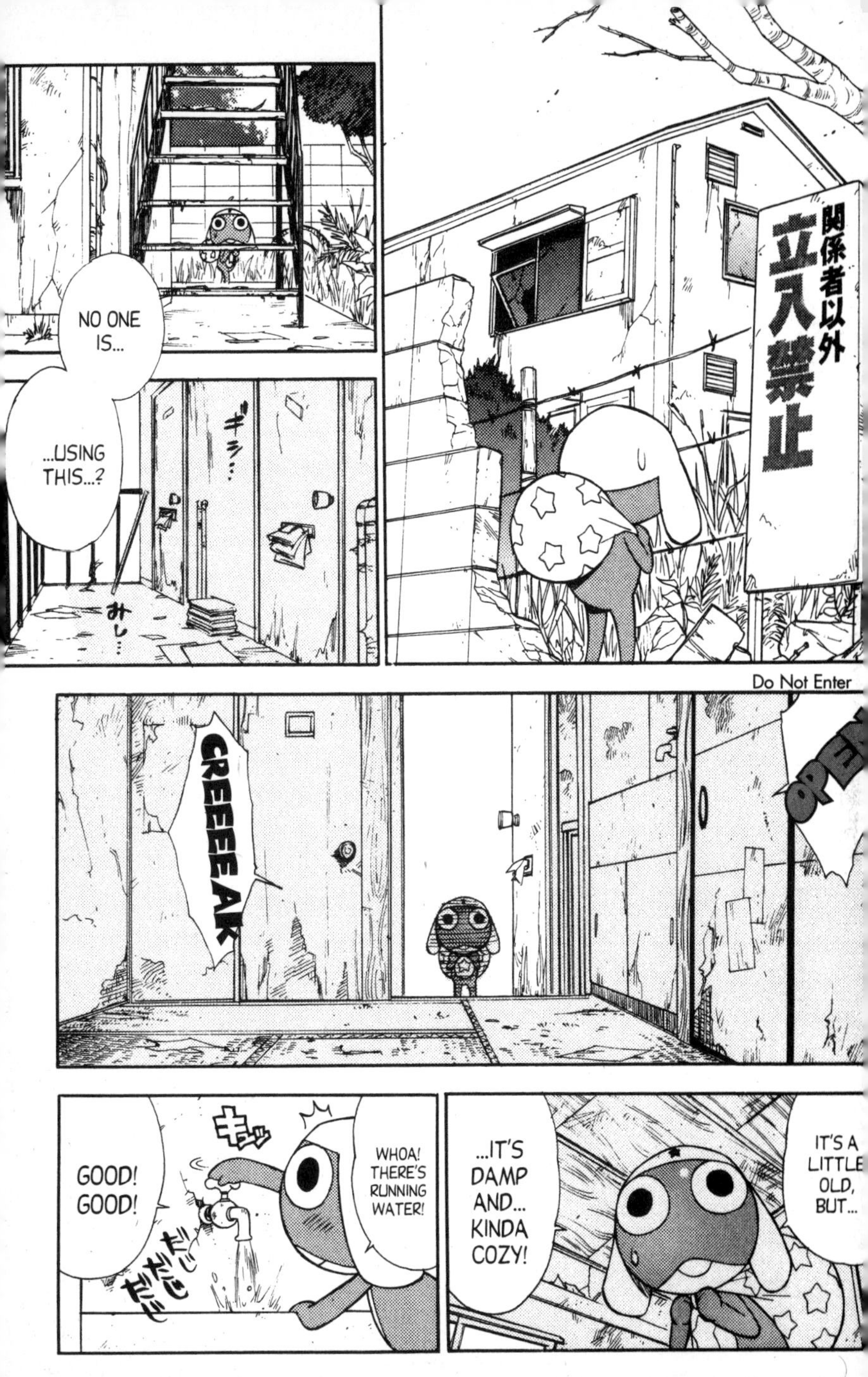
関係者以外立入禁止
Do Not Enter
NO ONE IS...
...USING THIS...?
みし…
CREEEEAK
IT'S A LITTLE OLD, BUT...
...IT'S DAMP AND... KINDA COZY!
WHOA! THERE'S RUNNING WATER!
GOOD! GOOD!

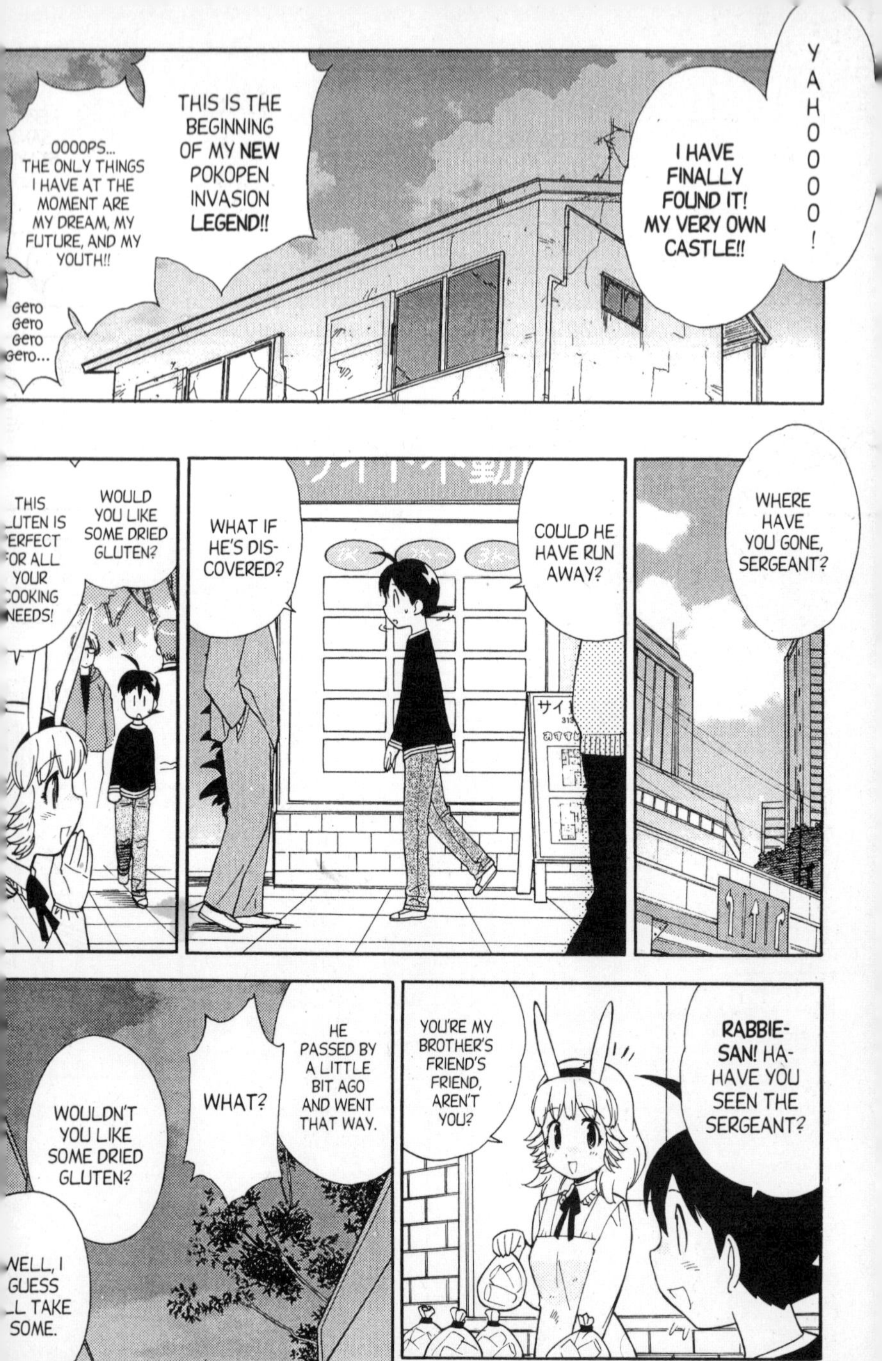
YAHOOOOO!
I HAVE FINALLY FOUND IT! MY VERY OWN CASTLE!!
THIS IS THE BEGINNING OF MY NEW POKOPEN INVASION LEGEND!!
OOOOPS... THE ONLY THINGS I HAVE AT THE MOMENT ARE MY DREAM, MY FUTURE, AND MY YOUTH!!
Gero Gero Gero Gero...
WHERE HAVE YOU GONE, SERGEANT?
COULD HE HAVE RUN AWAY?
WHAT IF HE'S DIS-COVERED?
WOULD YOU LIKE SOME DRIED GLUTEN?
THIS LUTEN IS ERFECT FOR ALL YOUR COOKING NEEDS!
RABBIE-SAN! HA-HAVE YOU SEEN THE SERGEANT?
YOU'RE MY BROTHER'S FRIEND'S FRIEND, AREN'T YOU?
HE PASSED BY A LITTLE BIT AGO AND WENT THAT WAY.
WHAT?
WOULDN'T YOU LIKE SOME DRIED GLUTEN?
WELL, I GUESS LL TAKE SOME.

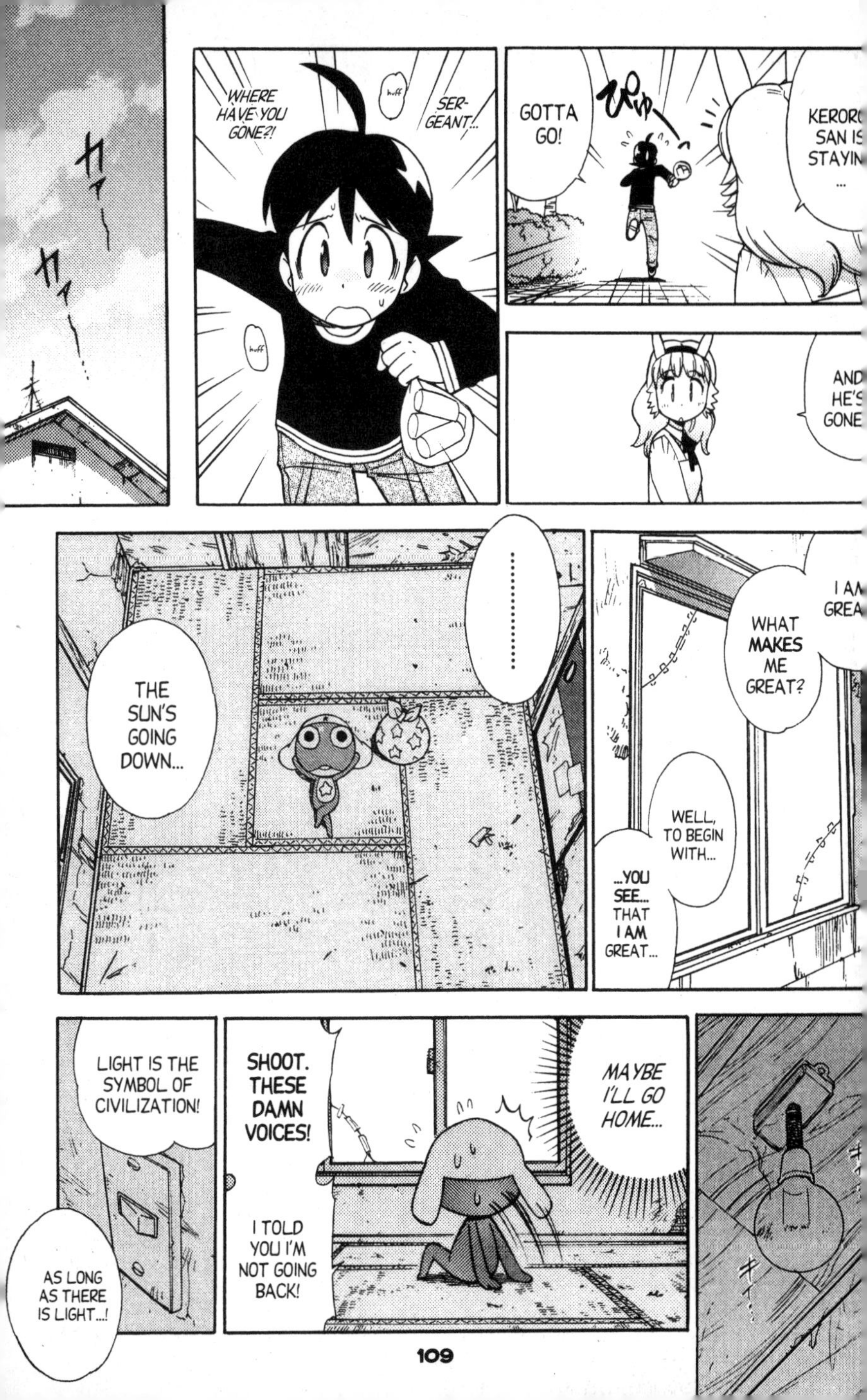

KEROR SAN IS STAYIN ...
GOTTA GO!
ぴゅー
AND HE'S GONE
SER-GEANT!...
huff
WHERE HAVE YOU GONE?!
huff
カァー
カァー
I AM GREA
WHAT MAKES ME GREAT?
WELL, TO BEGIN WITH...
...YOU SEE... THAT I AM GREAT...
......
THE SUN'S GOING DOWN...
キィ...
MAYBE I'LL GO HOME...
SHOOT. THESE DAMN VOICES!
I TOLD YOU I'M NOT GOING BACK!
LIGHT IS THE SYMBOL OF CIVILIZATION!
AS LONG AS THERE IS LIGHT...!

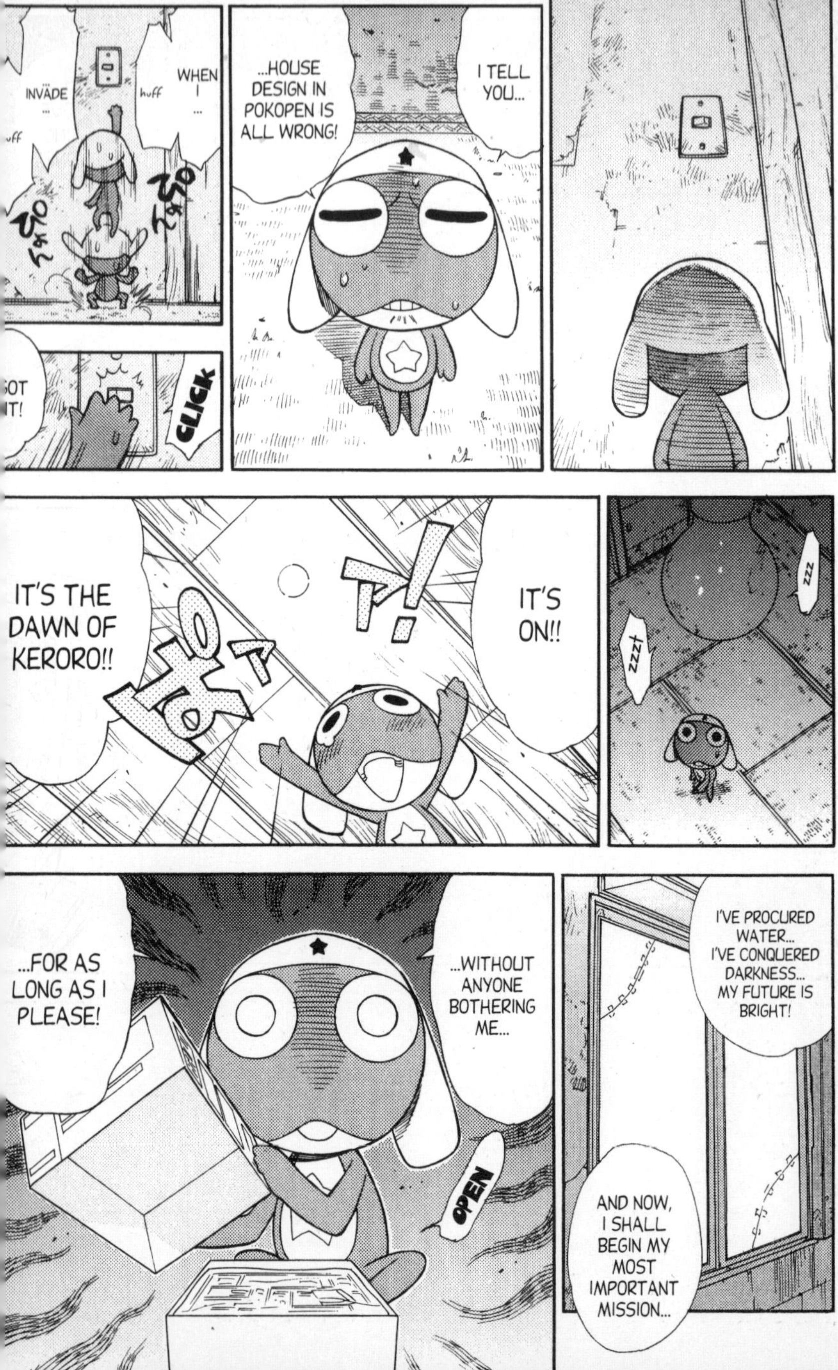
I TELL YOU...
...HOUSE DESIGN IN POKOPEN IS ALL WRONG!
WHEN I ...
huff
INVADE ...
huff
CLICK
OT IT!
zzz
zzz
IT'S ON!!
IT'S THE DAWN OF KERORO!!
I'VE PROCURED WATER... I'VE CONQUERED DARKNESS... MY FUTURE IS BRIGHT!
AND NOW, I SHALL BEGIN MY MOST IMPORTANT MISSION...
...WITHOUT ANYONE BOTHERING ME...
OPEN
...FOR AS LONG AS I PLEASE!

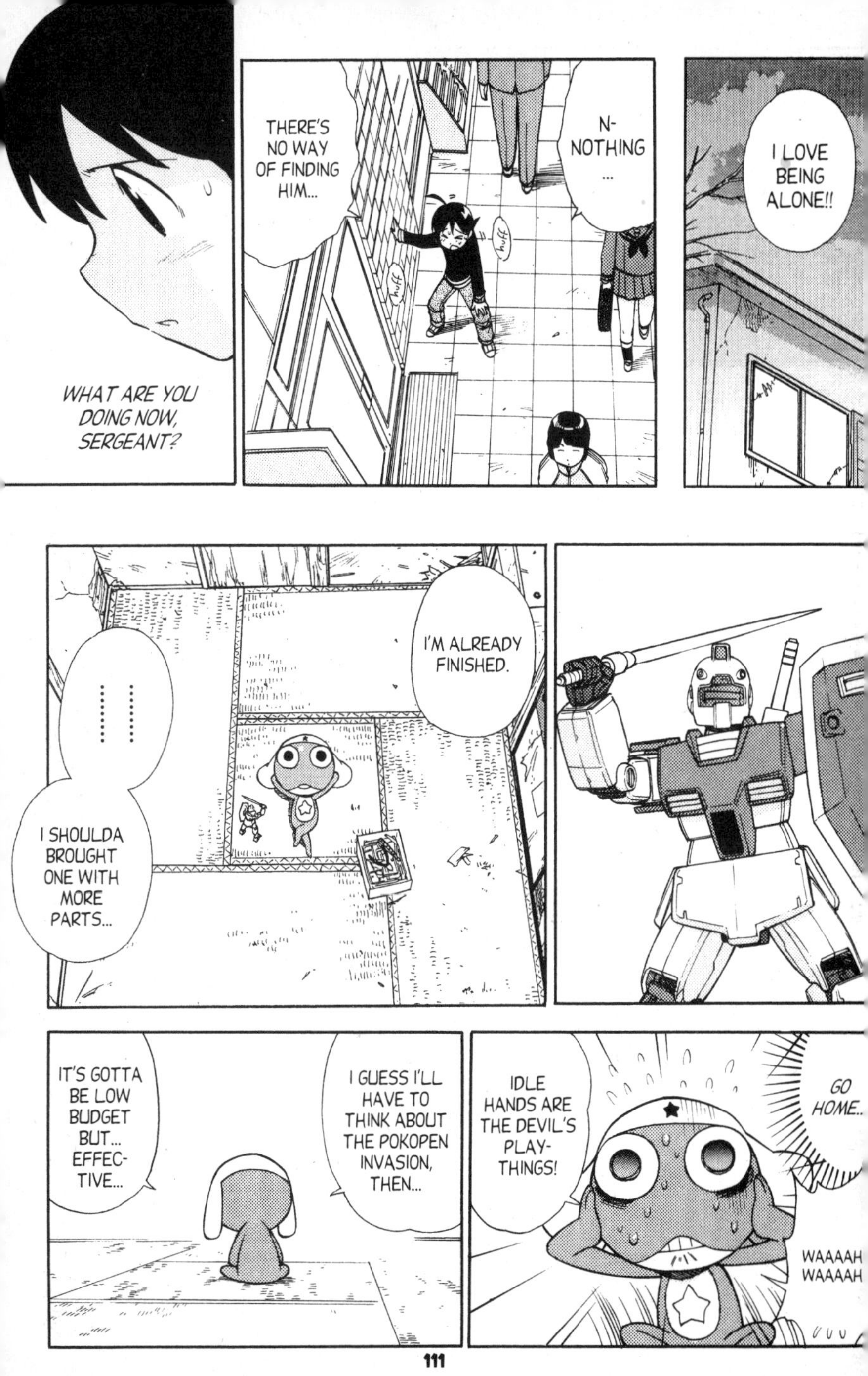
I LOVE BEING ALONE!!
N-NOTHING...
huff
huff
huff
THERE'S NO WAY OF FINDING HIM...
WHAT ARE YOU DOING NOW, SERGEANT?
I'M ALREADY FINISHED.
......
I SHOULDA BROUGHT ONE WITH MORE PARTS...
GO HOME..
IDLE HANDS ARE THE DEVIL'S PLAYTHINGS!
WAAAAH WAAAAH
I GUESS I'LL HAVE TO THINK ABOUT THE POKOPEN INVASION, THEN...
IT'S GOTTA BE LOW BUDGET BUT... EFFECTIVE...

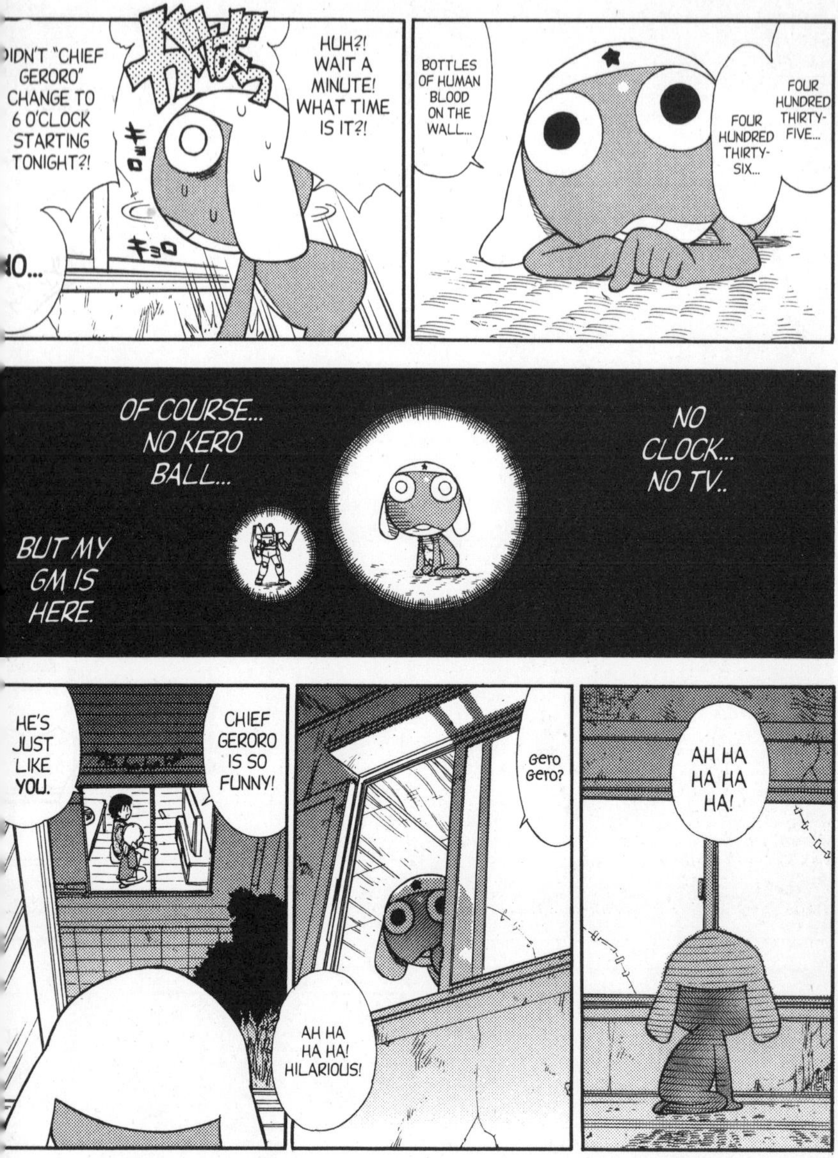
FOUR HUNDRED THIRTY-FIVE...
FOUR HUNDRED THIRTY-SIX...
BOTTLES OF HUMAN BLOOD ON THE WALL...
HUH?! WAIT A MINUTE! WHAT TIME IS IT?!
キョロ
キョロ
IDN'T "CHIEF GERORO" CHANGE TO 6 O'CLOCK STARTING TONIGHT?!
O...
NO CLOCK... NO TV..
OF COURSE... NO KERO BALL...
BUT MY GM IS HERE.
AH HA HA HA HA!
Gero Gero?
AH HA HA HA! HILARIOUS!
CHIEF GERORO IS SO FUNNY!
HE'S JUST LIKE YOU.

MAYBE I SHOULD GO HOME...?

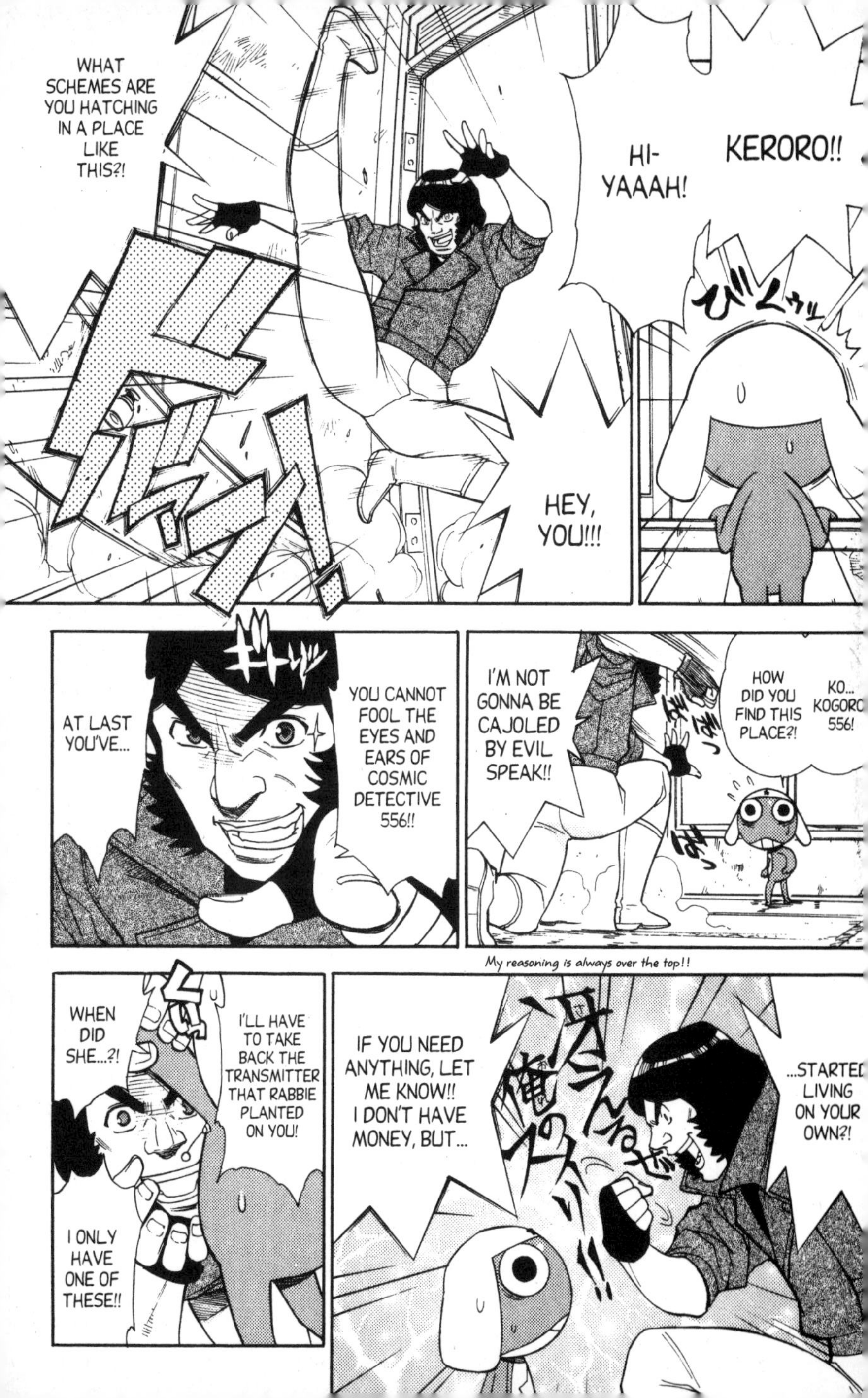
KERORO!!
HI-YAAAH!
HEY, YOU!!!
WHAT SCHEMES ARE YOU HATCHING IN A PLACE LIKE THIS?!
KO... KOGORO 556!
HOW DID YOU FIND THIS PLACE?!
I'M NOT GONNA BE CAJOLED BY EVIL SPEAK!!
YOU CANNOT FOOL THE EYES AND EARS OF COSMIC DETECTIVE 556!!
AT LAST YOU'VE...
My reasoning is always over the top!!
...STARTED LIVING ON YOUR OWN?!
IF YOU NEED ANYTHING, LET ME KNOW!! I DON'T HAVE MONEY, BUT...
I'LL HAVE TO TAKE BACK THE TRANSMITTER THAT RABBIE PLANTED ON YOU!
WHEN DID SHE...?!
I ONLY HAVE ONE OF THESE!!

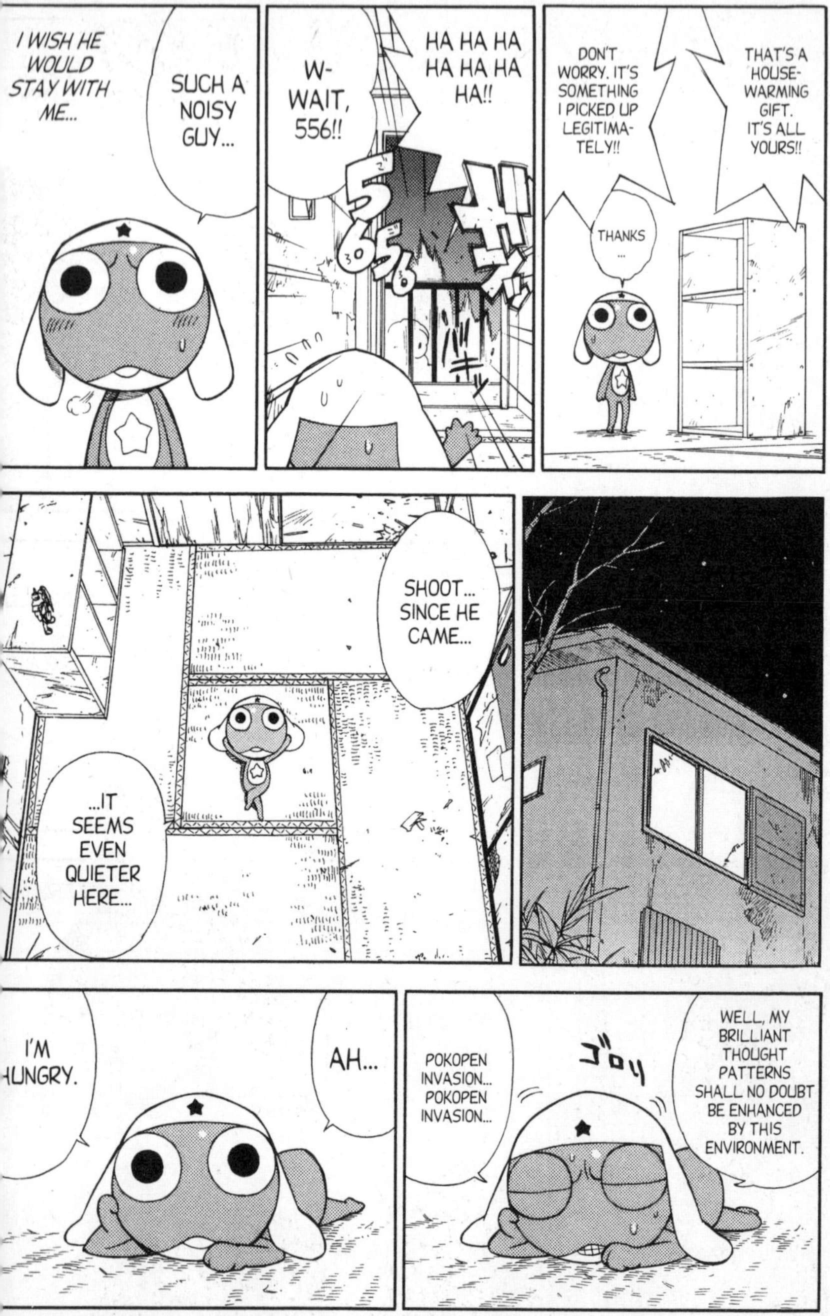
THAT'S A HOUSE-WARMING GIFT. IT'S ALL YOURS!!
DON'T WORRY. IT'S SOMETHING I PICKED UP LEGITIMA-TELY!!
THANKS...
HA HA HA HA HA HA HA!!
W-WAIT, 556!!
バキッ
SUCH A NOISY GUY...
I WISH HE WOULD STAY WITH ME...
SHOOT... SINCE HE CAME...
...IT SEEMS EVEN QUIETER HERE...
WELL, MY BRILLIANT THOUGHT PATTERNS SHALL NO DOUBT BE ENHANCED BY THIS ENVIRONMENT.
ゴロリ
POKOPEN INVASION... POKOPEN INVASION...
AH...
I'M HUNGRY.

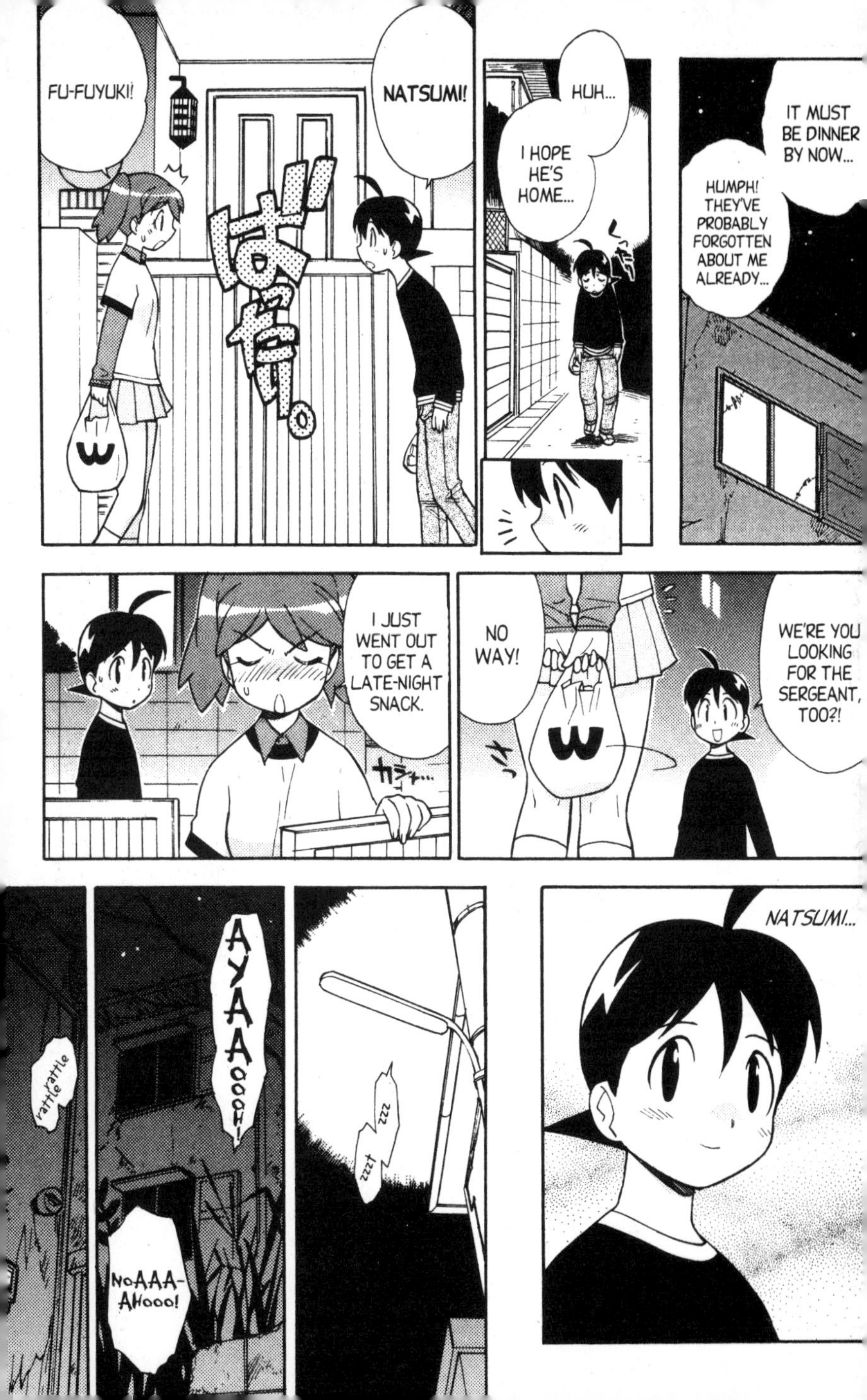

IT MUST BE DINNER BY NOW...
HUMPH! THEY'VE PROBABLY FORGOTTEN ABOUT ME ALREADY...
HUH...
I HOPE HE'S HOME...
NATSUMI!
FU-FUYUKI!
WE'RE YOU LOOKING FOR THE SERGEANT, TOO?!
NO WAY!
I JUST WENT OUT TO GET A LATE-NIGHT SNACK.
NATSUMI...
zzz
zzzt
AYAAAOOOH!
NoAAA-AHooo!
rattle rattle

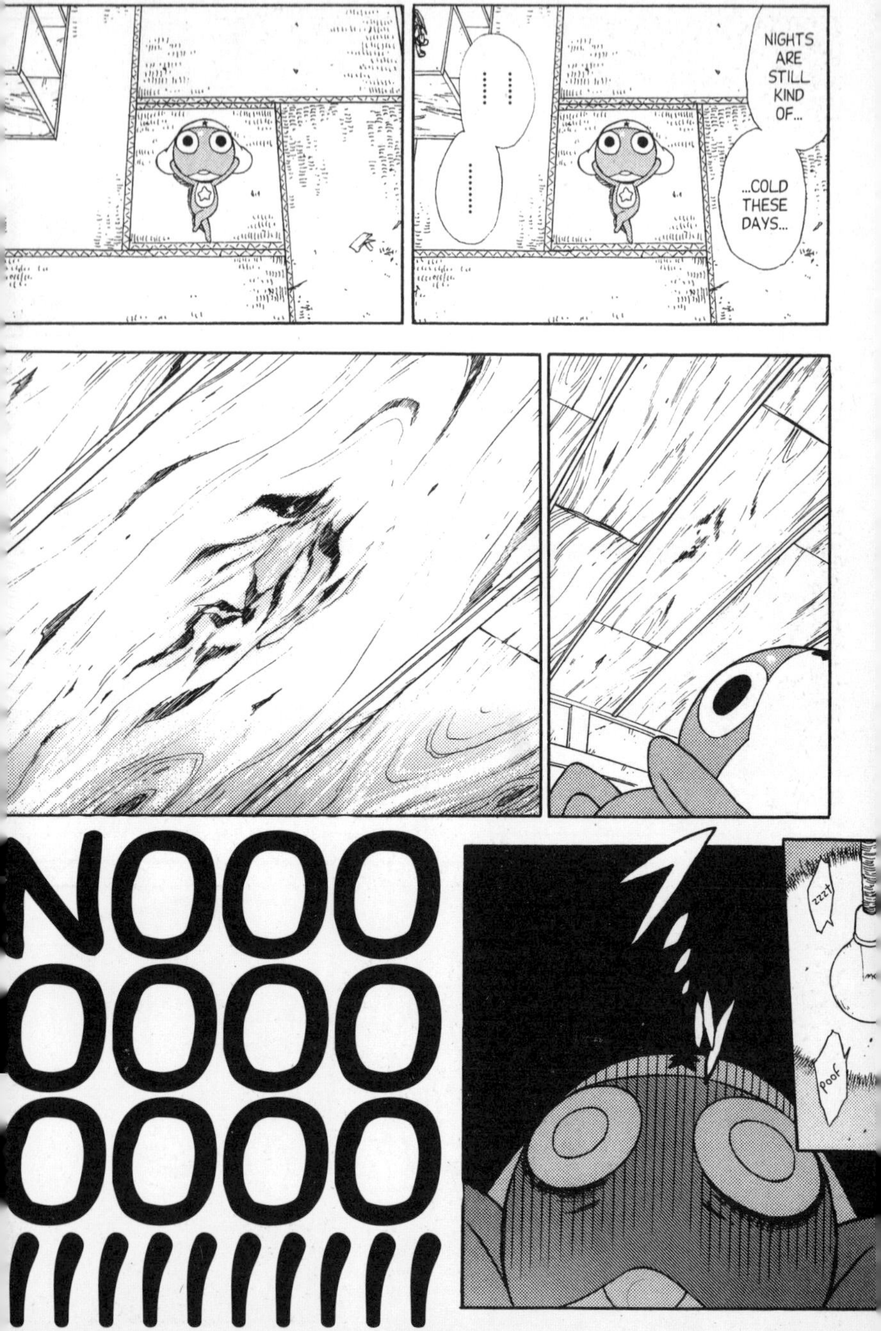
NIGHTS ARE STILL KIND OF...
...COLD THESE DAYS...
...
......
zzzt
poof
NOOOOOOOOOOOO!!!!!!!!!!

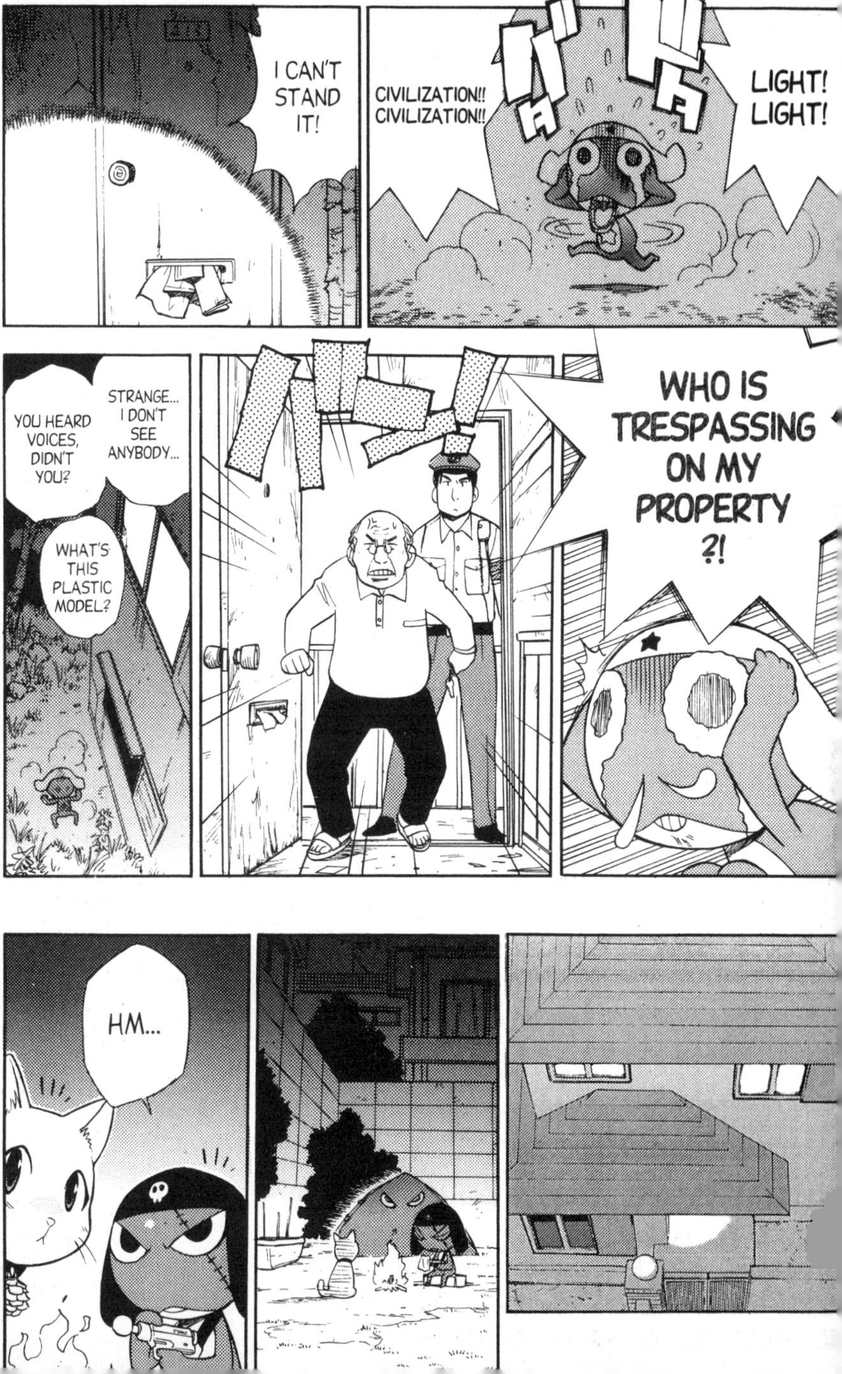
LIGHT! LIGHT!
CIVILIZATION!! CIVILIZATION!!
I CAN'T STAND IT!
WHO IS TRESPASSING ON MY PROPERTY ?!
STRANGE... I DON'T SEE ANYBODY...
YOU HEARD VOICES, DIDN'T YOU?
WHAT'S THIS PLASTIC MODEL?
HM...

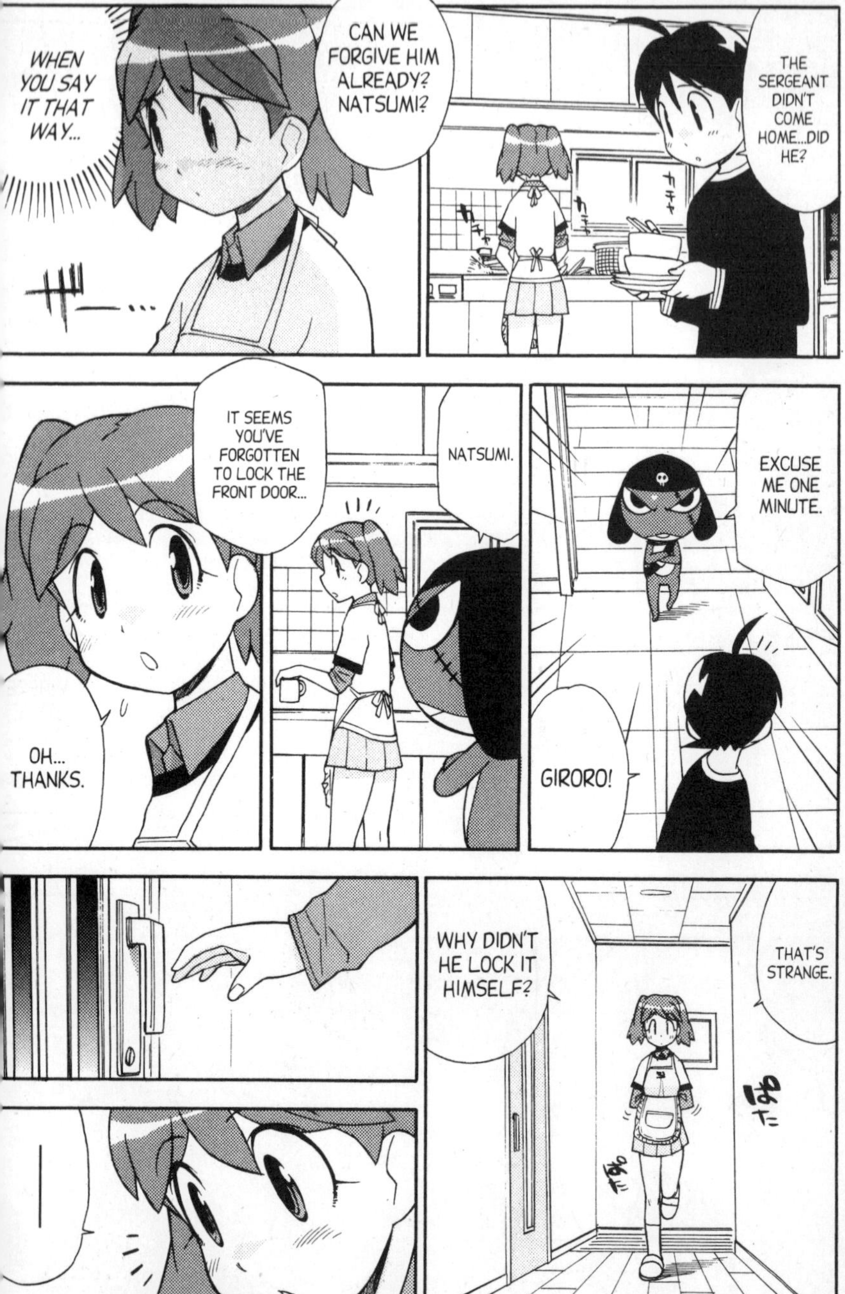
THE SERGEANT DIDN'T COME HOME...DID HE?
CAN WE FORGIVE HIM ALREADY? NATSUMI?
WHEN YOU SAY IT THAT WAY...
EXCUSE ME ONE MINUTE.
GIRORO!
NATSUMI.
IT SEEMS YOU'VE FORGOTTEN TO LOCK THE FRONT DOOR...
OH... THANKS.
THAT'S STRANGE.
WHY DIDN'T HE LOCK IT HIMSELF?

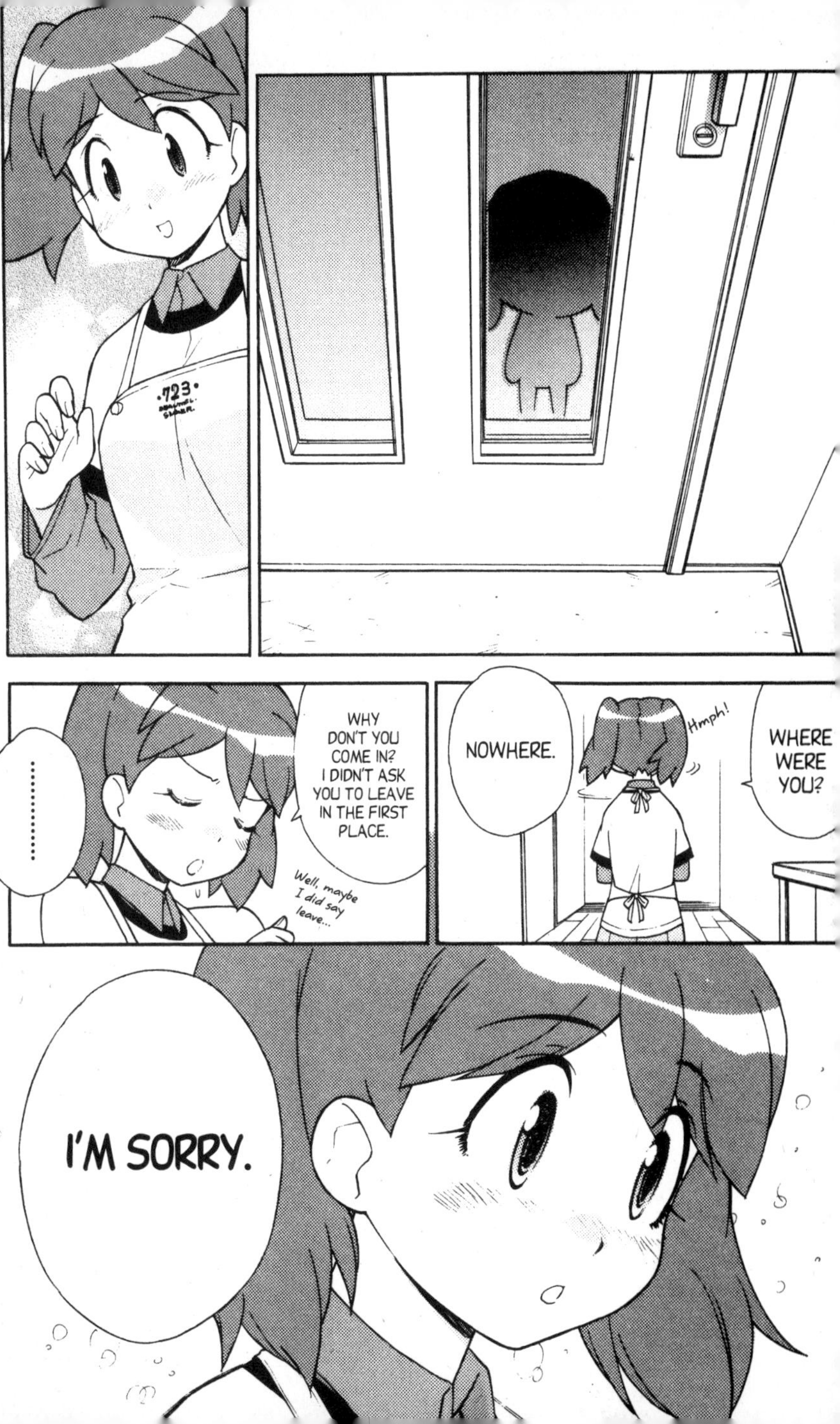
WHERE WERE YOU?
Hmph!
NOWHERE.
WHY DON'T YOU COME IN? I DIDN'T ASK YOU TO LEAVE IN THE FIRST PLACE.
Well, maybe I did say leave...
....
I'M SORRY.

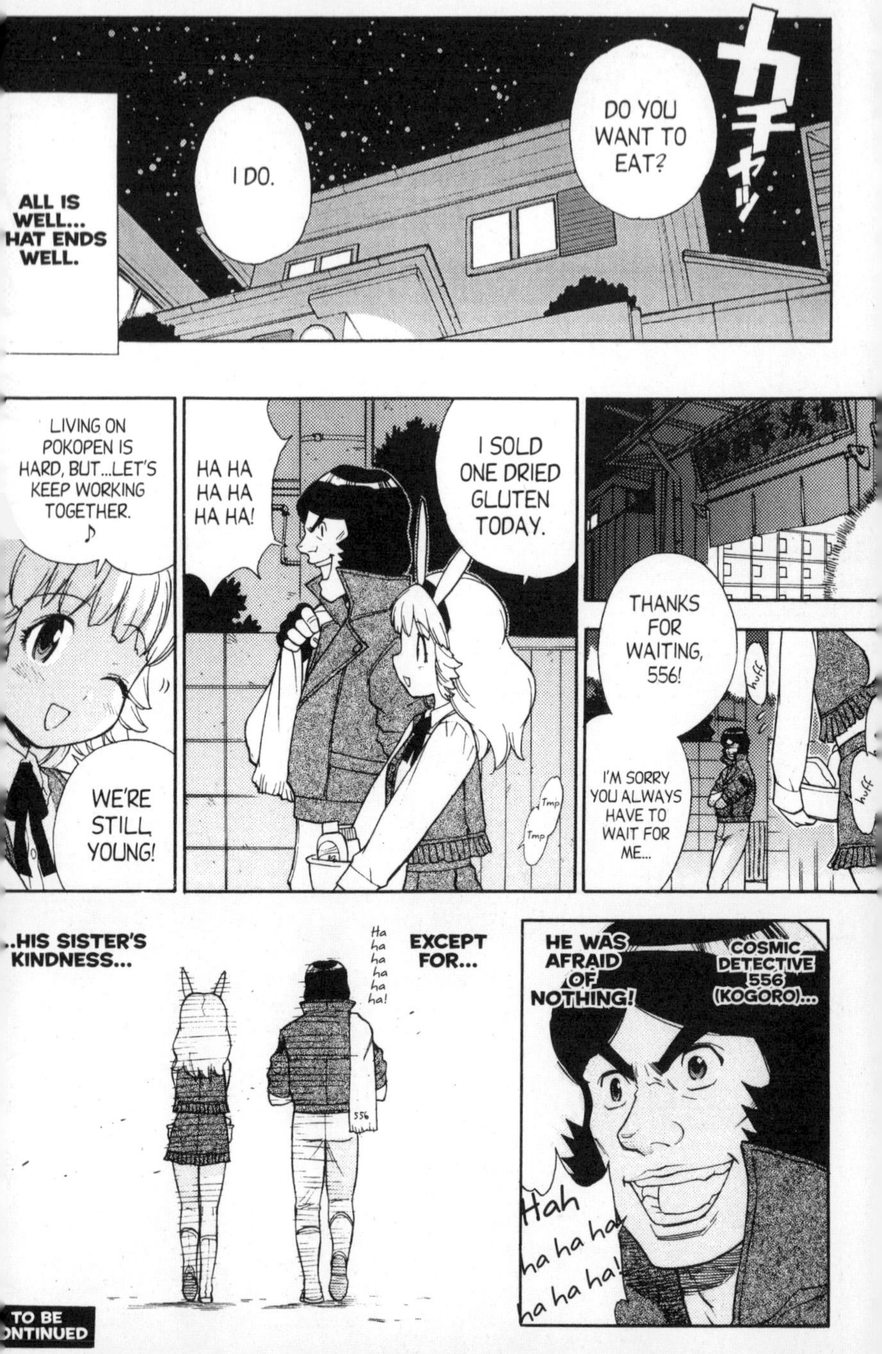

カチャッ
DO YOU WANT TO EAT?
I DO.
ALL IS WELL... HAT ENDS WELL.
THANKS FOR WAITING, 556!
huff
huff
I'M SORRY YOU ALWAYS HAVE TO WAIT FOR ME...
I SOLD ONE DRIED GLUTEN TODAY.
HA HA HA HA HA HA!
Tmp
Tmp
LIVING ON POKOPEN IS HARD, BUT...LET'S KEEP WORKING TOGETHER. ♪
WE'RE STILL YOUNG!
COSMIC DETECTIVE 556 (KOGORO)...
HE WAS AFRAID OF NOTHING!
Hah ha ha ha ha ha! ha ha ha!
EXCEPT FOR...
Ha ha ha ha ha ha!
556
..HIS SISTER'S KINDNESS...
TO BE ONTINUED

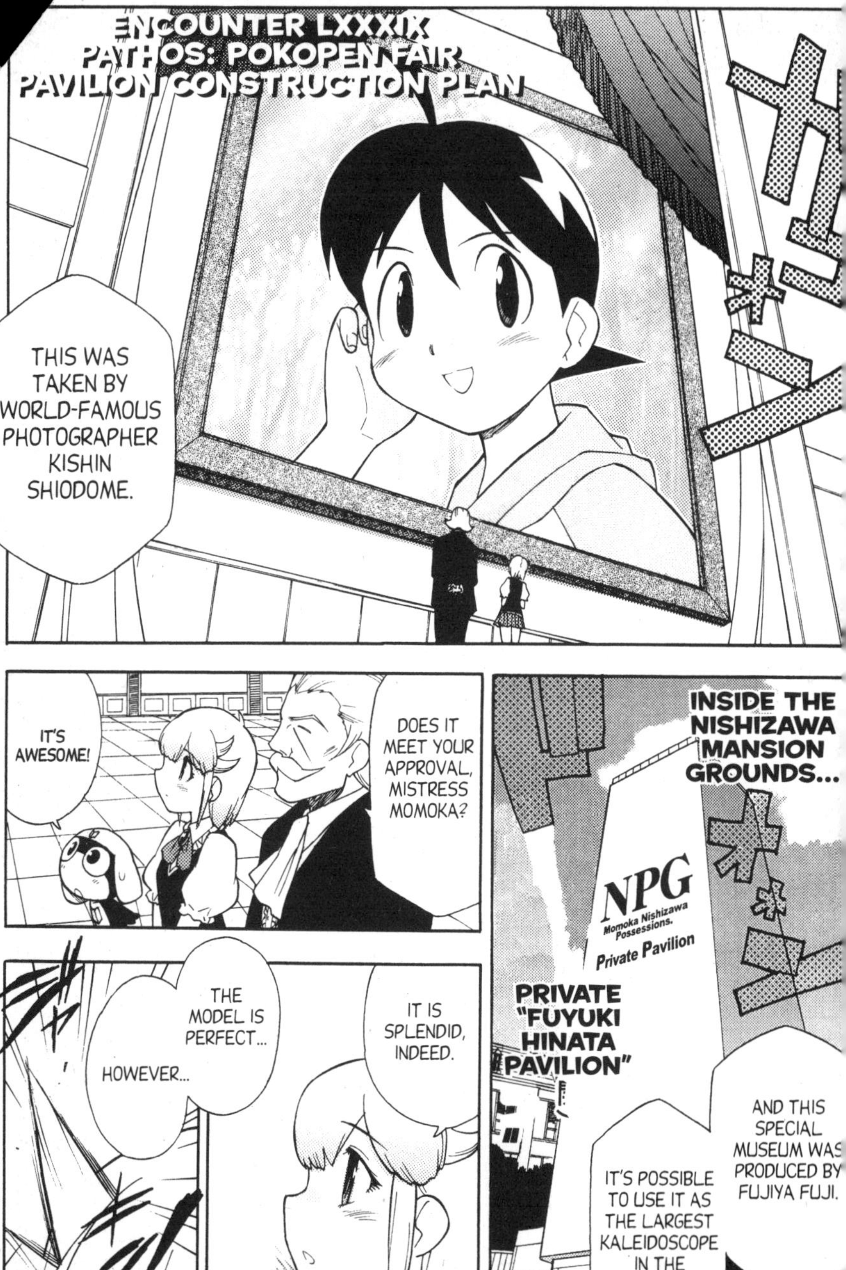
ENCOUNTER LXXXIX
PATHOS: POKOPEN FAIR PAVILION CONSTRUCTION PLAN
THIS WAS TAKEN BY WORLD-FAMOUS PHOTOGRAPHER KISHIN SHIODOME.
INSIDE THE NISHIZAWA MANSION GROUNDS...
NPG
Momoka Nishizawa Possessions.
Private Pavilion
PRIVATE "FUYUKI HINATA PAVILION"
AND THIS SPECIAL MUSEUM WAS PRODUCED BY FUJIYA FUJI.
IT'S POSSIBLE TO USE IT AS THE LARGEST KALEIDOSCOPE IN THE WORLD.
DOES IT MEET YOUR APPROVAL, MISTRESS MOMOKA?
IT'S AWESOME!
IT IS SPLENDID, INDEED.
THE MODEL IS PERFECT...
HOWEVER...

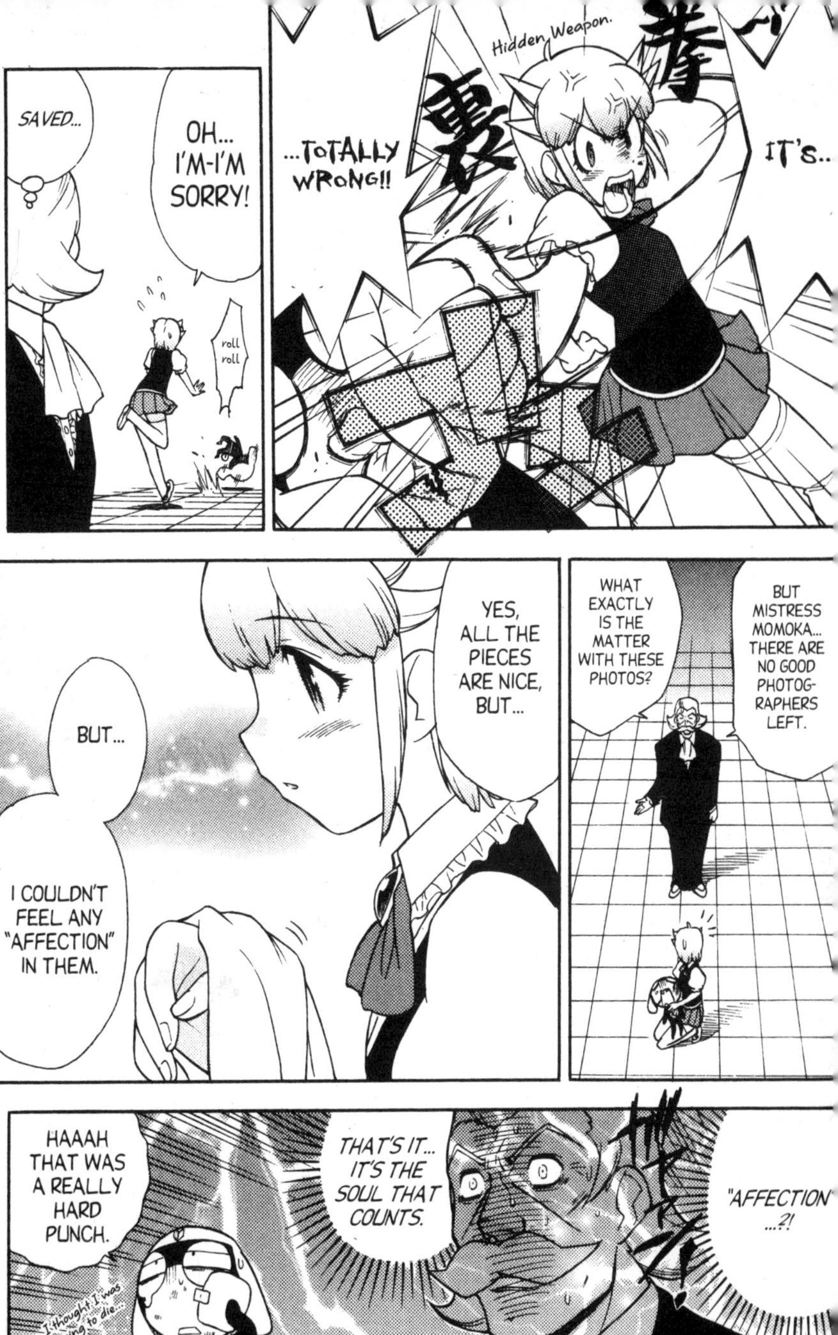
Hidden Weapon.
裏拳
IT'S...
...TOTALLY WRONG!!
OH... I'M-I'M SORRY!
roll roll
SAVED...
BUT MISTRESS MOMOKA... THERE ARE NO GOOD PHOTOGRAPHERS LEFT.
WHAT EXACTLY IS THE MATTER WITH THESE PHOTOS?
YES, ALL THE PIECES ARE NICE, BUT...
BUT...
I COULDN'T FEEL ANY "AFFECTION" IN THEM.
"AFFECTION" ...?!
THAT'S IT... IT'S THE SOUL THAT COUNTS.
HAAAH THAT WAS A REALLY HARD PUNCH.
I thought I was going to die...

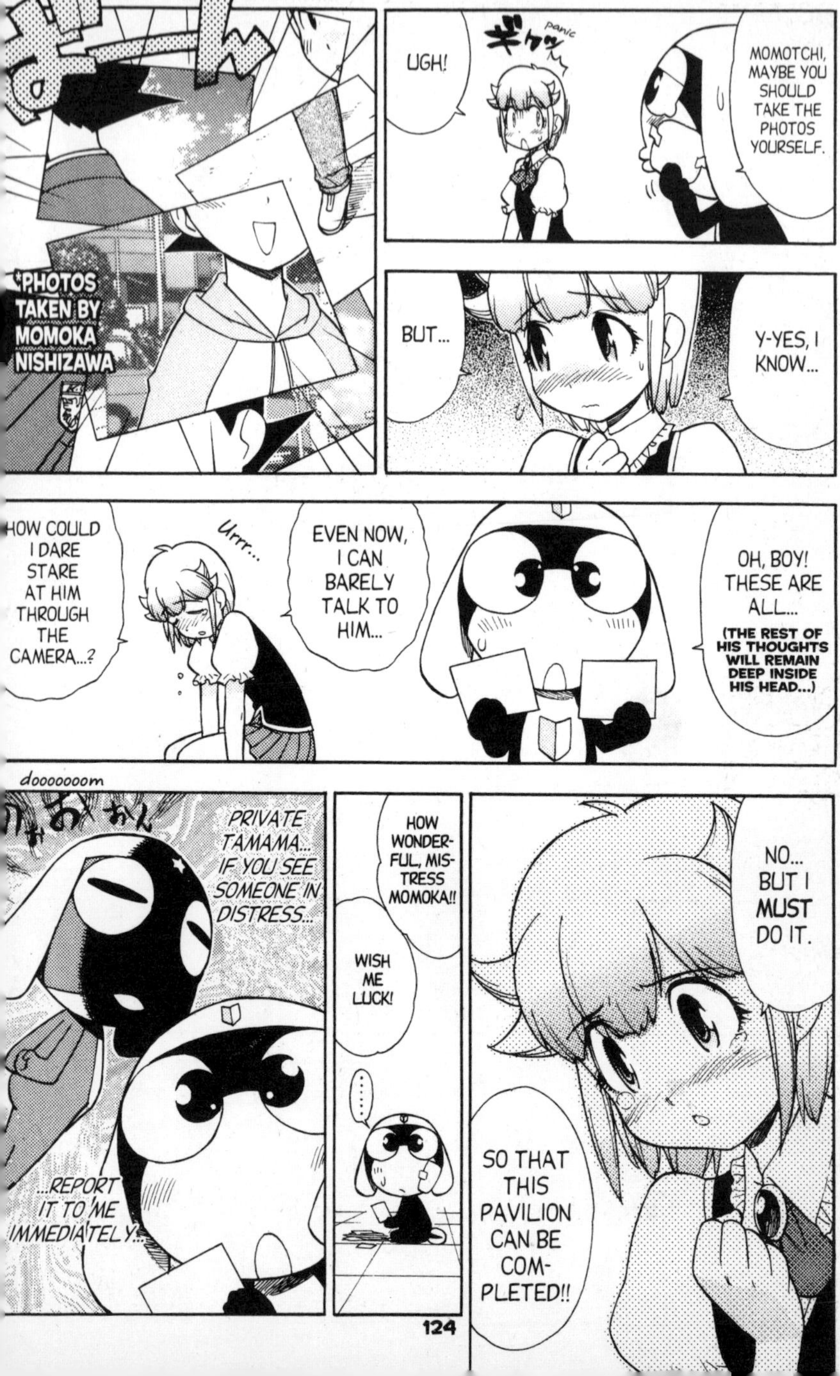
MOMOTCHI, MAYBE YOU SHOULD TAKE THE PHOTOS YOURSELF.
panic
UGH!
Y-YES, I KNOW...
BUT...
*PHOTOS TAKEN BY MOMOKA NISHIZAWA
OH, BOY! THESE ARE ALL...
(THE REST OF HIS THOUGHTS WILL REMAIN DEEP INSIDE HIS HEAD...)
EVEN NOW, I CAN BARELY TALK TO HIM...
Urrr...
HOW COULD I DARE STARE AT HIM THROUGH THE CAMERA...?
NO... BUT I MUST DO IT.
SO THAT THIS PAVILION CAN BE COM-PLETED!!
HOW WONDER-FUL, MIS-TRESS MOMOKA!!
WISH ME LUCK!
......
dooooooom
PRIVATE TAMAMA... IF YOU SEE SOMEONE IN DISTRESS...
...REPORT IT TO ME IMMEDIATELY...

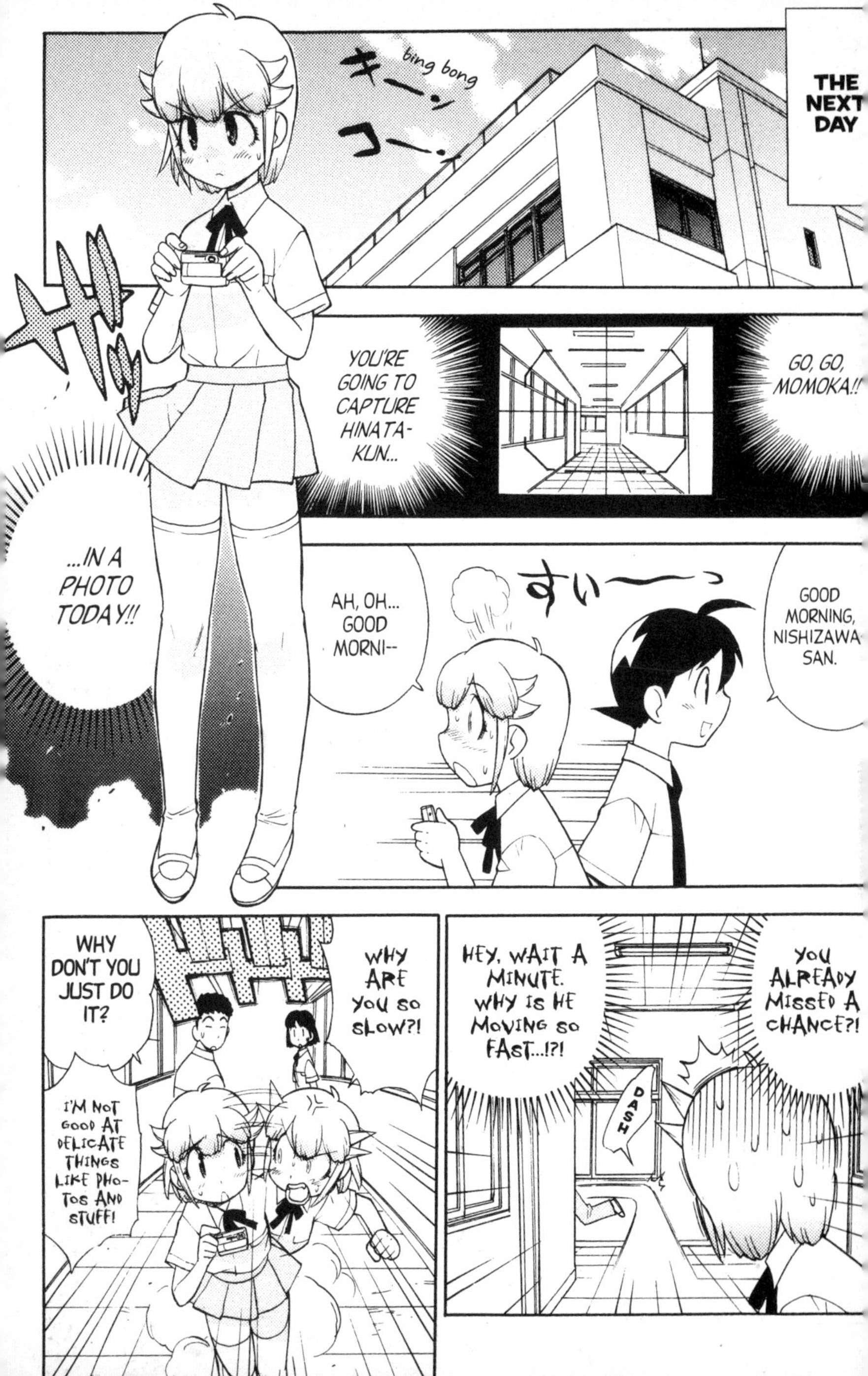
THE NEXT DAY
キ～ン
コ～ン
bing bong
GO, GO, MOMOKA!!
YOU'RE GOING TO CAPTURE HINATA-KUN...
...IN A PHOTO TODAY!!
GOOD MORNING, NISHIZAWA-SAN.
すい～～っ
AH, OH... GOOD MORNI--
YOU ALREADY MISSED A CHANCE?!
HEY, WAIT A MINUTE. WHY IS HE MOVING SO FAST...!?!
DASH
WHY ARE YOU SO SLOW?!
WHY DON'T YOU JUST DO IT?
I'M NOT GOOD AT DELICATE THINGS LIKE PHOTOS AND STUFF!

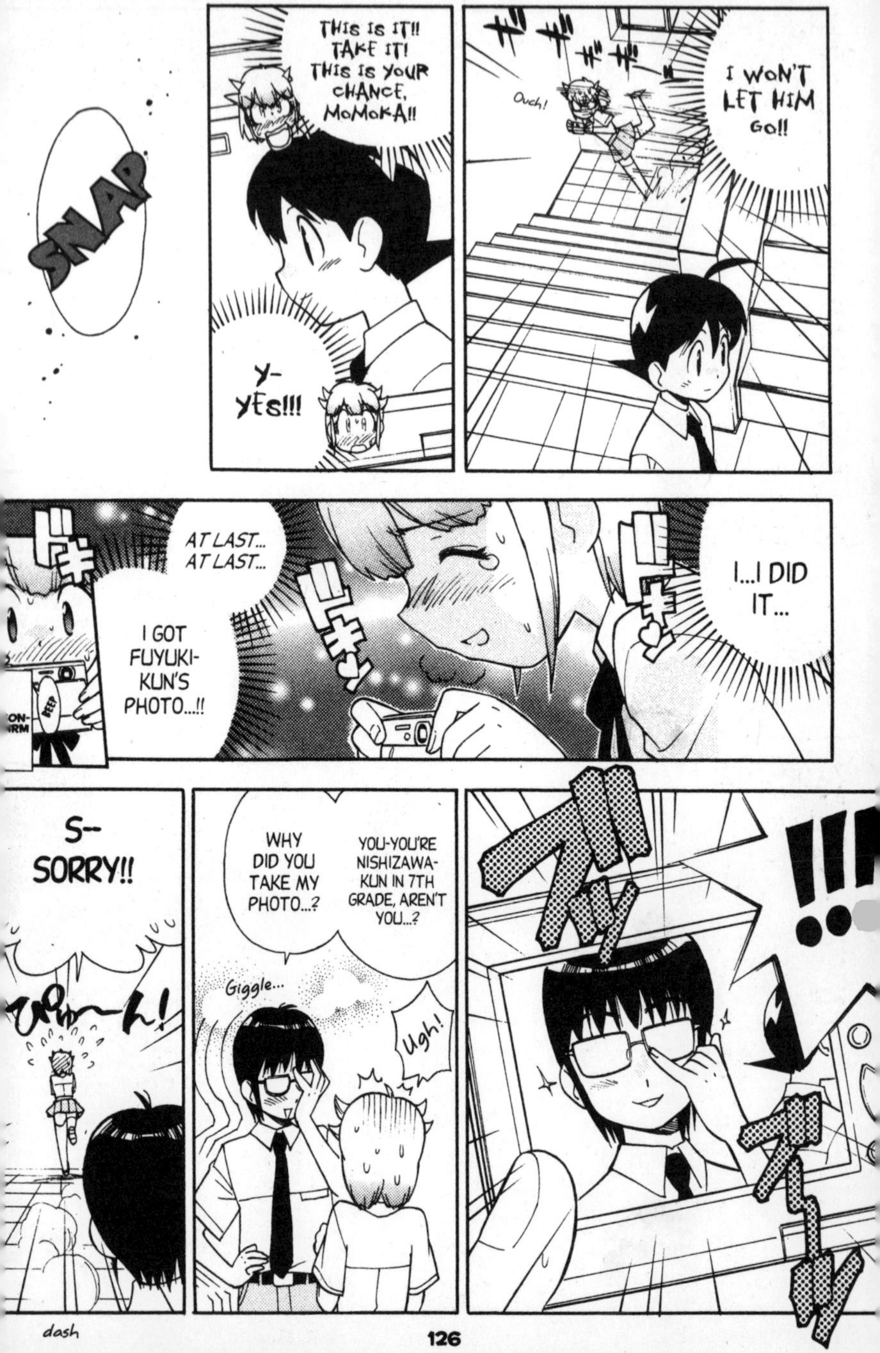
Ouch!
I WON'T LET HIM GO!!
THIS IS IT!! TAKE IT! THIS IS YOUR CHANCE, MOMOKA!!
Y-YES!!!
SNAP
I...I DID IT...
AT LAST... AT LAST...
I GOT FUYUKI-KUN'S PHOTO...!!
BEEP
!!!
YOU-YOU'RE NISHIZAWA-KUN IN 7TH GRADE, AREN'T YOU...?
WHY DID YOU TAKE MY PHOTO...?
Giggle...
Ugh!
S--SORRY!!

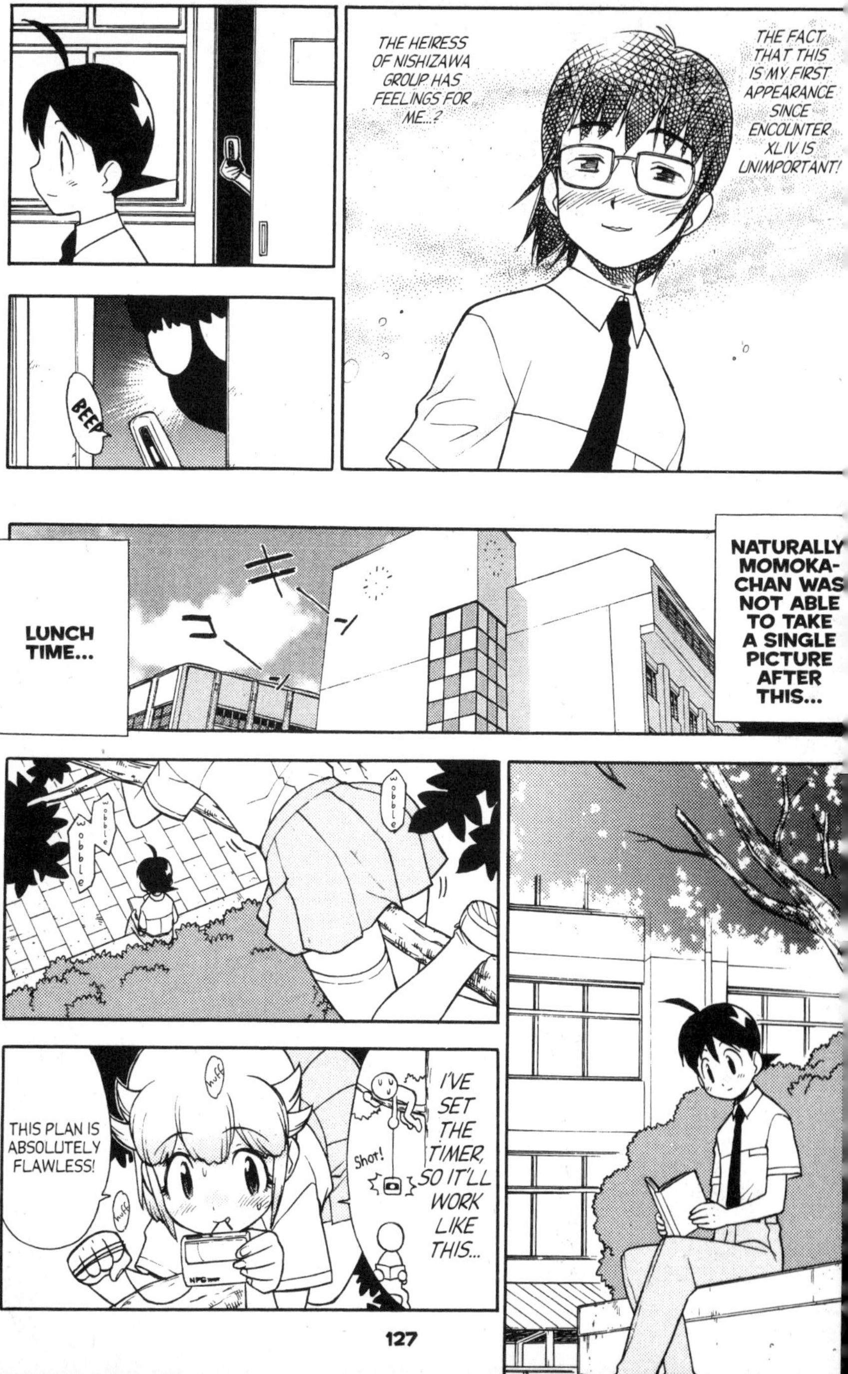
THE FACT THAT THIS IS MY FIRST APPEARANCE SINCE ENCOUNTER XLIV IS UNIMPORTANT!
THE HEIRESS OF NISHIZAWA GROUP HAS FEELINGS FOR ME...?
BEEP
NATURALLY MOMOKA-CHAN WAS NOT ABLE TO TAKE A SINGLE PICTURE AFTER THIS...
キーン コーン
LUNCH TIME...
wobble
wobble
wobble
I'VE SET THE TIMER, SO IT'LL WORK LIKE THIS...
Shot!
huff
THIS PLAN IS ABSOLUTELY FLAWLESS!
huff

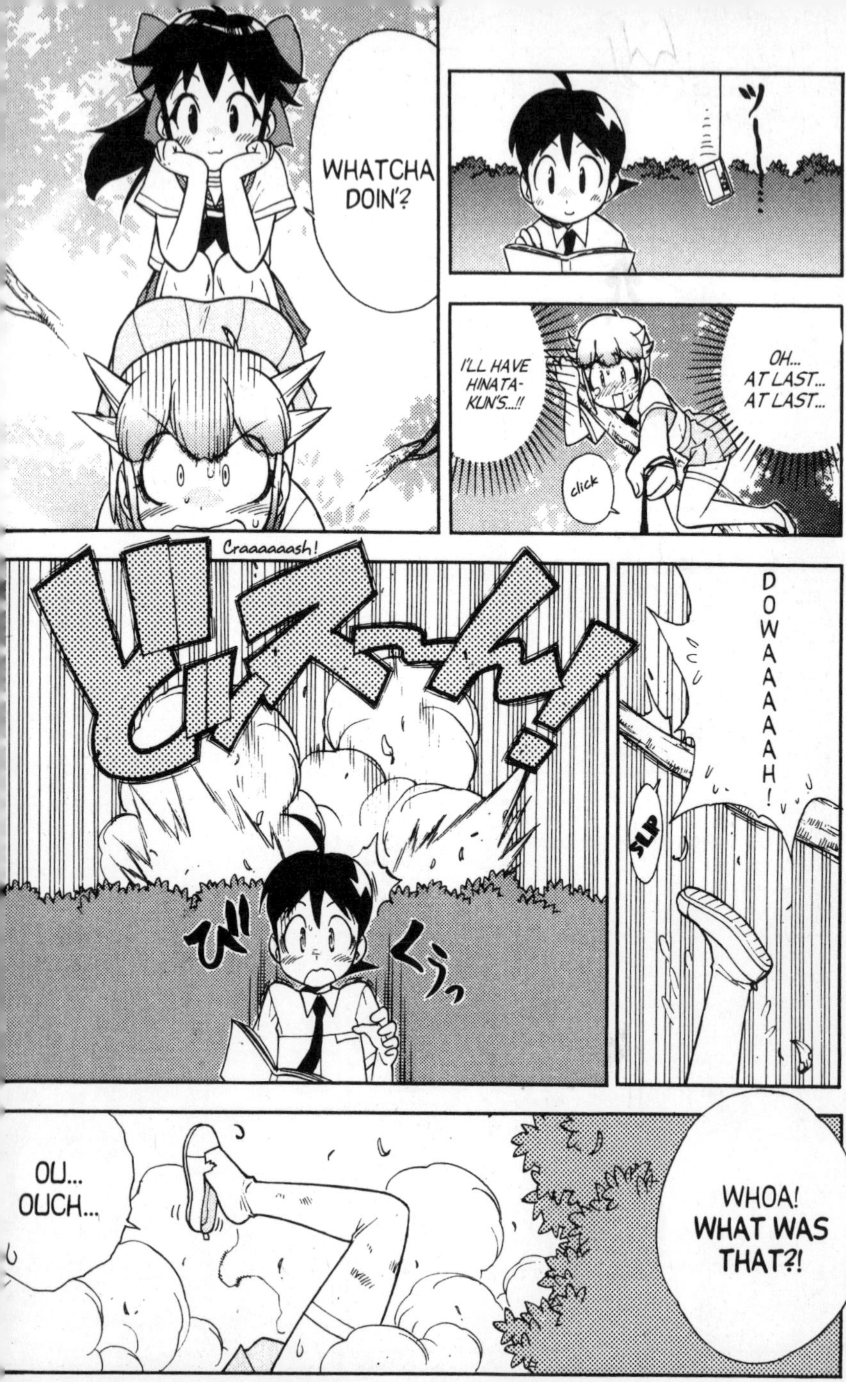
ツー
OH... AT LAST... AT LAST...
I'LL HAVE HINATA-KUN'S...!!
click
WHATCHA DOIN'?
DOWAAAAAAAAH!
SLIP
Craaaaaash!
どスーん!
びくぅっ
WHOA! WHAT WAS THAT?!
OU... OUCH...

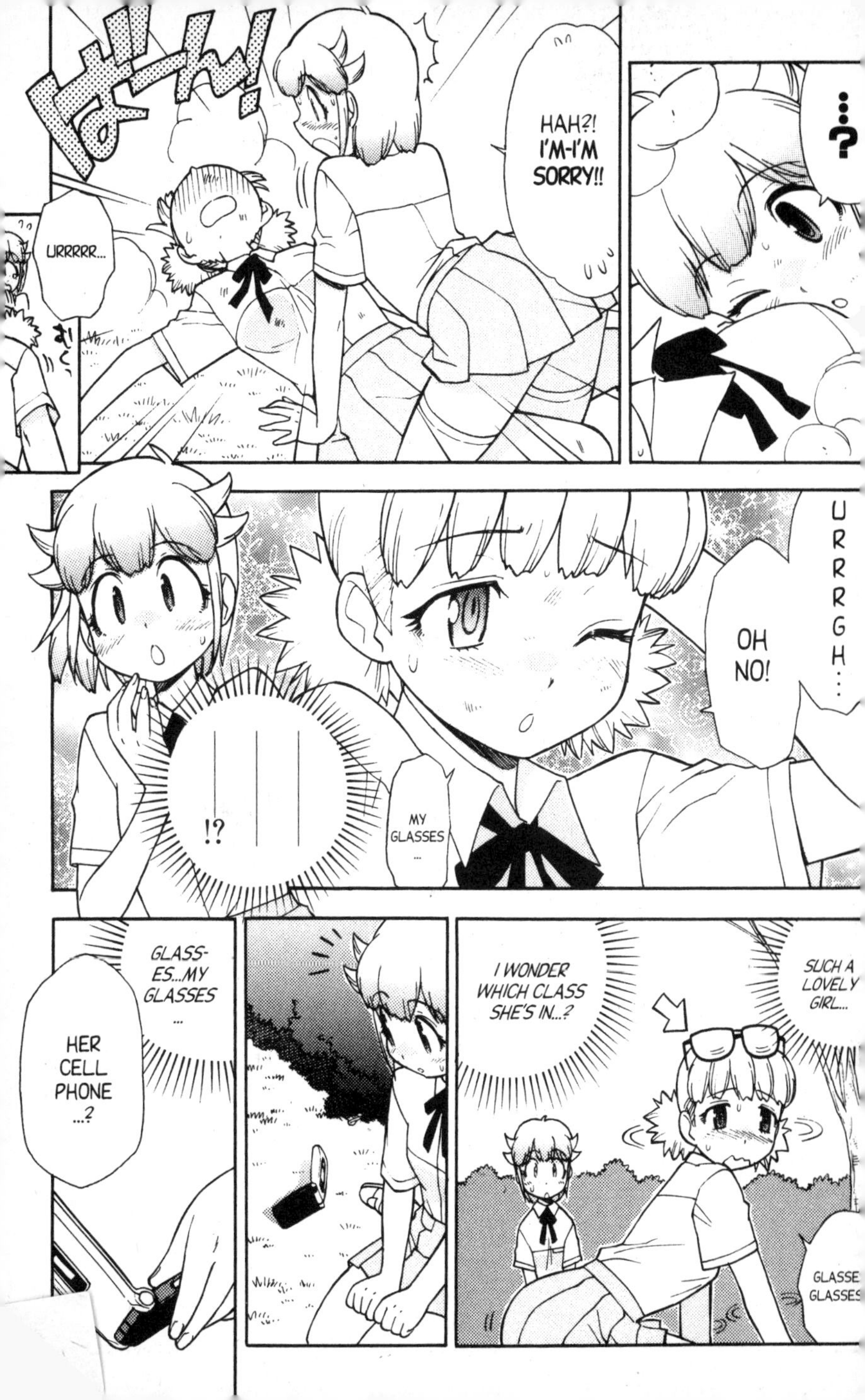
?...
HAH?! I'M-I'M SORRY!!
ばーん!
URRRRR...
URRRGH...
OH NO!
MY GLASSES...
!?
SUCH A LOVELY GIRL...
GLASSE GLASSES
I WONDER WHICH CLASS SHE'S IN...?
GLASSES...MY GLASSES...
HER CELL PHONE...?

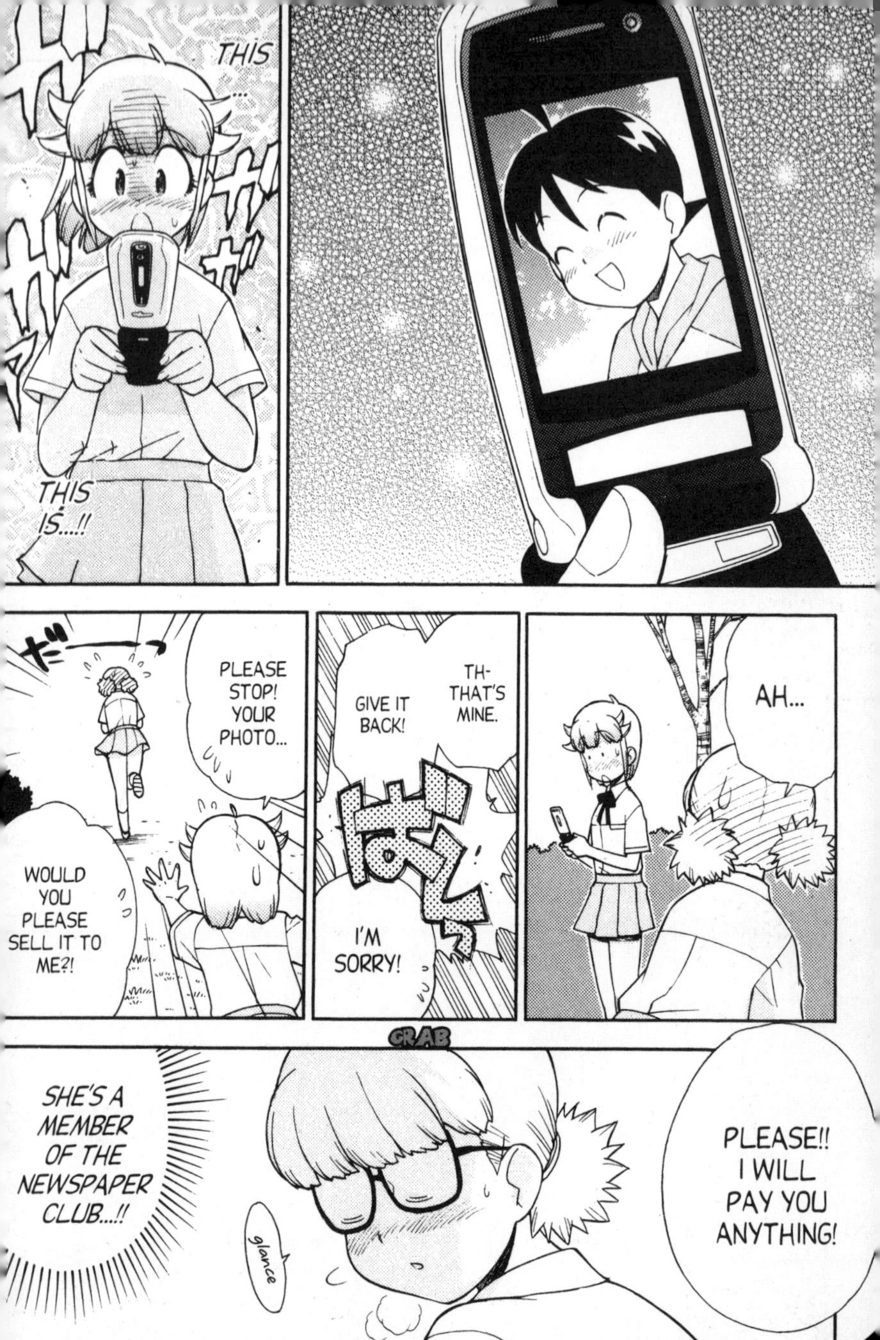
THIS ...
THIS IS...!!
AH...
TH- THAT'S MINE.
GIVE IT BACK!
I'M SORRY!
PLEASE STOP! YOUR PHOTO...
WOULD YOU PLEASE SELL IT TO ME?!
GRAB
PLEASE!! I WILL PAY YOU ANYTHING!
glance
SHE'S A MEMBER OF THE NEWSPAPER CLUB...!!

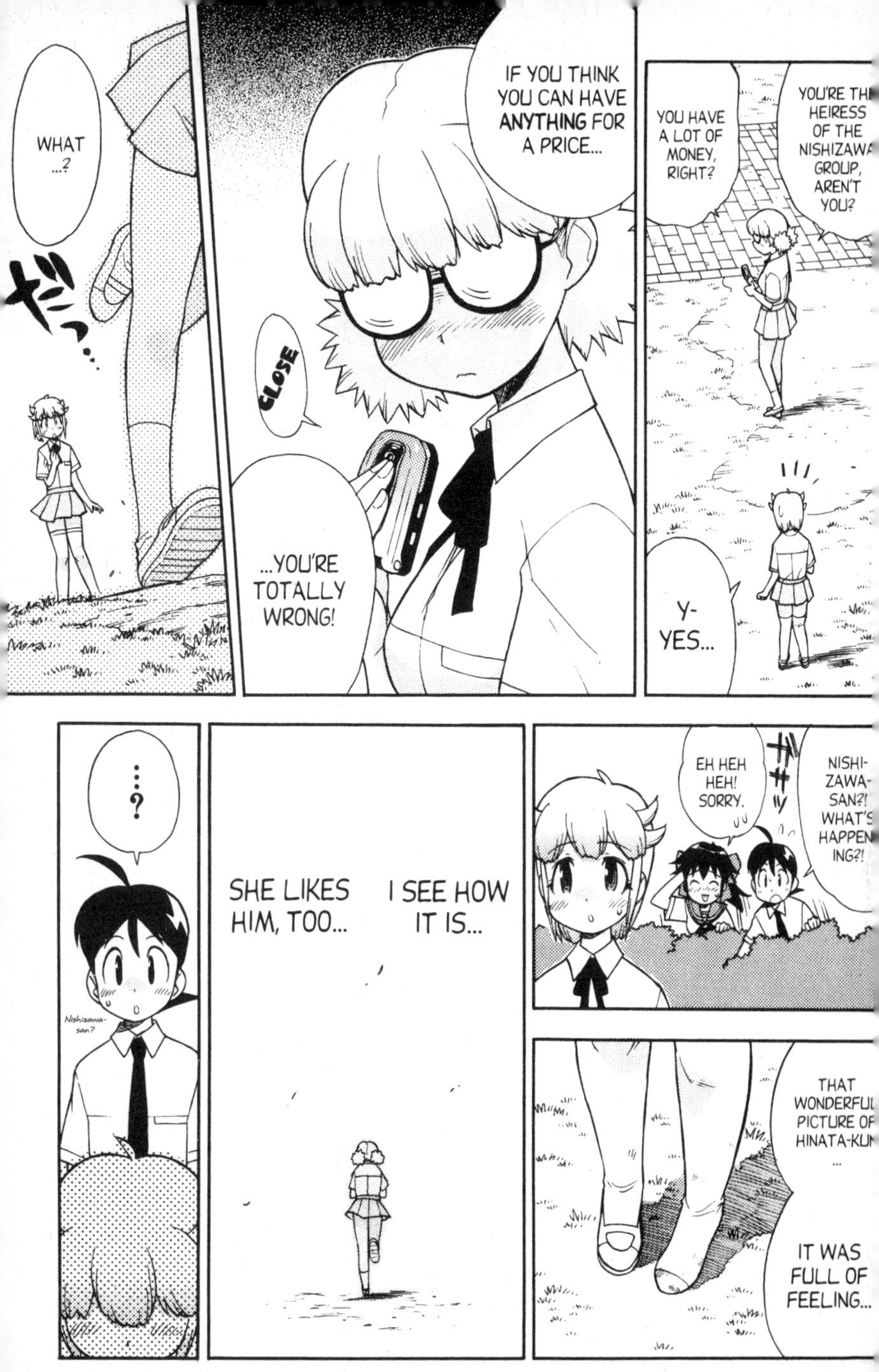
YOU'RE TH HEIRESS OF THE NISHIZAWA GROUP, AREN'T YOU?
YOU HAVE A LOT OF MONEY, RIGHT?
Y- YES...
IF YOU THINK YOU CAN HAVE **ANYTHING** FOR A PRICE...
CLOSE
...YOU'RE TOTALLY WRONG!
WHAT ...?
ダッ...
NISHI- ZAWA- SAN?! WHAT'S HAPPEN ING?!
EH HEH HEH! SORRY.
THAT WONDERFUL PICTURE OF HINATA-KUN ...
IT WAS FULL OF FEELING...
I SEE HOW IT IS...
SHE LIKES HIM, TOO...
...?
Nishizawa- san?

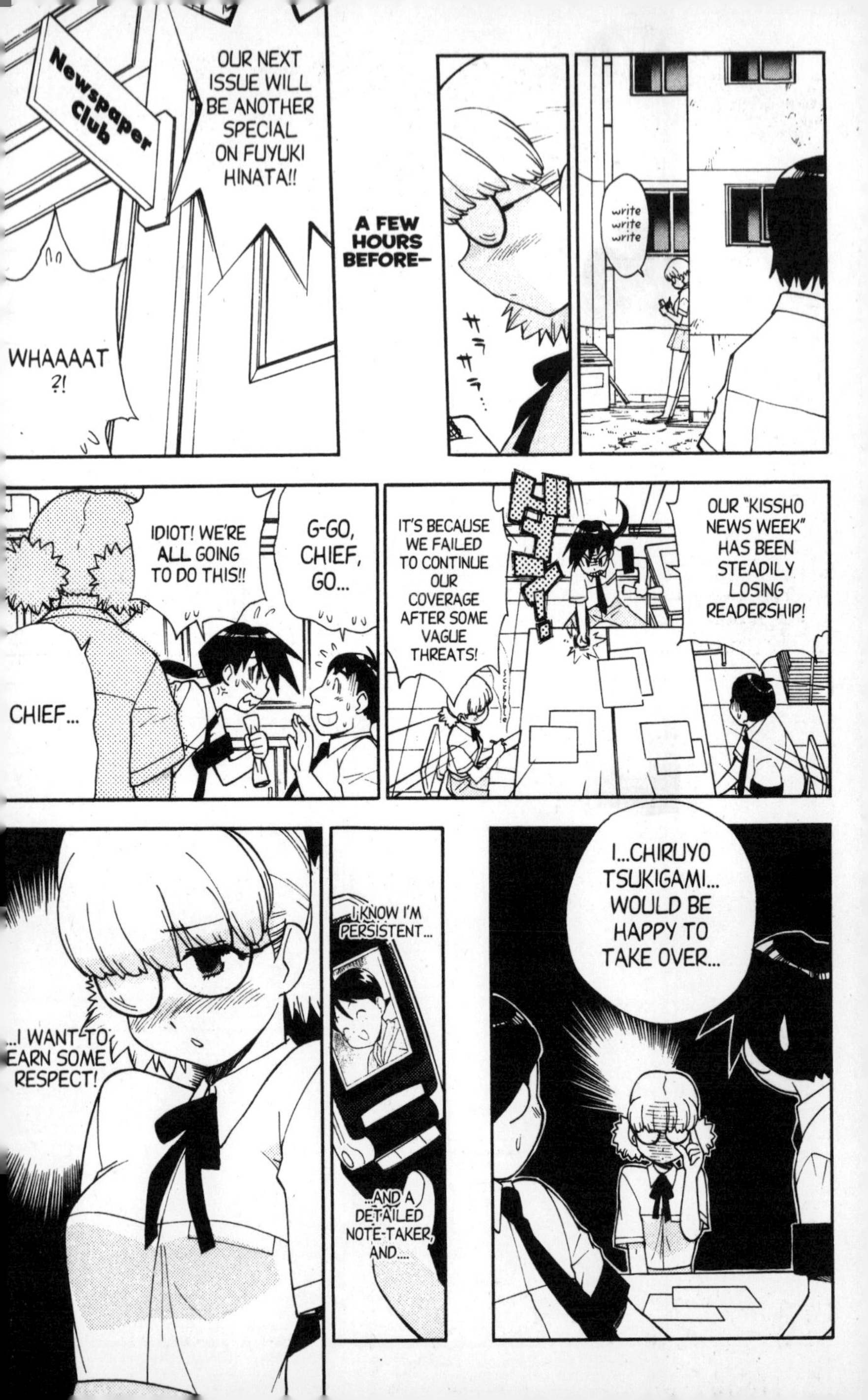
write
write
write
A FEW HOURS BEFORE—
OUR NEXT ISSUE WILL BE ANOTHER SPECIAL ON FUYUKI HINATA!!
Newspaper Club
WHAAAAT ?!
OUR "KISSHO NEWS WEEK" HAS BEEN STEADILY LOSING READERSHIP!
IT'S BECAUSE WE FAILED TO CONTINUE OUR COVERAGE AFTER SOME VAGUE THREATS!
G-GO, CHIEF, GO...
IDIOT! WE'RE ALL GOING TO DO THIS!!
CHIEF...
I...CHIRUYO TSUKIGAMI... WOULD BE HAPPY TO TAKE OVER...
I KNOW I'M PERSISTENT...
...AND A DETAILED NOTE-TAKER, AND....
...I WANT TO EARN SOME RESPECT!

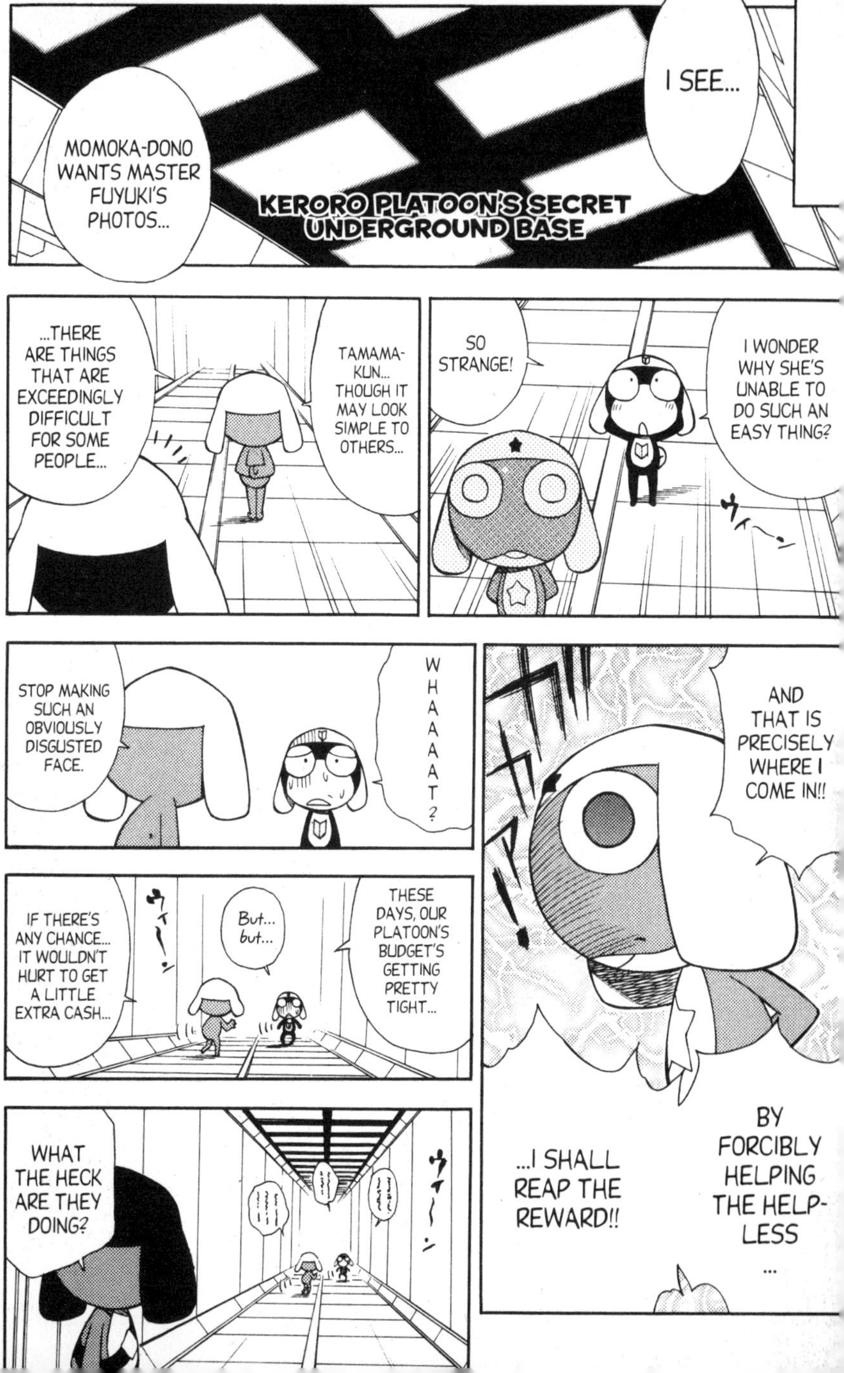
I SEE...
MOMOKA-DONO WANTS MASTER FUYUKI'S PHOTOS...
KERORO PLATOON'S SECRET UNDERGROUND BASE
I WONDER WHY SHE'S UNABLE TO DO SUCH AN EASY THING?
SO STRANGE!
ウィ～ン
TAMAMA-KUN... THOUGH IT MAY LOOK SIMPLE TO OTHERS...
...THERE ARE THINGS THAT ARE EXCEEDINGLY DIFFICULT FOR SOME PEOPLE...
AND THAT IS PRECISELY WHERE I COME IN!!
BY FORCIBLY HELPING THE HELP-LESS ...
...I SHALL REAP THE REWARD!!
WHAAAAAT?
STOP MAKING SUCH AN OBVIOUSLY DISGUSTED FACE.
THESE DAYS, OUR PLATOON'S BUDGET'S GETTING PRETTY TIGHT...
But... but...
IF THERE'S ANY CHANCE... IT WOULDN'T HURT TO GET A LITTLE EXTRA CASH...
ウィ～ン
ウィ～ン
WHAT THE HECK ARE THEY DOING?

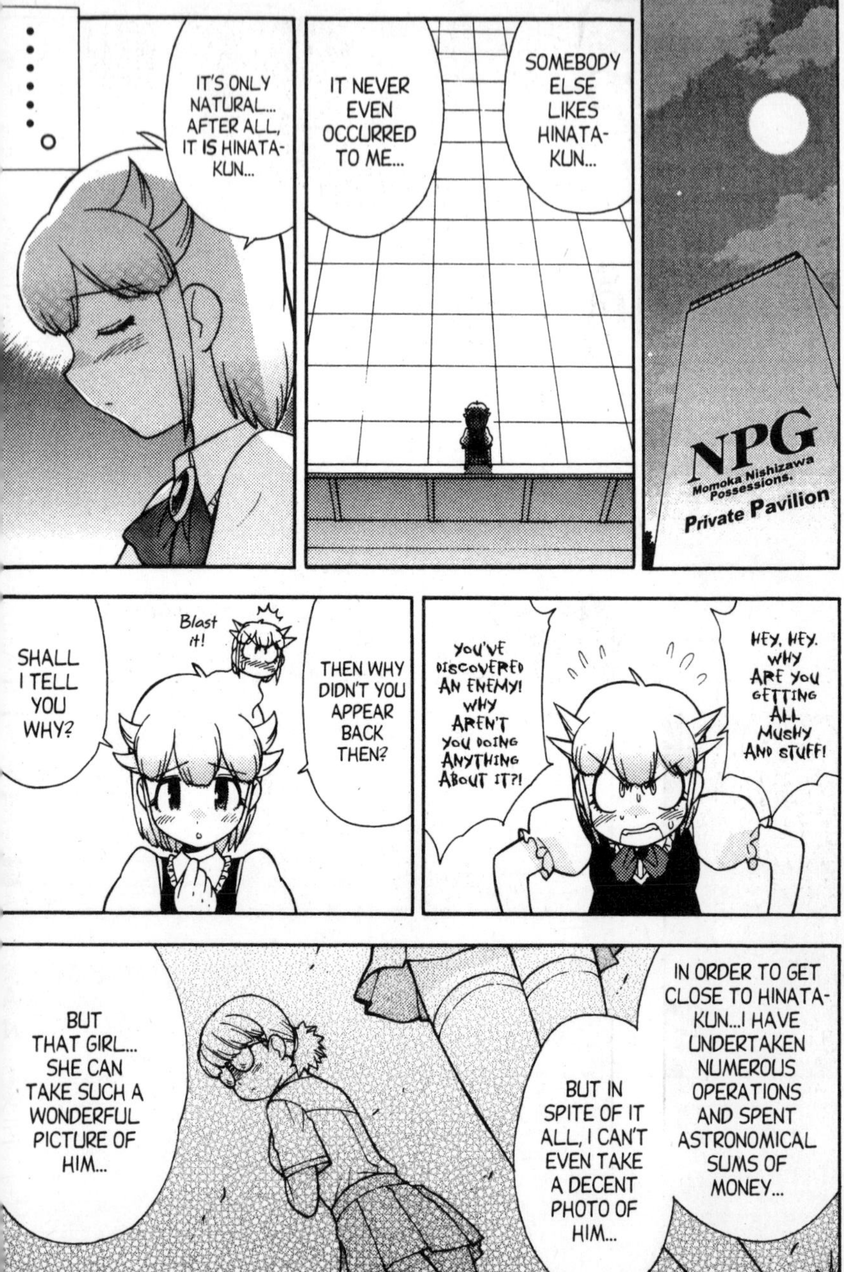
NPG
Momoka Nishizawa Possessions.
Private Pavilion
SOMEBODY ELSE LIKES HINATA-KUN...
IT NEVER EVEN OCCURRED TO ME...
IT'S ONLY NATURAL... AFTER ALL, IT IS HINATA-KUN...
......o
HEY, HEY. WHY ARE YOU GETTING ALL MUSHY AND STUFF!
YOU'VE DISCOVERED AN ENEMY! WHY AREN'T YOU DOING ANYTHING ABOUT IT?!
THEN WHY DIDN'T YOU APPEAR BACK THEN?
Blast it!
SHALL I TELL YOU WHY?
IN ORDER TO GET CLOSE TO HINATA-KUN...I HAVE UNDERTAKEN NUMEROUS OPERATIONS AND SPENT ASTRONOMICAL SUMS OF MONEY...
BUT IN SPITE OF IT ALL, I CAN'T EVEN TAKE A DECENT PHOTO OF HIM...
BUT THAT GIRL... SHE CAN TAKE SUCH A WONDERFUL PICTURE OF HIM...

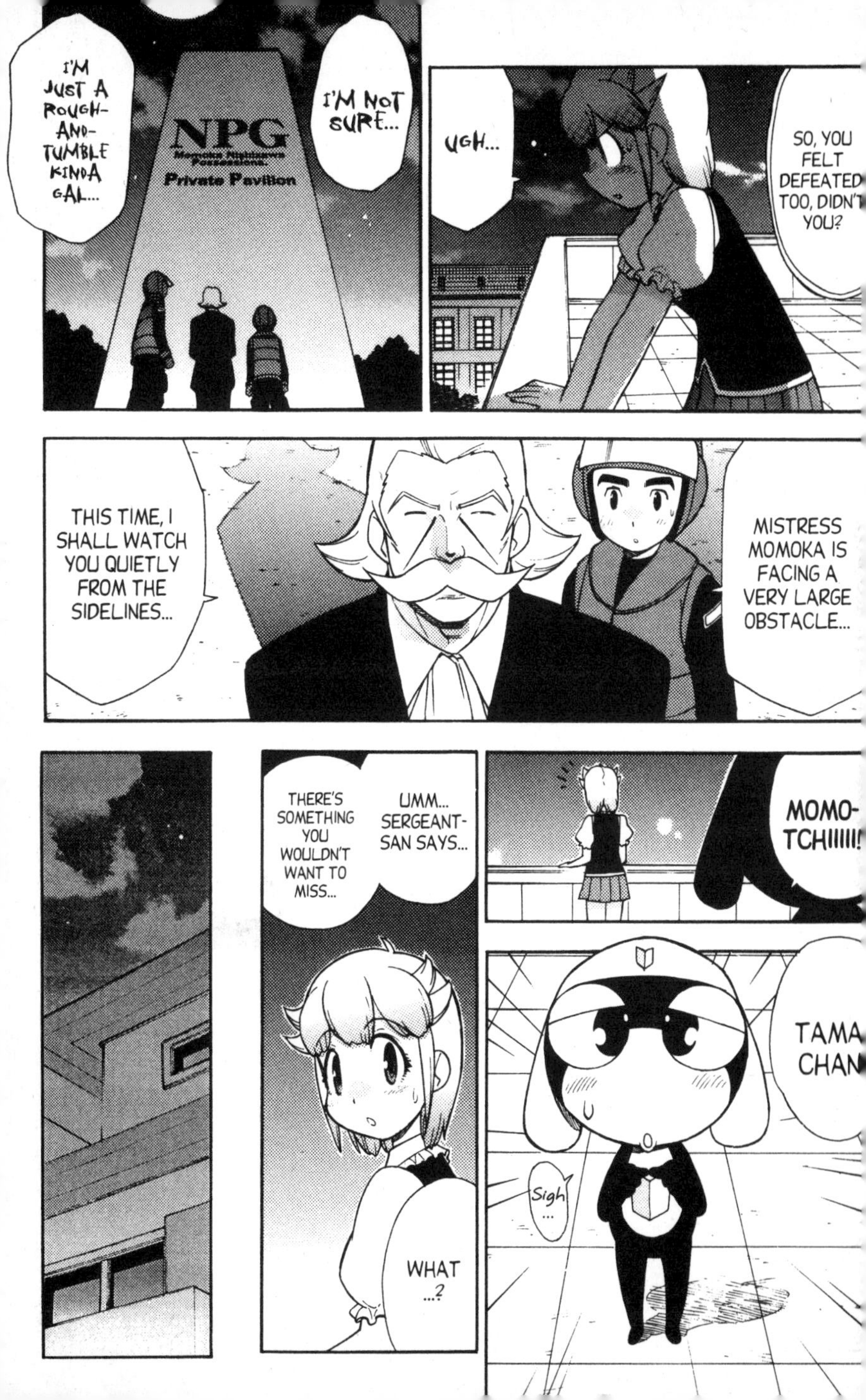
SO, YOU FELT DEFEATED TOO, DIDN'T YOU?
UGH...
NPG
Momoka Nishizawa Possessions.
Private Pavilion
I'M NOT SURE...
I'M JUST A ROUGH-AND-TUMBLE KINDA GAL...
MISTRESS MOMOKA IS FACING A VERY LARGE OBSTACLE...
THIS TIME, I SHALL WATCH YOU QUIETLY FROM THE SIDELINES...
MOMO-TCHIIIII!
TAMA CHAN
Sigh ...
UMM... SERGEANT-SAN SAYS...
THERE'S SOMETHING YOU WOULDN'T WANT TO MISS...
WHAT ...?

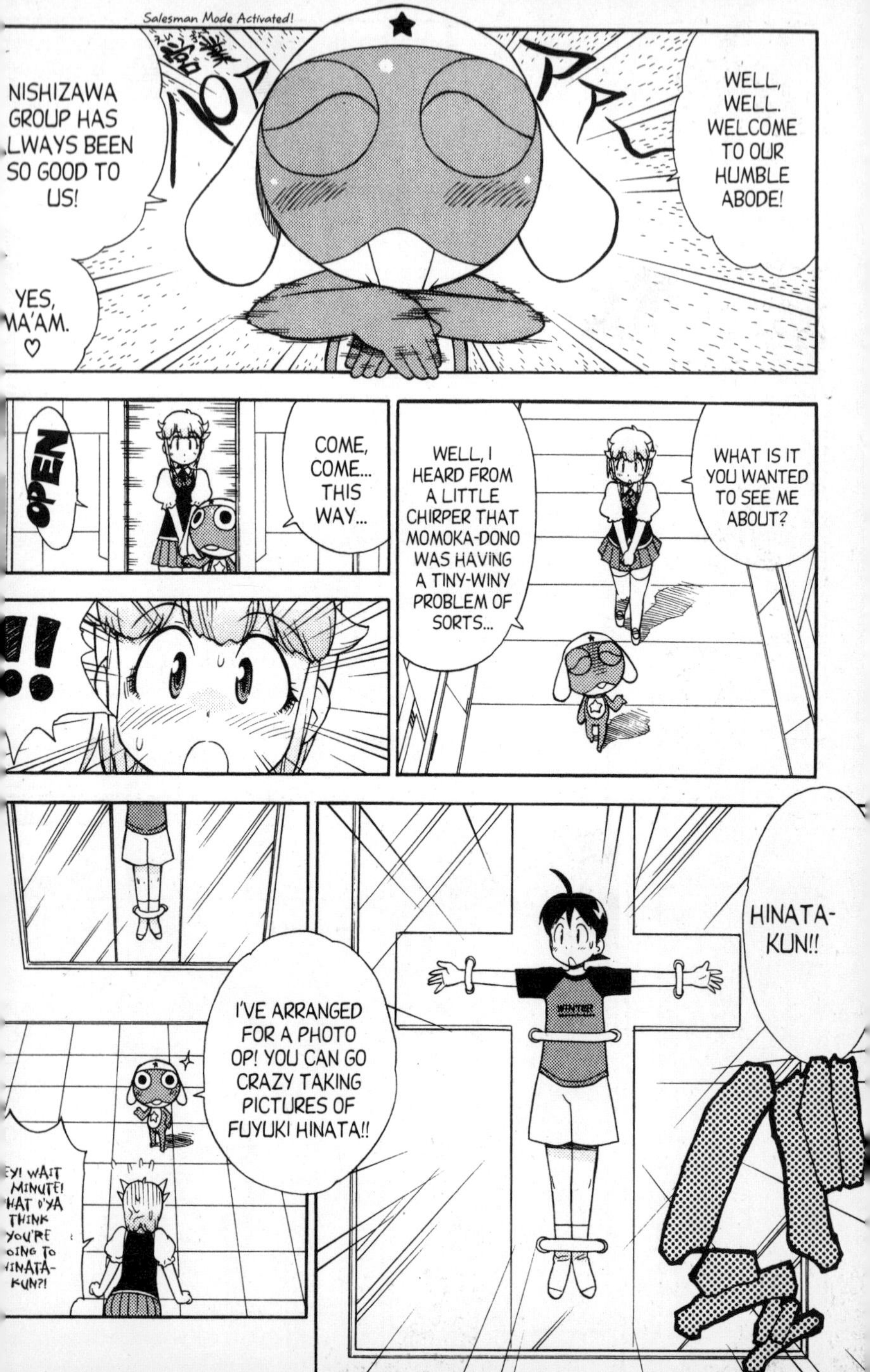
Salesman Mode Activated!
営業
PA
PA
WELL, WELL. WELCOME TO OUR HUMBLE ABODE!
NISHIZAWA GROUP HAS LWAYS BEEN SO GOOD TO US!
YES, MA'AM. ♡
WHAT IS IT YOU WANTED TO SEE ME ABOUT?
WELL, I HEARD FROM A LITTLE CHIRPER THAT MOMOKA-DONO WAS HAVING A TINY-WINY PROBLEM OF SORTS...
COME, COME... THIS WAY...
OPEN
!!
HINATA-KUN!!
WINTER
I'VE ARRANGED FOR A PHOTO OP! YOU CAN GO CRAZY TAKING PICTURES OF FUYUKI HINATA!!
EY! WAIT MINUTE! HAT D'YA THINK YOU'RE OING TO INATA-KUN?!

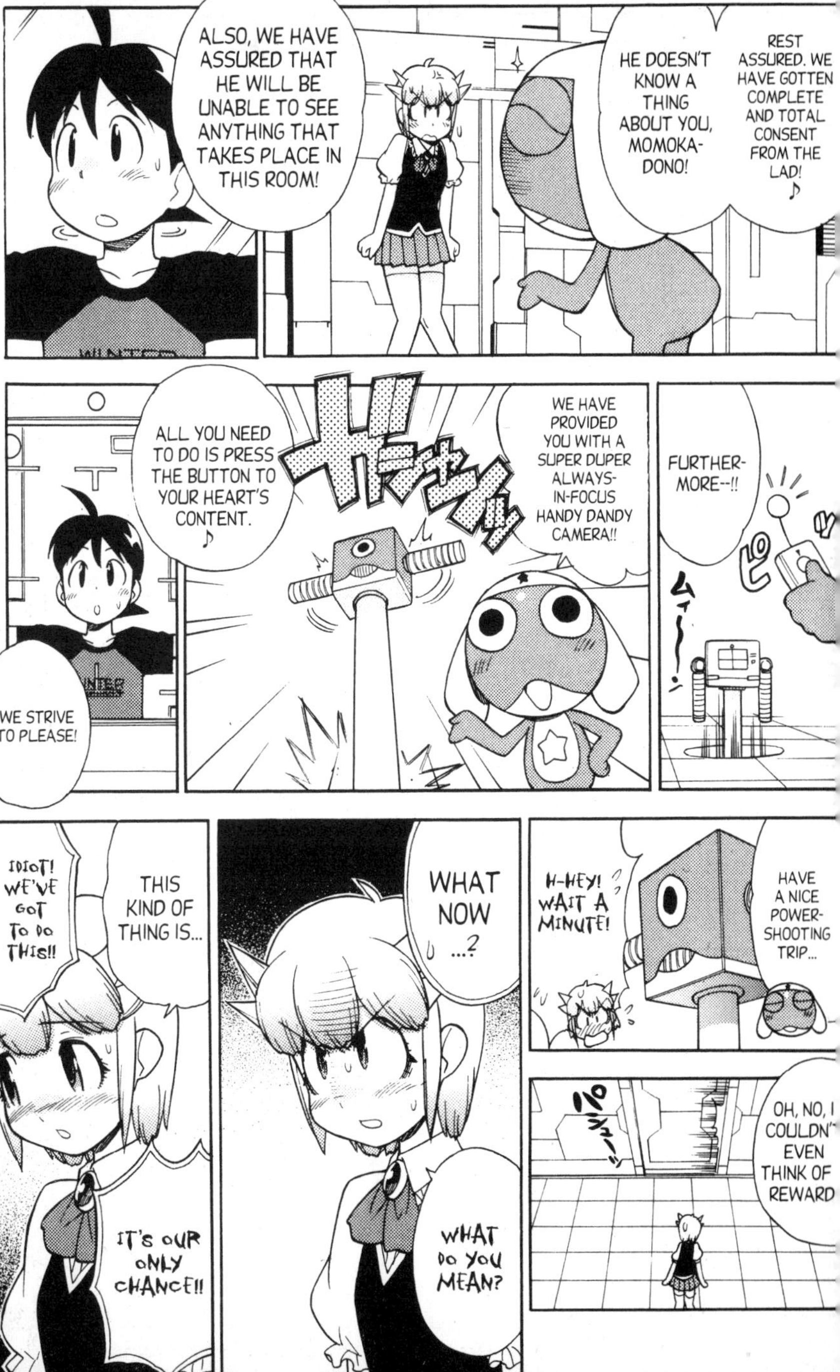
REST ASSURED. WE HAVE GOTTEN COMPLETE AND TOTAL CONSENT FROM THE LAD! ♪
HE DOESN'T KNOW A THING ABOUT YOU, MOMOKA-DONO!
ALSO, WE HAVE ASSURED THAT HE WILL BE UNABLE TO SEE ANYTHING THAT TAKES PLACE IN THIS ROOM!
FURTHER-MORE--!!
WE HAVE PROVIDED YOU WITH A SUPER DUPER ALWAYS-IN-FOCUS HANDY DANDY CAMERA!!
ALL YOU NEED TO DO IS PRESS THE BUTTON TO YOUR HEART'S CONTENT. ♪
WE STRIVE TO PLEASE!
HAVE A NICE POWER-SHOOTING TRIP...
H-HEY! WAIT A MINUTE!
OH, NO, I COULDN'T EVEN THINK OF REWARD
WHAT NOW ...?
WHAT DO YOU MEAN?
THIS KIND OF THING IS...
IDIOT! WE'VE GOT TO DO THIS!!
IT'S OUR ONLY CHANCE!!

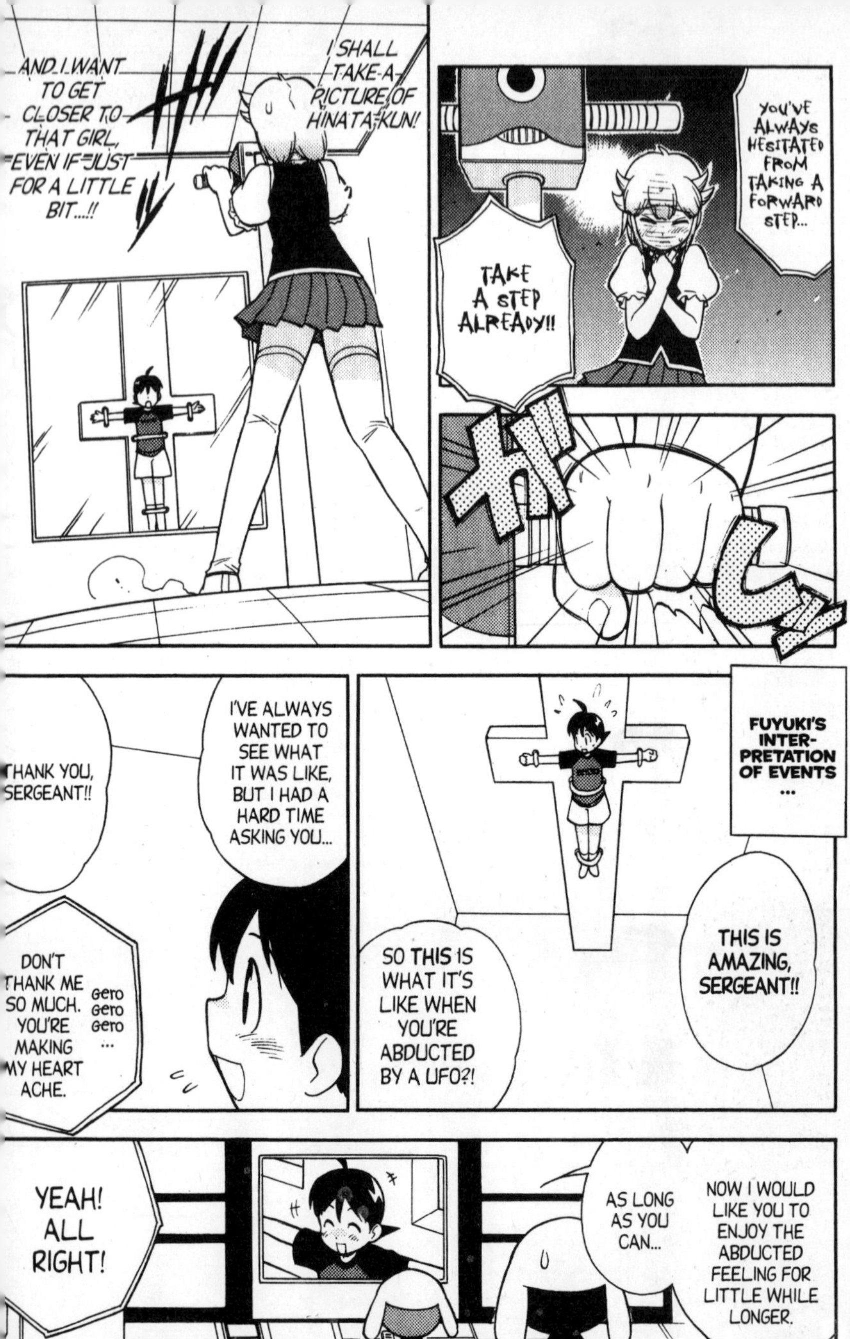
YOU'VE ALWAYS HESITATED FROM TAKING A FORWARD STEP...
TAKE A STEP ALREADY!!
I SHALL TAKE A PICTURE OF HINATA-KUN!
AND I WANT TO GET CLOSER TO THAT GIRL, EVEN IF JUST FOR A LITTLE BIT...!!
FUYUKI'S INTER-PRETATION OF EVENTS ...
THIS IS AMAZING, SERGEANT!!
SO THIS IS WHAT IT'S LIKE WHEN YOU'RE ABDUCTED BY A UFO?!
I'VE ALWAYS WANTED TO SEE WHAT IT WAS LIKE, BUT I HAD A HARD TIME ASKING YOU...
THANK YOU, SERGEANT!!
DON'T THANK ME SO MUCH. YOU'RE MAKING MY HEART ACHE.
gero gero gero ...
NOW I WOULD LIKE YOU TO ENJOY THE ABDUCTED FEELING FOR LITTLE WHILE LONGER.
AS LONG AS YOU CAN...
YEAH! ALL RIGHT!

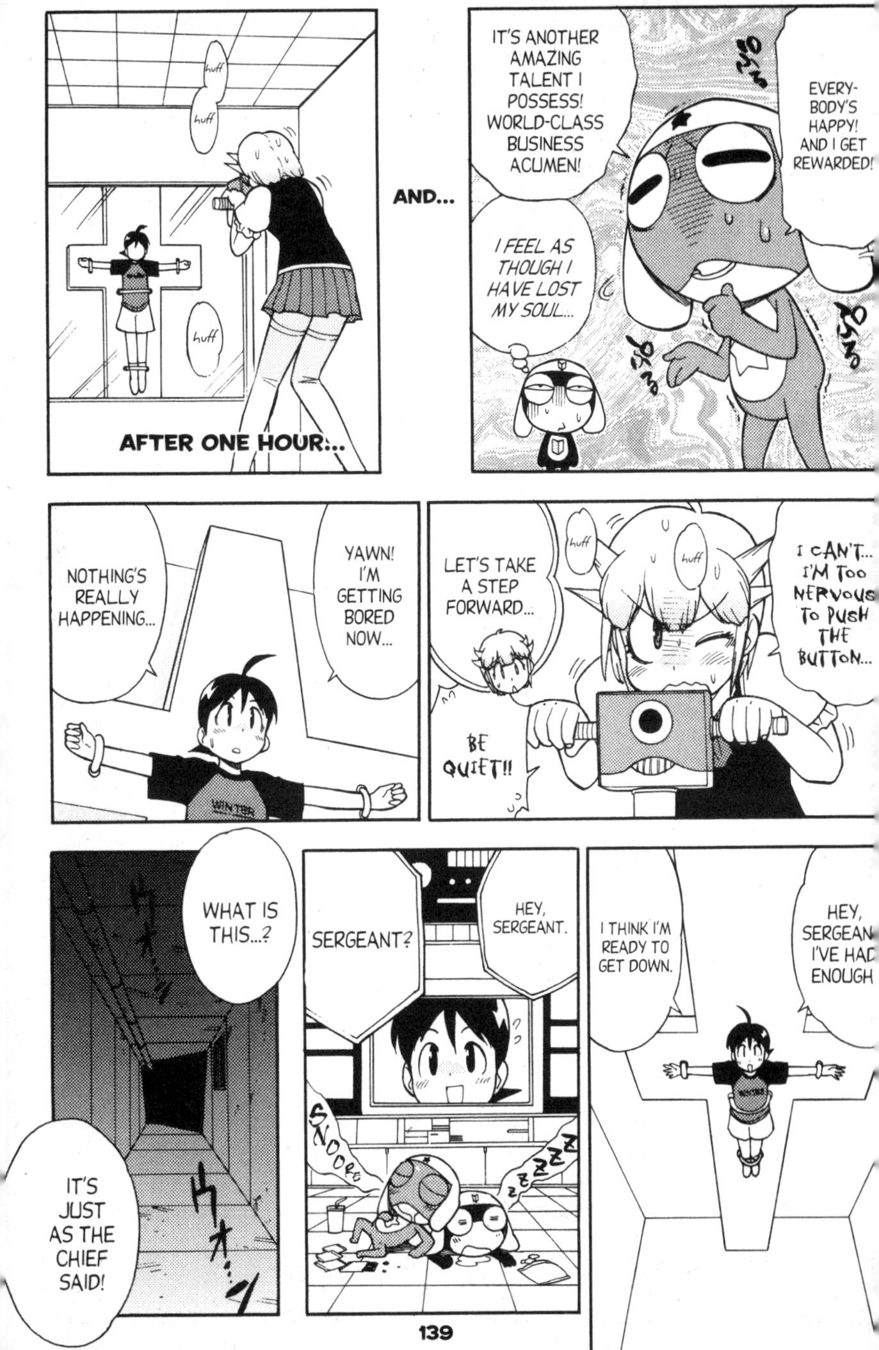

EVERYBODY'S HAPPY! AND I GET REWARDED!
IT'S ANOTHER AMAZING TALENT I POSSESS! WORLD-CLASS BUSINESS ACUMEN!
I FEEL AS THOUGH I HAVE LOST MY SOUL...
AND...
huff
huff
huff
AFTER ONE HOUR:..
I CAN'T... I'M TOO NERVOUS TO PUSH THE BUTTON...
huff
huff
LET'S TAKE A STEP FORWARD...
BE QUIET!!
YAWN! I'M GETTING BORED NOW...
NOTHING'S REALLY HAPPENING...
HEY, SERGEAN I'VE HAD ENOUGH
I THINK I'M READY TO GET DOWN.
HEY, SERGEANT.
SERGEANT?
ZZZZ
SNOORE
WHAT IS THIS...?
IT'S JUST AS THE CHIEF SAID!

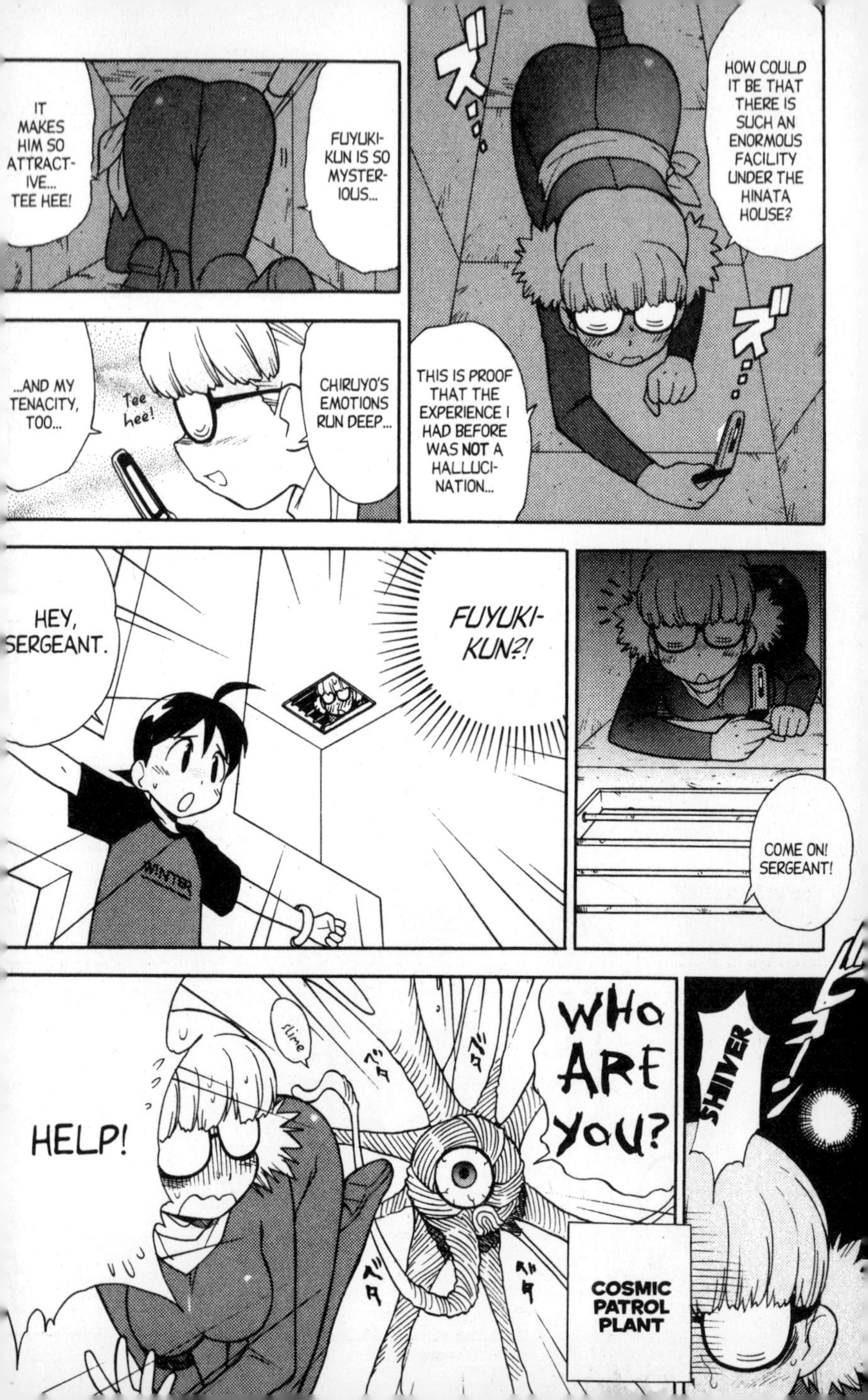
ズ…
HOW COULD IT BE THAT THERE IS SUCH AN ENORMOUS FACILITY UNDER THE HINATA HOUSE?
ズ…
THIS IS PROOF THAT THE EXPERIENCE I HAD BEFORE WAS NOT A HALLUCINATION...
FUYUKI-KUN IS SO MYSTERIOUS...
IT MAKES HIM SO ATTRACTIVE... TEE HEE!
CHIRUYO'S EMOTIONS RUN DEEP...
Tee hee!
...AND MY TENACITY, TOO...
COME ON! SERGEANT!
FUYUKI-KUN?!
HEY, SERGEANT.
SHIVER
WHO ARE YOU?
COSMIC PATROL PLANT
slime
HELP!

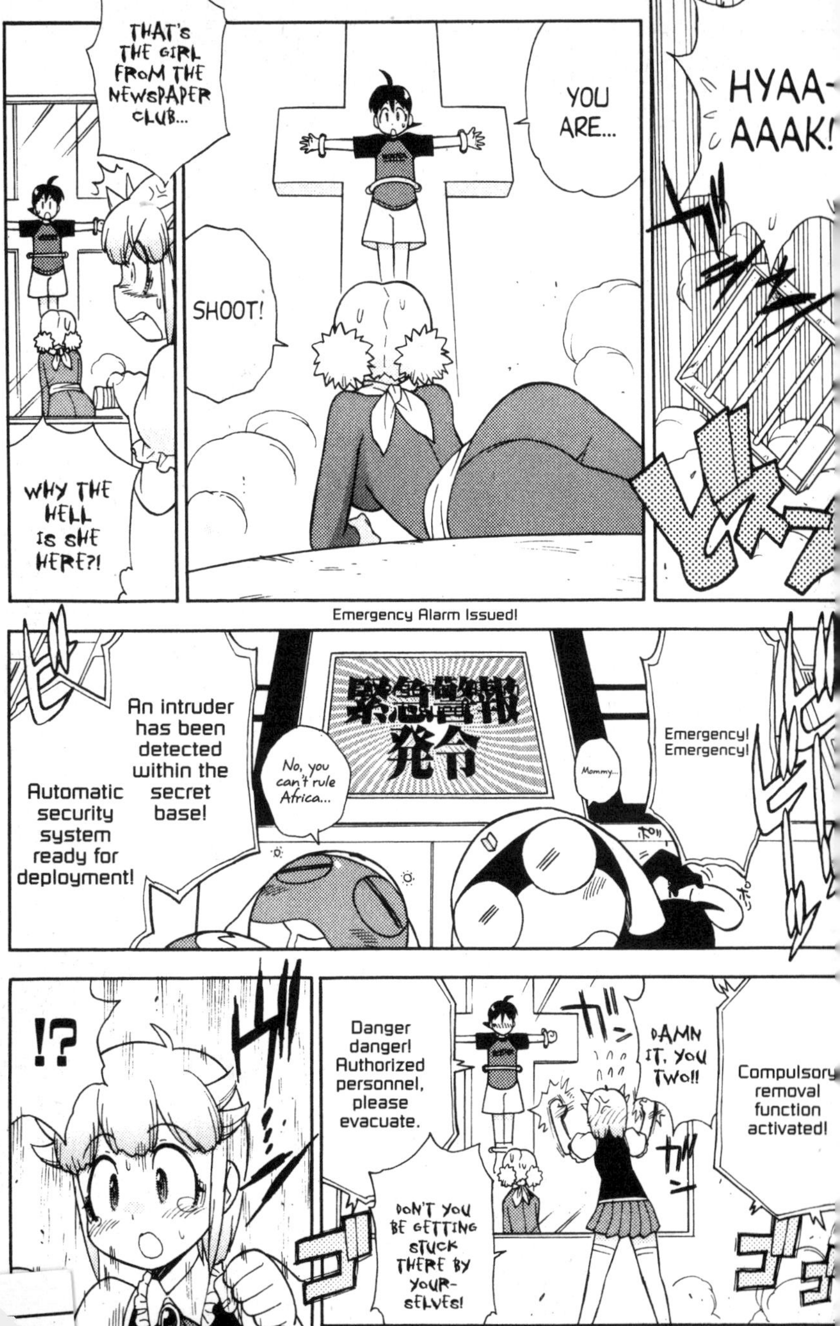
HYAA-AAAK!
YOU ARE...
SHOOT!
THAT's THE GIRL FROM THE NEWSPAPER CLUB...
WHY THE HELL IS SHE HERE?!
Emergency Alarm Issued!
緊急警報発令
Emergency! Emergency!
Mommy...
No, you can't rule Africa...
An intruder has been detected within the secret base!
Automatic security system ready for deployment!
Compulsory removal function activated!
DAMN IT, YOU TWO!!
Danger danger! Authorized personnel, please evacuate.
DON'T YOU BE GETTING STUCK THERE BY YOURSELVES!
!?

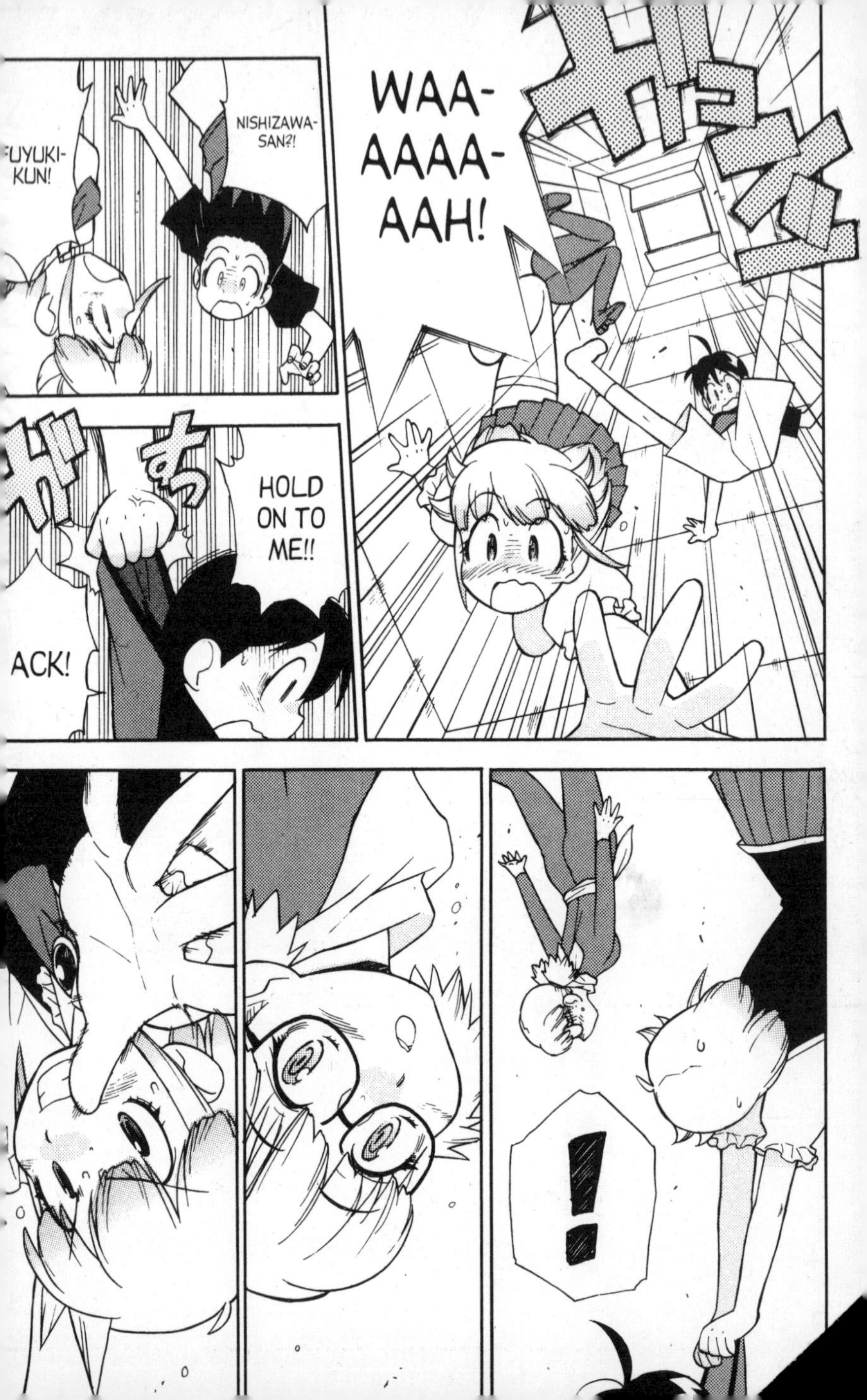
WAA-AAAA-AAH!
NISHIZAWA-SAN?!
FUYUKI-KUN!
HOLD ON TO ME!!
ACK!
!

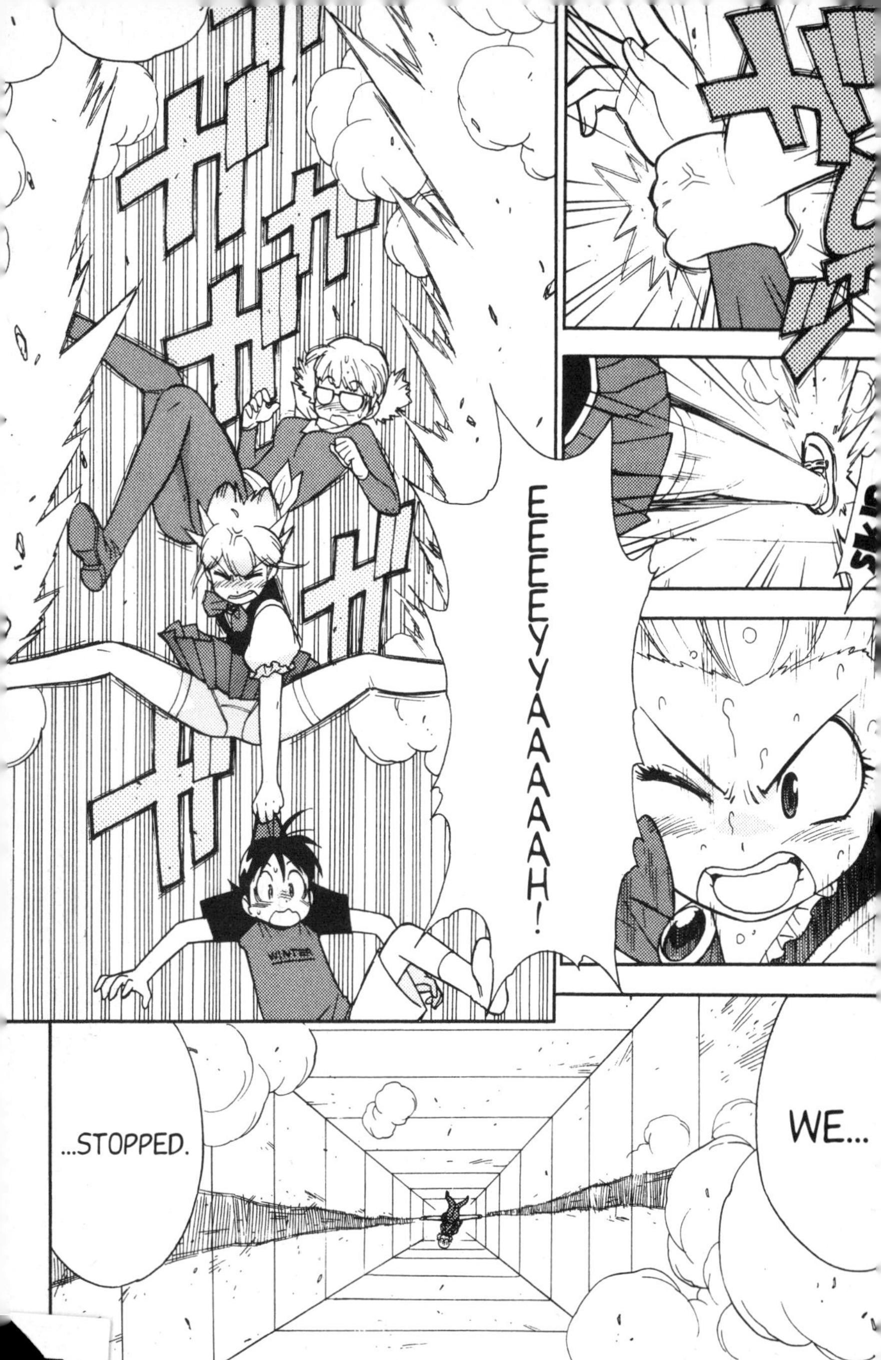
EEEEYYAAAAAH!
WE...
...STOPPED.

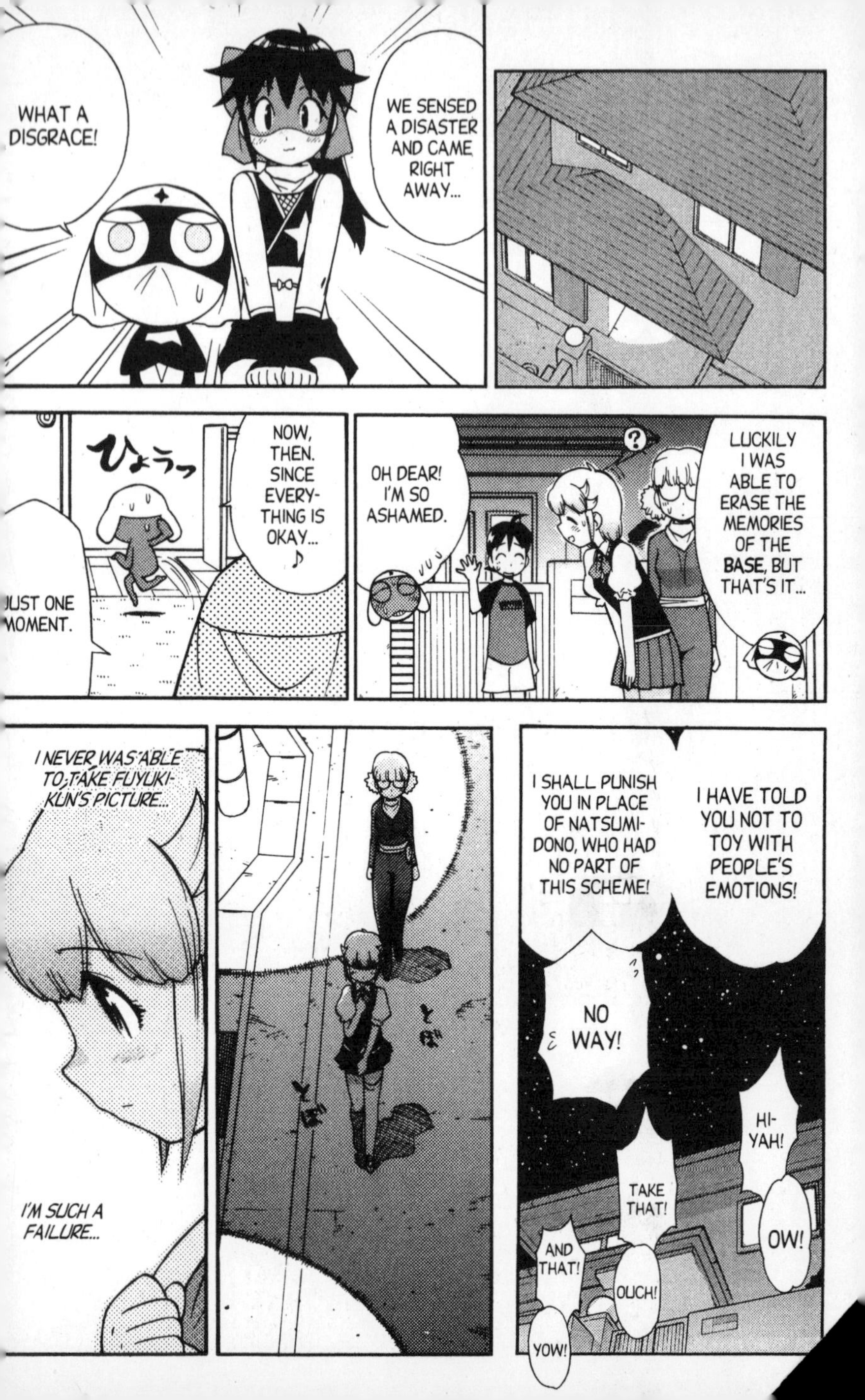
WE SENSED A DISASTER AND CAME RIGHT AWAY...
WHAT A DISGRACE!
LUCKILY I WAS ABLE TO ERASE THE MEMORIES OF THE BASE, BUT THAT'S IT...
OH DEAR! I'M SO ASHAMED.
NOW, THEN. SINCE EVERYTHING IS OKAY... ♪
JUST ONE MOMENT.
I HAVE TOLD YOU NOT TO TOY WITH PEOPLE'S EMOTIONS!
I SHALL PUNISH YOU IN PLACE OF NATSUMI-DONO, WHO HAD NO PART OF THIS SCHEME!
NO WAY!
HI-YAH!
OW!
TAKE THAT!
AND THAT!
OUCH!
YOW!
とぼ
とぼ
I NEVER WAS ABLE TO TAKE FUYUKI-KUN'S PICTURE...
I'M SUCH A FAILURE...

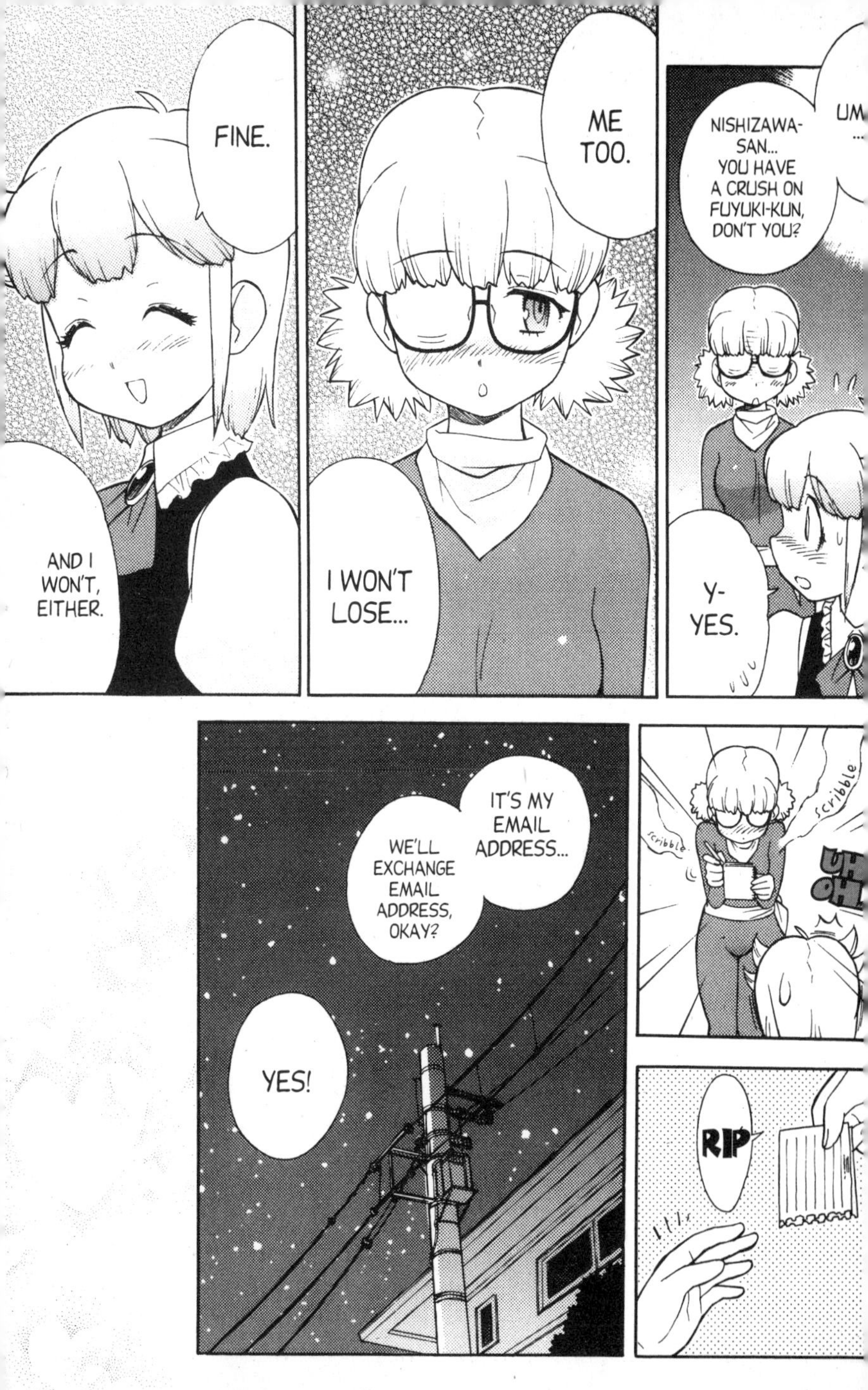
UM...
NISHIZAWA-SAN... YOU HAVE A CRUSH ON FUYUKI-KUN, DON'T YOU?
Y-YES.
ME TOO.
I WON'T LOSE...
FINE.
AND I WON'T, EITHER.
scribble
scribble
UH OH
RIP
IT'S MY EMAIL ADDRESS...
WE'LL EXCHANGE EMAIL ADDRESS, OKAY?
YES!

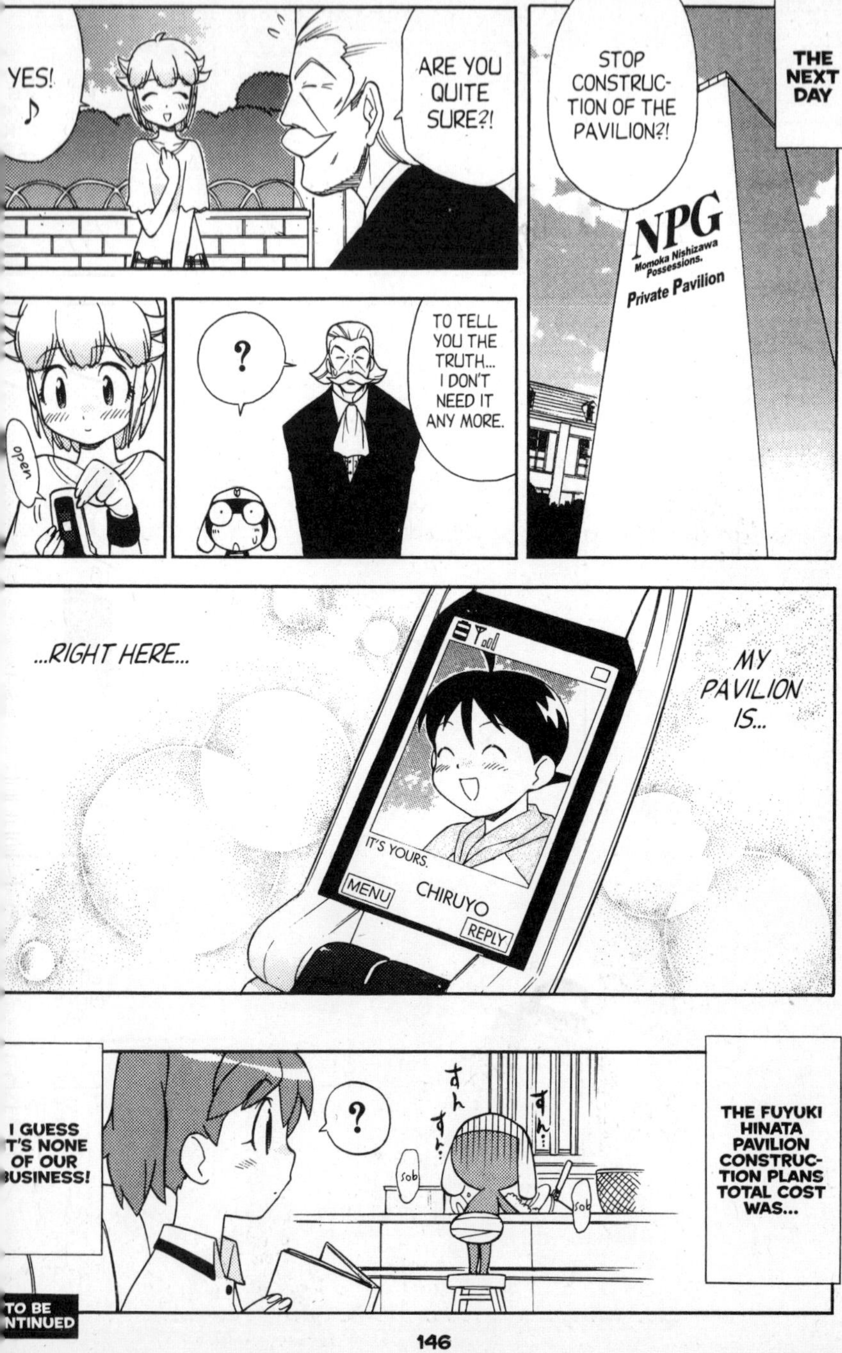
THE NEXT DAY
STOP CONSTRUC-TION OF THE PAVILION?!
NPG Momoka Nishizawa Possessions. Private Pavilion
ARE YOU QUITE SURE?!
YES! ♪
TO TELL YOU THE TRUTH... I DON'T NEED IT ANY MORE.
?
open
MY PAVILION IS...
...RIGHT HERE...
IT'S YOURS.
CHIRUYO
MENU
REPLY
THE FUYUKI HINATA PAVILION CONSTRUC-TION PLANS TOTAL COST WAS...
すん...
すん
すん
すん...
sob
sob
?
I GUESS T'S NONE OF OUR USINESS!
TO BE NTINUED

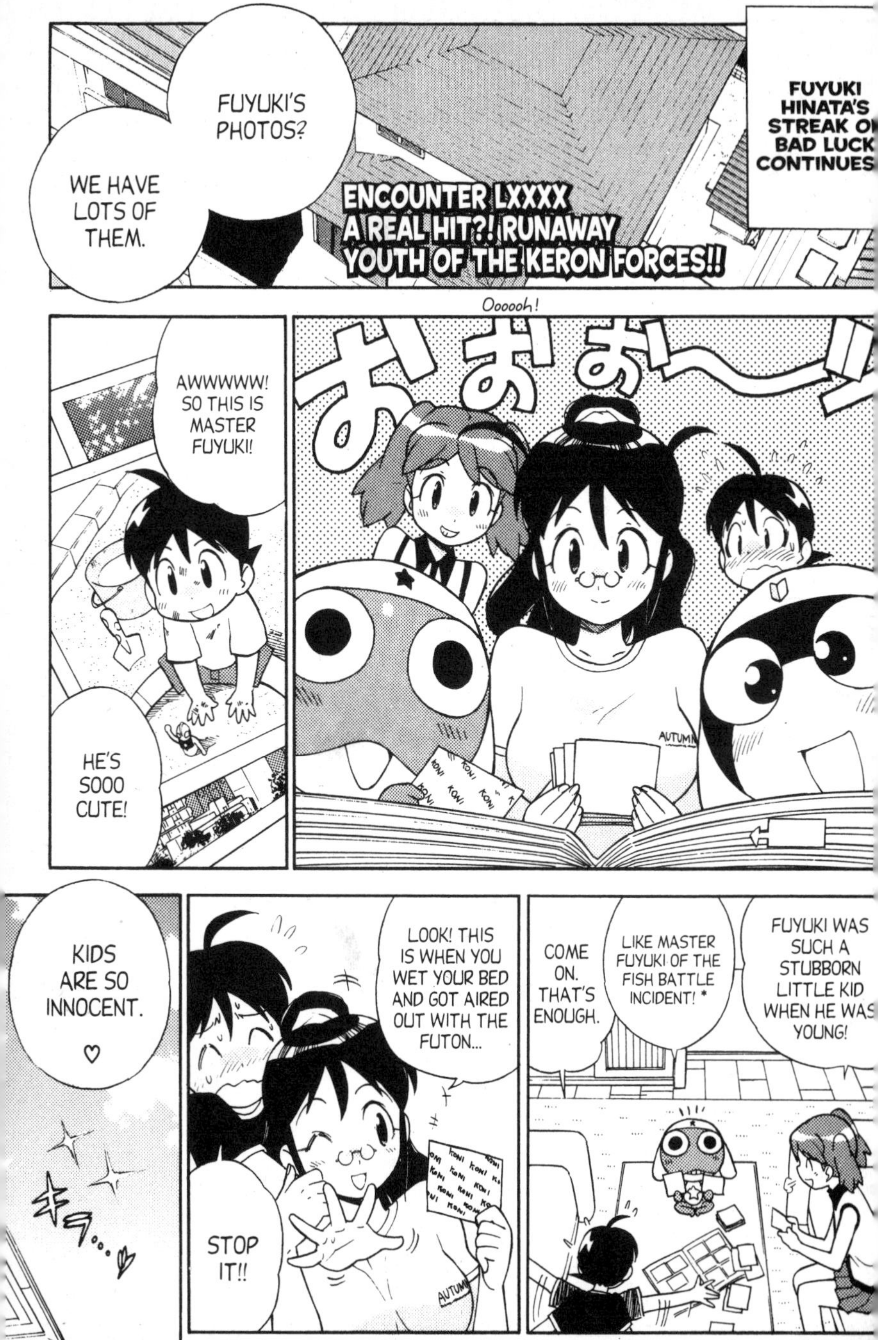

FUYUKI HINATA'S STREAK O BAD LUCK CONTINUES
ENCOUNTER LXXXX A REAL HIT?! RUNAWAY YOUTH OF THE KERON FORCES!!
FUYUKI'S PHOTOS?
WE HAVE LOTS OF THEM.
Oooooh!
AWWWWW! SO THIS IS MASTER FUYUKI!
HE'S SOOO CUTE!
FUYUKI WAS SUCH A STUBBORN LITTLE KID WHEN HE WAS YOUNG!
LIKE MASTER FUYUKI OF THE FISH BATTLE INCIDENT! *
COME ON. THAT'S ENOUGH.
LOOK! THIS IS WHEN YOU WET YOUR BED AND GOT AIRED OUT WITH THE FUTON...
STOP IT!!
KIDS ARE SO INNOCENT. ♡

* Please see Volume 9, Encounter LXXI

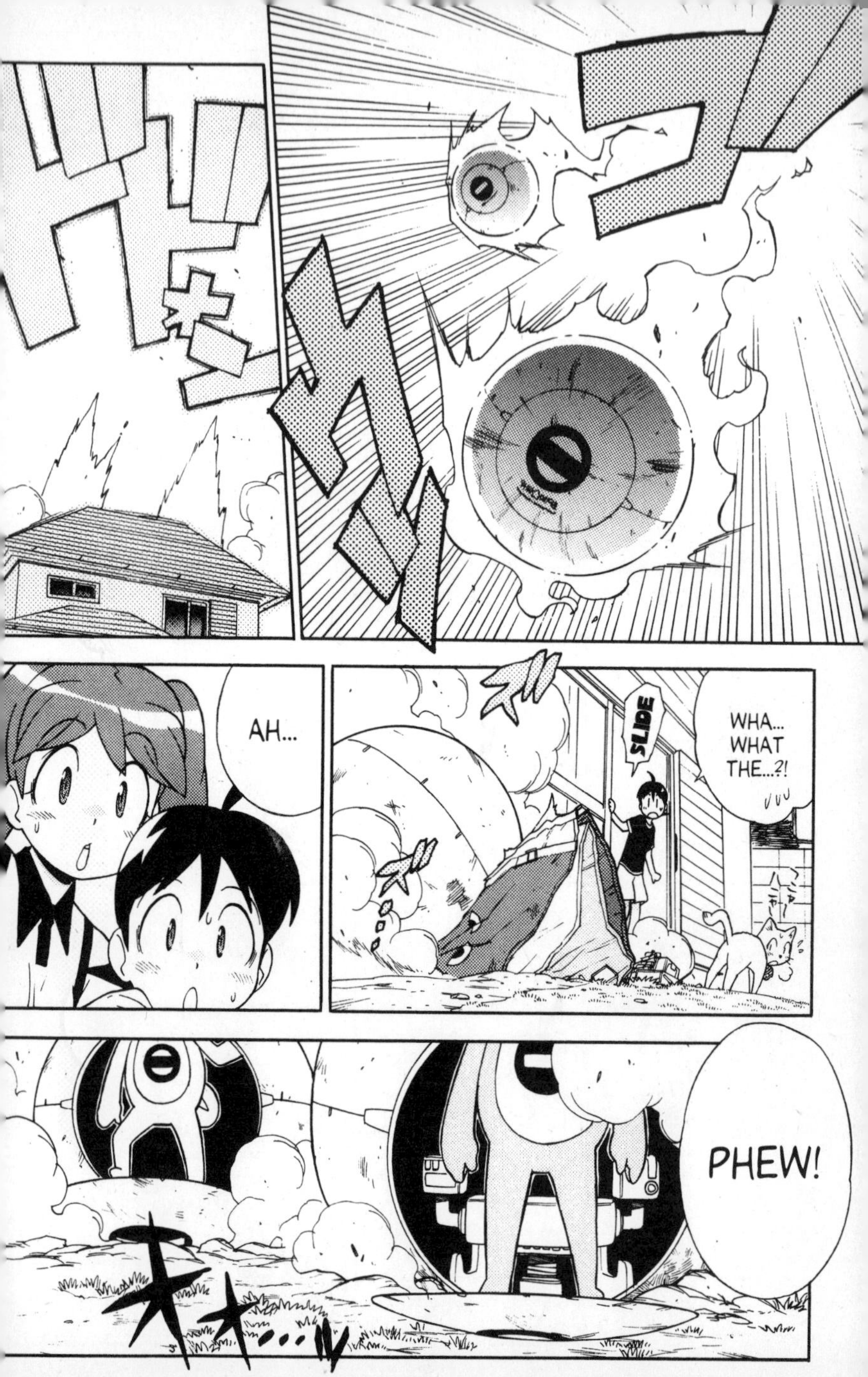
SLIDE
WHA... WHAT THE...?!
AH...
PHEW!

ENCOUNTER LXXXX
A REAL HIT?! RUNAWAY YOUTH OF THE KERON FORCES!!

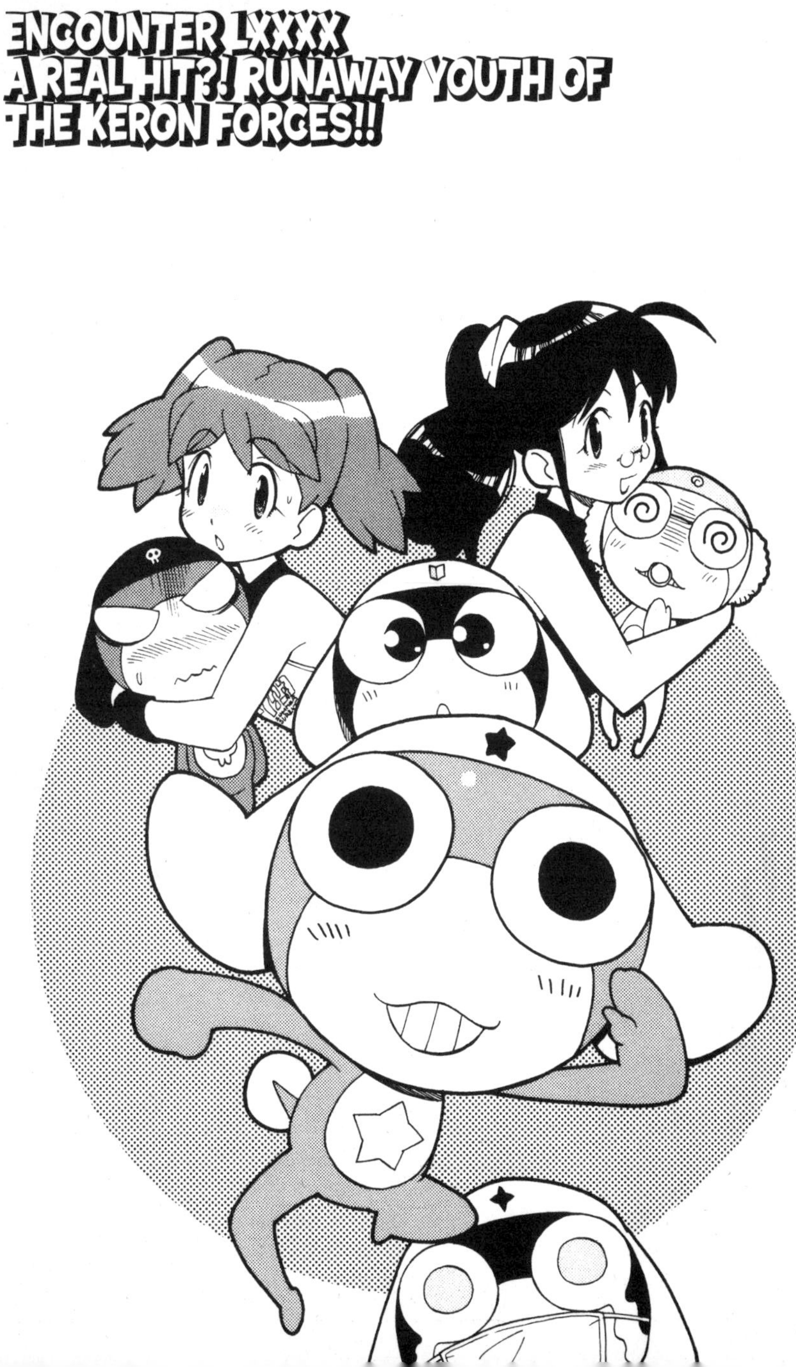

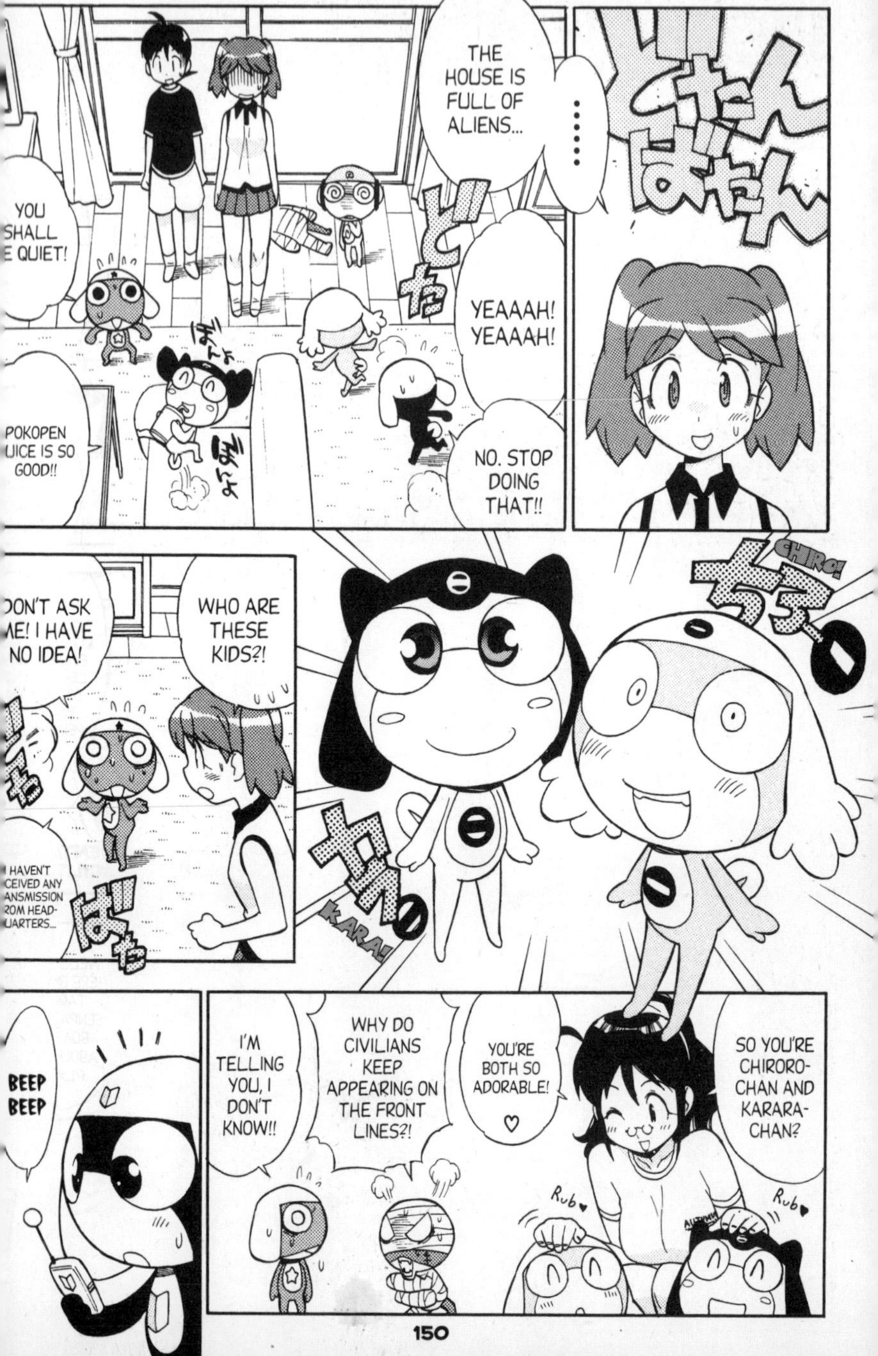
THE HOUSE IS FULL OF ALIENS...
......
YEAAAH! YEAAAH!
NO. STOP DOING THAT!!
YOU SHALL E QUIET!
POKOPEN UICE IS SO GOOD!!
CHIRO!
KARA!
WHO ARE THESE KIDS?!
DON'T ASK ΛE! I HAVE NO IDEA!
I HAVEN'T CEIVED ANY ANSMISSION ROM HEAD-UARTERS...
SO YOU'RE CHIRORO-CHAN AND KARARA-CHAN?
YOU'RE BOTH SO ADORABLE! ♡
WHY DO CIVILIANS KEEP APPEARING ON THE FRONT LINES?!
I'M TELLING YOU, I DON'T KNOW!!
Rub♥
Rub♥
BEEP BEEP

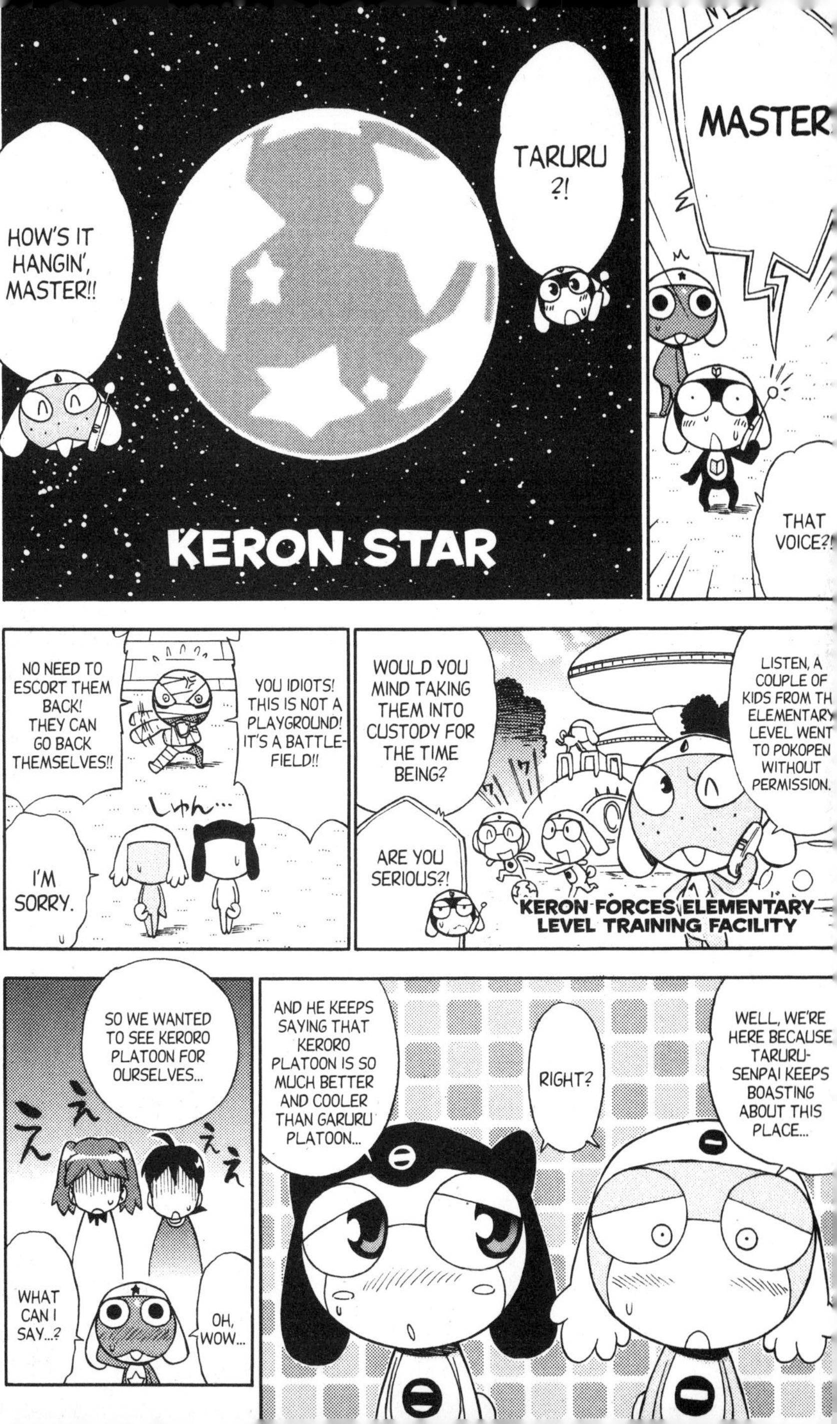
MASTER
THAT VOICE?!
TARURU ?!
HOW'S IT HANGIN', MASTER!!
KERON STAR
LISTEN, A COUPLE OF KIDS FROM TH ELEMENTARY LEVEL WENT TO POKOPEN WITHOUT PERMISSION.
WOULD YOU MIND TAKING THEM INTO CUSTODY FOR THE TIME BEING?
ARE YOU SERIOUS?!
KERON FORCES ELEMENTARY LEVEL TRAINING FACILITY
YOU IDIOTS! THIS IS NOT A PLAYGROUND! IT'S A BATTLE-FIELD!!
NO NEED TO ESCORT THEM BACK! THEY CAN GO BACK THEMSELVES!!
しゅん…
I'M SORRY.
WELL, WE'RE HERE BECAUSE TARURU-SENPAI KEEPS BOASTING ABOUT THIS PLACE...
RIGHT?
AND HE KEEPS SAYING THAT KERORO PLATOON IS SO MUCH BETTER AND COOLER THAN GARURU PLATOON...
SO WE WANTED TO SEE KERORO PLATOON FOR OURSELVES...
ええ
ええ
OH, WOW...
WHAT CAN I SAY...?

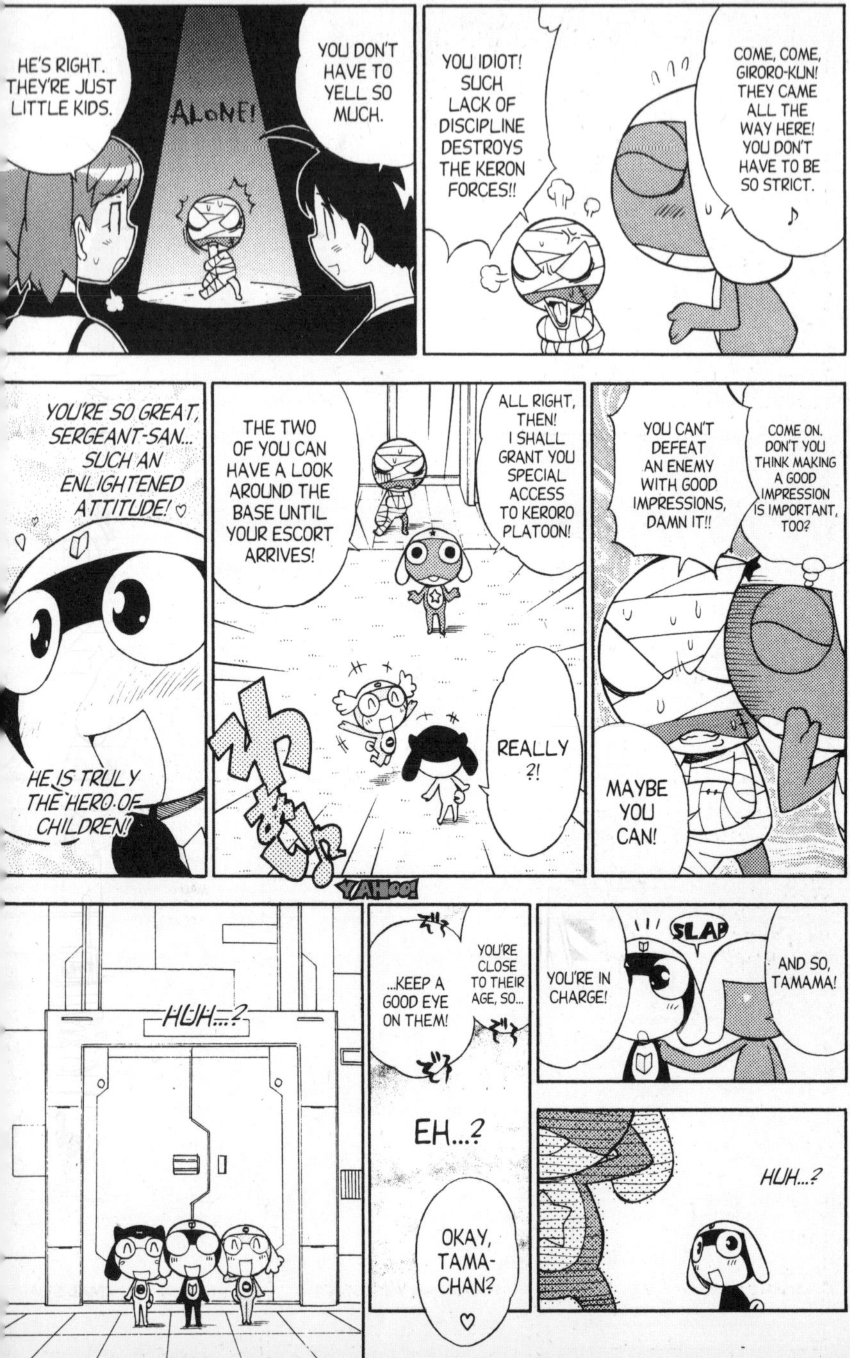
COME, COME, GIRORO-KUN! THEY CAME ALL THE WAY HERE! YOU DON'T HAVE TO BE SO STRICT. ♪
YOU IDIOT! SUCH LACK OF DISCIPLINE DESTROYS THE KERON FORCES!!
YOU DON'T HAVE TO YELL SO MUCH.
ALONE!
HE'S RIGHT. THEY'RE JUST LITTLE KIDS.
COME ON. DON'T YOU THINK MAKING A GOOD IMPRESSION IS IMPORTANT, TOO?
YOU CAN'T DEFEAT AN ENEMY WITH GOOD IMPRESSIONS, DAMN IT!!
MAYBE YOU CAN!
ALL RIGHT, THEN! I SHALL GRANT YOU SPECIAL ACCESS TO KERORO PLATOON!
THE TWO OF YOU CAN HAVE A LOOK AROUND THE BASE UNTIL YOUR ESCORT ARRIVES!
REALLY ?!
YAHOO!
YOU'RE SO GREAT, SERGEANT-SAN... SUCH AN ENLIGHTENED ATTITUDE! ♡
HE IS TRULY THE HERO OF CHILDREN!
AND SO, TAMAMA!
SLAP
YOU'RE IN CHARGE!
HUH...?
YOU'RE CLOSE TO THEIR AGE, SO...
...KEEP A GOOD EYE ON THEM!
EH...?
OKAY, TAMA-CHAN? ♡
HUH...?

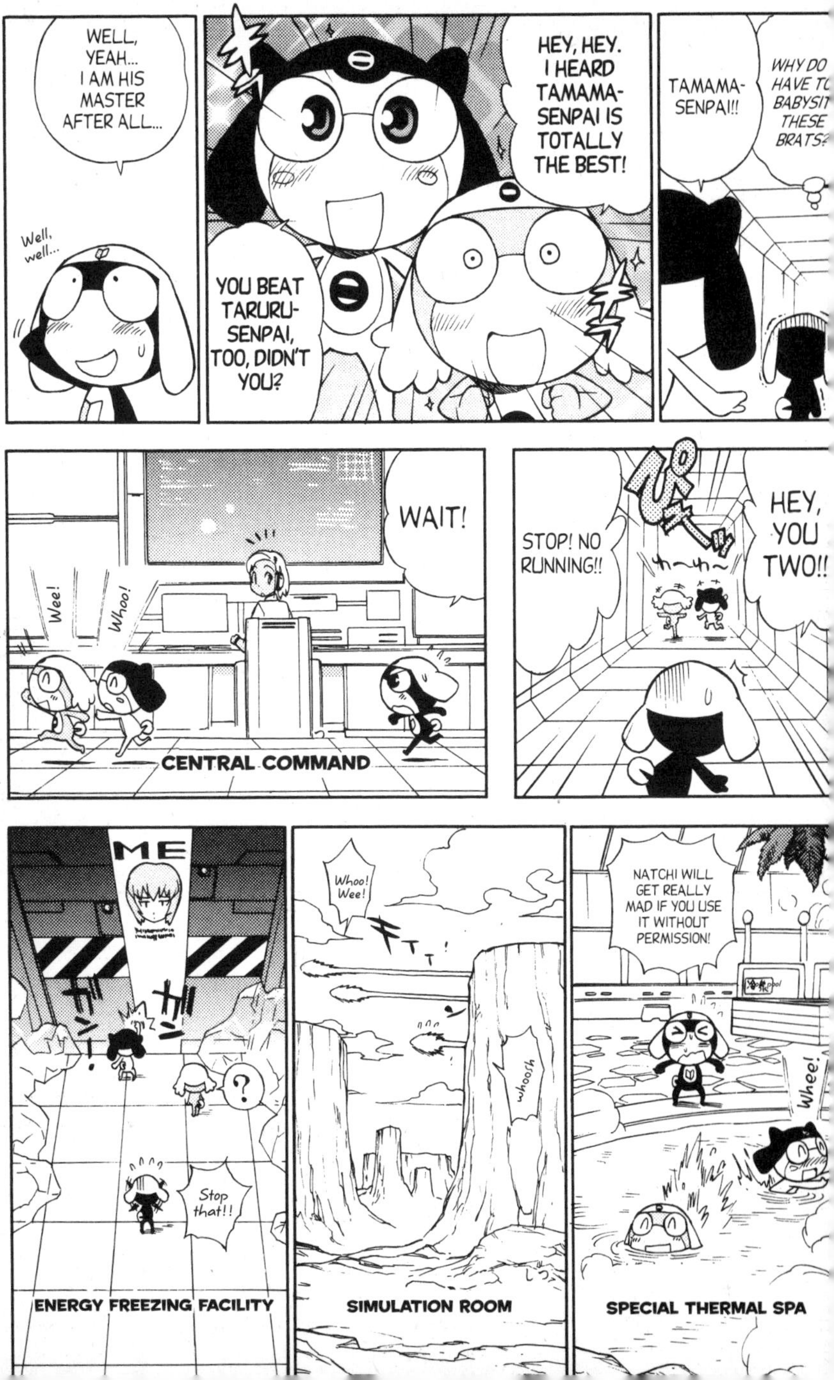
TAMAMA-SENPAI!!
WHY DO
HAVE T
BABYSIT
THESE
BRATS?
HEY, HEY. I HEARD TAMAMA-SENPAI IS TOTALLY THE BEST!
YOU BEAT TARURU-SENPAI, TOO, DIDN'T YOU?
WELL, YEAH... I AM HIS MASTER AFTER ALL...
Well, well...
HEY, YOU TWO!!
STOP! NO RUNNING!!
WAIT!
Wee!
Whoo!
CENTRAL COMMAND
NATCHI WILL GET REALLY MAD IF YOU USE IT WITHOUT PERMISSION!
Whee!
SPECIAL THERMAL SPA
Whoo! Wee!
whoosh
SIMULATION ROOM
ME
?
Stop that!!
ENERGY FREEZING FACILITY

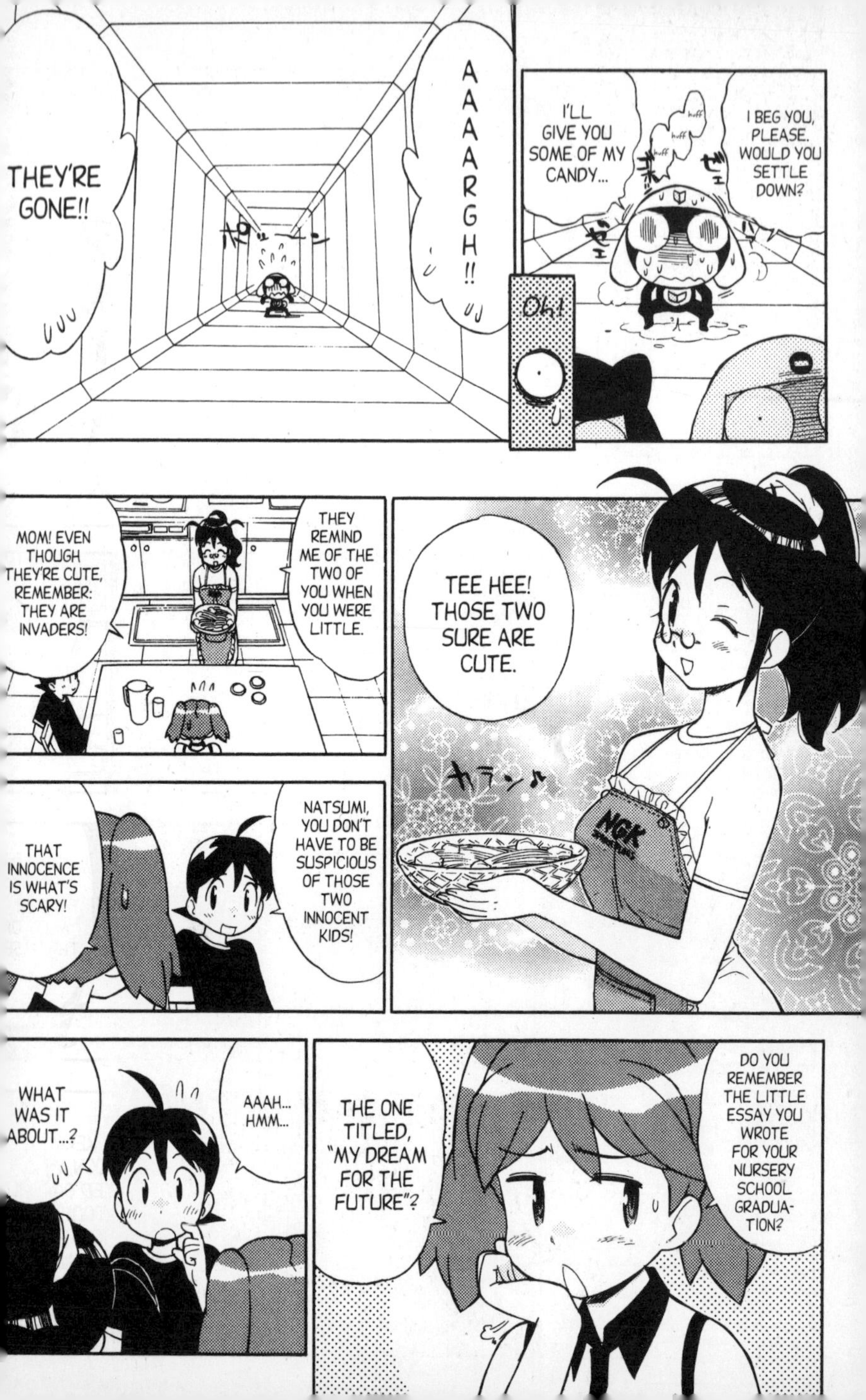
I BEG YOU, PLEASE. WOULD YOU SETTLE DOWN?
I'LL GIVE YOU SOME OF MY CANDY...
Oh!
AAAAARGH!!
THEY'RE GONE!!
TEE HEE! THOSE TWO SURE ARE CUTE.
THEY REMIND ME OF THE TWO OF YOU WHEN YOU WERE LITTLE.
MOM! EVEN THOUGH THEY'RE CUTE, REMEMBER: THEY ARE INVADERS!
NATSUMI, YOU DON'T HAVE TO BE SUSPICIOUS OF THOSE TWO INNOCENT KIDS!
THAT INNOCENCE IS WHAT'S SCARY!
DO YOU REMEMBER THE LITTLE ESSAY YOU WROTE FOR YOUR NURSERY SCHOOL GRADUATION?
THE ONE TITLED, "MY DREAM FOR THE FUTURE"?
AAAH... HMM...
WHAT WAS IT ABOUT...?

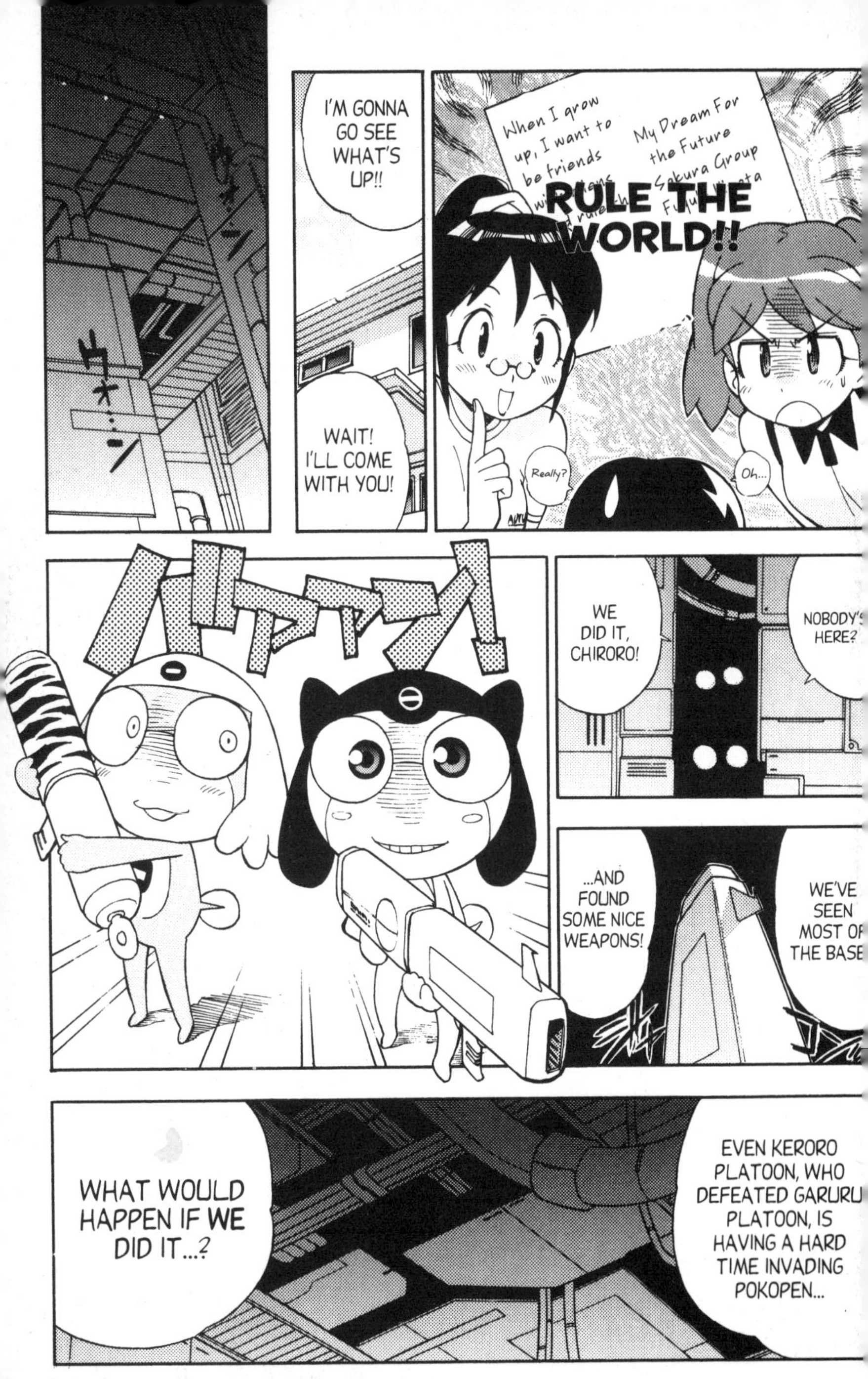
My Dream For the Future
Sakura Group
When I grow up, I want to be friends
RULE THE WORLD!!
Oh...
Really?
I'M GONNA GO SEE WHAT'S UP!!
WAIT! I'LL COME WITH YOU!
NOBODY'S HERE?
WE DID IT, CHIRORO!
WE'VE SEEN MOST OF THE BASE
...AND FOUND SOME NICE WEAPONS!
EVEN KERORO PLATOON, WHO DEFEATED GARURU PLATOON, IS HAVING A HARD TIME INVADING POKOPEN...
WHAT WOULD HAPPEN IF WE DID IT...?

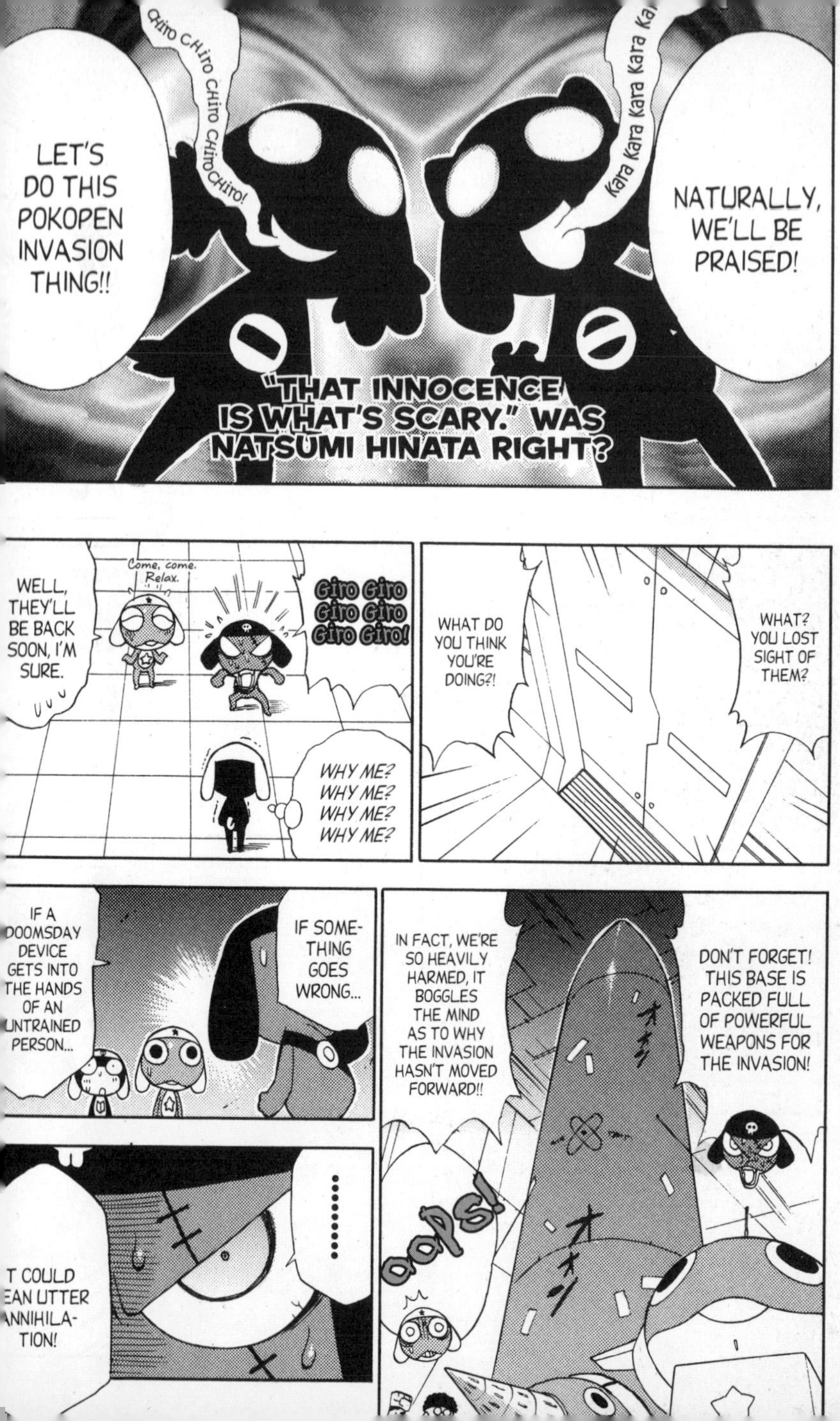

Kara Kara Kara Kara Kara
NATURALLY, WE'LL BE PRAISED!
Chiro Chiro Chiro Chiro Chiro!
LET'S DO THIS POKOPEN INVASION THING!!
"THAT INNOCENCE IS WHAT'S SCARY." WAS NATSUMI HINATA RIGHT?
WHAT? YOU LOST SIGHT OF THEM?
WHAT DO YOU THINK YOU'RE DOING?!
Giro Giro Giro Giro Giro Giro!
WHY ME? WHY ME? WHY ME? WHY ME?
Come, come. Relax.
WELL, THEY'LL BE BACK SOON, I'M SURE.
DON'T FORGET! THIS BASE IS PACKED FULL OF POWERFUL WEAPONS FOR THE INVASION!
IN FACT, WE'RE SO HEAVILY HARMED, IT BOGGLES THE MIND AS TO WHY THE INVASION HASN'T MOVED FORWARD!!
OOPS!
IF SOME-THING GOES WRONG...
IF A DOOMSDAY DEVICE GETS INTO THE HANDS OF AN UNTRAINED PERSON...
....
T COULD EAN UTTER ANNIHILA-TION!

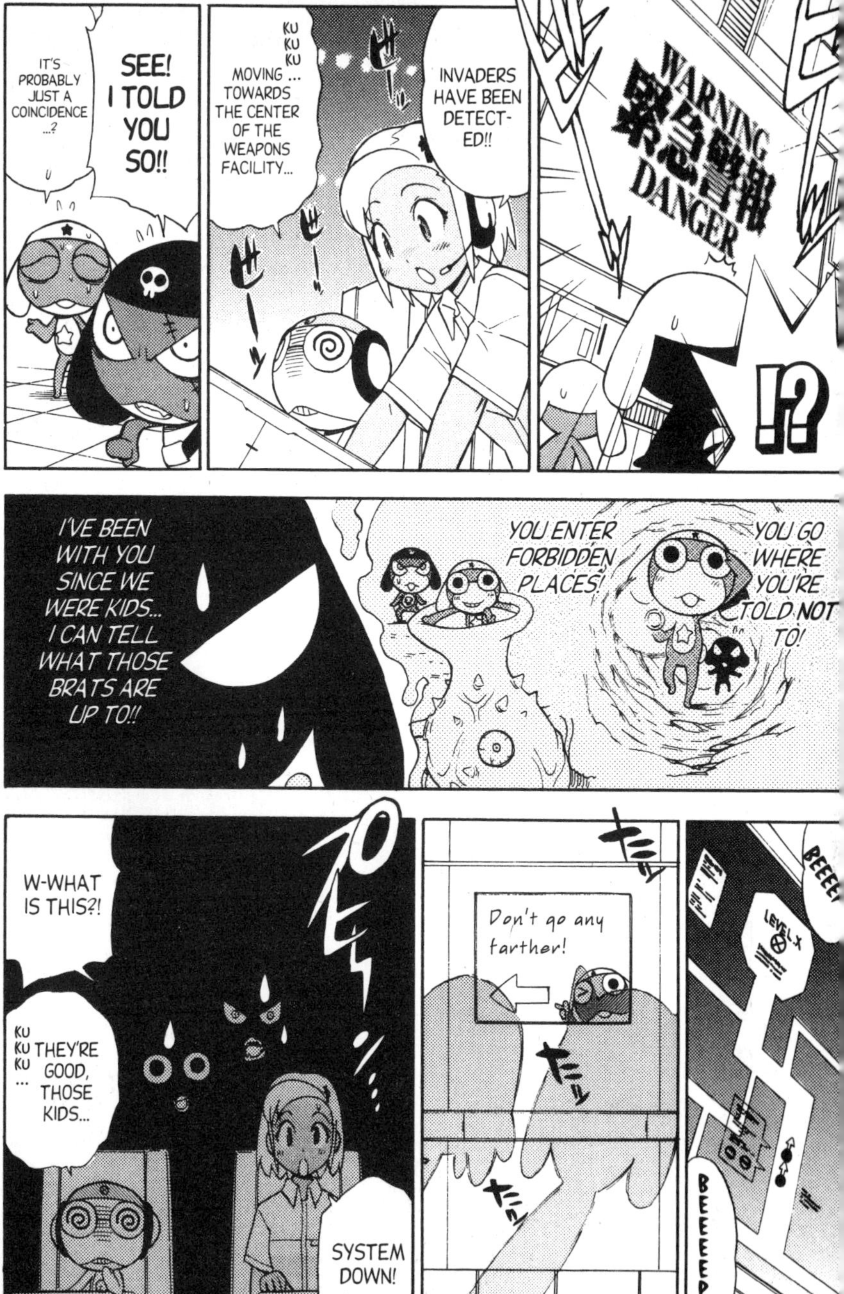
WARNING
緊急警報
DANGER
!?
INVADERS HAVE BEEN DETECT-ED!!
KU KU KU
MOVING ... TOWARDS THE CENTER OF THE WEAPONS FACILITY...
SEE! I TOLD YOU SO!!
IT'S PROBABLY JUST A COINCIDENCE ...?
YOU GO WHERE YOU'RE TOLD NOT TO!
YOU ENTER FORBIDDEN PLACES!
I'VE BEEN WITH YOU SINCE WE WERE KIDS... I CAN TELL WHAT THOSE BRATS ARE UP TO!!
BEEEE
LEVEL X
BEEEEEP
Don't go any farther!
W-WHAT IS THIS?!
KU KU KU ... THEY'RE GOOD, THOSE KIDS...
SYSTEM DOWN!

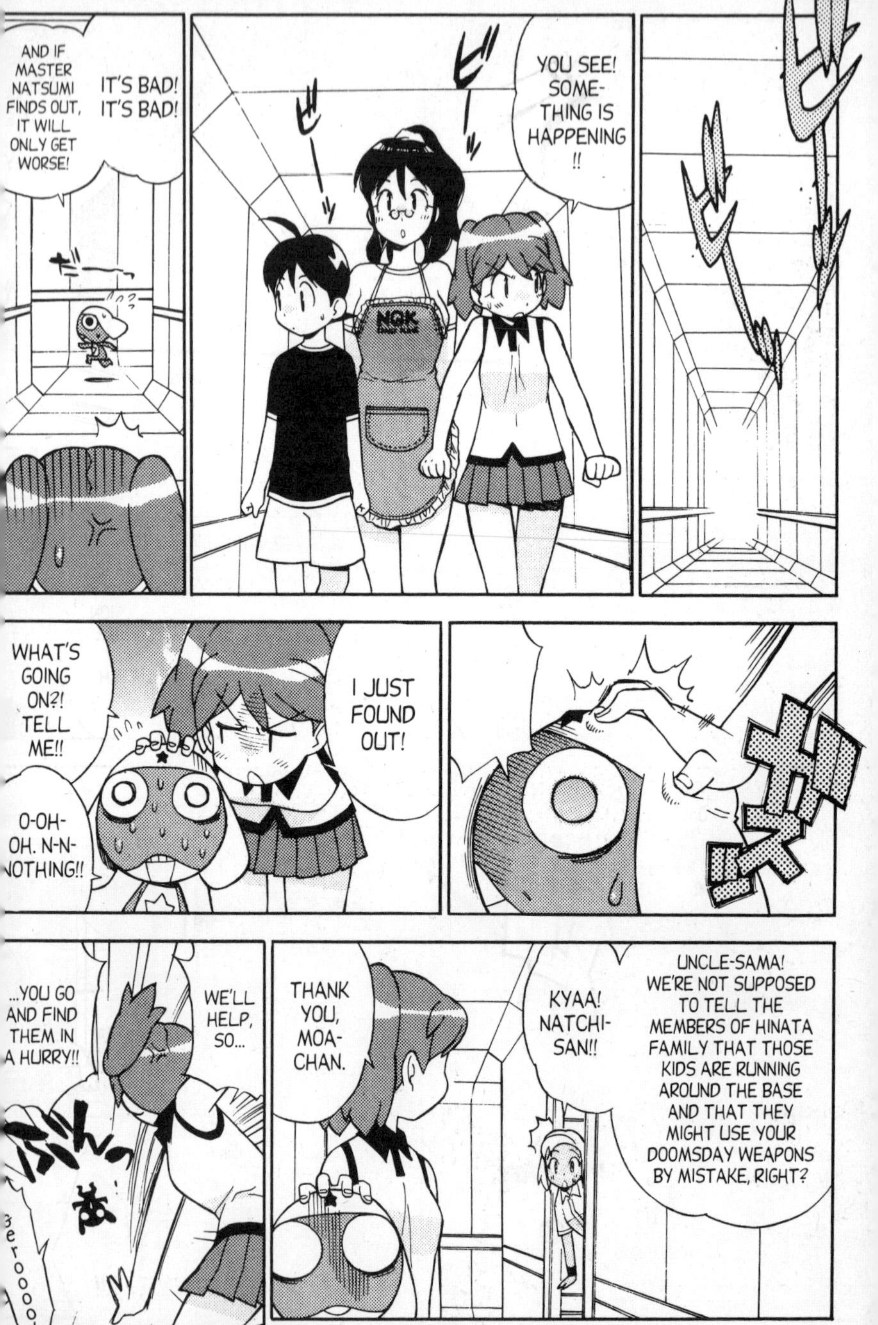

YOU SEE! SOME-THING IS HAPPENING!!
IT'S BAD! IT'S BAD!
AND IF MASTER NATSUMI FINDS OUT, IT WILL ONLY GET WORSE!
I JUST FOUND OUT!
WHAT'S GOING ON?! TELL ME!!
O-OH-OH. N-N-NOTHING!!
UNCLE-SAMA! WE'RE NOT SUPPOSED TO TELL THE MEMBERS OF HINATA FAMILY THAT THOSE KIDS ARE RUNNING AROUND THE BASE AND THAT THEY MIGHT USE YOUR DOOMSDAY WEAPONS BY MISTAKE, RIGHT?
KYAA! NATCHI-SAN!!
THANK YOU, MOA-CHAN.
WE'LL HELP, SO...
...YOU GO AND FIND THEM IN A HURRY!!

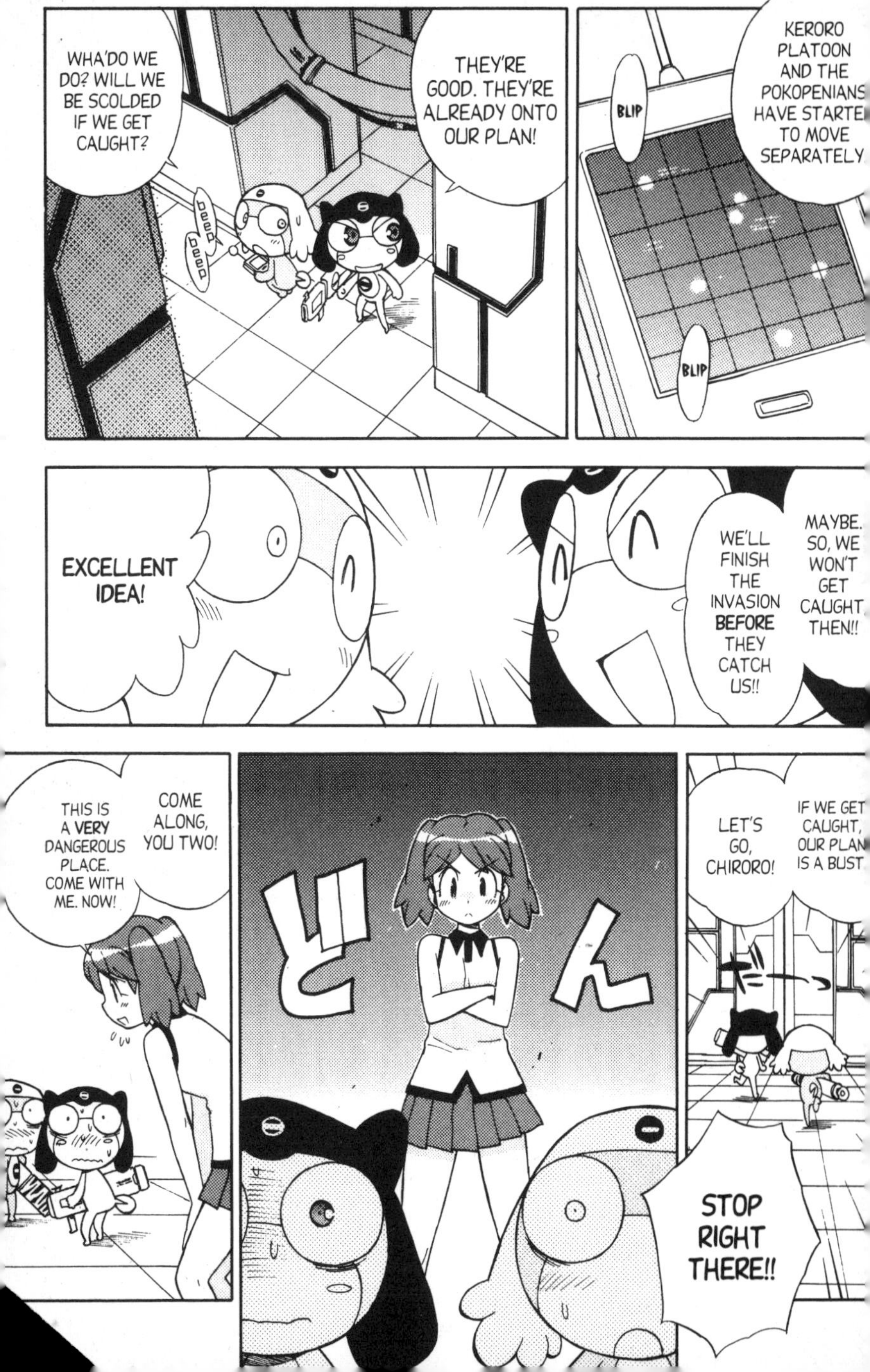
BLIP
KERORO PLATOON AND THE POKOPENIANS HAVE STARTE TO MOVE SEPARATELY.
BLIP
THEY'RE GOOD. THEY'RE ALREADY ONTO OUR PLAN!
WHA'DO WE DO? WILL WE BE SCOLDED IF WE GET CAUGHT?
beep beep
MAYBE. SO, WE WON'T GET CAUGHT THEN!!
WE'LL FINISH THE INVASION BEFORE THEY CATCH US!!
EXCELLENT IDEA!
IF WE GET CAUGHT, OUR PLAN IS A BUST.
LET'S GO, CHIRORO!
STOP RIGHT THERE!!
どん
COME ALONG, YOU TWO!
THIS IS A VERY DANGEROUS PLACE. COME WITH ME. NOW!

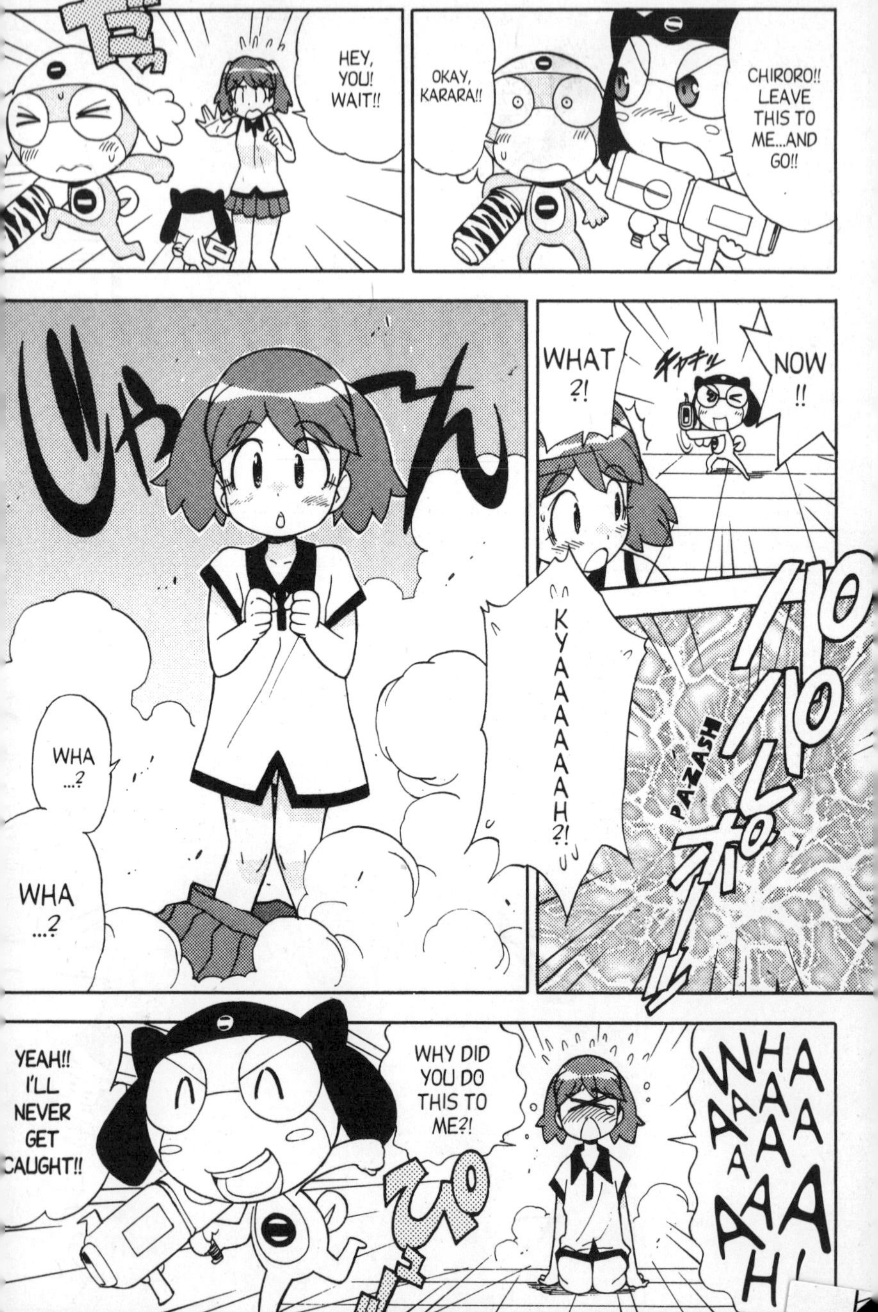
CHIRORO!! LEAVE THIS TO ME...AND GO!!
OKAY, KARARA!!
HEY, YOU! WAIT!!
NOW !!
WHAT ?!
KYAAAAAAAAH?!
PAZASH
WHA ...?
WHA ...?
WHAAAAAAAAAAAAAH!
WHY DID YOU DO THIS TO ME?!
YEAH!! I'LL NEVER GET CAUGHT!!

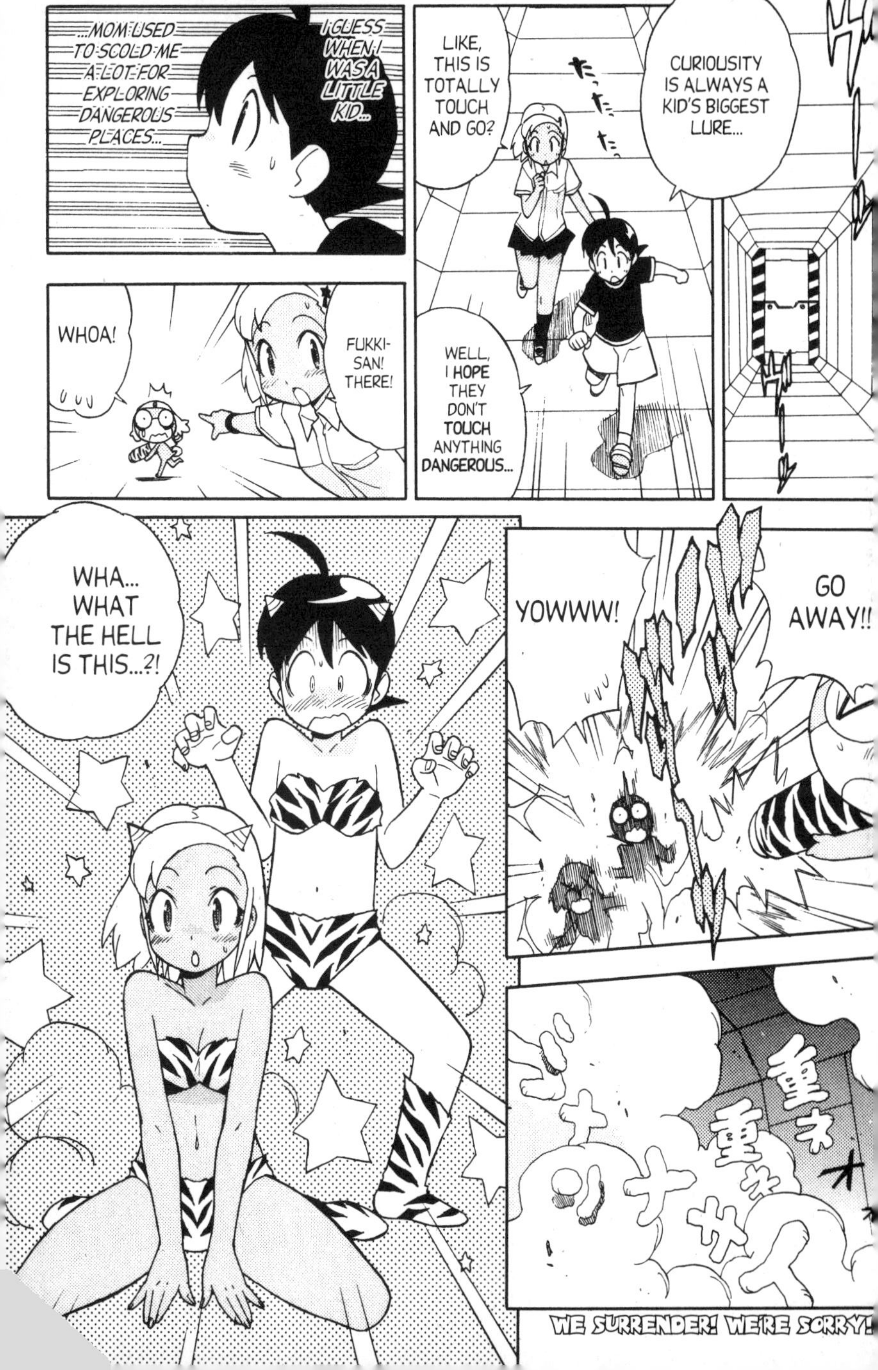

CURIOUSITY IS ALWAYS A KID'S BIGGEST LURE...
LIKE, THIS IS TOTALLY TOUCH AND GO?
WELL, I HOPE THEY DON'T TOUCH ANYTHING DANGEROUS...
I GUESS WHEN I WAS A LITTLE KID...
...MOM USED TO SCOLD ME A LOT FOR EXPLORING DANGEROUS PLACES...
FUKKI-SAN! THERE!
WHOA!
GO AWAY!!
YOWWW!
WE SURRENDER! WE'RE SORRY!
WHA... WHAT THE HELL IS THIS...?!

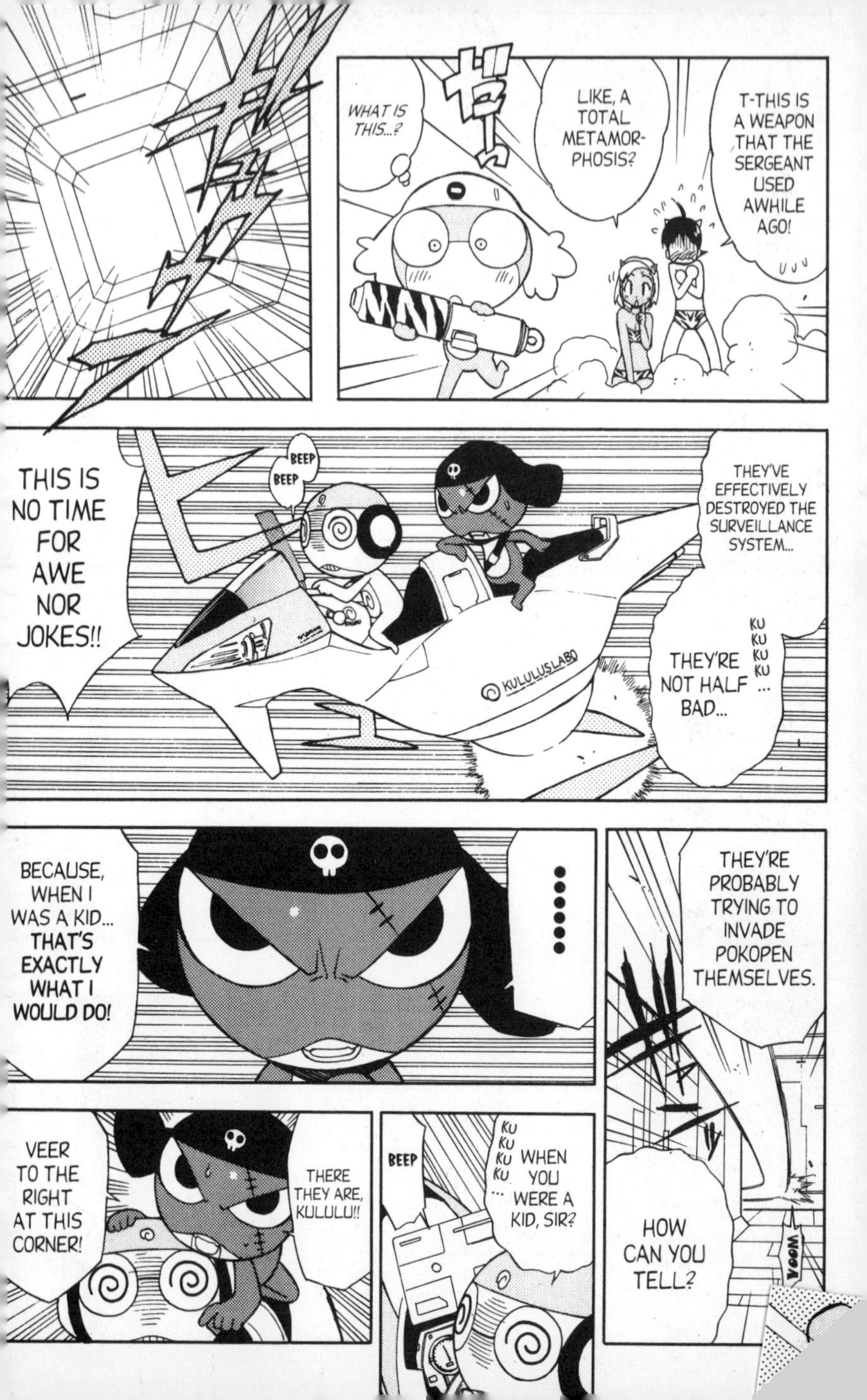

T-THIS IS A WEAPON THAT THE SERGEANT USED AWHILE AGO!
LIKE, A TOTAL METAMORPHOSIS?
WHAT IS THIS...?
THEY'VE EFFECTIVELY DESTROYED THE SURVEILLANCE SYSTEM...
KU KU KU KU...
THEY'RE NOT HALF BAD...
KULULUS LABO
BEEP BEEP
THIS IS NO TIME FOR AWE NOR JOKES!!
THEY'RE PROBABLY TRYING TO INVADE POKOPEN THEMSELVES.
HOW CAN YOU TELL?
VOOM
......
BECAUSE, WHEN I WAS A KID... THAT'S EXACTLY WHAT I WOULD DO!
KU KU KU KU...
WHEN YOU WERE A KID, SIR?
BEEP
THERE THEY ARE, KULULU!!
VEER TO THE RIGHT AT THIS CORNER!

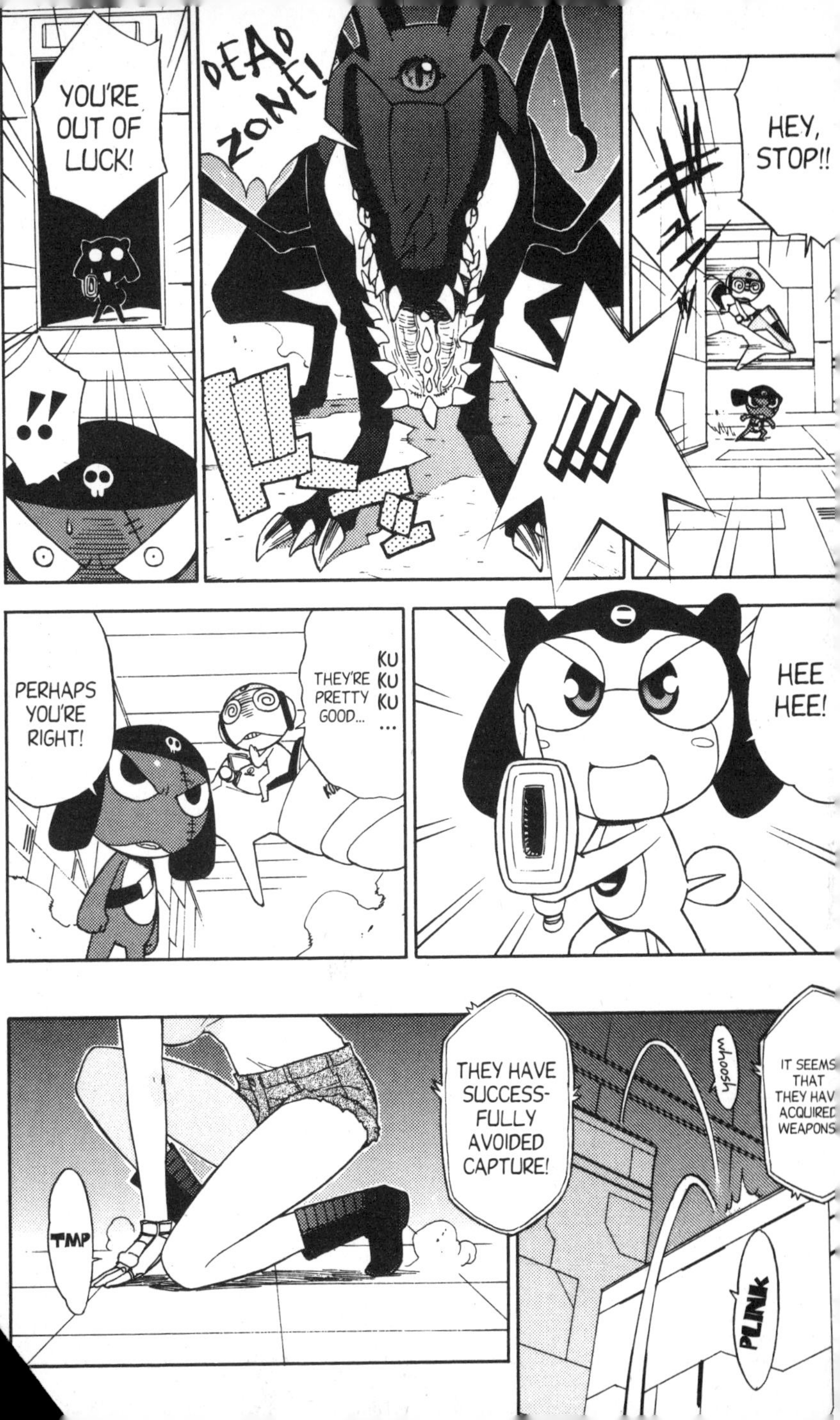
HEY, STOP!!
DEAD ZONE!
!!!!
YOU'RE OUT OF LUCK!
!!
HEE HEE!
THEY'RE PRETTY GOOD...
KU KU KU...
PERHAPS YOU'RE RIGHT!
IT SEEMS THAT THEY HAV ACQUIRED WEAPONS
whoosh
THEY HAVE SUCCESS-FULLY AVOIDED CAPTURE!
PLINK
TMP

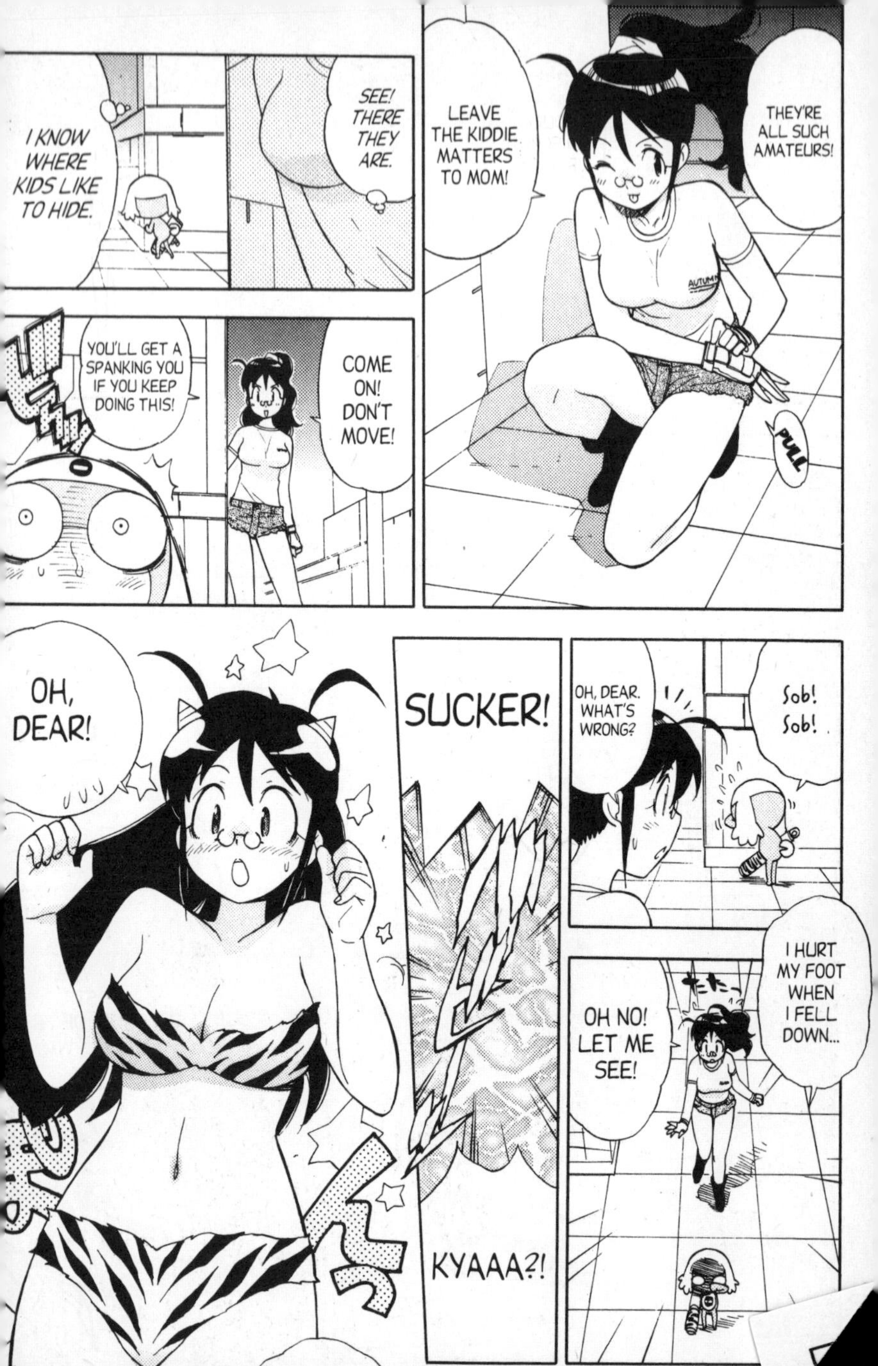
THEY'RE ALL SUCH AMATEURS!
LEAVE THE KIDDIE MATTERS TO MOM!
AUTUMN
PULL
SEE! THERE THEY ARE.
I KNOW WHERE KIDS LIKE TO HIDE.
COME ON! DON'T MOVE!
YOU'LL GET A SPANKING YOU IF YOU KEEP DOING THIS!
Sob! Sob!
OH, DEAR. WHAT'S WRONG?
I HURT MY FOOT WHEN I FELL DOWN...
OH NO! LET ME SEE!
SUCKER!
KYAAA?!
OH, DEAR!

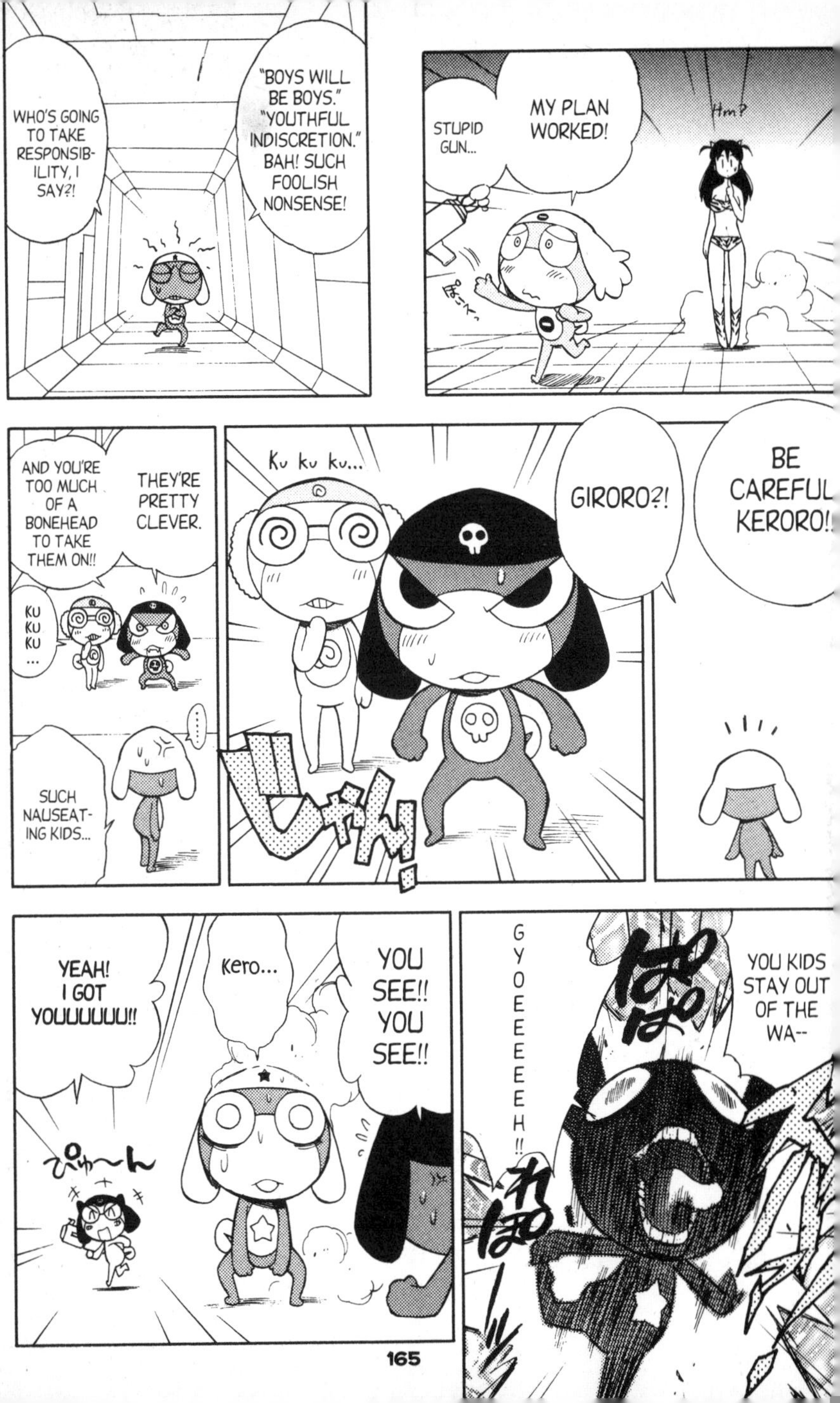
Hm?
MY PLAN WORKED!
STUPID GUN...
"BOYS WILL BE BOYS." "YOUTHFUL INDISCRETION." BAH! SUCH FOOLISH NONSENSE!
WHO'S GOING TO TAKE RESPONSIBILITY, I SAY?!
BE CAREFUL KERORO!!
GIRORO?!
Ku ku ku...
THEY'RE PRETTY CLEVER.
AND YOU'RE TOO MUCH OF A BONEHEAD TO TAKE THEM ON!!
KU KU KU ...
......
SUCH NAUSEATING KIDS...
YOU KIDS STAY OUT OF THE WA--
GYOEEEEEEEH!!
YOU SEE!! YOU SEE!!
Kero...
YEAH! I GOT YOUUUUUU!!

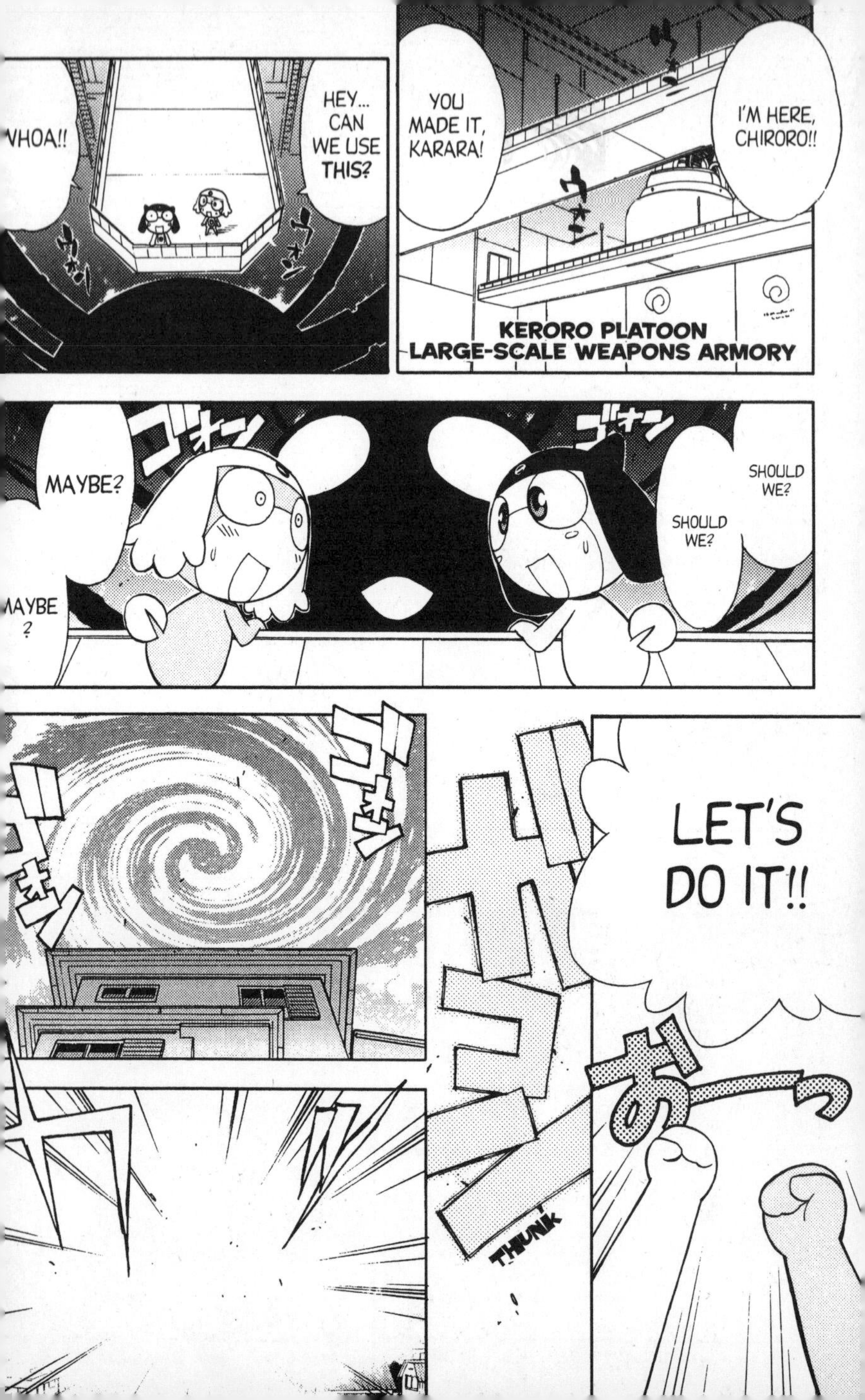
I'M HERE, CHIRORO!!
YOU MADE IT, KARARA!
KERORO PLATOON LARGE-SCALE WEAPONS ARMORY
HEY... CAN WE USE THIS?
SHOULD WE?
SHOULD WE?
MAYBE?
LET'S DO IT!!
THUNK

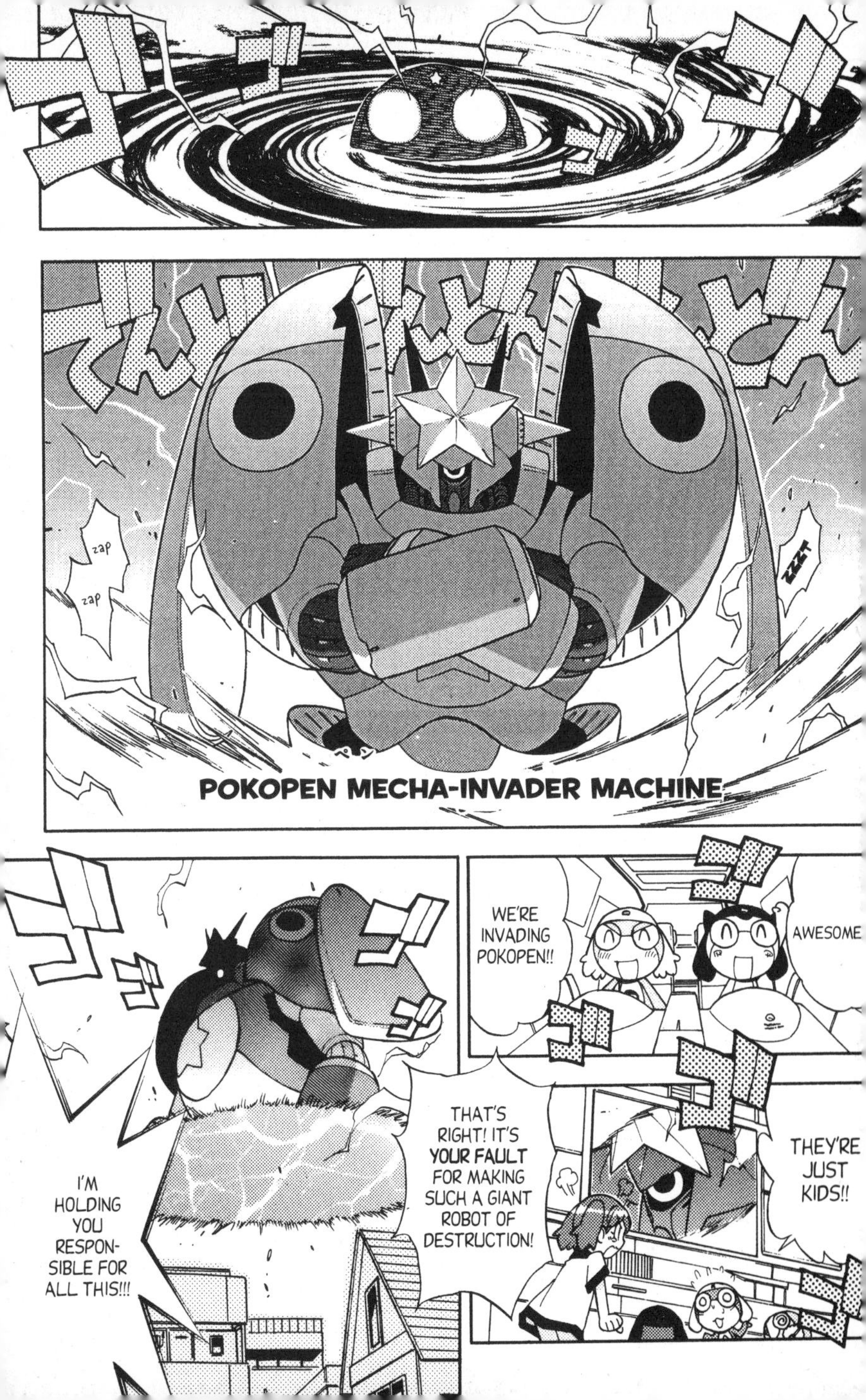
ZZZT
zap
zap
POKOPEN MECHA-INVADER MACHINE
AWESOME
WE'RE INVADING POKOPEN!!
THEY'RE JUST KIDS!!
THAT'S RIGHT! IT'S **YOUR FAULT** FOR MAKING SUCH A GIANT ROBOT OF DESTRUCTION!
I'M HOLDING YOU RESPONSIBLE FOR ALL THIS!!!

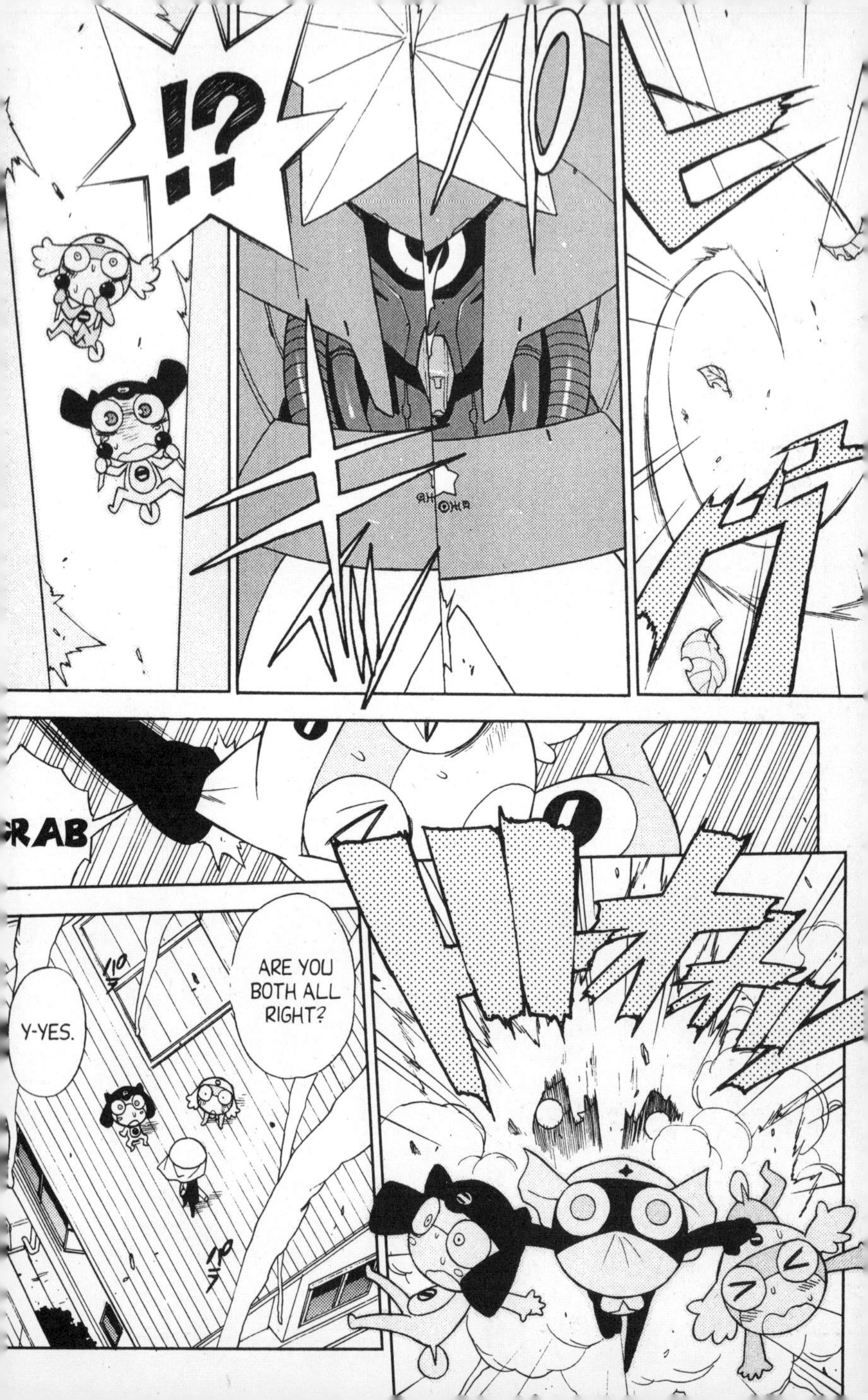

!?
GRAB
ARE YOU BOTH ALL RIGHT?
Y-YES.

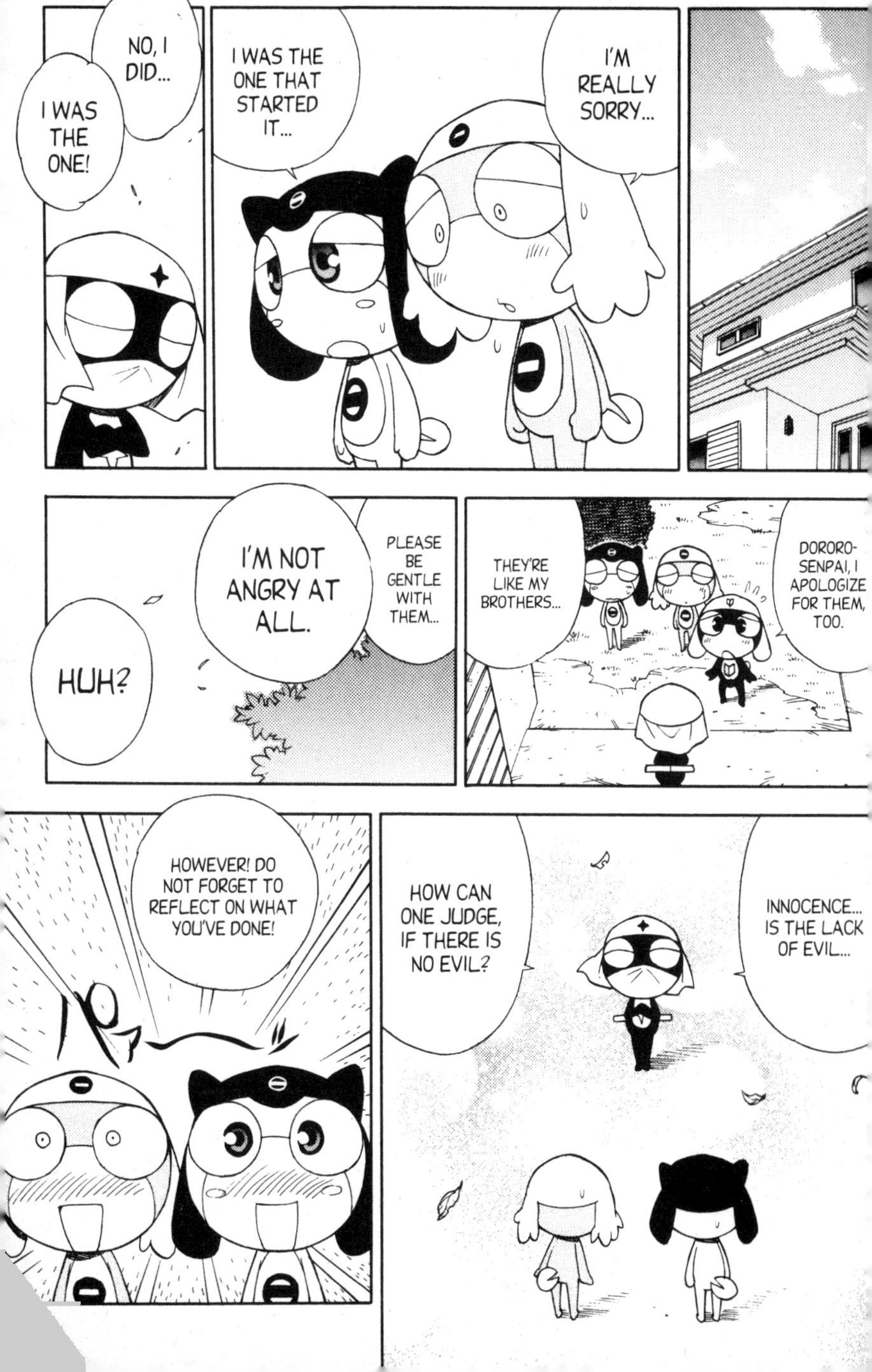
I'M REALLY SORRY...
I WAS THE ONE THAT STARTED IT...
NO, I DID...
I WAS THE ONE!
DORORO-SENPAI, I APOLOGIZE FOR THEM, TOO.
THEY'RE LIKE MY BROTHERS...
PLEASE BE GENTLE WITH THEM...
I'M NOT ANGRY AT ALL.
HUH?
INNOCENCE... IS THE LACK OF EVIL...
HOW CAN ONE JUDGE, IF THERE IS NO EVIL?
HOWEVER! DO NOT FORGET TO REFLECT ON WHAT YOU'VE DONE!

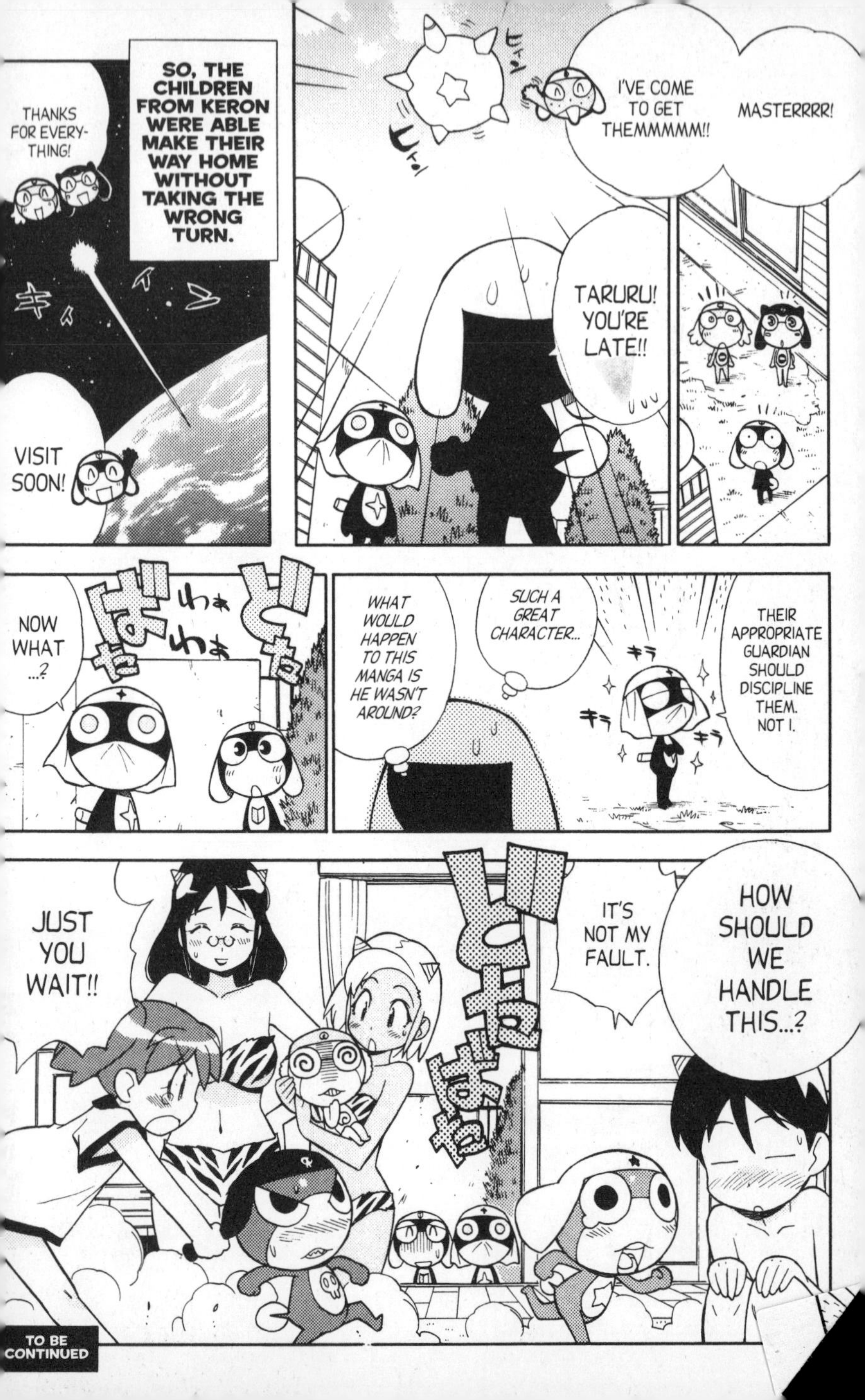
MASTERRRR!
I'VE COME TO GET THEMMMMM!!
TARURU! YOU'RE LATE!!
SO, THE CHILDREN FROM KERON WERE ABLE MAKE THEIR WAY HOME WITHOUT TAKING THE WRONG TURN.
THANKS FOR EVERY-THING!
VISIT SOON!
THEIR APPROPRIATE GUARDIAN SHOULD DISCIPLINE THEM. NOT I.
キラ
キラ
キラ
SUCH A GREAT CHARACTER...
WHAT WOULD HAPPEN TO THIS MANGA IS HE WASN'T AROUND?
NOW WHAT ...?
HOW SHOULD WE HANDLE THIS...?
IT'S NOT MY FAULT.
JUST YOU WAIT!!
TO BE CONTINUED

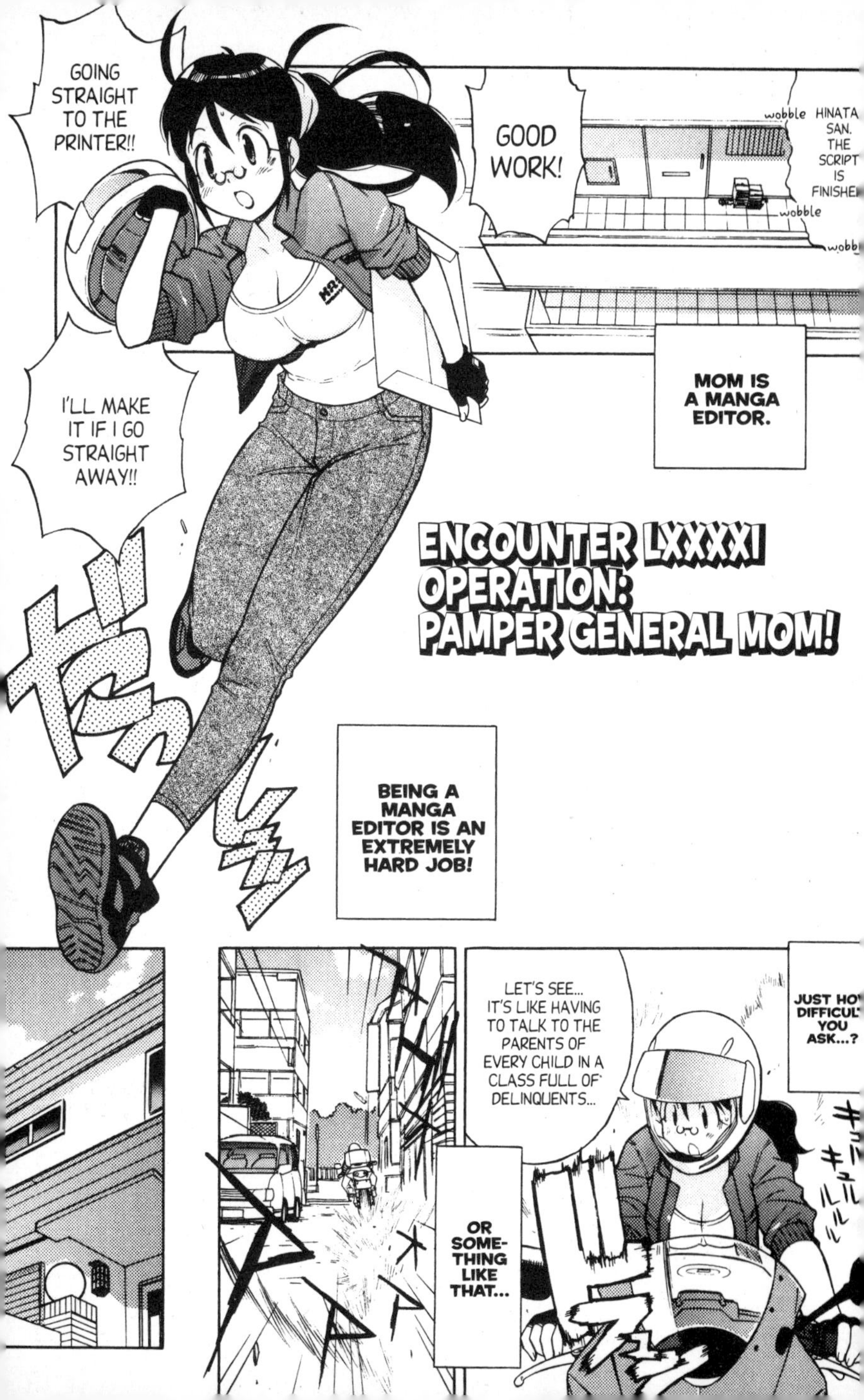
wobble
HINATA SAN. THE SCRIPT IS FINISHE
wobble
wobble
GOOD WORK!
GOING STRAIGHT TO THE PRINTER!!
I'LL MAKE IT IF I GO STRAIGHT AWAY!!
MOM IS A MANGA EDITOR.
ENCOUNTER LXXXXI
OPERATION: PAMPER GENERAL MOM!
BEING A MANGA EDITOR IS AN EXTREMELY HARD JOB!
JUST HO DIFFICUL YOU ASK...?
LET'S SEE... IT'S LIKE HAVING TO TALK TO THE PARENTS OF EVERY CHILD IN A CLASS FULL OF DELINQUENTS...
OR SOME-THING LIKE THAT...

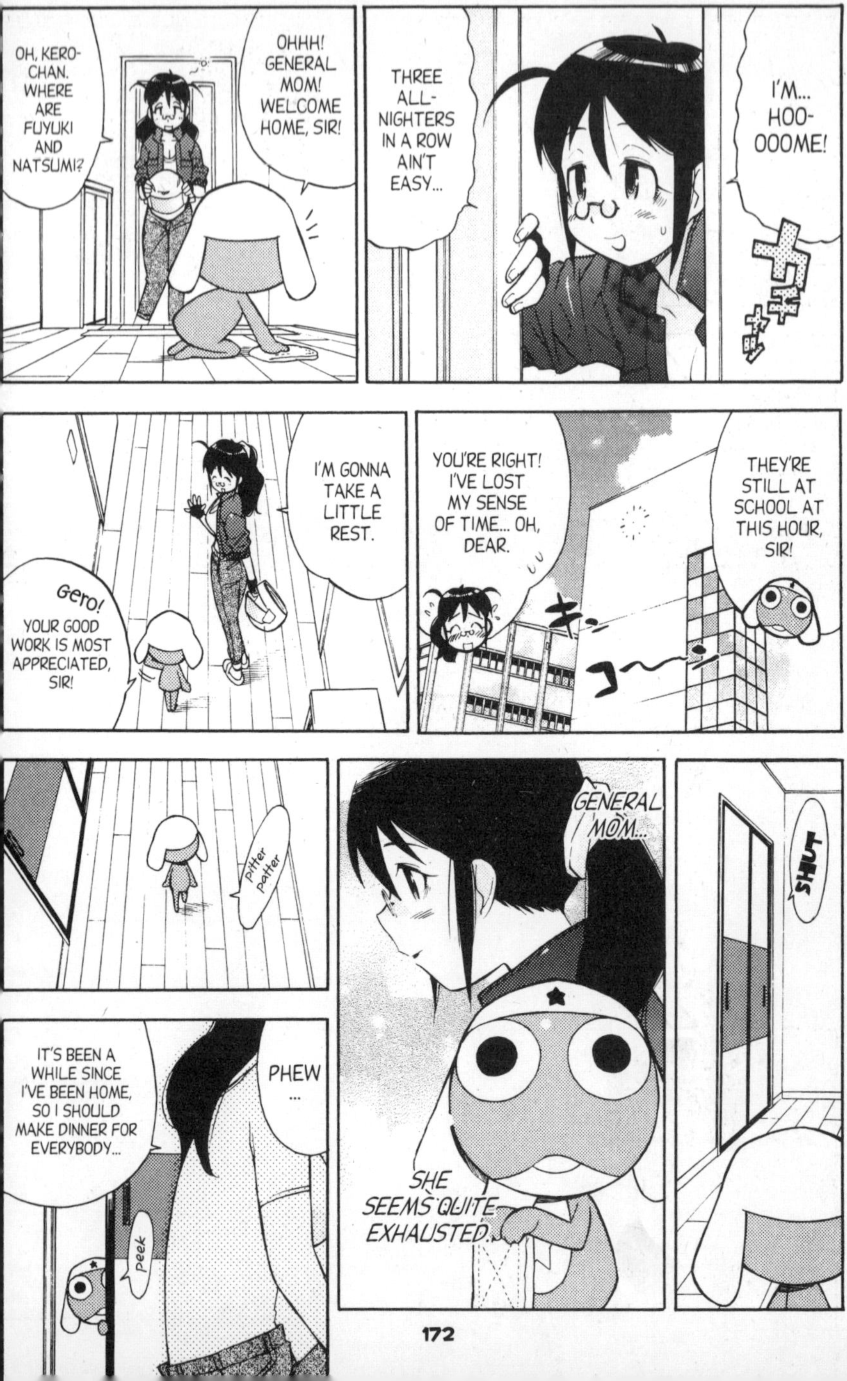
I'M... HOO-OOOME!
THREE ALL-NIGHTERS IN A ROW AIN'T EASY...
OHHH! GENERAL MOM! WELCOME HOME, SIR!
OH, KERO-CHAN. WHERE ARE FUYUKI AND NATSUMI?
THEY'RE STILL AT SCHOOL AT THIS HOUR, SIR!
YOU'RE RIGHT! I'VE LOST MY SENSE OF TIME... OH, DEAR.
I'M GONNA TAKE A LITTLE REST.
Gero! YOUR GOOD WORK IS MOST APPRECIATED, SIR!
SHUT
GENERAL MOM...
SHE SEEMS QUITE EXHAUSTED...
pitter patter
PHEW...
IT'S BEEN A WHILE SINCE I'VE BEEN HOME, SO I SHOULD MAKE DINNER FOR EVERYBODY...
peek

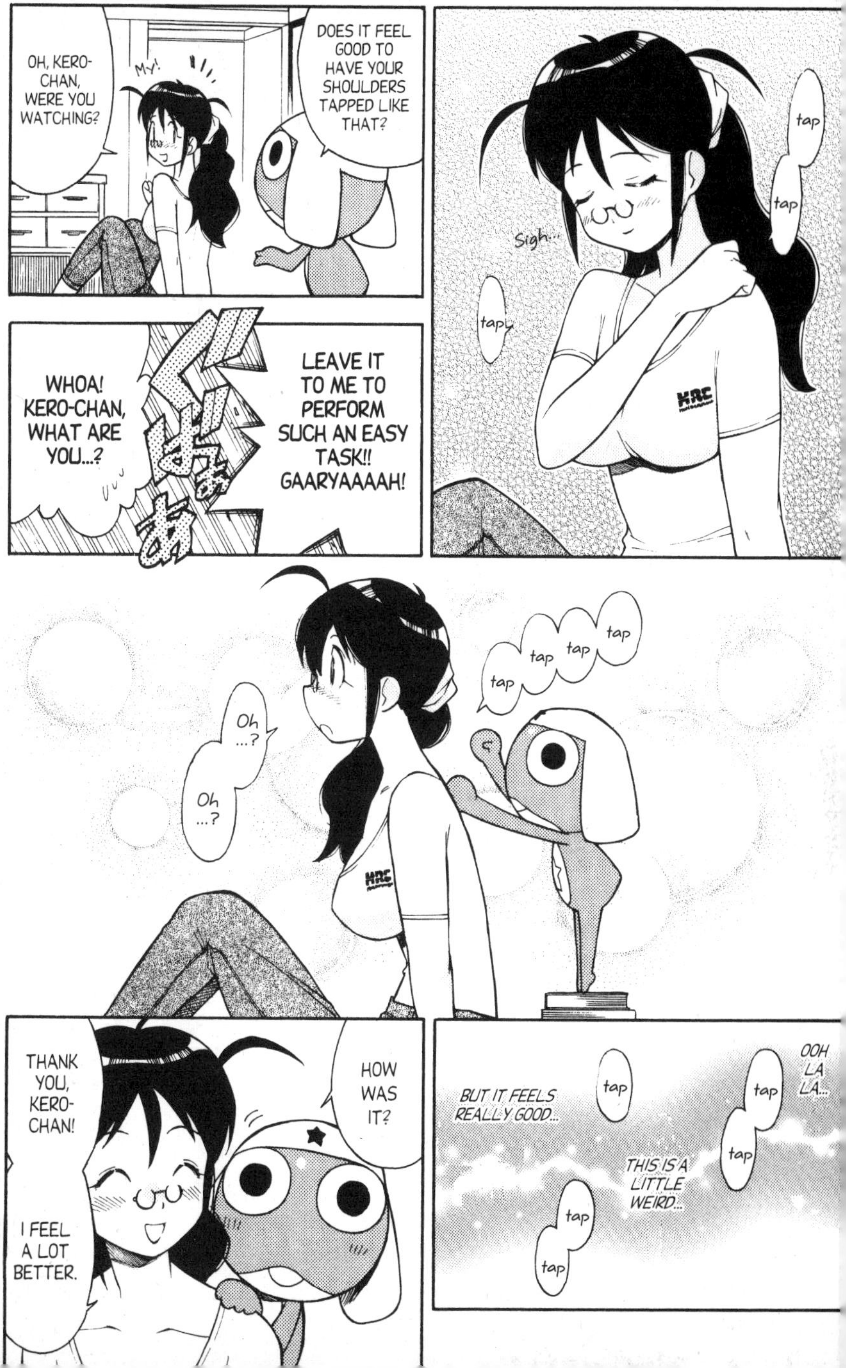
tap
tap
Sigh...
tap
DOES IT FEEL GOOD TO HAVE YOUR SHOULDERS TAPPED LIKE THAT?
My!
OH, KERO-CHAN, WERE YOU WATCHING?
LEAVE IT TO ME TO PERFORM SUCH AN EASY TASK!! GAARYAAAAH!
WHOA! KERO-CHAN, WHAT ARE YOU...?
tap
tap
tap
tap
Oh ...?
Oh ...?
OOH LA LA...
tap
tap
tap
BUT IT FEELS REALLY GOOD...
THIS IS A LITTLE WEIRD...
tap
tap
HOW WAS IT?
THANK YOU, KERO-CHAN!
I FEEL A LOT BETTER.

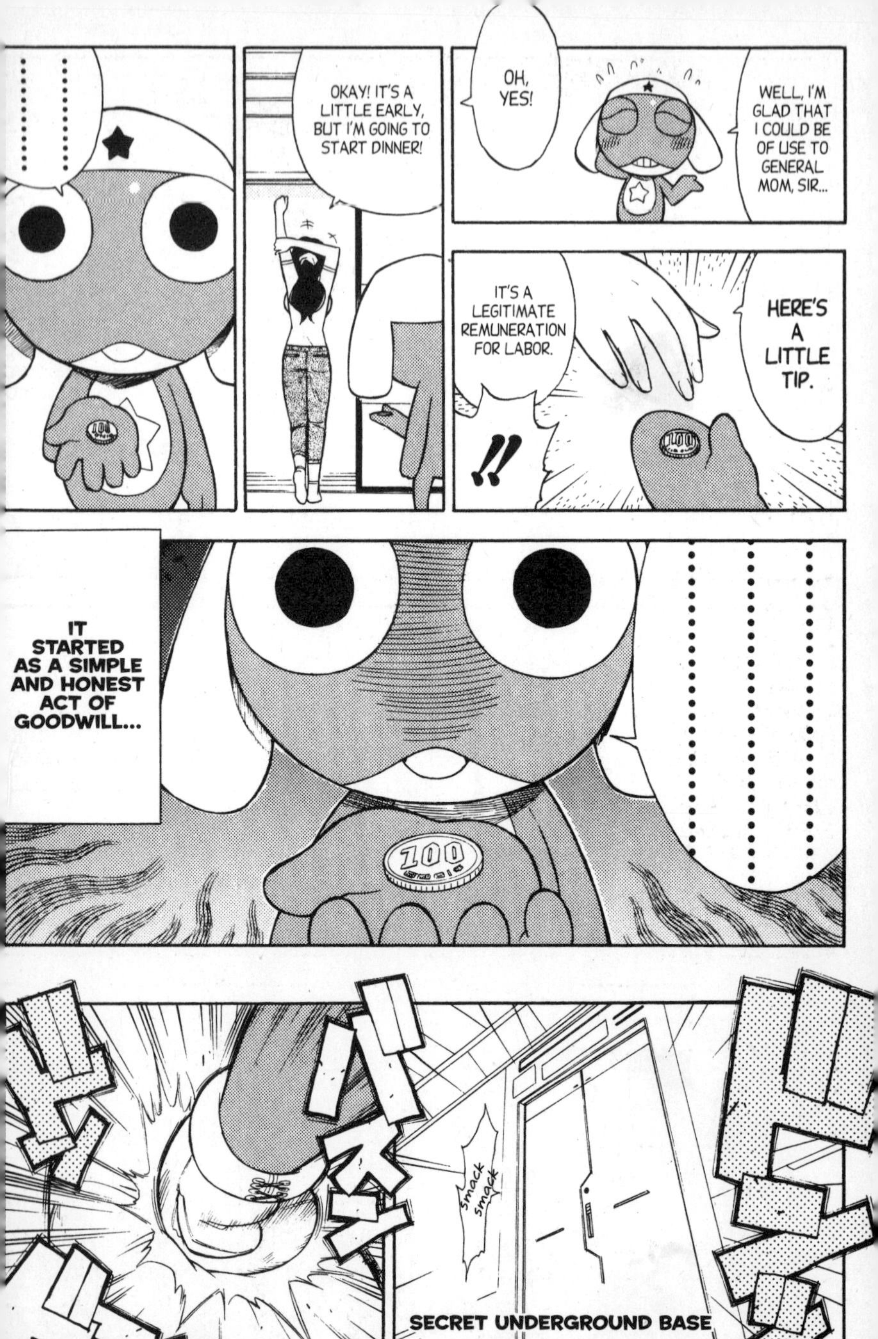

WELL, I'M GLAD THAT I COULD BE OF USE TO GENERAL MOM, SIR...
OH, YES!
HERE'S A LITTLE TIP.
IT'S A LEGITIMATE REMUNERATION FOR LABOR.
!!
OKAY! IT'S A LITTLE EARLY, BUT I'M GOING TO START DINNER!
......
......
IT STARTED AS A SIMPLE AND HONEST ACT OF GOODWILL...
SECRET UNDERGROUND BASE
Smack smack

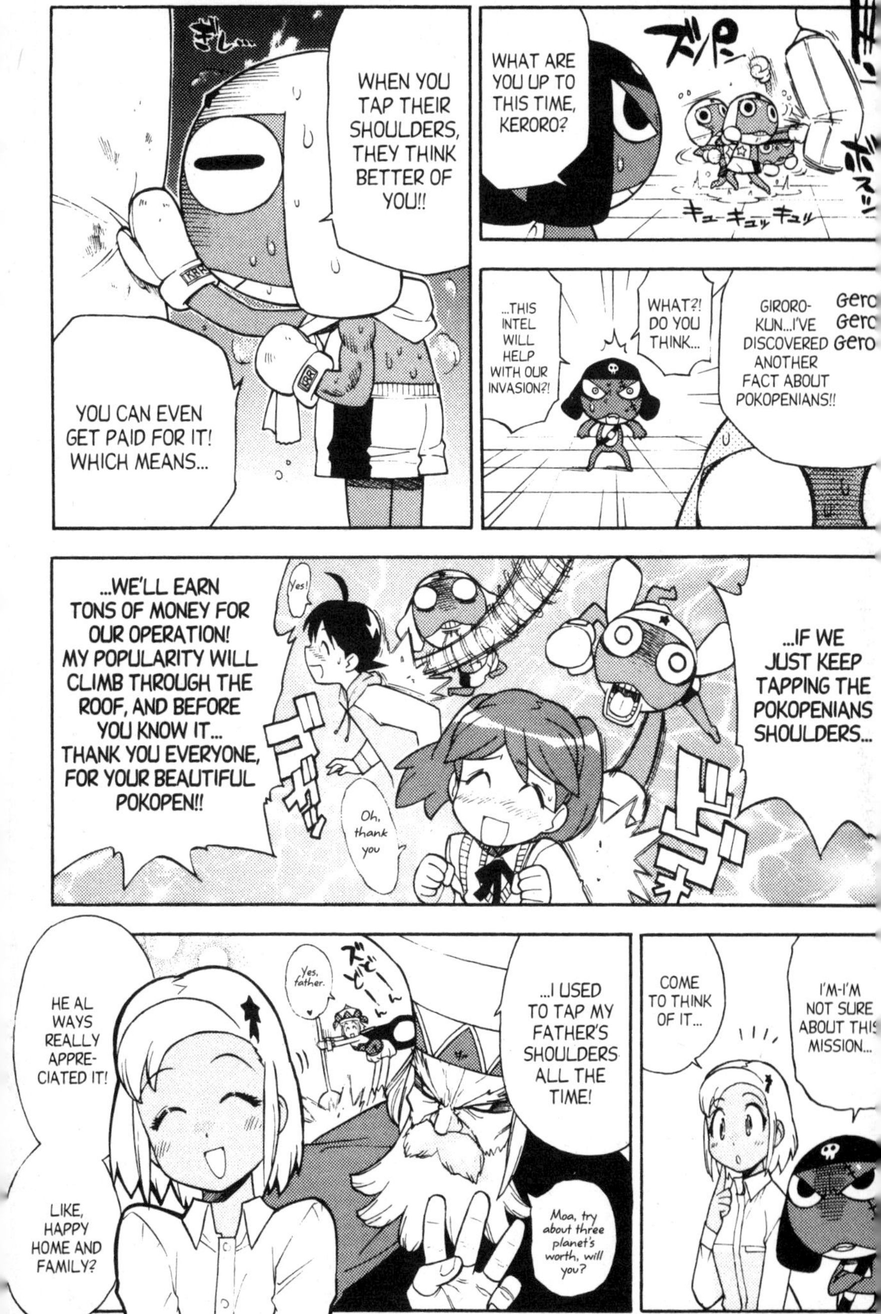
WHAT ARE YOU UP TO THIS TIME, KERORO?
GIRORO-KUN...I'VE DISCOVERED ANOTHER FACT ABOUT POKOPENIANS!!
Gero Gero Gero
WHAT?! DO YOU THINK...
...THIS INTEL WILL HELP WITH OUR INVASION?!
WHEN YOU TAP THEIR SHOULDERS, THEY THINK BETTER OF YOU!!
YOU CAN EVEN GET PAID FOR IT! WHICH MEANS...
...IF WE JUST KEEP TAPPING THE POKOPENIANS SHOULDERS...
...WE'LL EARN TONS OF MONEY FOR OUR OPERATION! MY POPULARITY WILL CLIMB THROUGH THE ROOF, AND BEFORE YOU KNOW IT... THANK YOU EVERYONE, FOR YOUR BEAUTIFUL POKOPEN!!
Yes!
Oh, thank you
I'M-I'M NOT SURE ABOUT THIS MISSION...
COME TO THINK OF IT...
...I USED TO TAP MY FATHER'S SHOULDERS ALL THE TIME!
Yes, father.
Moa, try about three planet's worth, will you?
HE AL WAYS REALLY APPRE- CIATED IT!
LIKE, HAPPY HOME AND FAMILY?

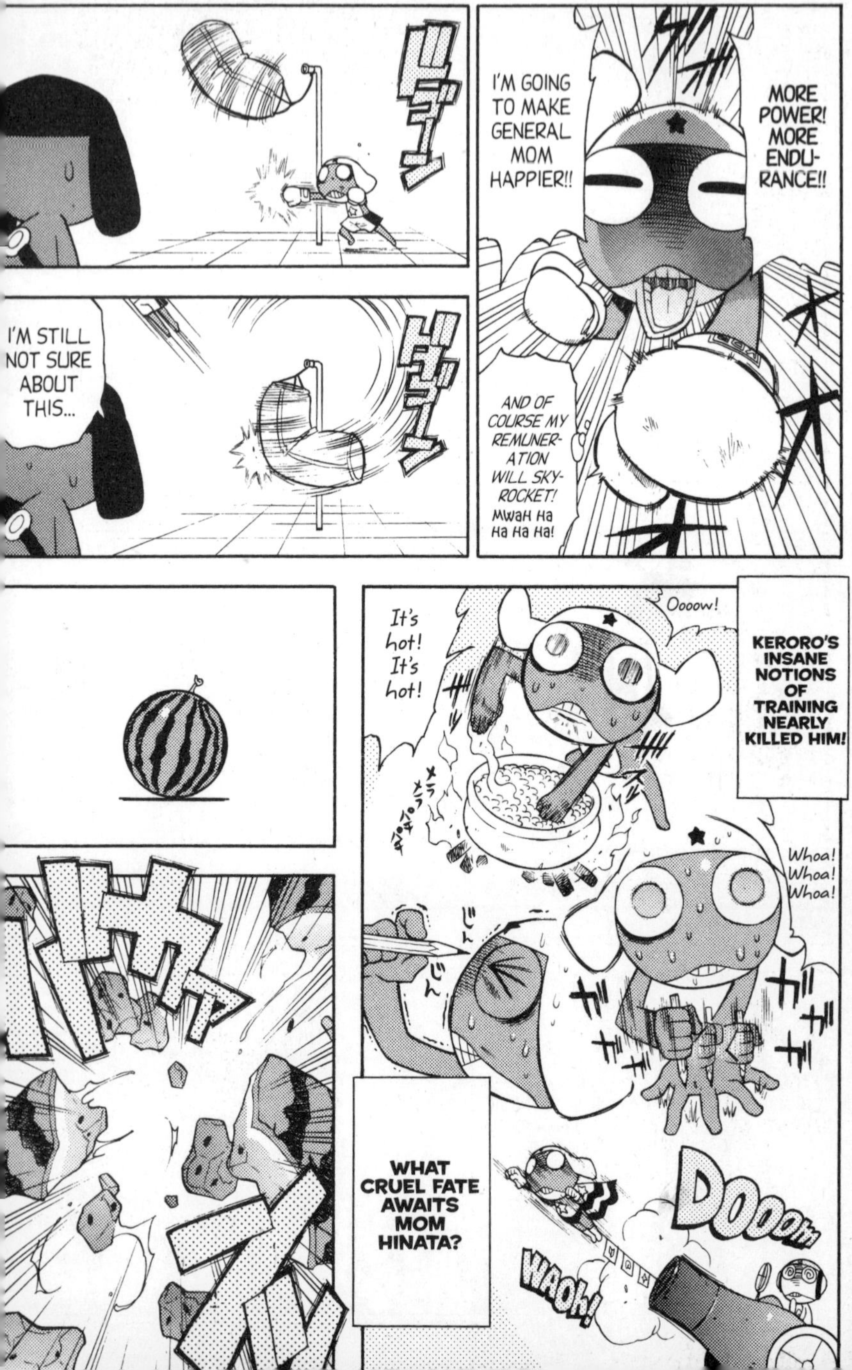
MORE POWER! MORE ENDU-RANCE!!
I'M GOING TO MAKE GENERAL MOM HAPPIER!!
AND OF COURSE MY REMUNER-ATION WILL SKY-ROCKET! MWAH HA HA HA HA!
I'M STILL NOT SURE ABOUT THIS...
KERORO'S INSANE NOTIONS OF TRAINING NEARLY KILLED HIM!
Oooow!
It's hot! It's hot!
メラメラパチパチ
Whoa! Whoa! Whoa!
じんじん
DOooom
WHAT CRUEL FATE AWAITS MOM HINATA?
WAOH!

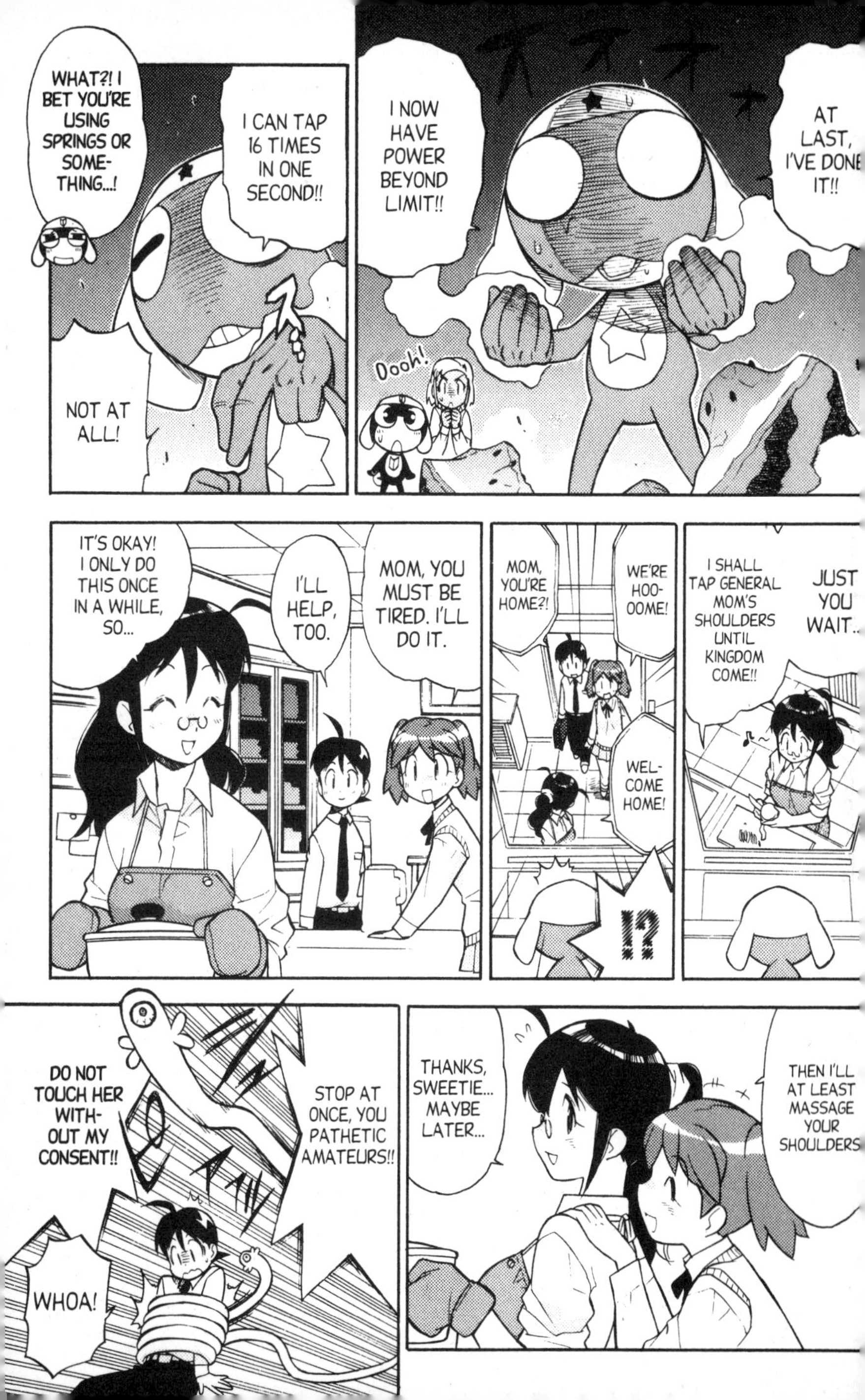
AT LAST, I'VE DONE IT!!
I NOW HAVE POWER BEYOND LIMIT!!
Oooh!
I CAN TAP 16 TIMES IN ONE SECOND!!
WHAT?! I BET YOU'RE USING SPRINGS OR SOME-THING...!
NOT AT ALL!
JUST YOU WAIT...
I SHALL TAP GENERAL MOM'S SHOULDERS UNTIL KINGDOM COME!!
WE'RE HOO-OOME!
MOM, YOU'RE HOME?!
WEL-COME HOME!
!?
MOM, YOU MUST BE TIRED. I'LL DO IT.
I'LL HELP, TOO.
IT'S OKAY! I ONLY DO THIS ONCE IN A WHILE, SO...
THEN I'LL AT LEAST MASSAGE YOUR SHOULDERS
THANKS, SWEETIE... MAYBE LATER...
STOP AT ONCE, YOU PATHETIC AMATEURS!!
DO NOT TOUCH HER WITH-OUT MY CONSENT!!
WHOA!

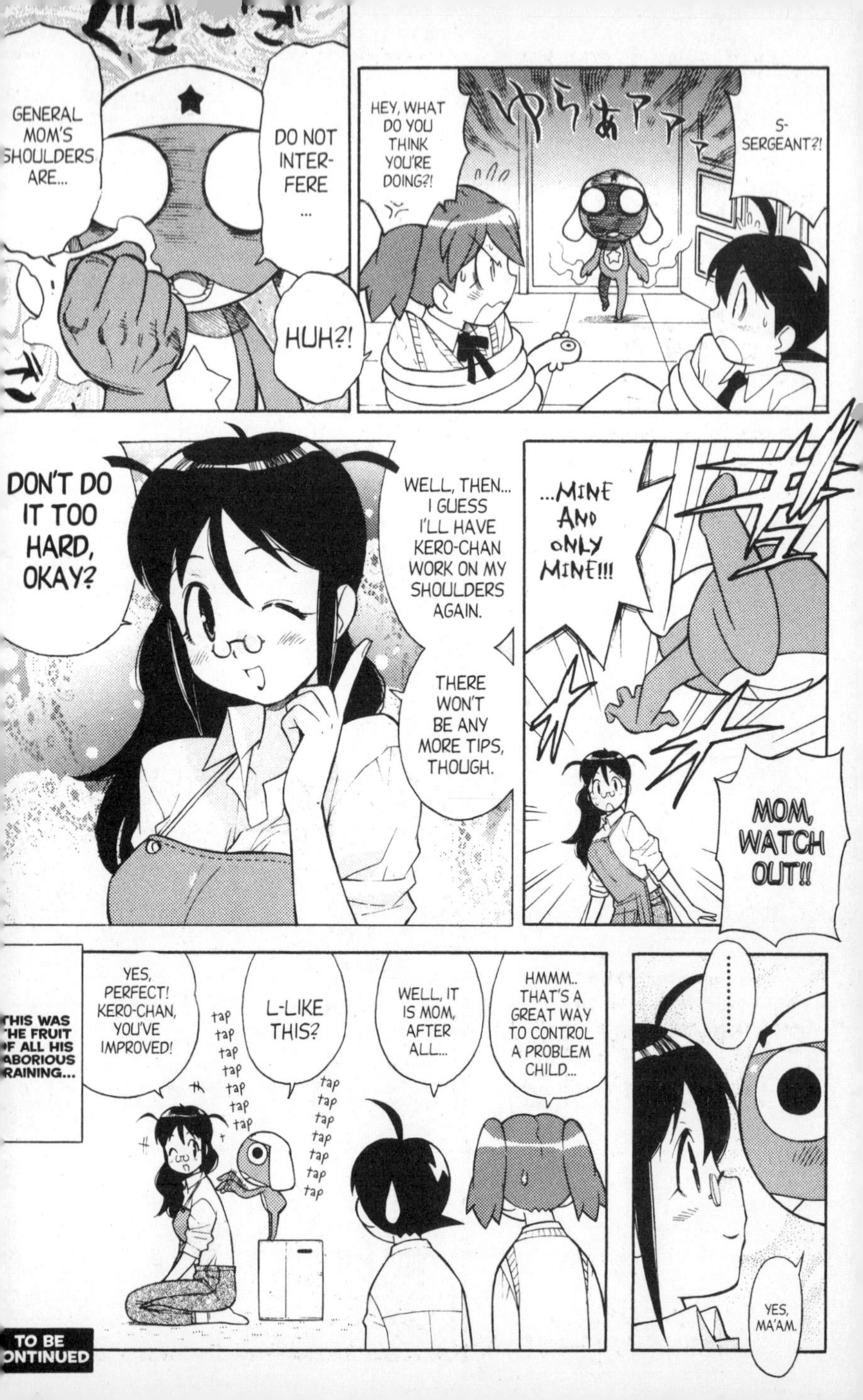
S-SERGEANT?!
ゆらぁアア
HEY, WHAT DO YOU THINK YOU'RE DOING?!
DO NOT INTERFERE ...
GENERAL MOM'S SHOULDERS ARE...
HUH?!
...MINE AND ONLY MINE!!!
MOM, WATCH OUT!!
WELL, THEN... I GUESS I'LL HAVE KERO-CHAN WORK ON MY SHOULDERS AGAIN.
THERE WON'T BE ANY MORE TIPS, THOUGH.
DON'T DO IT TOO HARD, OKAY?
......
YES, MA'AM.
HMMM.. THAT'S A GREAT WAY TO CONTROL A PROBLEM CHILD...
WELL, IT IS MOM, AFTER ALL...
tap tap tap tap tap tap tap
L-LIKE THIS?
tap tap tap tap tap tap tap
YES, PERFECT! KERO-CHAN, YOU'VE IMPROVED!
THIS WAS THE FRUIT OF ALL HIS LABORIOUS TRAINING...
TO BE CONTINUED

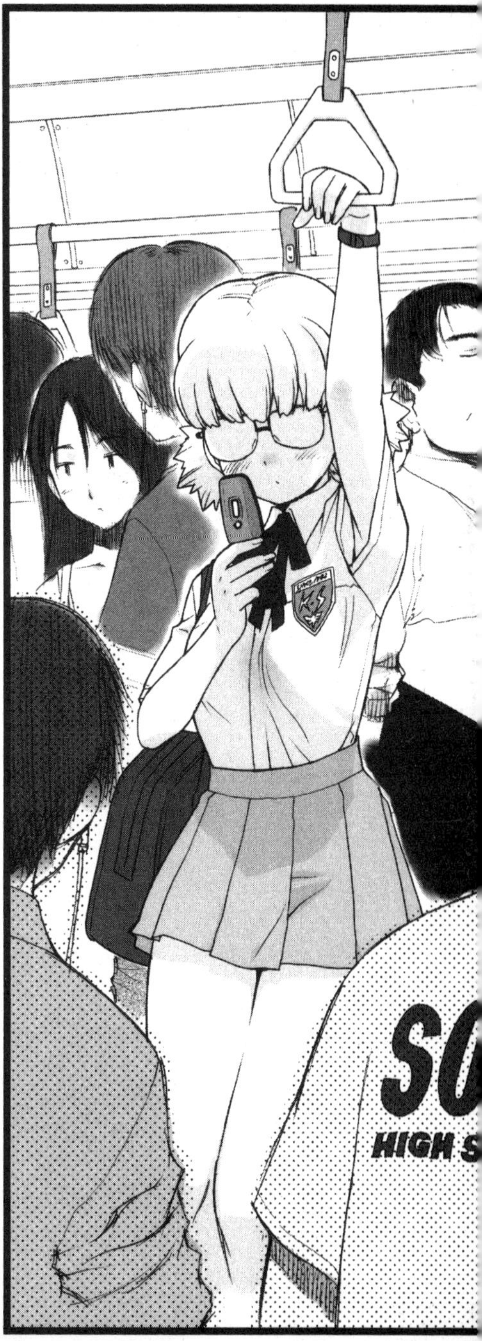

PAN STAFF

CREATOR
MINE YOSHIZAKI

BACKGROUNDS
OYSTER

FINISHES
GOMOKU AKATSUKI
ROBIN TOKYO
TOMMI NARIHARA
634
EIJI SHIMOEDA

TO BE CONTINUED IN VOL 12

CHIRUYO TSUKIGAMI-CHAN

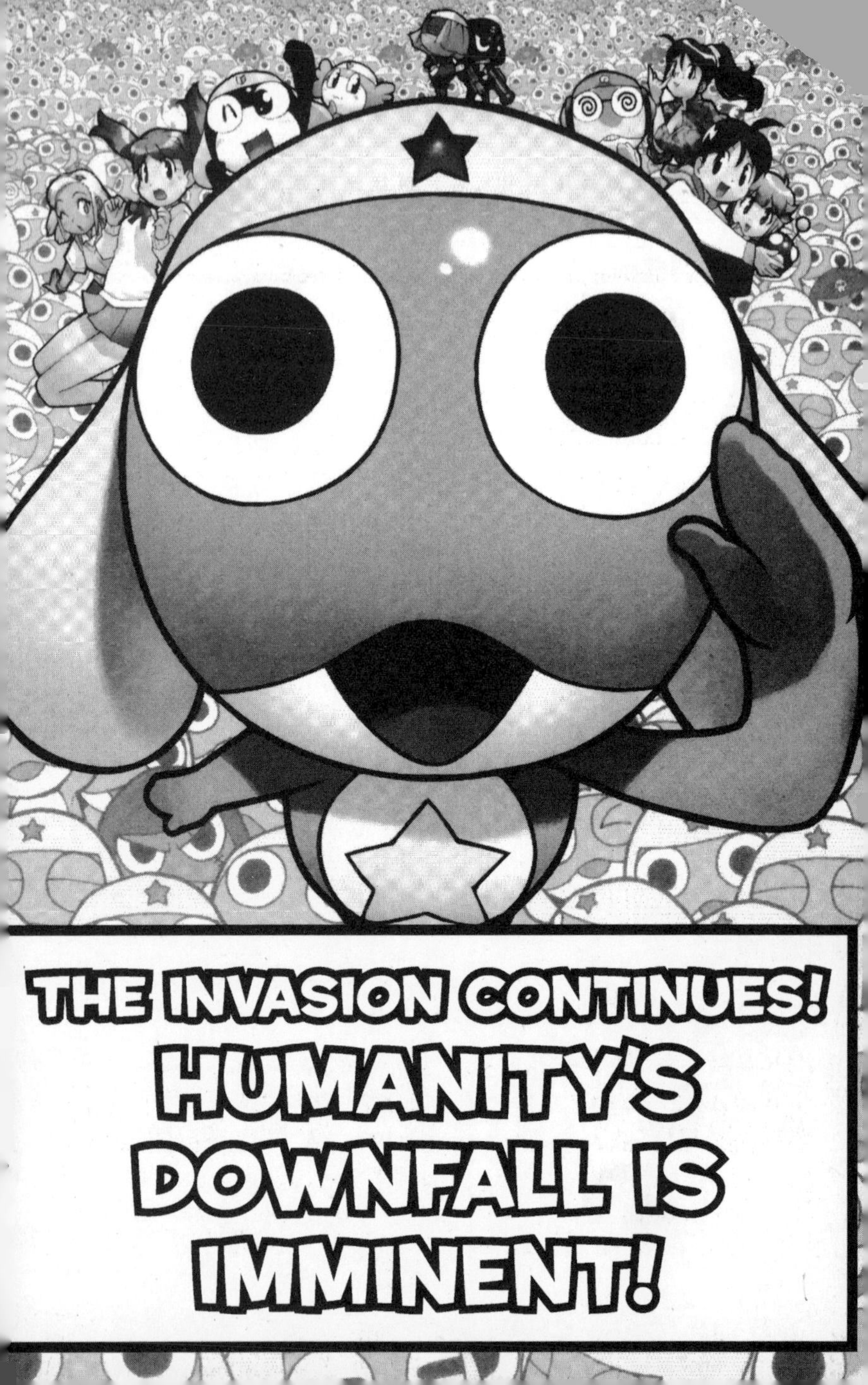

THE INVASION CONTINUES!

HUMANITY'S DOWNFALL IS IMMINENT!

GERO! GERO! GERO!

GREETINGS, POKOPENIANS! HAVE YOU MISSED
ANY EXCITING DETAILS SURROUNDING YOUR EVENTUAL
SUBJUGATION? FEAR NOT. VOLUMES 1 THROUGH 10 OF
SGT. FROG WILL BRIEF YOU. AND READING ABOUT ALL OF
MY FAILED PLOTS AND SCHEMES WILL ONLY LULL
YOU INTO A FALSE SENSE OF SECURITY!

SGT FROG

KERORO GUNSO

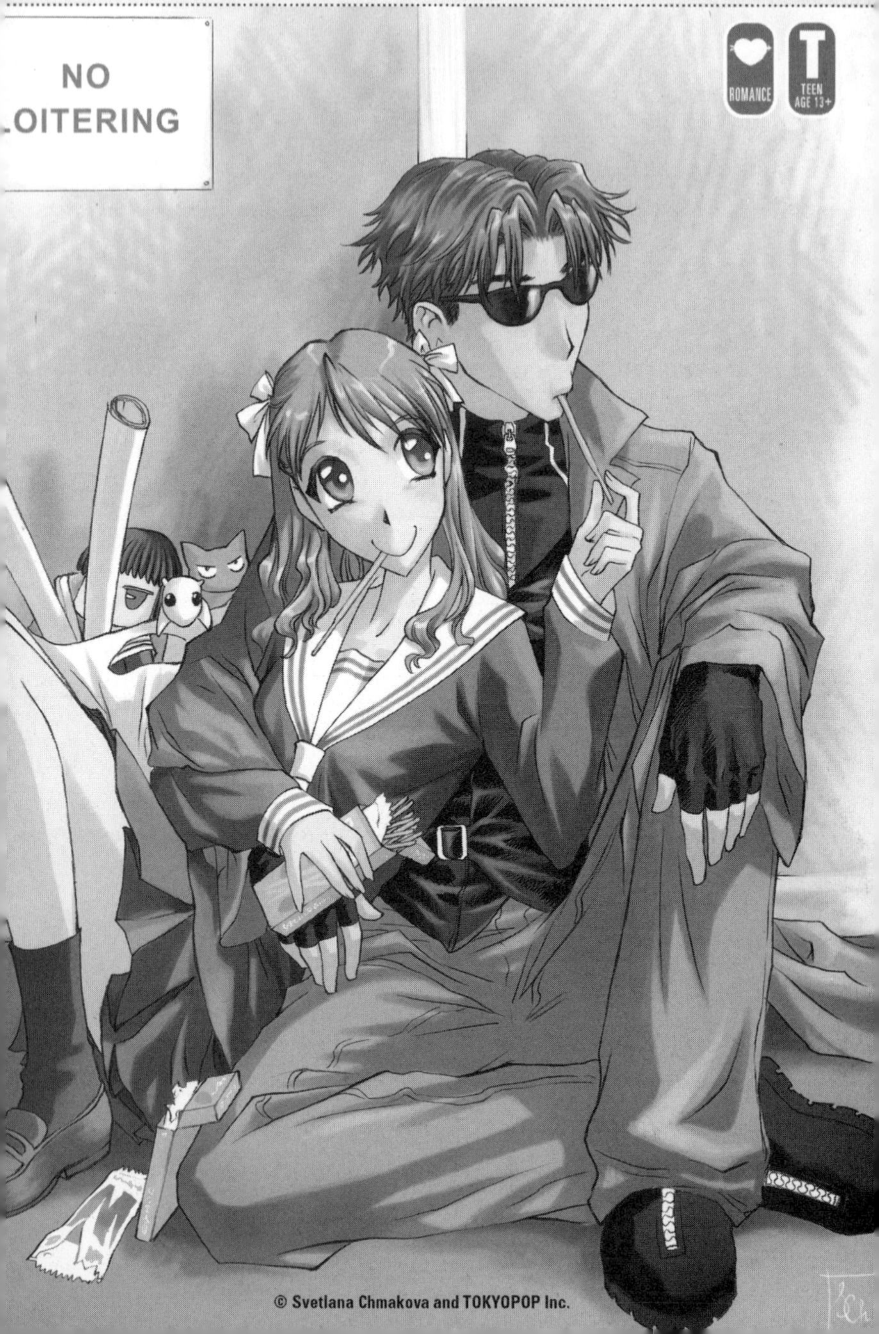
NO
LOITERING
ROMANCE
T
TEEN
AGE 13+

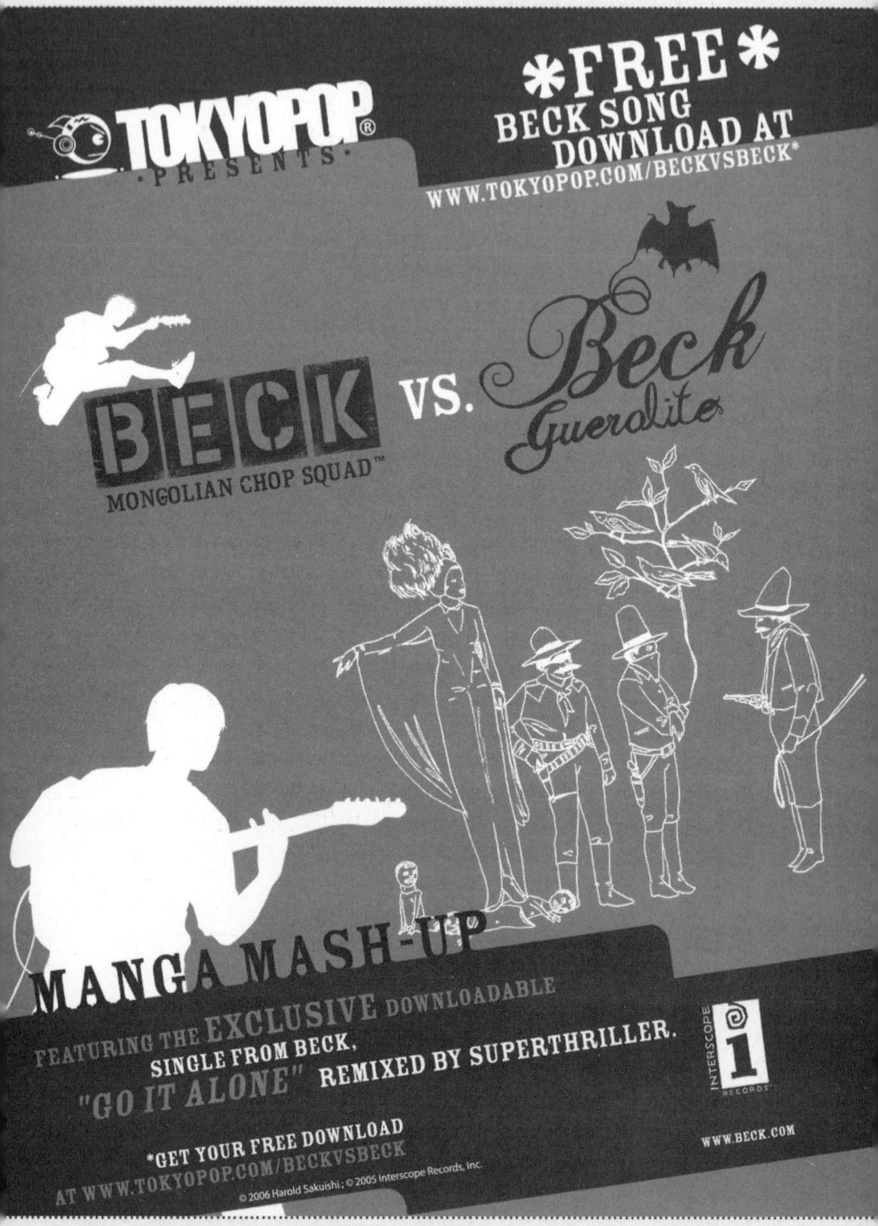
TOKYOPOP®
·PRESENTS·
FREE
BECK SONG
DOWNLOAD AT
TOKYOPOP.COM/BECKVSBECK*
WWW.TOKYOPOP.COM/BECKVSBECK
BECK
MONGOLIAN CHOP SQUAD™
VS.
Beck
Guerolito
MANGA MASH-UP
FEATURING THE EXCLUSIVE DOWNLOADABLE
SINGLE FROM BECK,
"GO IT ALONE" REMIXED BY SUPERTHRILLER.
INTERSCOPE
RECORDS
*GET YOUR FREE DOWNLOAD
AT WWW.TOKYOPOP.COM/BECKVSBECK
© 2006 Harold Sakuishi.; © 2005 Interscope Records, Inc.
WWW.BECK.COM

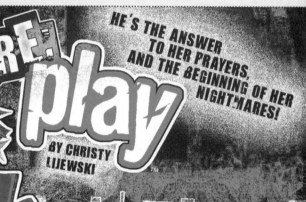

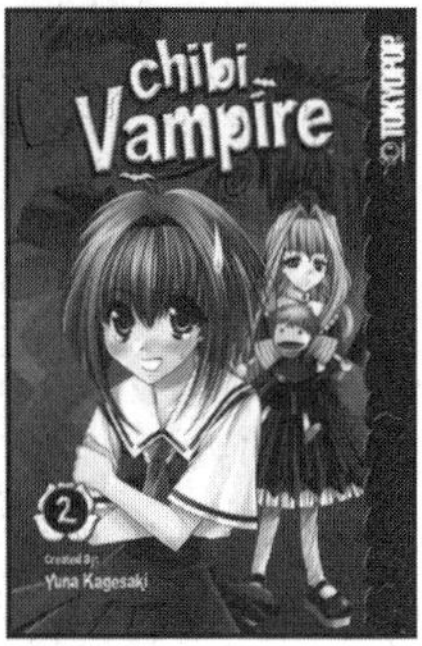
chibi Vampire
TOKYOPOP
2
Created By:
Yuna Kagesaki

CHIBI VAMPIRE VOLUME 2

BY YUNA KAGESAKI

This bloody-good vampire has a big crush on her prey!

COMEDY | OT OLDER TEEN AGE 16+

Inspired the hit anime!

DEVIL MAY CRY 3 VOLUME 2

BY SUGURO CHAYAMACHI

The secret of the seven seals will release the demon world unto the earth!

It's good against evil... and brother against brother!

ACTION | OT OLDER TEEN AGE 16+

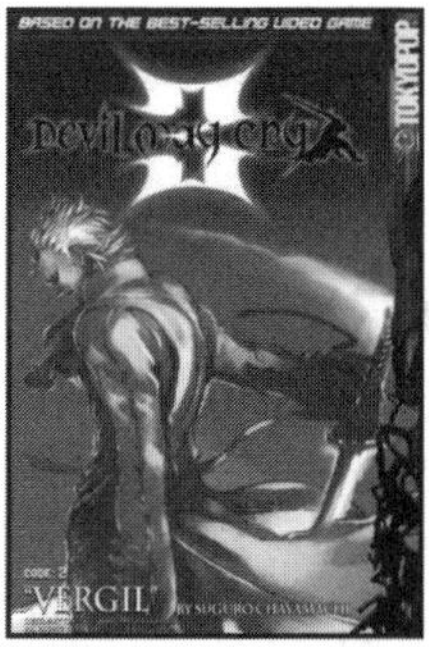
BASED ON THE BEST-SELLING VIDEO GAME
TOKYOPOP
Devil May Cry
"VERGIL"

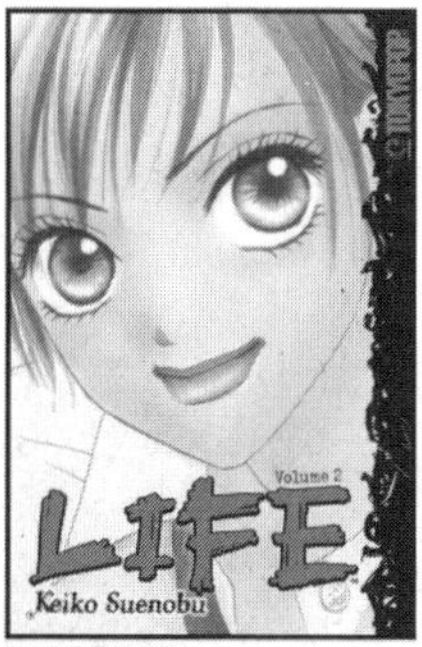
TOKYOPOP
Volume 2
LIFE
Keiko Suenobu

LIFE VOLUME 2

BY KEIKO SUENOBU

It's about real teenagers...
real high school...
real life!

DRAMA | OT OLDER TEEN AGE 16+

**Every life has a story...
Every story has a life of its own.**

STOP!

This is the back of the book.
You wouldn't want to spoil a great ending!

This book is printed "manga-style," in the authentic Japanese right-to-left format. Since none of the artwork has been flipped or altered, readers get to experience the story just as the creator intended. You've been asking for it, so TOKYOPOP® delivered: authentic, hot-off-the-press, and far more fun!

DIRECTIONS

If this is your first time reading manga-style, here's a quick guide to help you understand how it works.

It's easy... just start in the top right panel and follow the numbers. Have fun, and look for more 100% authentic manga from TOKYOPOP®!